1979

AN INTRODUCTION TO CORRECTIONS:

A POLICY AND SYSTEMS APPROACH

AN INTRODUCTION TO CORRECTIONS:

A POLICY AND SYSTEMS APPROACH

David Duffee
The Pennsylvania State University

Robert Fitch
The Pennsylvania State University

Goodyear Publishing Company, Inc.
Pacific Palisades, California

Library of Congress Cataloging in Publication Data
Duffee, David.
    An introduction to corrections.

    Bibliography: p. 376
    Includes indexes.
    1. Corrections.   2. Criminal justice, Administration of.
I. Fitch, Robert, 1926–   joint author.   II. Title.
HV8665.D83   364.6   75-19931
ISBN 0-87620-465-5

Library of Congress Catalog Card Number: 75-19931

ISBN: 0-87620-465-5
Y-4655-0

Current Printing (last digit):
10 9 8 7 6 5 4 3 2 1

Printed in the United States of America

TO CYNDI AND ALICE

Contents

Foreword

Fads and fashions are not restricted to the trivial and superficial aspects of life; indeed, fashion itself can be a very serious business. There are fashions in the applications of the scientific method as there are trends in gentlemen's suits. Being up with the latest trend is not necessarily reprehensible, since some fashions are clearly utilitarian.

Among the current fashions in the social sciences and related areas is the systems theory approach. This book takes a systems theoretic approach to the correctional operations and agencies within the criminal justice system, the authors stressing the *inter-connectedness* of the procedures. The concept of system is often far removed from the original ideas of those who first introduced it, and it is, of course, many years since the procedures for dealing with persons accused and convicted of crime were designated as "the criminal justice system." But the procedures seem more adequately described as an administrative potpourri: a collection or sequence of operations arbitrarily called a "system."

The criminal justice system has one feature that conforms with the general idea of a system, namely, that what is done in one part of the process affects persons or events in another part of the network of procedures—the hip bone is more or less connected to the thigh bone. But the nature of the interconnectedness in the administrative potpourri is a thin, weak line—the thread traced by a very small proportion of offenders who "go through" the whole sequence from arrest to parole. Most of those who enter the network branch off at various points—the many decision nodes on the route—for various reasons (or accidents).

When one talks about a system one usually has in mind a richly interconnected network that has a specific purpose. The term "purpose" is used in the same way as we would describe a piece of machinery as having a purpose: It does not connote the idea of intent. When mention is made of a system it is inappropriate to inquire, as one would of a complex piece of apparatus, "What is it for?" or "What is it designed to do?" If criminal justice processes constitute a system it should be easy to answer these questions with regard to the set of processes *as a whole*. It may be possible to answer such questions with regard to the activities of the police, the prosecutor's office, probation, or the parole board, but it is doubtful that each would give the same statement of purpose. As the authors note, it is sometimes more appropriate to see the criminal justice machinery as a set of subsystems that do not mesh together to produce a product. Both the descriptive and the prescriptive elements of the procedures of criminal justice are disordered. There is not much agreement on the kinds of products that should be produced or that *are* being produced.

There are many who are calling for tougher penalties for all or particular kinds of offenses, while at the other extreme there are those who would have us plan for the total abolition of prisons. It is not surprising that with these widely divergent proposals for action there is little or no agreement on policy or purpose.

The authors have found their way through much of this maze to elaborate the nature of the interconnectedness that *does* characterize the processes from the perspective of correctional objectives and agencies. They are not content merely to describe the present procedures, but correctly, in my view, argue that more of the same can only lead to disaster. Innovative change is essential to achieve social control in a rapidly changing environment. The authors are not extreme radicals nor are they reactionary; they are glorious optimists. They would not build bigger and better prisons nor would they abolish the whole treatment concept; they would see the transmogrification of prisons and correctional agencies to a system with a mission to correct not only the rejects of society but society itself.

Leslie T. Wilkins

Preface

This book is an introduction to corrections in the United States. Our first title for the manuscript, *Correctional Strategies*, we later rejected because it might mislead prospective readers into expecting an advanced, rather than an introductory, work. Nevertheless, we still feel that "correctional strategies" is descriptive of our basic theme. It was our intent to approach corrections from a broad focus, one that would include the interface of the correctional process and organizations with the preconviction process and organizations. Indeed, we really desired to go further than that: to posit that the entire criminal justice system is really a series of *correctional* or *remedial* strategies. Crime *prevention*, in contrast, is primarily a function of other social service systems or other social institutions such as the schools or the political process.

Two major threads throughout the book are 1) an emphasis on the interorganizational and interagency networks that are coordinated for the accomplishment of correctional programs and goals and 2) the major variables, structural characteristics, and beliefs that are crucial to the creation and stabilization of desired change in the correctional system. The discussion in most cases operates on two distinct levels. On one level we describe, as accurately as possible, the present nature of the operation of the correctional system. On another level, we describe the changes in the system that appear necessary if correctional organizations are to accomplish certain goals that are currently seen as desirable or that are likely to become paramount in the next ten to twenty years. While it was a painstaking process, we have attempted to distinguish the foregoing from the dimension of optimum or desirable functioning. The reader should be aware, however, that the beliefs, ideologies, and goals of correction that some experts see as optimal will affect current practices by redirecting their broad aims or by conflicting with one another and producing conflicts in the operational structure of the system.

THE PLAN OF THE TEXT

The text is organized somewhat like a sandwich. The specifics, or the meat of the book, are in the middle. There are two chapters on each end to help the reader hold the middle together. From our point of view, it is this organization of both general and specific coverage that is the unique contribution of our text to correctional literature.

Chapter 1 deals at some length with our idea of "correctional strategies" and provides an overview both to the correctional process and to the rest of the book. Chapter 2 outlines the precorrection phases of the criminal justice system in terms of how the organization of police and court agencies and their relationships to the correctional system influence the nature of correctional intake. Chapter 3 focuses on sentencing, a part of the decision-making process that, in the last ten years, has increasingly fallen within the purview of correctional experts and correctional policy making. Chapter 4 covers institutional corrections, its history and current characteristics. Chapters 5 and 6 describe probation and parole, respectively, and Chapter 7 considers other forms of community supervision and treatment. Chapter 8 is, to our knowledge, the most comprehensive synthesis of correctional policy, programming, and organizational structure that is currently available. Almost all of the policies, programs, and organizational variations presented in Chapters 3 through 7 of this text are related as parallel tracks under four generic policy types. The development of the correctional typology itself is dealt with at length so that the reader can decide for himself the appropriateness of our final categorization. Last, Chapter 9 moves on from the policy and program level to a discussion of models of the total criminal justice process and relates the projected consequences for the future of corrections to two very distinct system models.

It would be difficult to thank all the people whose help contributed to the completion of this work. The book grew out of informal friendships and formal responsibilities of both the authors in the Division of Community Development, Law Enforcement and Corrections major. Of equal weight were the general influence and ideas of Professor Vincent O'Leary. The correctional policy model, which we expanded in Chapter 8, was originally his. We would like to thank Kay McClellan for accurate and rapid typing. The editorial and production staffs of Goodyear Publishing were both supportive and extremely thorough.

Most of all we wish to thank our wives, who had different, but significantly important, duties in controlling the different excesses of their husbands.

David Duffee
Robert Fitch

The Criminal Sanction and Social Control 1

Invoking the criminal sanction is only one way of achieving or restoring social control. The criminal justice system—the police, the courts, and the correctional agencies that are responsible for implementing the criminal law—is usually called on only when more important methods of social control are failing. Generally, society depends on its primary institutions for the maintenance of social order. These political, economic, educational, religious, and family institutions, within which the most frequent events of social interaction occur, are ordinarily the most powerful forces by which to keep social interactions bunched together in the normal part of the distribution of social exchange activities. The institution of criminal justice usually becomes involved only with social interactions occurring at the fringes of this distribution.

Some social theorists have suggested that the agencies of criminal justice are a part of the "political institution" of society. They mean, perhaps, that the criminal has broken the laws of a state or has gone against the wishes of its government. Other theorists have argued that the criminal justice system is part of the economic institution, because it pulls out of the social order the poor and disenfranchised and protects the legal and established means of obtaining wealth. Still other theorists have argued that the criminal justice system is part of the educational institution of society, because it educates free citizens about the dangers of committing criminal acts and reeducates criminals about proper ways to behave.

We find entering this debate, let alone settling it, inconsequential to the present study and to solution of the pressing problems facing a society that is dependent on the current criminal justice system. We do find it extremely important, however, that a student of these

1

problems should view the entire criminal justice system, and certainly any lesser part of it, as a minor collection of agencies, compared with the vast array of other social structures that determine the trends and alter the quality of modern life. An equally important point follows from this first one. Since there are many ways of generating social order before the criminal justice system is set in motion and, consequently, many and diverse paths to social disorder before society pronounces the discord criminal, the criminal justice system is probably not the best way to deal with disorder and probably not the best way of engineering social control.

An analogy may help to illustrate this point. It would be a rare critic indeed who would attribute the awesomeness of the tragedy of Shakespeare's *King Lear* to the skill of the players. Certainly poor players detract from the potential of any performance, but it takes stellar performances to parallel the quality of the playwright's design. Likewise, the participants in the criminal justice system appear on the stage long after the roles are structured and the ultimate tragedy has been assured. They even have difficulty keeping pace with their parts. The officials in charge of enforcing the law and carrying out justice never seem to confront the factors that structured the interactions they are supposed to change. They deal with murderers, but rarely with the forces that culminate in murder. They deal with alcoholics, but rarely with the forces that converge as alcoholism. They argue with a few delinquents, but rarely have a chance to speak to the problem of delinquency. These actors on the social stage seem compelled to convince some audience of the importance of the roles they play. Hence, they often speak in ideal terms expressing the underlying values personified in the cast. As this process continues, both the characters on stage and the public audience tend to forget that the performance deals with human beings and that the forces that brought them together generally tend to remain unchanged by the events on stage.

In short, the criminal justice system usually deals with people rather than with the problems that have identified the people as victims and criminals. The same problems seem to occur over and over again because there are usually new people to play the old roles. Thus, while the invocation of the criminal punishment is usually viewed by the actors as an act *for society*, the actors are usually those curious critics who concentrate on the players rather than the play. We hope that the student using this book will keep in mind that the major variables influencing social interaction exist in the design of the interaction rather than in the personal attributes of the people undertaking any particular performance. It is through this fundamental shift in perspective that we can hope to understand how to change the design and resolve some of the problems that bring these people together.

TRADITIONAL GOALS OF THE CRIMINAL SANCTION

Throughout history, there have been many different ways of explaining why an apprehended criminal is punished for his actions. Several reasons have usually existed within any one culture at any one point in history, but these reasons have received different emphasis depending on the evolutionary status of the society in question. Four commonly recognized goals of the criminal sanction are retribution, deterrence, incapacitation, and rehabilitation. It is not easy to separate these goals, and any sophisticated analysis will probably lead to as many overlaps as distinctions. Recognizing this problem, we can attempt preliminary definitions.

Retribution

When someone hits someone else, a fairly common reaction is to hit back. When this reaction is motivated by the desire to return the first wrong, it is considered an act of retribution. The philosophy of an eye for an eye, a tooth for a tooth is retributive because it is aimed at returning a past wrong rather than stopping future wrongs. It is the goal of the retributive act to punish the criminal because he did something wrong. Hence, we can justify on retributive grounds some forms of punishment that may escalate a conflict instead of resolving it or may punish a wrongdoer who is physically incapable of acting wrongly again.

Deterrence

When someone hits someone else to stop the other person from striking again, this may be considered an act of deterrence. The offender is punished so that he will weigh the consequences if he should consider committing a similar offense in the future. This is usually called *specific deterrence*, because it is directed at the individual offender in retaliation for the specific kind of act he has already committed. In contrast, we speak of *general deterrence* as punishing the act of one offender so that other people contemplating similar acts will consider the likelihood of similar retaliation. Specific deterrence assumes that the criminal will be influenced by his past experience in governing his own behavior. General deterrence assumes that potential offenders will be influenced by the experience of the punished offender in governing their future behavior.

Incapacitation

When someone hits someone else and he is locked up so that he cannot physically engage in the act again, he has been incapacitated. In Elizabethan England, the hands of pickpockets and the tongues of slanderers were cut off. A principal advantage of these forms of corporal punishment was thought to be that they made it impossible for the criminal to repeat his crime. Corporal punishment is no longer legal in the United States, but incarceration serves the same purpose—to contain the criminal.

Rehabilitation

When someone hits someone else and the response is to attempt to change the offender's values, perceptions, or personality so that he will not want to hit again, we can call the punishment an act of rehabilitation. A current view of rehabilitation opposes it to punishment, but we would define rehabilitation as a *type* of punishment because it may be legally applied only after the criminal is convicted. Offenders rarely want to undergo rehabilitation, and the government may not intervene, even for the purpose of rehabilitation, unless the action is preceded by a legal conviction.

THE TIME ORIENTATION OF THE TRADITIONAL GOALS

As we previously warned, it is probably impossible to make clear-cut distinctions among the goals of punishment or to clearly identify different types of punishment. Both specific deterrence and rehabilitation are attempts to change the offender's desire to reoffend by changing his perceptions of the value of the criminal act. Deterrence may be defined as a threat applied to an unchanged offender who is inclined to repeat the offense, but whose fear that the punishment will be repeated keeps him from committing the act. In contrast, rehabilitation can be defined as the manipulation of the offender so that when he is confronted with the possibility of repeating the criminal act, he will not *want* to commit it. We can also try to distinguish deterrence from rehabilitation on the basis that deterrence requires surveillance by the state of likely offenders and of places where crimes are likely to occur so that the possibility of punishment remains high and the deterrent threat remains in force, while rehabilitation requires no surveillance of the criminal once the punishment is completed. Rehabilitation should last as long as the change in the individual endures. Deterrence, as a goal of the criminal sanction, lasts only as long as the state is committed to enforcement of the threat.

In comparison with deterrence, the preventive effect of incapacitation is even more limited in duration. Incapacitation is a preventive measure only as long as the offender remains physically controlled by the state. Of course, the effect of incapacitation may be prolonged by increasing the length of a prison sentence, but we can assume that the effect of incapacitation exists wholly outside the offender and will not last beyond the sentence itself, as rehabilitation and deterrence are supposed to do.

Lastly, retribution, unlike the other three goals, is usually seen as "backward-looking" rather than "forward-looking." According to this view, retribution is a goal of the criminal sanction that is interested in only the past act of the offender rather than his future acts. Although in the simple sense this is correct, a more critical appraisal makes it fairly unlikely that society would engage in retribution if it had significance only for acts that have occurred in the past. While retribution is not concerned with the future acts of the offender, it is obviously concerned with the present state of mind of the victim or the present condition of the government acting for the victim. When society commits an act of retribution and punishes a criminal because he was wrong, the most logical explanation seems to be that social order is disturbed by the criminal act, and retribution is needed to restore that order.

In its Preliminary Report,[1] the New York State Governor's Special Committee on Criminal Offenders called this aspect of retribution "the prevention of anomie." Anomie is normlessness—a social condition that exists when people no longer find support for the norms by which they have lived. According to the Committee, anomie would result if the government did not visibly punish criminals, because citizens would no longer feel protected by sanctions against criminal behavior.

Thus, while the four goals have frequently been distinguished from one another in terms of their time perspective, this approach is not entirely accurate. We prefer to speak of retribution as being concerned with the present state of society and committed against the offender, but directed toward society. Incapacitation is concerned with the present state of society, committed against the offender, and directed toward his physical movement. Deterrence is concerned with the future state of society, committed against an offender, and directed at him (specific deterrence) or at others with similar inclinations (general deterrence). Rehabilitation is concerned with the future of society, committed against the offender, and directed at him.[2]

THE EFFECTIVENESS OF THE CRIMINAL SANCTION

It is common knowledge that something is wrong with our present criminal justice system. The correctional institutions attract as much criticism as any other part of the system, and many of the critical viewpoints conflict. Either prison officials are harsh, inhuman, and unwilling to change, or they are bleeding hearts unwilling to treat criminals in the harsh manner that they deserve. This is not to suggest that the correctional agencies are really all right, but that one of their difficulties may lie in the contradictory demands that are made of them and the conflicting purposes to which they are put. Is it possible, for example, that a prison can deter one criminal while it is rehabilitating another? Or, perhaps even more complex, is it possible to deter and rehabilitate the same individual? Frequently prisons are expected to do these jobs concurrently, and it is not surprising that few of them are performed well.

The picture is further beclouded by the fact that correction actually begins long before the judge pronounces sentence. It begins when the legislature enacts laws proscribing certain acts as crimes and enacts other laws establishing the correctional organization that will deal with the lawbreaker. For example, when the state legislature passes a bill proscribing burglary, it does so in order to deter such behavior. The judge, however, when passing sentence on a convicted burglar, may have the goal of retribution in mind. The prison that accepts the burglar may diagnose a personality problem and attempt to rehabilitate the offender. Later, a parole agent may revoke the burglar's parole in order to incapacitate him. How can we evaluate any of these actions when none of them seems to have been carried through to completion?[3]

The causes of crime and the goals
of the criminal sanction

Although it is difficult to find empirical demonstrations of the effectiveness of the different criminal sanctions, we can assume that if most of the goals of punishment are to be accomplished, they must have some relationship to the *causes* of crime. With the exception of retribution, all of these goals are related to the *prevention* of crime. It would be difficult to prevent an act if we intervened in ways that had nothing to do with the reasons for which the act was committed.

The effectiveness of deterrence would seem to depend on the manner in which the criminal reaches his decision to commit a crime. Deterrence is a threat to make the consequences of the crime not worth the trouble of committing it. Thus, if the criminal is to be deterred, he must be in a state of mind to rationally consider the consequences of the crime before committing it. There is not much evidence about how criminals decide to commit crimes, but we could probably rule out the effectiveness of deterrents for some crimes of passion involving marital infidelity and jealousy or bar fights brought on by anger and alcohol. It is unlikely, for example, that the fifty-year-old husband, home after a late office conference, stops to weigh the various consequences of shooting his wife after stumbling upon her infidelity. These and other violent crimes that occur under extremely emotional circumstances are poor material for the threats of deterrence. Likewise, thefts that occur on the spur of the moment or vandalism that occurs when children egg one another on would seem less deterrable than rational crimes.

A crime that might be deterrable would be income tax evasion, where the offender knowingly misreports income, taking the calculated risk that his report will not be scrutinized too carefully or, if it is, that the penalty will not be too great. Ironically, legislatures and judges frequently react to this kind of crime in ways that confirm the offender's perceptions about the chances of getting away with it.

This example brings up a second problem of deterrence. While there would seem to be some undeterrable acts, such as certain kinds of murder, the probability of deterring more rationally considered offenses also depends upon the probabilities of capture and conviction. A legislature or a judge may intend to deter crime through their actions, but their chances of success are small if the criminal knows that he is unlikely to be caught. For example, Herbert Packer points out the absurdity of a New York City ordinance that prohibits smoking in hotel room beds.[4] How, asks Packer, is such an act to be influenced by the ordinance if there is no reasonable way of enforcing the rule?

A related but different problem of deterrence is that different people are probably rational with different results. The legislature, in stiffening a penalty for armed robbery, may be rational in thinking that a stiffer sentence would make offenders consider more carefully the consequences of armed robbery. But the person who is likely to commit an armed robbery may live under circumstances that are very different from those of the legislators in the state capitol. He could be just as rational as any legislator and still consider the benefits of the robbery worth the possible costs, given his alternatives. If he is poor and without a job, he may be willing to accept unfavorable odds as he commits an offense, because he perceives even these odds as better than his other avenues of action.

We can complicate this matter even further by postulating that some criminal activity takes place in a social situation that makes it rational to do something simply *because* the probable costs of committing the act are great. One reason for a city gang fight, for example, is that the fight provides the gang members with an opportunity to gain a reputation. The greater the risk they take, and the more illegal the act they are willing to commit, the more they can add to their prestige. In this situation, the more the legislators and the police attempt to deter a crime, the more desirable that act might appear to a gang member who is seeking to add to his status in the group. Thus, the rational, deterrent activity of lawmakers may backfire if they expect to control the commission of crimes among people who are rational in their own way, but who place a positive value on things negatively valued by the legislature.[5]

The effectiveness of incapacitation as a goal would appear to be easier to observe and measure. Unfortunately, this is not really so. First of all, incapacitation is applicable only to the minority of offenders who are caught and imprisoned at least once. Second, if incapacitation is to be of any value, it must be based on an accurate prediction that the incapacitated offender, if he had been left to his own devices, would have committed another crime. Obviously, incapacitation is unnecessary if it is applied to an individual who would not repeat the crime if he were free. Unfortunately, if the system officials err by incarcerating an offender who would not reoffend, there is no way for that error to come to light. In contrast, the error of releasing someone who should have been incarcerated is embarrassingly evident to the officials who make the decisions. Thus, there might be some pressure in the system to incapacitate, not because it is an effective use of the criminal sanction, but because it is one for which evaluations are ineffective.[6]

Another problem with incapacitation is that it is rarely done in such a way as to prevent crimes against other inmates. Incapacitation merely changes the location of the next crime rather than reducing the probability of the next crime.[7] Of course, many would argue that it is better that criminals offend against other criminals than against free and law-abiding citizens. This belief may be acceptable only if society is willing to pay the ultimate price for confining all offenders in the same space for a period of years. The price may be that the incapacitated criminal, upon his release, will be more likely to engage in criminal behavior because even fewer alternatives are open to him after incapacitation than before. Likewise, the old practice of separating the pickpocket from his hand not only separated the offender from his illegal trade but also effectively curtailed his chances for honest employment. Thus, the Elizabethan pickpocket, once caught, probably switched to robbery or some other form of crime that required less dexterity.

Another aspect of incapacitation (which we shall mention again later) has to do with new techniques of behavior modification by which an offender can be incapacitated physiologically, or mechanically, without resorting to incarceration. It is possible, for example, to monitor parolees by implanting on them an electronic transmitter monitored by a central control. If the signal indicates that the parolee has entered a forbidden area, such as a bar, or is wandering about when he should be in bed, the monitor may push a button that will shock the parolee into behaving himself.[8]

Perhaps the epitome of this approach to crime control is portrayed by Anthony Burgess in *A Clockwork Orange*. In this film the protagonist undergoes a treatment that nauseates him whenever his criminal or sexual inclinations overtake him. This kind of behavior control is not science fiction; it can be accomplished today.[9] But even if it is possible, is it ethically desirable? Does the commission of a criminal act justify society in remaking the criminal as an automaton? It is arguable that such incapacitation is ethical if it stops a dangerous offender from committing further heinous acts. The opposite argument is that this new kind of behavior control has not really overcome the ineffectiveness of the Elizabethan mutilation process. If we take from a man the capacity for criminal acts, we probably also take from him the capacity for positive, law-abiding acts.[10]

Another difficult question concerns the effectiveness of rehabilitative goals. To some extent the effectiveness of rehabilitation may depend on factors opposite to those that would make deterrence effective. If deterrence depends on the rational criminal, rehabilitation is often an attempt to deal with the irrational criminal. While there are many modes of rehabilitation, therapy usually entails demonstrating to the patient that his view of himself and of the world is inaccurate and should be replaced with the view preferred by the therapist. Thus, if the criminal has a perfectly rational explanation for his commission of a crime—if his picture of the world that led him to commit the crime is accurate—then the therapist is hard put to change such perceptions.

A weakness of rehabilitation is the difficulty in identification of those criminals whose acts are predicated on inaccurate rather than accurate perceptions of their situation. We do not know much about this area of criminality, and the irrational criminal may be the least likely person to help us with this selection process. What often happens is that therapists in the correctional system recommend therapy for almost all criminals on the assumption that the commission of crime is proof that the criminal is irrational. This approach suffers from the same mistake made by people who favor deterrence: it lumps all crimes together as stemming from one underlying cause. This suggestion is as absurd as the idea that all noncriminal behavior has the same cause.[11]

Another problem with the idea of rehabilitation is that it is usually based upon the idea that there "is something wrong with the offender." In other words, rehabilitation is usually based upon a "medical model" by which criminality is viewed as a condition contracted by the criminal and treatable as a doctor would treat a disease. Unfortunately, the analogy of sickness and criminality breaks down rather rapidly. If a patient goes to a doctor for a sore throat and the condition is diagnosed as a streptococcus infection, it can be treated with penicillin. The existence of the infection can also be demonstrated because the streptococcus bacilli can be identified under a microscope. The criminal condition, however, cannot be extracted from the offender and treated with a remedy that is known to have, with a high degree of probability, the desired effect on the condition. Perhaps even more important, the patient with the strep throat shows up at the doctor's office voluntarily. The doctor has even done away with house calls because the patients are so willing to see him. The criminal does not go willingly to the therapist. The criminal does not believe he needs therapy. That he does need treatment is a decision made by somebody else because the criminal has done something that has bothered other people. While the therapist may speak of the offender having a condition of which the crimes are symptoms, it is doubtful that, the crime absent, anyone would bother about the condition—if it existed at all. In short, one problem with rehabilitation may be that, rather than dealing with offenders' inaccurate perceptions of the world, rehabilitation may be based on an inaccurate perception of the offender. If this is the case we cannot expect rehabilitation to be very effective.[12]

The problem of defining the target of correctional action

Throughout the discussion of causes of crime and of the motivations for invoking the criminal sanction, a recurring theme is the difficulty in locating exactly what should be altered in order to stop crime or to make society less subject to disturbance by criminal actions. So far we have suggested that some goals of the criminal sanction may be ineffective because they are unrelated to the causes of crime. In a broader sense, the criminal sanction is ineffective because it does not deal with the reduction of criminal activity except by intervening in the lives of specific criminals. Arresting and convicting particular criminals deals with *persons* and has very little to do with the prevention of *events* that are crimes. Thus, if society desires to prevent crime, rather than to prevent anomie, by acting symbolically on people, it is probably depending on the wrong system to do its work. When a policeman arrests a criminal, the crime rate has gone up because another crime has been committed. In order for the occurrence of crime to decrease, we must devise ways of affecting the incidence of crime on a wholesale basis, rather than affecting on a retail scale the people who have already committed a crime. Frequently we do not bother with strategies that might substantially alter a crime rate—other than the artificial strategy of changing the definition of crime categories or failing to report crime. Because society *believes* that interfering with the criminal may change the crime rate, there has not been much opportunity to develop sound preventative measures. There have been some technological experiments with cars that are more difficult to steal and with plate glass windows that will not break, but there has been little study of the way a society might be structured so that the probability of deviance will be reduced.[13]

The most headway in this respect seems to have been made in the area of "victimless crimes." The Supreme Court of the United States has declared abortion legal in specified circumstances, and several legislatures have reduced the sanctions for the use of marijuana. Some states have taken most consensual sexual crimes off their books, and other states have been experimenting with legalized gambling. What has happened is that some of the rules by which society is constrained have been changed so that certain kinds of behavior are no longer defined as deviant.

It is less arguable that more traditional common law crimes, such as robbery and homicide, should be relegislated. But other kinds of social controls have been overlooked. For example, it is commonly recognized that rewards are more effective than punishment in influencing behavior. But society tends to frown on rewarding those who are "not deserving." Thus, many undeserving people seek rewards illegally, and some of them are punished. Finding such people opportunities to be rewarded legally is a social alternative that is implemented only in rare cases. There is always the success story of the criminal turned prize fighter. The sentence of the folksinger Leadbelly was commuted because he sang so well. But American society has not found ways of structuring the reward distribution system so that people will have greater access to legal opportunities than to illegal opportunities.[14]

A principal difficulty with this kind of restructuring process is that while it might prove highly effective in preventing crime, it seems to run headlong into the goal of retribution: the value of effective crime prevention conflicts with the value of punishing people who do not behave like the rest of us. We may be in a dilemma in that effective crime prevention (that is, the restructuring in the distribution of rewards) will increase anomie in the general population, and prevention of anomie will increase the crime rate because it relies on negative rather than positive sanctions.

Secondary difficulties in using the criminal sanction

Another problem in connection with the invocation of the criminal sanction has to do with side effects. Even when the criminal justice system is effective in reducing the frequency of some kinds of crimes or in changing certain kinds of offenders in the desired direction, there are sometimes consequences for the system itself that make the enforcement practice of doubtful value. For example, the Knapp Commission investigating corruption in the New York City Police Department disclosed the problems that narcotics investigation can create for discipline and order within the police department.[15] In brief, investigation of victimless crimes leads police frequently into unethical situations, such as accepting bribes or gaining information from offenders by promising to ignore crimes they have committed. Even when actual corruption is not an issue, it is true that many of the Supreme Court cases dealing with improper police procedure have stemmed from the investigation of victimless crimes.[16] Furthermore, while drug abuse and gambling may be engaged in by all sectors of society, laws against these offenses are primarily enforced only in sectors of society where there is less opportunity for the offense to occur in private.[17] Thus one serious side effect of the invocation of the criminal sanction, regardless of its effectiveness against the offense itself, may be that certain crimes lend themselves to selective and discriminatory enforcement patterns that act as a catalyst to greater social disorder.[18]

The police are by no means the only persons influenced by these unintended consequences of the structure of enforcement activity. Where a certain kind of offense or offender has caused the police some unusual problems, these disturbances in the operation of the system are likely to wash through to its later phases as well. Where the immorality of something illegal is in doubt, or where the propriety of the criminal sanction as an antidote is in question, the prosecutor is frequently tempted to set the charge at some level other than the one dictated by the evidence about the offense. When offenses of drug selling are notoriously hard to prove, or where the seller was really only a user making a casual sale, the prosecutor is likely to reduce charges and seek a guilty plea, where the issue of police practice will not be raised. When the prime motivation for discretionary decisions relates to the smooth operation of the system rather than to the issues of guilt and innocence, this tends to reduce both the quality and the quantity of information that will be available at later stages of the proceedings. The effects of such practices upon the information that follows the offender through the system are multiplied at each decision point, until the actual reasons for the presence of the offender in a prison setting may become unknown and unascertainable to prison officials; or, as Erving Goffman has said about mental patients, the institutionalization process is better explained in terms of the contingencies of the case than by the fact of mental illness.[19] Likewise, the contingencies are often as important to the disposition of offenders as the decision about guilt or innocence. An important study in the effectiveness of the criminal justice system, then, is the study of the characteristics of offenders, *other than their guilt*, that make them susceptible to processing in the system when the criminal sanction is not invoked against other guilty offenders.

THE LOCATION OF THE CRIMINAL SANCTION IN THE CRIMINAL JUSTICE PROCESS

The flow chart location

In a strictly formal and mechanistic way, we can locate the criminal sanction in the criminal justice process as occurring after conviction—beginning with the pronouncement of sentence. There is in the American system of justice, to use the Latin phrase, *nulla poena sine lege*.[20] Or, to state that principle in terms of the Constitution, no man shall be deprived of life, liberty, or property without due process of law.[21] Thus it is illegal and unconstitutional to incarcerate a man until there has been a legally binding decision about his guilt.

Under this strict interpretation of when the criminal sanction applies, the criminal sanction is felt by a small number of people. It has been estimated that, on any given day, 1,200,000 people are serving out sentences in the United States. Roughly one-third of this number are incarcerated.[22] Four hundred thousand is not a great number of people compared to the number who have been institutionalized for other reasons.[23] Nor does the total of 1.2 million people under some sort of supervision at any one time constitute a large number of people compared to the number who were charged with a crime at arraignment, and it is considerably smaller still when compared to the number of people who were arrested.

The location of the sanction in the decision-making process

In terms of how decisions are made in the criminal justice system, the influence of the criminal sanction is in operation long before we run across the sentencing decision in the flow chart. In its 1967 report, the President's Commission on Law Enforcement and the Administration of Justice emphasized that each part of the criminal justice system affects every other part. The Commission considered it imperative to try to understand the whole system before analyzing any of its parts.[24] It is in terms of understanding the whole system that we can see the location of the criminal sanction quite differently than the flow chart examination might lead us to believe.

An idea that may help to clarify this "systemic location" is the concept of feedback. Feedback is basically a simple principle which can be used to explain the impact of the criminal sanction on our system of justice. Very simply, feedback is a process by which the output of a system loops back into the system. For example, many rock music groups have experimented with feeding the output from their electric guitars back through the amplifying system. An electronic amplifier itself is a feedback system in which a small initial sound is recycled until it reaches a proper intensity. At its most rudimentary level, feedback in the criminal justice system is not very different from feedback through an electronic system. The kinds of things that are put out and fed back are human beings, and the consequences that concern us are social rather than electronic.

The criminal sanction begins to have an effect, in the systemic sense at least, when the prosecutor decides to charge an offender with a crime, if not sooner. At that point the prosecutor has not only decided that there is probable cause to prosecute for a crime, but he has also made a decision about what the crime is, and about the possible consequences of a conviction for the crime. This, of course, is common knowledge. But frequently things that are common knowledge are overlooked. How is it that a consequence of prosecution has influenced the prosecution decision itself? The prosecutor is making a current decision in anticipation of a future decision of a judge. Or, in system terms, the output of prosecution is feeding back into the system and is changing those parts of the criminal justice process that occur before the sentence.

In simple language, we can say that the prosecutor "anticipates" the sentence. But the idea of "anticipation" probably does not convey the same impression of structural change in the system as does the idea of feedback. Anticipation can be understood as something that the prosecutor has in his mind. But the feedback of the criminal sanction to the prior parts of the system is really a more objective phenomenon than that. It is not something that exists only in the prosecutor's mind; it also influences in remarkably similar fashion the behavior of the defense attorney and the defendant—and anyone else involved in the case.

Observers have noticed that, to prison inmates, "time" is a strangely concrete and objectified thing. "Time" is something one does. There is easy time and hard time. Some people can do time "standing on their head." Time is very real in the system of criminal justice. Time is, therefore, real in its social consequences. For example, if too many people are doing time in a given place, word reaches the judge that fewer people should be sentenced to do it. If the police suddenly increase the number of people arrested, feedback will reach them from the courts that the rate should decrease. In fact, one person has estimated that the amount of time "being done" in the United States has remained constant for a good number of years— that only the place of incarceration has changed.[25]

One of the major areas where feedback from the sanction itself reenters the system is in the process of plea negotiation. Whether the prosecutor and the defense bargain on reduction of counts and charges or bargain on a recommendation for sentence, the primary issue is how much time the offender must serve for agreeing to plead guilty. Since, as Skolnick points out, negotiation about the plea can even affect police behavior[26] and may continue through the initiation of trial proceedings,[27] the influence of the criminal sanction over the preconviction behavior of the system is tremendous.

Additional sanctions short of conviction

Finally, we should point out that the criminal sanction has a "halo effect," i.e., it affects more people than those who eventually serve a sentence. It affects those who are formally prosecuted but not sentenced. It affects the innocent sometimes as much as or more than the guilty. A poor man who is acquitted at trial after spending a year in jail in lieu of bail has lost a job, most of his social contacts, and perhaps even his family. Frequently, American employers ask not whether a prospective employee has been *convicted* but whether he has been *arrested*; whereas in Sweden a man can serve a prison sentence and return to his former position with much less difficulty.[28] Thus, many penalties short of conviction are attached to involvement with the American criminal justice system, and most of these penalties are generated by the social perception of the criminal sanction itself.

CORRECTIONAL STRATEGIES IN THEIR BROADEST SCOPE: DISCRETIONARY JUSTICE

It should be obvious by now that correctional activity does not begin at the prison door. The concept of correction implies a change process and, hence, a duration through time. It refers not to one action but to a set of actions. Because those actions are supposedly related to attaining a goal in a specific case, the correctional activity involves "tactical" decisions. Because these tactical decisions are related to the achievement of longer-range goals, a plan or strategy is implicit in the correctional activity. A strategic course of action is a complex set of plans in which the effects of a variety of short-run tactical missions are integrated to achieve the effectiveness of the entire group of activities.

We have been careful to point out relationships between pre- and postconviction activity to demonstrate that *the criminal justice system itself is a strategy*. It is a complex set of activities that, taken together, provide one alternative in dealing with certain social problems.

In the broadest sense of correctional strategy, then, the study of corrections involves the study of when the criminal justice strategy is called upon in response to community problems. The importance of this aspect of the system is being increasingly recognized and is frequently termed "discretionary justice."[29] This term refers to the fact that the officials of the system, beginning with the police, make decisions about whether or not to use the criminal process as a correctional strategy. For example, the policeman who decides not to arrest someone after investigating a complaint has, in effect, made a strategic decision. He has decided that the social disorder represented by the complaint will not be effectively corrected by the invocation of the criminal justice process.

Keeping people out of the system

Despite the great variety of motivating factors in the discretionary decision, the decision to invoke or not to invoke the criminal sanction has its boundaries. The most obvious constraint is the substantive criminal law. The correctional strategies afforded through criminal justice are not available to most social disorders—only to those disorders rigorously proscribed by the material elements of the criminal act as described in statutes. The legislative constraints, however, are very broad. They leave officials with the power, for example, to ignore back-alley crap games and bingo parties or to arrest all gamblers, petty and professional.

Another set of constraints has to do with the tolerance limits of certain communities concerning what is and what is not deviant. James Q. Wilson has done an admirable job of analyzing the discretionary activity of six police departments according to the ways in which they are influenced by the social, political, and economic character of their respective communities. He points out that the discretionary handling of legally similar offenses, such as drunkenness, simple assault, vagrancy, and disturbing the peace, varies widely in the six cities studied. These variations clustered similarly in certain communities depending on similar underlying factors such as the form of municipal government, the type of party politics, and so on. Wilson called the three major clusters of variation in the discretionary decisions the *styles of policing*. He named the styles "Legalistic," "Service," and "Watchman."[30] The Watchman style probably keeps more people out of the system than any other, because the police act as enforcers of local standards of morality rather than as enforcers of the law; i.e., if illegal behavior is normal within a certain area, it may well be ignored, or "contained." The Service style exists in homogeneous communities, where crime rates are generally low anyway, but where the invocation of the criminal sanction is not seen as a proper way to handle social problems. In the Legalistic style many more persons may be processed through the system, because laws are interpreted strictly and enforced rigorously.

Invoking the criminal sanction

Wilkins gives an even more generalized model for the analysis of the discretionary invocation of the criminal sanction. He suggests that we can view all acts of society on a continuum in terms of their frequency. He assumes that the frequency distribution of social events is likely to approach a normal curve: the great majority of acts will fall in the middle, and the distribution will taper off with equal infrequency as we locate acts that are considered very bad or very good in society. This model may help us perceive the independence of the judgments about an act from the act itself. An act is usually judged as good or bad. It is unusual to speak of acts as rare or common. And we usually judge those acts that are common as good and those acts that are rare as bad. In other words, the model demonstrates that a moral judgment about an act is, to a great extent, a reaction to its relative frequency. Very bad acts, such as murder, and very good acts, such as self-sacrifice for the good of the country, are both very rare. Normal acts, or those that fall toward the center of the curve, maintain the status quo, but are neither very functional nor very dysfunctional for society.

Wilkins speaks of all categories of "bad" acts as cutting points on this continuum. In general, we can compare social reactions to deviance in terms of the distance from the mean at which the social reaction to an act is likely to be a formal one. Some social groups seem to be fairly flexible or have relatively large tolerance for deviant activities. Other social groups seem to react more quickly to deviant activity as dangerous or undesirable.[31]

It may be helpful to think of the criminal justice system as the social alternative that is invoked when an event falls beyond the tolerance limits of a society. The quantity of tolerance would then be crucial to the number of events that the system would be called upon to handle and to the nature of the acts that would fall within the purview of the system.

Obviously, the police, the prosecutor, and other people responsible for invoking the criminal sanction are affected by the relative tolerance or intolerance of the entire community to infrequent events. As Wilson points out, arrests for simple assault are rare in the city of Amsterdam, New York, although assaults occur frequently. Arrests for the same behavior in Oakland, California or Syracuse, New York are much more frequent.[32] Thus, two important constraints on any particular criminal justice system are (1) the legal definitions observed within the jurisdiction and (2) the related social definitions of the situation that emerge in particular communities. In other words, the officials of a criminal justice system are not independent agents who can take a fixed stand toward the occurrence of disorder. They are also members of society who define their organizational roles and responsibilities within a larger communal context.

Redefining social boundaries

We should not end the study of discretion in the system by asserting that official actions are predicated on social antecedents. One characteristic of complex organizations is that they are relatively autonomous entities that can control, to a certain extent, how their external environment will influence internal operations. Furthermore, the criminal justice organizations in a particular area are often the final deciding factor in whether a community will react to an act as deviant and illegal. Thus, while a policeman takes some of his cues from the community, the citizens of a community are seeking expert assistance in how to deal with a difficult situation. The policeman is viewed as a representative of society who is responsible for knowing how to deal with difficult situations. His method of intervening is variable. Depending on how he enters the situation when called to help, the citizens will alter their own perceptions of the situation (in either direction), and community tolerances for rare events may also change.

Likewise, the prosecutor, the defense attorney, the judge, the defendant, and other actors in the criminal justice system can alter community tolerances by interacting in different ways. We do not know to what degree, or in what direction, internal operations of the system affect the community's formal or informal reactions to deviant acts. But we do know enough to stipulate that the organizational actors and the community are interdependent. There are mutual actions and reactions, and it is the complex results of these activities that define the correctional strategies that will finally be employed.

Remaking an organization

So far we have been discussing discretion as it shapes the boundaries of the criminal justice system—how officials interact with the community to take in or reject social problems as appropriate to criminal justice intervention. Another kind of discretion that is also very important to the study of correctional strategies involves discretion *within* the system, as it affects offenders against whom the criminal justice sanction has already been levied.

It is well recognized by now that decisions in the correctional end of the criminal justice process have generally had low visibility. Officials are seldom asked to explain why they have done such and such. Indeed, these officials have discovered from time to time that they only get into trouble when they do enunciate their reasons for a decision. Until recently the courts have ignored correctional activity by using, among other excuses, the explanation that prison discipline must be "left to the experts."[33] Curiously, starting with the judge's sentencing decision, the demand for articulated reasoning has been so low that it is difficult to understand how anyone in the field was known to be an expert. But now the demand is increasing for rational and defensible decisions that can be evaluated. As this demand has arisen, officials have found themselves in the embarrassing position of contradicting one another about what were the best correctional policies, or of admitting that there is not much reliable information about what has been going on or what should be changed. As officials begin the task of reformulating correctional strategies at a more visible and vulnerable level, these kinds of things are bound to happen. It will take much conflict, revision, and rethinking before some kind of consensus about correctional strategies can be reached.

We would be mistaken, however, to think that as correctional goals gradually are clarified and correctional programs are structured more consistently, discretion within the system will disappear. It is important for judges and correctional authorities to remember, as sentencing and supervisory policies are developed, that the lower level workers and inmates will not respond as cogs in a complex human machine. Even the clearest directives from managers will meet with reinterpretation and change by the people who actually carry out the work.

Discretion is necessary in a correctional system because people rather than objects are being processed. People are doing things to other people. Unlike an inanimate object, a person can always say no. Regardless of how coercive a correctional system may be, the men who supervise the inmates must somehow gain the cooperation of those inmates. In order to do so, they will need discretion—room to make choices depending on situations that cannot be determined in advance.[34]

Organizations that require discretion at their lowest staff levels are frequently called "front-line" organizations. They have in common the characteristic that the front-line personnel frequently have more information and more discretion than centrally located managers, at least about particular cases or events. Social welfare agencies, police departments, and prisons are alike in this manner.[35] The front-line workers in all these organizations follow policy set by managers, but the workers have the freedom to apply principles enunciated by managers in ways that make sense in the particular situation as perceived by the workers.

Many times the correctional officer or counselor or work supervisor may follow policy exactly as the managers have anticipated. But if the front-line interpretation of policy is poor, or incomplete, or rebellious, then the activity of the front-line is, in effect, a reformulation of policy. Because the offender as well as the correctional worker frequently exercises discretion, the question of what a correctional strategy is becomes very complex. We cannot look simply at social definitions, legal definitions, or managerial definitions. A correctional strategy in its broadest sense is clearly a complex system of interactions, and understanding it is an exercise in synthesis rather than analysis.

CORRECTIONAL STRATEGIES IN THE TRADITIONAL VIEW

While it is becoming increasingly important to understand the systemic interactions making up the correctional strategies that are employed, it is also important to understand the formal boundaries within which these interactions occur. A traditional definition of a correctional strategy would probably refer to the alternatives open at sentencing and/or the alternative custodial and treatment modes open to the correctional authority.

Sentencing

When one considers how long sentencing has been going on, it is surprising how few alternatives are available to the judge as he decides on a proper sentence for a convicted offender. The most common sentencing alternatives are the levying of a fine, probation, incarceration, or some combination of these. Considerably less frequently, there may also be other community resources to which the judge can refer the convicted offender. While it is not legally a sentence, the practice of dismissing a case when the evidence seems probative of guilt might also be considered a correctional strategy if the judge does so because he feels the offender will suffer too much if convicted and is unlikely to commit an offense again.

FINE

The fine is by far the most common punishment in the United States, where it is the usual consequence of conviction for all petty and minor offenses. The legal attention given to this seemingly simple device has increased lately and will continue to do so. This rising interest is related both to the new judicial intervention into discretionary correctional matters and to the increasing importance of the Equal Protection clause of the Fourteenth Amendment.

It is now illegal to incarcerate a man who has not had benefit of counsel in his defense. This decision of *Argersinger* v. *Hamlin*[36] is the logical outgrowth of *Gideon*,[37] where it was stated that the kind of trial a man receives should not depend on how much money he has. This attitude of the Supreme Court has implications for the use of a fine as a punishment. Should the fine be proportional to the gravity of the offense or to the ability of the offender to pay? If a fine cannot be paid by the poorest offender, should this alternative be available to anyone? What is a reasonable expectation of someone's ability to pay? What happens if someone fails to pay? What happens if the penalty for failure to pay is incarceration, but the defendant had no lawyer when convicted?

PROBATION

American judges are using probation with increasing frequency. While there are many good reasons for considering probation a punishment, just as a fine or incarceration is a punishment, in many states probation is not legally a punishment. In these jurisdictions, probation is considered to be in lieu of sentence. If conditions of probation are broken by the probationer and probation is revoked, the judge may then impose the original sentence without crediting the time spent on probation. Hence, if a probationer commits a new crime after two years on probation, the judge may sentence for the full-term imposed for the original crime, regardless of those two years.

Probation is usually considered a more serious alternative than a fine and is usually imposed in more serious offenses. The consequence of breaking probation regulations is more serious than non-payment of a fine, since the judge's response is likely to be more severe. Furthermore, probation does involve some restriction of freedom, because the probation staff has the legal right to intervene in the probationer's life, even if they never actually do so.

INCARCERATION

Perhaps the greatest reason for the increasing use of probation is the growing dissatisfaction with incarceration as a sentencing alternative. Incarceration for a misdemeanor is usually limited to one year, which is served in the local jail. Incarceration for a felony is usually restricted to terms of more than a year, which are served in a state prison.

The quality of prison administration was once completely ignored by the courts, but two prison systems (in Arkansas and in Philadelphia County) have recently been declared unconstitutional because their operation violates the prohibition against cruel and unusual punishment.[38] Most prisons are more humane than the extremes cited in these two cases, but even in the most humane prison there now appear to be limits to official discretion and limits to the prisoner's loss of rights.[39]

As the prison population goes down, there is a possibility that trouble in prisons will increase. As probation keeps more and more offenders out of prison and as paroling authorities release prisoners more routinely, it will be the least compromising and most unmanageable inmates who remain behind bars. At this time, however, the greater problem still seems to be the needless incarceration of men who are not dangerous to the community and who would fare better under some sort of community supervision.

Correctional alternatives

In some states, if the offender is sentenced to be incarcerated, the judge's disposition specifies to which prison facility he is allocating the prisoner. In other states, however, prison facilities have been centralized under a department or bureau. In such cases, the sentencing judge usually sentences an offender to a certain term in the place decided upon by the correctional authority. This design allows prison officials more flexibility in the allocation of offenders. Most central correctional authorities have also established a diagnostic and reception center to which the incoming offender is channeled until a more definitive decision is made about his placement.

When a statewide correctional authority makes the placing and programming decisions concerning the offender, the correctional officials obviously have more leeway than when the judge makes such decisions. Correctional departments have slowly been capitalizing on these allocation options by broadening the choices of facilities in which an offender may be placed. Frequently, however, the diagnostic sensitivity of the initial reception surpasses the alternatives available within a correctional department. These alternatives can usually be classified into three main categories: community supervision, institutionalization, and a small variety of halfway houses, group houses, and other innovative measures.

COMMUNITY SUPERVISION

Generally, the community supervision occurring within the correctional department takes the form of parole after a period of institutionalization. Frequently probation and parole are treated together by criminal justice scholars because the techniques of community supervision employed by probation and parole officers are similar. Although this similarity exists, it should be clearly understood that 1) probation is legally an alternative to punishment in many states; 2) probation is frequently seen by judges as a way of keeping offenders *out* of the correctional system rather than as a correctional method itself; and 3) probation is usually separate from the state correctional authority and is frequently part of a county organization under control of the judge. For these reasons, the community supervision strategies available to most state correctional authorities do not usually include probation.

Parole is one area of corrections that is rapidly changing. Supervision and discipline of prison inmates are still largely matters of administrative discretion. In contrast, the amount of freedom that a parolee has makes the change from parole to prison status (and vice versa) less discretionary and of more interest to the courts. The constitutional provision that no man shall be deprived of life, liberty, or property without due process now applies to parolees who face *revocation* of parole.[40] It is possible that in the future, similar rights will be applied to the *granting* of parole.

In addition to parole, other types of community supervision are used to a limited extent. Three common types are work release, study release, and furlough. All three involve temporary or periodic release from an institution for a specific purpose.

Work and study release involve releasing the offender for part of the day to employment, a school, or a college, after which he returns to the prison each day. These programs are growing and sometimes involve the transfer of state prisoners to local jail facilities or the construction of work release centers close to the employment or study opportunities.

Furlough is a temporary release to the community which it is difficult to call a form of supervision. Nevertheless, furlough (even for the usual twenty-four or forty-eight hour periods) is meant to be used by the inmate for specific purposes such as working out family problems or interviewing for a job. In theory, therefore, furlough is part of the casework design and part of the supervision process.

INSTITUTIONAL TREATMENT

Just as probation, as a form of supervision, is normally not an alternative open to a state correctional authority, jail is usually precluded as a form of institutional treatment. Most jails are county facilities intended for the detention of persons awaiting trial and persons sentenced on misdemeanor charges. A few states still allow the incarceration of serious offenders in jails for extended periods; but some of those states, such as Pennsylvania, are revamping the relationship between county and state facilities, in order to get the long-term offender out of jail and into state facilities. At the opposite extreme, several states such as Connecticut and Vermont have done away with the county as a legal entity, and the state department of corrections has taken over jail administration. These state correctional authorities do have the jail option and can transfer offenders from one kind of facility to another without being restricted by the legal classification of the crime.

The variations on prison facilities have grown over the years. The two original models for prison, the Eastern State Penitentiary in Pennsylvania and the Auburn Prison in New York, were both maximum security institutions. Some states now have three security risk gradations: maximum, medium, and minimum. Perhaps more important, states with more than one prison are beginning to specialize in different kinds of programs within each institution.

From the judge's point of view at sentencing, the major problem underlying incarceration is that of deciding who should be sent to prison and who should remain in the community. From the point of view of prison officials, the problem is what to do with the people they receive. Perhaps the most common aspect of this problem, regardless of what the prison officials are trying to provide, is their isolation from the rest of the criminal justice system and from the community, and their lack of influence over either. As long as prisons were basically places for physical restraint of offenders, the isolation of prisons was satisfactory, or even desirable. But now prisons are supposed to facilitate changes in offenders, and the physical, political, and social isolation of the prisons has become a crippling handicap. On the other side of the coin, it should be noted that there still is little evidence that community supervision is any more effective than institutional treatment in the reduction of recidivism.[41]

RECENT INNOVATIVE MEASURES

Recently, the distinction between community treatment and institutional treatment has become blurred. Forty years ago, most offenders were released from prison only after serving their full terms behind bars. With no parole system to help them make the transition, they returned without supervision to communities that had often become strange and different to them. Parole (which has become widely used in the last forty years) has lessened the shock of reentry somewhat, but a major problem for both parole supervision staff and institutional officials has been the legal distinction between prison and parole status. On occasion the prison officials feel an inmate would fare better in the community, but the autonomous parole board will not agree to parole. On other occasions, the parole staff may feel that an offender needs more continual supervision than is available on parole, but that revocation is too drastic a measure. Halfway houses, group homes, and other half-way-in or half-way-out programs have begun to spring up on both sides of the parole decision. In many states this has meant the duplication of services. With the increasing attention to economic efficiency of governmental activity, it is probable that parole and prison supervision will merge as the legal distinctions between them give way to financial considerations.

There are many strong arguments in support of programs that combine the community contact available on probation or parole with the opportunity for in-depth counseling and a sustained group life. Community facilities to which offenders may be diverted without going to prison or to which they can return after serving a prison sentence seem to offer the advantages of prison and parole settings while avoiding the disadvantages of both. Whether this is true can be decided only after a longer time has elapsed and more sophisticated evaluations have been made.

CORRECTIONAL STRATEGIES FROM A SYSTEMIC PERSPECTIVE

If we are interested in correctional strategies rather than disjointed and isolated attempts at change, an important question to raise here is, Why have the sentencing and correctional alternatives remained so unsophisticated in concept and fragmented in practice? Unless correctional authorities are completely hypocritical in their claims to rehabilitative goals, it would seem likely that the development of the correctional organization is being frustrated by something outside itself. We know quite well, for example, that correctional budgets have for years been neglected in legislatures. Although police and court organizations may also be under-budgeted, corrections has suffered proportionally greater poverty. It is also common knowledge that correctional authorities run into their greatest opposition when they seek to change the traditional relationships between the convicted offender and the community. It is still difficult to reduce the stigma of a criminal conviction. The job of *correction* is still viewed as relatively unimportant compared to other goals of the criminal justice system. Preventing crime is still not considered as important as catching and convicting offenders. In short, getting offenders out of society has been emphasized much more than getting them back into society.

NOTES

1. Governor's Special Committee on Criminal Offenders, *Preliminary Report* (New York: State of New York, 1968), pp. 29–30.
2. For a concise review of these four goals of the criminal sanction see John Kaplan, *Criminal Justice* (Mineola, N. Y.: Foundation Press, 1973), pp. 9–31. For a more detailed discussion see Herbert Packer, *The Limits of the Criminal Sanction* (Stanford: Stanford University Press, 1968), pp. 35–61.
3. For an interesting discussion of conflicting directives in a prison setting see Donald Cressey, "Contradictory Directives in Complex Organizations: The Case of the Prison," *Administrative Science Quarterly* 4 (June 1959): 1–19; and Richard Korn, "Of Crime, Criminal Justice and Corrections," *University of San Francisco Law Review* 6 (October 1971): 27–75.
4. Packer, note 2, supra, pp. 271–272.
5. See Claude Brown, *Manchild in the Promised Land* (New York: Signet, 1965) for an autobiographical description of the reasons for fighting gang behavior in Harlem.
6. On this decision game as played by parole boards see the reports of the Parole Decision Making Project, National Council on Crime and Delinquency Research Center, Davis, California (Law Enforcement Assistance Administration grant NI 72–017–G).
7. See Kaplan, note 2, supra, p. 26.
8. See Ralph Schwitzgebel, "Limitations on the Coercive Treatment of Offenders," *Criminal Law Bulletin* 8, no. 4 (1972): 267–320.
9. Ibid.
10. Perhaps the most eloquent statement of this proposition is Emile Durkheim, *The Rules of the Sociological Method* (Glencoe, Ill.: Free Press, 1950), pp. 65–75.
11. See Travis Herschi and Hanan Selvin, *Delinquency Research* (New York: Free Press, 1967).
12. On the Medical Model and its dangers see Nicholas Kittrie, *The Right to Be Different* (Baltimore: Penguin Books, 1973); and David Duffee and Vincent O'Leary, "Models of Correction: An Entry in the Packer-Griffiths Debate," *Criminal Law Bulletin* 7, no. 4 (May 1971): 329–352.
13. In the area of changing the environment to make crime more difficult see Oscar Newman, *Defensible Space* (New York: Collier Books, 1973).
14. See Robert Merton, "Social Structure and Anomie," in R. Merton, *Social*

Theory and Social Structure (Glencoe, Ill.: Free Press, 1949), pp. 125–133; and Richard Cloward and Lloyd Ohlin, *Delinquency and Opportunity* (Glencoe, Ill.: Free Press, 1960).

15. Commission to Investigate Allegations in Police Corruption, *Final Report* (New York: George Braziller, 1973).

16. Kaplan, note 2, supra; Packer, note 2, supra.

17. Michael Katz, "Patterns of Arrest and the Dangers of Public Visibility," *Criminal Law Bulletin* 9, no. 4 (1973): 311–324.

18. National Advisory Commission on Civil Disorders, *Final Report* (New York: Bantam Books, 1968), pp. 299–322.

19. Erving Goffman, *Asylums* (Garden City, N. Y.: Doubleday, 1969), p. 135.

20. No punishment without a law (violated).

21. "Due Process" clauses are found in both the Fifth and Fourteenth Amendments.

22. See National Council on Crime and Delinquency Survey, "Correction in the United States," Data Summary in President's Commission on Law Enforcement and the Administration of Justice (hereafter cited as President's Crime Commission), *Task Force Report: Corrections* (Washington, D.C.: Government Printing Office, 1967), pp. 191–192.

23. See Kittrie, note 12, supra, pp. 32–44.

24. President's Crime Commission, *Challenge of Crime in a Free Society* (Washington: Government Printing Office, 1967), pp. 7–12.

25. See material in Wolfgang, Savitz, and Johnston, *The Sociology of Crime and Delinquency* (New York: Wiley, 1962), pp. 35–68.

26. Jerome Skolnick, *Justice Without Trial* (New York: Wiley, 1967), pp. 104–179.

27. See Donald Newman, *Conviction: The Determination of Guilt or Innocence Without Trial* (Boston: Little, Brown, 1967); and Peter Goldman and Don Holt, "How Justice Works: The People vs. Donald Payne," *Newsweek*, 9 March 1971, pp. 20–37.

28. See John Conrad, *Crime and Its Treatment* (Berkeley: University of California Press, 1965).

29. Kenneth Culp Davis, *Discretionary Justice* (Baton Rouge: Louisiana State University Press, 1969).

30. James Q. Wilson, *Varieties of Police Behavior* (Cambridge: Harvard University Press, 1968), pp. 140–226.

31. Leslie Wilkins, *Social Deviance* (Englewood Cliffs, N. J.: Prentice-Hall, 1965), Chapter 4.

32. Wilson, note 30, supra, pp. 92–98.

33. See President's Crime Commission, *Task Force Report: Corrections* (Washington: Government Printing Office, 1967), Chapter 8; and Fred Cohen, "The Legal Challenge to Corrections" (Consultant's paper for the Joint Commission on Correctional Manpower and Training, Washington, D.C.: Government Printing Office, 1967).

34. See Cressey, note 3, supra, and Gresham M. Sykes, *The Society Of Captives* (Princeton, N. J.: Princeton University Press, 1971).

35. Gilbert Smith, *Social Work and the Sociology of Organizations* (Boston: Routledge and Kegan Paul, 1967).

36. 92 S. Ct. 2006 (1972).

37. Gideon v. Wainwright 372 U.S. 335 (1963).

38. Holt v. Sarver, 309 F. Supp. 362 (E.D. Ark., 1970); and Jackson v. Hendrick, 40 *Law Week* 2710 (Ct. Comm. Pls. Pa. 1972).

39. See Hazel Kerper and Janeen Kerper, *Legal Rights of the Convicted* (St. Paul: West, 1974); and Cohen, note 34, supra.

40. Morrissey v. Brewer 408 U.S. 471 (1972).

41. Leslie Wilkins, *The Evaluation of Penal Measures* (New York: Random House, 1971).

The Impact of Preconviction Operations on the Correctional Strategies 2

This chapter is not about "corrections" in the traditional sense of the term. It is about the preconviction system, and it covers topics that ordinarily would fall under a discussion of police operations, police management, the role of lawyers and judges, and court organization. For this reason it may appear to be a review; but it is not intended as a review. We are not interested in this text in saying things about police or about courts *except as those components of the criminal justice network perform the function of selecting the offenders* who will be subjected to the available correctional strategies. This chapter is an examination of the *input* to the correctional system.

Even in this regard, however, this chapter reaches farther back into the preconviction process than previous systematic coverages of corrections have done. In 1940, for example, Donald Clemmer was careful to examine the input to the prison he was studying.[1] But he did so largely by describing the variety of demographic and biographic information he discovered about the inmates of the prison community. For example, he discussed the differences between the inmate with a primarily rural background and the inmate with a primarily urban background. He examined the complexities of family relationships. What he did not do, however, was examine the *process by which certain offenders became inmates and other offenders did not.* He was interested in *differences among inmates.* But the range of differences he looked at and the impact this range had upon the prison social system were restricted by the fact that *all the offenders he examined were inmates.* He did not, in contrast, compare differences between new inmates and defendants who were arrested and later released, and he did not look at the difference

28

between offenders sent to prison and those sent to probation. He focused on *characteristics of inmates.* We are focusing on *characteristics of the preconviction process.* We will certainly be interested in the nature of inmates, but we will be equally interested in the nature of officials and the structure of the process that reduces the probability of conviction and punishment in some cases and increases the probability in other cases.

The underlying reasons for taking this "long way around" are important to comprehend, if for no other reason than that this comprehension can provide valuable insights into how a correctional operation works when its managers do *not* have this understanding. The importance of the preconviction process can perhaps be better understood through the use of an oversimplified analogy. Rather than talk about the characteristics of inmates, let us consider the characteristics of chicken eggs. Eggs are categorized in the retail market in terms of size. We can, to a certain extent, understand what an extra-large egg is by opening a carton and noting that the variety within that dozen (all different) have an average weight. After opening two or three cartons in the same category, we will be fairly sure of what we are talking about, and reasonably willing to bet that the next carton of extra-large eggs contains a distribution of about the same mean weight with the same deviation from the mean.

An egg buyer who knows nothing more about extra-large eggs than this, however, is really in the dark. He knows something about a certain population of eggs, but he doesn't know what was *not* placed in the carton. He can only find this out by looking in cartons of other size categories. If he does that, then he knows not only the average weight of extra-large, but the relationship between this category and those eggs that have not made the grade. Moreover, if he were to do a study of wholesale prices or of the farm economy rather than worry about what eggs to select for the breakfast table, he would understand that these categories are not "natural" differences, but *conventions* agreed upon by farmers and wholesalers. If he were to study the mechanisms by which an egg arrives in one carton or another in terms of these conventions, he would also see that the inherent traits of eggs—or of chickens—are no more "responsible" for the final destination of eggs than the decisions made about them by chicken raisers, buyers, and consumers. The raisers, for example, do *not* decide that all eggs laid of a certain type and size make the market. Because the farmer has a longer-range goal than making a one-time profit, he does not sell some eggs at all. Instead, he calls in other resources and plans to have some special eggs become chickens.

Like many retail egg buyers, many correctional officials and many students of correction stop with the discovery of the allowable variation within the first box of extra-large eggs. For them this is the discovery of the usual variation within the first prison or parole caseload. Somehow, the similarities between these offenders and all those who are not selected are forgotten; and the fact that the *offenders* arrived at their respective destinations because of the conventions established among police and court officials and certain community groups is also forgotten. Of course, if the job of the correctional officials is merely to handle in some way the shipments they receive, this ignorance of the system relationships is not too important. But supposedly, the correctional officials are going to do something with these shipments—something based on the conventions accepted by other people. Unless the correctional official knows what these conventions are, he may not react toward the shipment in terms of the differences that, to other officials, mattered the most. And since the correctional official deals with human beings rather than eggs, he will be doubly ineffective, because the conventions matter not only to the police, the court, and the community, but also to the offender. Thus (to take one instance of inmate-staff conflict) the correctional official who lacks this knowledge of the preconviction system is at a loss to deal with the offender who insists that he has been mistakenly thrown in with the wrong lot. If the correctional official does not know about these other lots or about the decisions by which these lots are arrived at, he will probably assume that the offender is a "trouble-maker." The offender *will be* a trouble-maker. But the official is likely to locate the trouble within the offender— "this egg is bad"—rather than between the offender and the preconviction officials—"this egg was poorly selected."

In this chapter we will study the "non-correctional" parts of the system. But we will not look at all that goes on there. Rather, we are interested in the conventions or patterns of behavior that have a direct bearing upon what the correctional system can and cannot expect, and what it can and cannot do.

CATEGORIES OF POLICE BEHAVIOR

In discussing the police contribution to the correctional selection process, we have divided the major factors into two different categories. In this section we will discuss the individual police officer in terms of how he interacts on the street with citizens, suspects, and offenders. In the next section (Organizational Pressures on Police Discretion) we will discuss how the behavior of the individual officer is constrained by police organization and how that organizational structure contributes to differential treatment of people susceptible to prosecution.

The model for categorizing police behavior has been developed by Michael O'Neill.[2] It is a typology based on two dimensions that were posited as theoretically significant to the policeman's decision about how he should behave. The first dimension is that of activity. Some policemen believe that they should be very active in the community, that they should intervene in a variety of situations whether or not their assistance has been solicited. Other policemen believe that they should maintain a "low profile," that the community should be free of their influence as long as the normal pattern of community behavior is maintained. They will respond to calls for assistance, but even in these situations they believe it is their prerogative (if not their duty) to turn down some requests for intervention because they do not see the problem as severe or as police business.

Perpendicular to the dimension of activity, O'Neill places the dimension of formalism. This dimension refers to police beliefs about the *way* in which they should intervene, and about what justifies intervention. Some policemen, for example, see every occasion for intervention as justification for invoking the criminal sanction. There are many legal prohibitions, some of them vague enough to permit any intervention opportunity to be classified as an opportunity for arrest. Other officers see their role in a much more informal light. The opportunities for arrest may be there, but these officers perceive many of these opportunities as "false." In other words, they see the formal legal "solutions" to certain community problem situations as irrelevant. These officers believe that their role in the community is to handle problem situations *without* enforcing a law. They may use the power of their uniform or the threat of legal intervention as a basis for their intervention authority, but the solutions in their repertoire are generally informal and do not involve arrest.

These two dimensions and the typological identities of these kinds of officers are given in Table 1.

Table 1

VARIETIES OF POLICE ROLE PERCEPTION

	High	Crime Fighter	Law Enforcer
Formalism			Social
	Low	Watchman	Agent
		Low	**High**
			Activity

O'Neill constructed a questionnaire that measured the dimensions of formalism and activity and administered the form to policemen in a large west coast city. He found, to the surprise of many, that these four role perceptions were to be found among all traditional categories of officers. Belief did not seem to be affected by the officers' race, age, education, length of service, shift, or area of the city patrolled. The one significant correlate of these belief patterns was the peer group within the department to which the officer belonged. This does not mean that the officer's peer group is a cause of his beliefs. It is possible that, somehow, like-minded officers manage to find one another within the department and wangle job assignments that bring them all into physical proximity and foster the primary group interaction.

However one wants to explain the different attitudes of the police, the existence of these attitudes poses interesting (but at this point untested) possibilities for the correctional system. Before we look at these belief patterns, it should be remembered that they can be assumed to result in few action differences when the nature of the intervention opportunity presented is both severe and relatively infrequent. Thus, all four types of officers might be expected to behave about the same in response to a shooting, an armed robbery, or a murder. But these are rare events in the policeman's world. Most of his intervention opportunities are common, routine events in which the public is not certain of the right or wrong in the situation, where the policeman's duty is not clearly defined, and where his own discretion weighs heavily in the kind of action that results.[3] Thus, cases of vagrancy, public drunkenness, assault, malicious mischief, and so on, are events that are not completely defined until the officer himself has made a decision. And these decisions are influenced by what he perceives as important in police work.

Consequently, the existence of these patterns of belief within one legal jurisdiction presents many possibilities for unequal and differential enforcement of the law. The low activity of Crime Fighters and Watchmen, for example, reduces the frequency of police intervention in community life and thus the frequency of arrests. The high formalism of Crime Fighters and Law Enforcers ensures that many interventions will result in arrest. In contrast, the Social Agents and Watchmen see themselves as community agents, but not as the front line of the criminal justice system. To look at what happens from a potential offender's viewpoint, he is much "closer" to the correctional system if patrol in his area is handled by Law Enforcers than by Watchmen. Potential offenders in an area patrolled by Social Agents may come under scrutiny of the police, but their behavior will be handled informally until they commit very serious crimes.

The importance of police enforcement patterns to the court and correctional system is probably not clearly perceived because most of the offenders arrested by different groups of officers will come together into a single court system for processing. Thus, the influence of the police decision on the selection of the criminal justice input becomes diffused. It is perceived in the courtroom, for example, "that all vagrants come from the same area of the city," rather than that "all vagrants who are arrested are arrested by the same (Law Enforcer) policemen." Even this observation is not so interesting as the possibility that "all vagrants in the patrol area of group X (Social Agent) are taken to a soup kitchen or shelter, or are referred to a social agency" or that "all vagrants are ignored by group Y (Crime Fighter), while group Z (Watchmen) either ignores vagrants or redirects them to skid row." Because such perceptions are seldom made, we really do not know how those patterns influence the criminal justice system. But if James Q. Wilson is correct that the front-line policeman is trusted with the discretion to make these very different approaches to vagrancy (because the front-line man is on the scene while his supervisors are not),[4] then the effects of these decisions can be important. Vagrants, for example, will or will not fill the county jail, depending on which police group beliefs are dominant in the most disorganized sections of the city. If this particular section of the community is patrolled by Law Enforcers, the jail will have to accommodate a larger number of minor offenders than if the area is patrolled by Watchmen or Social Agents. If the jail must hold many minor offenders, then jail administrators cannot use their limited resources in other ways, such as developing more humane conditions for serious offenders awaiting trial or developing work release programs for convicted offenders with families and vocational potential.

The differential enforcement problem is much more severe in other areas. A major problem in large cities, for example, is the detention of juveniles. It is a severe problem because detention facilities for juveniles are usually poorly administered and overcrowded. More important, the juvenile, unlike the fifty-year-old vagrant, has the opportunity for many more years of contact with the system. His future contacts and his attitudes toward society, toward education, toward the law, and so on, are still developing. We can expect that a juvenile's brushes with the law in minor matters, such as illegal driving, joy-riding, experimentation with alcohol and marijuana, will be exacerbated by the Law Enforcer, ignored by Watchmen and Crime Fighters, and handled informally by Social Agents. If, as some delinquency theorists argue, much delinquent behavior is the juvenile's search for limits, ignoring his behavior is not a satisfactory response.[5] But if labeling theorists are also correct that the juvenile will respond by acting to achieve the label placed on him by officials, then the Law Enforcer will contribute to a solidification of a delinquent identity.[6] Again, the kind of police behavior with which the juvenile interacts would seem to be very important.

The future operation of the juvenile court and juvenile corrections will be influenced by the present police interaction with juveniles. And there does not seem to be very much control over which kind of police behavior will have the greatest impact.

To take the same problem from the output side of corrections, we can imagine other very significant impacts of correctional goals and operations on police. If it is a correctional trend to reintegrate offenders into the community through half-way houses, work release, and parole mechanisms, we should anticipate very different consequences for these programs as they interact with different police behavior patterns. Crime Fighters and Law Enforcers, for example, might look upon offenders in the community as a serious risk, and their surveillance activity might alter the offender's perceptions of his chances to make it in the community. Watchmen might see these correctional programs as contrary to the norms of the community or as disruptive of the cultural patterns they seek to conserve. Lastly, Social Agents may cooperate with such programs, but since they do not see themselves as members of the criminal justice system, their cooperation with state correctional agencies may not be satisfactory to correctional officials.

In conclusion, it is not the goal of correctional strategists to turn policemen into correctional agents. But correctional strategies will be influenced considerably by different kinds of police role behavior. Certainly there is a great need for research in this area and for increasing the dialogue among correctional officials, offenders, and the policeman on the street. There should be policy sessions between correctional officials and police managers (which are virtually nonexistent at present). And in these policy sessions, there should be ways of using the analysis of police discretion discussed here for redeployment of the different police groups to enhance the development of various correctional strategies.

ORGANIZATIONAL PRESSURES ON POLICE DISCRETION

We have been analyzing the possible effects of different police role performances on the selection of input into the criminal justice system. It is apparent that there can be major differences among individual policemen in the way they handle the minor, routine events that make up the bulk of their work. The possibility of recognizing these differences formally, and planning correctional and police policy with the understanding that these differences exist, brings up the relationship between correctional strategies and the police organization in its entirety. The individual officer as the front-line worker has considerable discretion, because he has firsthand information and frequently must make decisions without supervisory review. In a sense, then, police policy is made in the street by the officer. But police managers should influence the policeman's use of discretion much more than they now do, by setting guidelines or setting up constraints beyond which the patrolman cannot go without risking negative sanctions.

The demand has become stronger that police managers take a more active role in policy making. For example, the Supreme Court of the United States has in several of its opinions urged state legislatures and police managers to take a more active role in setting specific police goals and structuring ways to achieve them.[7] To some extent, this kind of activity is foreign to both the legislative process and to the police manager. State legislators have traditionally taken a piecemeal approach to enacting criminal laws and the procedural regulations that govern agencies. They have reacted to one crisis after another, one wave of public sentiment after another, by prosecuting specific acts and relegislating criminal penalties, without much regard to how all these pieces might fit together in terms of how the police department should enforce the law. Moreover, police managers have also taken a case-by-case approach to problems. One of the major reasons, perhaps, is that police managers in most departments are not professional managers who have been trained in integrating and coordinating the activity of many people. It is much more likely that they have been trained as policemen to handle particular events. The notion that the police manager might structure his organization to achieve long-range goals by codifying events into categories and predicting their occurrence is relatively new to police work.

Within the last ten years or so, police departments have become increasingly interested in the applicability of operations research, computerized communications systems, and so on.[8] The goal of much of this activity has been to give the centralized police administration greater control over the widely dispersed front-line workers. There have been many complex studies, for example, about the optimum way to deploy policemen so that there is maximum police patrol coverage in high crime areas or at times of the week with high crime frequency. The central theme of this kind of study appears to be the growing concern with *efficiency*—how to get the highest output or return for the lowest possible input or cost.

There has been much less concern with the idea of *effectiveness*. Without this broader concern for effectiveness, many advances of police science have been achieved without sufficient attention to the way in which the efficiently run operations contribute to desirable social goals of the police organization,[9] of the criminal justice system, or of other community systems. There is evidence, for example, that increased police efficiency in the apprehension of criminals has reduced the policeman's ability to communicate effectively with various portions of a city population.[10] There is also evidence that police efficiency has been increased without attention to the demand in the unit for certain procedural regularities, so that efficient apprehension tactics have conflicted with efficient prosecution tactics.[11] And neither police nor court officials have considered how changes in their operating patterns might affect the operations of correctional agencies, which are supposed to reduce the probability that arrested offenders will return to crime.[12]

It becomes necessary, therefore, to consider how existing police organizational structures and policy decisions (or lack of them) will influence the effectiveness of present correctional strategies and how conflicts between these strategies and police organization might be mimimized through adaptation of the correctional system. We will look at three related areas of police organization in order to suggest the outlines and utility of this kind of assessment:

1) the structure of the front-line role in relation to management, community structure, and criminal justice goals
2) the maintenance of the police organization in terms of recruitment, training, and socialization into police work
3) the effect of current criteria for the evaluation of police organizational performance

The structure of the policeman's role

We have looked at several ways in which the patrolman in a police department views his role responsibilities. So far, however, we have not discussed the basic characteristics of the police role itself, as it affects all policemen. Two major figures in this area of study are Jerome Skolnick, author of the now classic *Justice Without Trial*,[13] and James Q. Wilson, whose contribution is the equally important *Varieties of Police Behavior*.[14] The two authors are in essential agreement about the organizational and cultural constraints that form the basic outline of the policeman's job. The dominant characteristics that they identify are:

1) the fundamental bifurcation of police activity into the function of order maintenance and the function of law enforcement
2) the apprenticeship nature of the police socialization process
3) the dominance of the policeman's reference to values related to craftsmanship

Skolnick and Wilson argue that the history of police organization and the nature of interaction on the street maintain a distinction for policemen between tasks that are related to keeping order in a particular area of the city and tasks that are related to enforcing the law. Both men argue that the recent emphasis on LAW'N'ORDER has beclouded public and police awareness of the major demands and distribution of time in police work.

Wilson points out that police forces in the United States originally had the responsibility of watchmen. For example, it was their duty in Boston, in 1820, to patrol the streets at night in order to keep public travel free of obstacles. It was not the police duty to go out and apprehend persons suspected of crimes. Originally that duty was reserved to officers of the court or to the citizens at large. The term "hue and cry" for example, refers to the practice by the victim of a crime, or witnesses to a crime, of yelling for public assistance in chasing down a suspect. All the people on the block were supposed to drop what they were doing and rush out in hot pursuit. When prisons were first built in the United States, there was no specialized group whose job it was to seek out and deliver suspects. In 1820, the criminal justice system began with the prosecution process.[15]

It was only as the eastern seaboard cities began to grow and the new urban governments became more established that policemen took on the job of catching criminals. Their original duties were not to change the social order by seeking out suspects and preventing crime, but rather to maintain whatever social order existed in a particular district. The police were hired to prevent major social disturbances, such as riots, but if picking pockets or burglary were common in an area of a city, it was not the job of the police to change these social norms.

Wilson points out that in terms of time spent per function, the major task of the police is still to maintain order. He found in the city of Syracuse, New York, for example, that 90 percent of police dispatches involved routine calls for assistance of some sort. Only 10 percent of police dispatches involved high probability of serious criminal activity.[16] The order-maintenance function of police activity is very much in evidence in the police role perceptions we have examined. The Watchman Style, for example, is a vestige of the original police role. The policeman is seen as a guardian of existing social order, not an agent of law enforcement. The Social Agent seems equally affected by this tradition. The policeman is supposed to intervene in problem situations, but he does not view the criminal sanction and formalized correctional strategies as basic tools in this task. The Crime Fighter also seems to be affected in the sense that he has rejected the order-maintenance function as his duty and perceives this traditional police service as the task of other social agencies. The Law Enforcer seems to be affected in a different way. Perhaps giving in to the recent pressures for professionalization or for LAW'N'ORDER, this kind of policeman has merged the order maintenance and law enforcement functions. In a sense, the traditional police virtue of "handling the situation" or "keeping a quiet beat" is no longer in the Law Enforcer's repertoire.

The major impact of this police tradition on corrections is that the police organization is not structured to be an integral component of the criminal justice system. Until very recently, communities, particularly urban communities, have utilized the police force as part of the primary institutional structure of the social system rather than as a specialty service that is called in to deal with social disorder. In other words, the police force has been viewed as part of the governmental structure that keeps things right rather than as an agency that fixes things gone wrong. According to this outlook, we can categorize most police behavior in the same boxes that include public schools, city politics, industrial and economic organizations, and so forth. The fact that the police initiate prosecution by arresting people means that they are also responsible for remedial action or "correctional" activity.

This is a fairly unusual situation for major or primary social institutions. For example, if the public schools are incapable of dealing with a particular student, the student is usually relegated to increasingly less challenging and prestigious areas of the curriculum until he finally drops out or is expelled. Until very recently, public schools were not required to commence remedial action with such a student. It was the school's job to educate the vast majority who conformed and were educable within the traditional institutional processes. If the poor student flunked and/or dropped out, remedial action was ignored. This function was relegated to commercial vocational schools, or it was taken up by training schools and reformatories which received poor students who also committed crimes.

In contrast, the police organization is not only required to keep order in the community, it is also required to recognize when this activity has been performed inadequately or incompetently and to initiate remedial action. In some sense, this second function might be a welcome addition to both school and police systems. It might be a change in the right direction, for example, if the school system were legally bound to identify problems in its normal operation and to continually test alternatives until some means was found for satisfying all students' educational needs.[17] In police work, however, a frequent result of this dual function is that the signals for remedial action are seen as reflecting on the individual who gives the police department trouble, rather than on the contribution of existing police strategies and tactics to the occurrence of social disorder. This is *not* to suggest that suspects identified by the police may not be guilty. Of course they may be guilty; crimes are committed by individuals. But the fact that an individual has committed a crime and is caught has little to do with improving the effectiveness of the crime prevention or the order maintenance function. Those functions have little to do with interactions between police and suspects. Catching a criminal after a crime is a retail business. Preventing crime and maintaining social order is a wholesale business in which the police must concentrate on certain variables of community structure rather than on individual offenders.

The high probability of apprehending an offender in the immediate future should signal a switch in roles for the policeman: at that point it is no longer his task to maintain order, but to start remedial action with an individual. There is little reason, of course, why the ordinary patrolman, with the usual training and socialization into police work, should understand the difference between these two functions. But more often than not, the apprehension of the individual offender symbolizes to the policeman the achievement of his goals.[18] Catching the crook becomes a substitute for keeping the peace, and the suspect becomes a scapegoat—the personification of all the forces in the city that lead to the incidence of crime. Thus, the apprehension of the offender is treated by police departments as a victory—as the end of the peace-keeping game, rather than as the beginning of the remedial game. In summary, the police seem to understand arrest as the end of their peace-keeping duties, rather than as a signal requiring another set of behaviors on their part that would be congruent with remedial goals.

Given this reversal in the police perception of the remedial sequence (i.e., that the arrest "solves the case"), the police organization cannot be well coordinated with judicial and correctional components of a justice system. To the police, the phases of the criminal justice process that follow the arrest cannot make a great deal of sense. If the offender is the personification of all the evil forces in the city, deliberation over his guilt or innocence can seem like a wasteful drama of ideals; and if correctional officials treat as a redeemable individual someone whom the police perceive to be a manifestation of criminogenic forces, the correctional process can appear as total nonsense.

It must be said here that the police are not the only branch of the justice system to perceive the offender as a symbol of social disorder rather than as a person with problems. Newspapers and political figures frequently decry lenient judges, as if using remedial action with an individual were a direct threat to community stability. Judges also have ambivalent feelings, particularly at sentencing. They may understand the social norm of treating the offender as a symbol of socially rejected ways of behaving. For the correctional officials who may strive to understand the convict as a person, this vision is usually confounded by social beliefs about protecting society by isolating an individual.

In summary, the police role in society is a very complex one in which the two major functions conflict. The ultimate objective of maintaining order in a community should be order and the reduction of crime, rather than merely the apprehension of individual offenders. The remedial process, of course, does not end with the police at all, but with adjudication and correction. Therefore, effective corrections is considerably more difficult, if not impossible, when the police organization performing the apprehension or selection function treats this activity in and of itself as functional for community stability.

Maintenance of the organization

In their analysis of the maintenance of the police organization, the interest of Skolnick and Wilson in police training and socialization processes takes on paramount importance. According to both men, the majority of police officers—those who are responsible for the front-line duties of order maintenance—are not professionals. They do not learn to do what they do through a rigorous educational experience like the one to which doctors and lawyers are subjected. Their competence and knowledge is not codified in a set of academic and professional principles, the mastery of which governs their behavior in particular instances. Their loyalty is not to a professional organization that governs the conduct of its members through a canon of ethics.

The policeman's loyalty is usually to the police organization in which he works and to his superior. Unlike the professional, the policeman cannot travel from job to job and perform the same set of tasks in different geographic and economic areas. The policeman is usually locked into a career of limited vertical mobility within one department. If he does travel to another department, he must learn all over the skills and reaction patterns that will be most effective in the new setting.

Some police do become professionalized in certain areas, of course; but front-line, on-the-street activities are not segmented in such a way that the ordinary policeman can become professional. He must remain a generalist who reacts quickly to a high variety of situations as they present themselves.[19] As Skolnick and Wilson put it, the police job is learned through apprenticeship—through watching more experienced officers handle situations.[20] In his training and socialization the policeman is akin to plumbers, electricians, carpenters, and others engaged in guild-like activities in which people learn by doing.

If this perception of the police training process is true, we can expect the police to be a very close-knit group. The policeman's basic reference as to whether he is doing his job well or not is other policemen. In essence, this means that a good policeman is one who follows the social norms of the group rather than scientific or legal principles that define the best way to accomplish a task. Given this reference for achievement, we can understand why it might be difficult for the policeman to understand what elements contribute to an effective prosecution or on what basis the Supreme Court criticizes police behavior. To the policeman, a good arrest is the one that is conducted as most of the officers in the group conduct arrests. For lawyers, a good arrest is one that provides legally admissible evidence in a court room. Similarly, this organizational maintenance pattern may make it difficult for the police to understand the complexities of a contemporary sentencing decision. Sentencing is not based on the policeman's perceptions of what contributes to a good arrest (for him, an end product) but on the perception of the judge and his staff of what will contribute to effective remedial action (for the court, a means to an end).

Similarly, the pressures on the police to maintain the normative perception of apprehension as an end in itself raises many possibilities of conflict with the traditional agencies of correction. It makes sense, for example, that the police perceive probation and parole functions as primarily those of protecting the community. Having located the sources of community disorder as coming, at least symbolically, from *within the offender*, the police are less likely to understand and cooperate with probation and parole provisions of service. Even though many probation and parole staffs are overworked and many individual agents perceive surveillance of the client as more important than service, most correctional field agents interact with probationers and parolees within a frame of reference very different from that which influences policemen.

The basic difference in the frame of reference, of course, has to do with the commitment of the policeman to order maintenance (and hence, to the control of events) and the commitment of the correctional field staff to remedial action (and hence, to the control of people). The policeman, for example, is likely to give a citizen a second chance, following a confrontation, if he believes that this is the best way to handle the situation and/or that the possibility that the citizen will repeat his mistake is rather slim. From an officer's point of view, the granting of a second chance usually means that the utility of arrest is questionable because the evidence is not really clearcut, the infraction is *de minimus,* or the situation is clearly under control despite infraction of the law.

The perception of the "second chance" by the probation and parole officer is considerably different. While the field agent may also pride himself on "handling the situation," the parameters of his situation are different, the tools he uses are different, and the rewards the agent receives are different. The patrolman, for example, may be rewarded for "hauling someone in." The field worker who hauls someone in, however, may have his own skills called into question. It was the agent's job, after all, to keep the offender in the community. The policeman is likely to view the probationer or parolee in the community as a threat to the situation that he is trying to maintain. The correctional field worker, in contrast, may perceive the patrolman's surveillance of his client as a threat to the situation he is trying to maintain.

To summarize the conflict, the correctional worker, no matter how conservative, is charged with changing community norms to some extent. He is the guardian of the tail end of a remedial correctional strategy (probation or incarceration and parole) that succeeds when the previously identified offender and the community find some way of adapting to each other. This kind of success is foreign to a police department that perceives its goals as accomplished when it takes people out of the community.

Agency-specific efficiency rates

The conflicts between correctional strategies and police goals and socialization patterns can be tied together with the concept of performance evaluation. Perhaps the most typical method of evaluating the department as a whole is in terms of fluctuations in the crime rate. The crime rate in a city is an amorphous, inaccurate statistic that is a function of many things besides criminal behavior and police behavior. Furthermore, it is very unclear what kinds of police activity affect crime rates, and what those effects are. Nevertheless, the police are supposed to spend most of their time reducing the crime rate or maintaining a low one. Unfortunately, there are few ways in which the police supervisor can evaluate his personnel in terms of how individual performances contribute to the overall goal. He might rely on reports from citizens in a precinct about the conduct of officers on particular beats. But the police typically lack confidence in this kind of evaluation since citizens may have many different motives for calling officers good or bad, and the police manager is unlikely to have the methodological sophistication needed to sort out reliable or valid evaluations from unreliable and biased ones. Moreover, as we discussed in the last section, police typically do not accept outside evaluations of their performance as valid; instead, they refer to their peers.[21]

Thus, as Skolnick sees it, police management faces a dilemma. There seem to be no objective criteria that measure a policeman's contribution to major police goals; but without some objective criteria, police managers would receive many internal complaints about unfairness and favoritism in the distribution of promotions and other rewards.[22] Skolnick suggests, then, that the police department more or less invents "objective" evaluation criteria, not because they are accurate indices of departmental accomplishment, but because hard numbers serve as a better justification for rewards than subjective evaluations.[23] Police managers feel that it is wiser to appear certain than to admit uncertainty, not only because admitting uncertainty could play into the hands of opposing external forces (such as the opposition political party), but also because it undermines the policeman's confidence in the reasons why he receives the kinds of rewards he does.

A major example of the kind of evaluation criterion used by the police is the "arrest rate" or the "clearance rate." The clearance rate is simply a ratio arrived at by dividing the numbers of *crimes solved by police* by the number of *crimes known to police*. Actually, the clearance rate does not even enjoy the mathematical status of a ratio, since, in reality, "crimes solved" is the number of *persons* arrested plus the number of crimes these arrested persons are willing to accept as their responsibility. As Skolnick points out, many crimes are cleared very quickly after one arrest because the offender, if he is convicted on the evidence against him in the arrest crime, knows that he will not be additionally punished for other crimes he admits. In fact, says Skolnick, the offender may be rewarded for cooperating.[24]

Thus, an evaluation criterion such as the clearance rate involves two major problems: 1) It bears no real relationship to peace in the community (the crime rate and the arrest rate are not directly related); and 2) it bears little relationship to the effectiveness of individual officers. What it *does* do is provide a basis in (manufactured) numbers for grading the accomplishment of different policemen and different police units. The difficulty with this arrest rate, if we look at the two problems together, is that it pressures policemen to respond to a short-term statistical *measure of performance* rather than to long-term, fundamental goals of peace-keeping; and it reinforces the notion that arrest is an end in itself rather than a means to a remedial end. To the extent that such agency-specific efficiency rates are enforced, the possibility of integrating criminal justice system operations is reduced and the means to order-maintenance in the community is ignored. The result is that police are led to believe in the efficacy of something that is not only poor bookkeeping, but is an entry in the wrong book! If anything, the clearance rate is a measure of input to the courts rather than a measure of the peace-keeping function. It isolates the police from the community and from more accurate measures of their job, and it shortens the policeman's time perspective so that he cannot comprehend the duration of the remedial process or the effects on that remedial process that are generated by police intake decisions.[25]

PROSECUTORIAL DECISIONS: THE MAKING OF THE CORRECTIONAL CLIENT

The major initiator of the criminal justice process in most cases is the district attorney and his staff. It is important to understand that the court, unlike the police or correctional departments, is not one organization. The district attorney is an independent agent in the system, subordinate only to the constituency that elects him. In large cities, the elected D. A. is a manager of a complex organization of appointed assistants. Whether the prosecutor's organization is large or small, his role is crucial in the selection of offenders for the application of correctional strategies.

While there are many arguments for and against the discretion of the policeman, it is accepted that the prosecutor has the discretion to seek or reject implementation of the criminal sanction. One major difference between the discretion of the prosecutor and that of a policeman is that the prosecutor is an elected official whose authority is supposedly under close scrutiny by the body politic. Supposedly, the decisions of the prosecutor have much higher visibility than the decisions of a policeman, and if the prosecutor demonstrates a serious misuse of discretion he places his job in jeopardy. Whether these fundamentals of representative government actually function in practice is debatable, particularly in a large urban office where most of the decisions are made by assistant district attorneys under superficial, if any, supervision by their elected superior.[26]

There are innumerable ways in which a prosecutor may affect the selection of correctional strategies to be used and their effectiveness, but we will limit ourselves here to three key issues that highlight the structure of a prosecutor's office in relationship to correctional goals:

1) the selection and socialization of the prosecutor; 2) the criteria of evaluation used to judge his performance; and 3) the ways in which the prosecutor contributes to the manipulation of the pre-arraignment system in order to obtain a conviction.

Socialization of the prosecutor

Unlike most police and correctional officials, the prosecutor is a professional in the traditional sense of the term. He is a lawyer who has undergone a more or less rigorous educational experience and has also passed an examination admitting him to practice. Contrary to the training received by policemen, the prosecutor has received most of his training *off* the job and away from the organization in which he works.

In comparing the difference between the entry process into a police department or correctional organization and entry into a pro-secutor's office, it is helpful to contrast the organizational activities of *selection* and *socialization*. Amitai Etzioni postulates that the amount of time spent on these two activities is inversely correlat-ed.[27] The greater the degree of selection, the less an organization needs to socialize its recruits; the less it is able to be selective, the greater the socialization pressure placed upon the recruit. The valid-ity of this point can be easily seen by comparing socialization efforts in institutions that, by statute, must accept everyone eligible with socialization efforts in institutions that do not have that restraint. For example, the socialization efforts in public primary and secondary schools is high compared to the efforts of selective private schools, and much higher compared to colleges that admit only academically qualified candidates. Likewise, the socialization of inmates entering a state prison is considerably more rigorous than socialization pres-sures in private institutions that can select the delinquents they want to treat. Similarly, the socialization process as one enters a police force as a patrolman is considerably higher than the socialization necessary to make people trained as lawyers behave as prosecutors.

In the instances where selectivity is high, presumably much of the socialization effort has gone on elsewhere: in this case, in the law school. On the other hand, the kind of socialization process that has taken place in law school deserves some scrutiny. Several legal writ-ers recently have noted that very few law schools are actively in-terested in the criminal justice process. In most first-class law schools, most good students seem to be pressured toward corporate or private practice. There are both academic and financial reasons for this trend. Academically, the criminal law is only a minor part of the normal law school curriculum. There are many other areas of the law to be covered, and these other areas are frequently seen as more interesting, more complex, and, hence, academically more rewarding.

Financially, the criminal law does not hold great promise for a law student, who may have run up considerable indebtedness to pay for his education, and whose social status or social aspirations may not make running around jails and criminal courts for lower-class defendants an enjoyable prospect. Furthermore, the defendant in the criminal process is rarely a rich man. Guilty or innocent, he is unlikely to have the financial resources that will allow the defense lawyer to use many outside resources in preparing the case, nor is the ultimate monetary reward very great. Consequently, the law students who stand highest in their class are usually uninterested in criminal practice either as defense lawyers or as prosecutors. Most frequently, the law students who go on to handle criminal cases upon graduation are at the bottom of their law school class.

In his study of the Manhattan criminal courts Blumberg notes this background of criminal lawyers, but he hypothesizes that poor academic standing may be influenced by other factors than lack of academic ability. Blumberg suggests that assistant prosecutors, particularly, have been law students who have had a long-standing interest in politics. They perceive a first job in a prosecutor's office as a good port of entry into local politics. Blumberg postulates that these lawyers may have received poor grades in law school because their political activism had taken them away from their studies. He also suggests that while their political interest gets these men into the prosecutor's office, it also gets them out. They expect careers as politicians, not as prosecutors. For them, the prosecutorial role is a temporary one in which they hope to pick up some trial experience, make a name, and establish the right connections.[28]

In summary, a large prosecutor's office has a high turnover rate, and many of the assistant prosecutors do not see the criminal justice system as a final career placement. Conversely, we might expect that the assistants who do stay on are persons whose vertical mobility has for one reason or another been limited. While they may be dedicated, it is equally likely that they are typical bureaucrats who have replaced their original goals with the routine rewards of office. In either case, it would seem that many prosecutors have chosen to perform that role in order to accomplish goals that are more or less tangential to the systematic and effective prosecution of cases.

It would be a mistake, however, to interpret this analysis of the socialization pressures on the prosecutor as evidence of corruption or of the dominance of ulterior motives behind every decision a prosecutor makes. This is not the case at all. There is a long-standing tradition in the United States that prosecutors should be publicly elected officials, responsive to the people, and committed to a career of public service. The second-class status of the criminal law in law schools and the use of a legal education as a political stepping stone are really commensurate with that tradition. *The current perspective is that prosecutors should be career professionals whose primary goal is the effective management of criminal justice.* It is not surprising that the systems perspective introduced by the President's Crime Commission should require socialization patterns and training opportunities that are foreign to most prosecutors.

However, now that society has apparently adopted the system model for application to criminal justice, we must be aware of the consequences of our traditions for the effective implementation of that model.

The basic consequence for correctional strategies is that the prosecutor, the key official in the selection of correctional input, is not sufficiently aware of the way in which his decisions about prosecution affect the prospects for effective correctional activity. Standard law school texts in the criminal law, such as Paulson and Kadish, *Criminal Law and its Processes,*[29] do not cover corrections. And widely acclaimed jurisprudential treatments of the criminal justice process such as Packer's *Limits of the Criminal Sanction*[30] do not treat corrections as part of that process. A major reason for this limitation, it would seem, is the dependence in legal circles on classical criminology as a basis for much of the writing about social control and punishment.[31]

Classical criminologists such as Bentham, for example, built their theories of criminal behavior on a "rational" model of man. In this school of thought, the criminal act is treated as a rational decision by the offender that the profit of a crime outweighs the severity of punishment and the chances of being apprehended. Hence, the punishment for crime is supposed to be severe enough to outweigh the illegal profit. In a word, the aim of the law is deterrence. The prosecutor is the person who implements deterrence by prosecuting the crime and demonstrating that the criminal gain is not worth the effort. It is *presumed* that control is effective if the conviction and the ensuing pronouncement of punishment are sufficient demonstration of severity to make the "rational" man reject that particular criminal act as unprofitable.[32] Given this model of the criminal and this mechanism of social control, the prosecutor does not have to be a correctional strategist. The strategy—that of deterrence—has already been decided by the legislature in its pronouncement of specific punishments. Thus, the prosecutor needs only to be a tactician—a person skilled in the application of the general strategy in the given instance. Being a tactician, the prosecutor's role ends with the conviction. The effectiveness of that tactic has been assumed *a priori*.

Naturally, this view of the prosecutorial role conflicts with many of the current goals of the contemporary correctional process. The field of corrections has been influenced by, among other factors, the positive school of criminology, in which a crime is seen not as a rational calculation by a rational man but as an event in an individual's life that must be interpreted in accordance with other events in the offender's career. In this model, what might dissuade one man from criminal acts might be irrelevant to preventing the same act by another, or might even *increase* the likelihood of further criminal behavior in another. Strategies based on this view, rather than the classical view, *require a decentralization of strategic thinking.* The legislature cannot decide *a priori* what is required to stop all offenders from committing a particular act. Criminals must be categorized according to particular behavior patterns and treated accordingly. Little headway has been made up to now in establishing these categories of treatment,[33] however; and the ideological and role conflicts between prosecutors and correctional officials hamper the communication between the prosecutorial and correctional phases of the process that would aid in this investigation.

Organizational ratings of the prosecutor

Another important influence on the prosecutor's behavior, and thus another factor with impact on corrections, has been the fact that the prosecutor is evaluated first and foremost at the ballot box. In other words, political durability is more important than performance as a prosecutor. But this criterion is unlikely to be used much longer independently of the decisions that the prosecutor makes on the job and independently of the outcome of those decisions. The prosecutor is elected to represent the "will of the people" concerning the application of public funds to the maintenance of social control. It is the prosecutor's job to gain convictions. But it is also his job to balance the cost of prosecution against the possible gains. If the prosecutor decides, for any of a variety of reasons, that prosecution of an apparently guilty man may do the state and the offender more harm than good, it is his duty to refuse to prosecute. Similarly, if the prosecutor feels that chances of conviction are slim, he should have second thoughts about initiating a lengthy and costly process even if the crime in question is a serious one. The prosecutor's job is one of "obtaining justice" or "enforcing the law" at a satisfactory level and at a minimum price.

It is in watching the daily implementation of this goal that people have begun to complain about the "market place" or the "assembly line" of criminal justice. Typically, the prosecutorial response to the demand for justice at a minimal cost is to undertake the cases that will lead to the easiest convictions. The easiest convictions are those that present the least chance of litigation. It is the courtroom battle, the demand that the state actually put its evidence to the test, that is expensive. Thus, as most students, officials, offenders, and even much of the general public are now aware, most convictions are obtained by pleas of guilty. When the defendant convicts himself the risk is taken out of the prosecution and considerable money and energy are saved.[34]

The social costs of the guilty plea and the mechanisms for obtaining it will be mentioned in the next section. Here we want to concentrate on the conviction and the guilty plea in terms of how they become the evaluation criteria that shape the prosecutor's role. The most common single standard is the prosecutor's "batting average" (number of cases won/number of prosecutions initiated). Presumably, the higher one's batting average, the more frequently has justice been done, and, simultaneously, the more frequently has the people's money been spent wisely. Equally important, if not more important than the batting average or the rate of conviction, is the number of cases handled within a certain time. Several scholars have pointed to "clearing the calendar" as the judge's principal concern; moving cases along is also a major goal of the prosecutor. A 100-percent conviction rate would be unsatisfactory if each case went through a full trial and a hundred cases were stuck waiting to come up. The longer a case takes, the more expensive it is; time *is* money, and the goal of prosecution is a high conviction rate with rapid turnover of cases. Rapid turnover, of course, requires the plea of guilty and, most frequently, the negotiation process that precedes the guilty plea.

These criteria, like the police clearance rate discussed earlier, are often used as measures of "efficiency," and the goal of the prosecutor is to be as efficient as possible. We could ask some very pointed questions about what goals are efficiently achieved by the guilty plea system, but at this point the main issue for us is how this alleged efficiency affects later stages of the criminal justice process.

The main effect would seem to be the lack of system integration that this type of performance evaluation provides. If the prosecutor is rated or evaluated in terms of his efficiency, and the efficiency rate is defined in terms of conviction, then there is minimal organizational pressure on him to consider the needs and constraints of the correctional system or the needs and wants of the offender. The prosecutor's main concern would seem to be with those characteristics of offenders and those operations of the system that retard case flow and reduce efficiency. What offenders do in the future or what criminal justice officials do after conviction is not, then, of direct interest to the prosecutor.

There are, of course, exchanges between different parts of the system. When prisons become overcrowded there will be a call for increased use of both probation and parole. If the judge's sentencing capacities are taxed, there may be pressure to slow down prosecution or, more likely, to reduce the number of cases. And if the prosecutors decide more frequently not to prosecute, police may decide more frequently not to arrest. Shock waves may be set up forward and backward in the system as rates and content of decisions vary at any particular point. But this kind of system interaction is not planned and purposive in any particular instance, and it does not even adhere to general principles such as the "check and balance" principle by which the three branches of American government were structured.[35]

Thus, there is an interaction pattern—perhaps even a predictable one—between prosecutorial and correctional processes, but the major constraints on the prosecutor's behavior do not include a rating of his contribution to the effectiveness or efficiency of the correctional system. The prosecutor is the main actor in obtaining guilty pleas (and other convictions) and thus in obtaining correctional fodder, but his main concern in prosecution is not "correctability" or even "punishability" of the defendant. His main concern is "convictability."

Now this concern would be fine, from the standpoint of corrections, if the primary factors that result in a defendant's convictability were also the factors that made him most suitable (in society's view) for correctional treatment. Unfortunately, perhaps, this does not seem to be the case.

Selection of "role-ready" defendants

Now that we have seen some of the socialization and evaluation pressures that constrain the way in which the prosecutor acts, let us look at the way he acts vis-a-vis the offender. Which defendants help the prosecutor to achieve high ratings?

First, it is a fairly widespread assumption that *most* of these defendants (i.e., the ones who plead guilty) are guilty of *something*. Most students of the criminal justice process assume that an innocent person would object quite strenuously to the prospect of conviction and that he would not plead guilty except in very rare instances.[36] An example of the concern for this rare instance is the case of *North Carolina* v. *Alford*.[37] Mr. Alford pleaded guilty to second degree murder while insisting simultaneously on his innocence. The U. S. Supreme Court accepted the constitutionality of the plea in this case and, in so doing, strengthened the constitutionality of plea bargaining. The court pointed out that there was ample evidence against Alford, perhaps enough to support a first-degree murder charge. Given this evidence, the Court said, a man claiming his innocence may rationally and freely choose to plead guilty to a reduced charge with a maximum penalty of life imprisonment in order to avoid going to trial on a charge for which a conviction might mean the death penalty.

Some people might question whether this choice was really free of coercion, but the Supreme Court apparently had sufficient respect for the evidence to make it seem unlikely that an innocent man had been convicted. However, if it is in the rare murder charge where penalties are highest and we might expect the innocent man to object the most, what might happen in more mundane kinds of crimes? John Kaplan, for example, cites an instance where the cost of pleading guilty was less than the cost of pleading not guilty. Specifically, the event involved two black men mistakenly arrested for loitering, trespassing, and failure to identify themselves on a street at night in San Francisco. They were both taken to jail, neither could make bail, and the prosecutor would not drop the case. After discussion with the prosecutor, the public defender offered the following alternatives:

1) plead guilty, prosecutor recommends suspended sentence and probation, defendants go home same day
2) plead not guilty, spend 10 days in jail awaiting trial before a judge
3) plead not guilty, spend 30 days in jail awaiting trial before a jury

The innocent defendants chose to plead guilty and go home.[38]

No one knows exactly where the dividing line for the innocent may be between insisting on innocence at all costs and pleading guilty because it is cheaper. Certainly it is different for each defendant. But the uniqueness of individuals has no value for the officials of criminal justice. What is profitable is finding the right boxes, the right similarities in individuals. As in the case of the two innocent black men pleading guilty, the characteristics of the defendant that make him proper material for conviction are not his guilt so much as contingencies surrounding the possibility of guilt. Where the criterion of prosecution is convictability, the characteristics of the defendant that become important are not guilt but the defendant's social status, education, retention of a lawyer, and so on.

Just as we have seen that prosecutors are socialized and gradually take on a particular role, prosecution from the defendant's standpoint is also a socialization process. As prosecution continues, the suspect becomes a defendant who becomes a convict. People in the system must come to some minimal agreement that the decisions made about the defendant are accurate and appropriate. This agreement is much easier when the defendant manifests the proper behavior for the new roles that he is assigned. Thus, with great frequency, it will be the "role-ready" defendant that the prosecutor will send on to the correctional process.

Research findings from the Vera Institute, the New York Legal Aid Society, the University of Pennsylvania Law School, and other sources suggest a broad outline for the role-ready defendant.[39]

1) He is generally a man who cannot make bail. (A man who can pay his bond can go back to his family or to work or into an active preparation of his defense. In any event, the defendant who is on the street can wait the system out and create higher costs because he is not losing during this wait. Furthermore, the man on the street has a very clear picture of what freedom is and why it should be maintained.) The man in jail has lost his social ties, has no money, and is suffering in jail under worse conditions than he will endure in a state prison. He is, before conviction, a jailbird. The longer he stays in jail, the greater the pressure on him to plead guilty, and the less he has to lose by pleading guilty (since jail time may be considered toward sentence).

2) He is often a man with a prior conviction (no matter how minor) and/or a man with no family or fixed abode. The more geographically mobile he is and the greater his rapsheet, the less his chance of release on recognizance (or nominal bail). Again, the man remains in jail. Also, a man with a record is less likely to want to risk going to trial. He is much more aware that full court process may mean a more severe sentence, because the judge will take his previous record into consideration. Furthermore, a man with previous court experience is also aware that there is some leniency, or apparent leniency, for cooperating and pleading guilty.

3) He probably lives in a city, because it is in cities that the system backlog is greatest and the pressures for the guilty plea are strongest.

4) He is frequently a minority group member, not only because whites tend to escape to suburbs but because ghetto living condi-

tions present a higher visibility of crime than is true in suburbs or in middle-class kinds of crime. Concomitantly, this defendant is also poor and uneducated. He has had trouble finding jobs and he will have more trouble in the future.[40]

5)   He either waives representation or is assigned a lawyer. He cannot afford to hire one and would probably not know where to find a good one anyway. If he does not receive a Legal Aid lawyer or Public Defender, he may end up with one of the "court regulars"— criminal lawyers who hang around court soliciting cases and making their money through low fees and high turnover (that is, "pleading clients guilty").[41]

6)   He is probably guilty of *some* crime—either the one charged or the one from which the charge was reduced in return for the plea or the one committed a few days ago that the police did not discover. As Casper says, defendants frequently have a sense of "generalized guilt" (i.e., they may not be guilty of the crime for which they have been apprehended, but accede to prosecution because "they had theirs coming."[42]

7)   He has committed and/or been charged with a run-of-the-mill crime. Spectacular crimes and heinous criminals are rare, and if the infamous criminal did not object to regular prosecution tactics, the public would probably object to the guilty plea and lighter sentence. The role-ready defendant is a nobody, legally and illegally. In broad categories, the offenses most frequently committed are (1) crimes against individual victims who are most likely not much better off than the offender or (2) crimes of status and/or "self-abuse" such as vagrancy, heroin use, and public intoxication.

Since these are the kinds of criminals that prosecutors are most likely to be able to convict, these are the people whom a judge must sentence most often, and these are the people that probation, prison, parole, and other correctional agencies most frequently accept. It is with these offenders, therefore, that correctional strategies tend to be concerned. This tendency severely limits the range and quality of correctional strategies. These criminals do not arouse the greatest human enmity nor the greatest human compassion and concern. (Indeed not! That is exactly why they are there!) These are not the offenders, generally, who would seem to be ripe material for deterrence. For them, occasional criminal punishment is perceived as part of the life cycle. Moreover, they have no *legal* alternatives that offer outcomes of any greater profit. On the other hand these are not, generally, sick offenders whose criminal activities can (at least with a layman's understanding) be classified as symptoms of some psychological dysfunction. On the contrary, they would seem to be fairly normal individuals operating under fairly normal circumstances. But they would *not* seem to be people who expect their crimes to be excused because of their circumstances.

The late George Jackson, for example, who was a normal run-of-the-mill defendant at the beginning of his incarcerated life (although certainly not at the time of his death), did not *excuse* the acts of criminals, even in his later letters. He considered the excusing of criminal acts just as much a ploy of the establishment as the punishment of those acts. Jackson suggested that the mechanism in which run-of-the-mill offenders victimize run-of-the-mill victims is a capitalistic plot to defuse a revolutionary force. Jackson might have condemned our most habitual convicts for their stupidity rather than for their crime, but he would have found them guilty.[43]

Without accepting Jackson's neo-Marxist politics, we can probably agree with his notion that the average offender (rather than manifesting psychological symptoms) is really *himself* a symptom of the fundamental nature of the criminal justice system. The kind of defendant described above as a "nobody—legally and illegally," is a symptom of the social, political, economic, and technological constraints placed first on our police, then on our prosecution, and finally on our correctional practices. While these people may be guilty, there is no evidence that they are more *frequently* guilty than others who go unapprehended or unprosecuted. And while the former may be convictable, there is ample evidence that the kinds of crime they commit result in *considerably less* social cost than, for example, white collar, corporate, or organized crime.[44]

These defendants, in other words, are the kind that most communities and most governments are willing and organizationally able to prosecute. The effort invested in their prosecution is evidently all that society is willing to expend on law enforcement and the achievement of justice in the criminal area.

If this is true, it would seem that the values, such as fairness, privacy, and equal justice, symbolized in the criminal justice process and long assumed to be cherished, are not so terribly important any more.[45] There is at least one recent major jurisprudential argument to that effect. In his major work, *The Right to be Different*, Nicholas Kittrie hypothesizes and documents the "divestment of criminal justice."[46] He points out that a variety of social problem areas (such as drug abuse, juvenile delinquency, and alcoholism) that have traditionally fallen within the realm of the criminal law, are being rapidly transferred to other realms—generally the civil law of the "therapeutic state"—where the question of guilt does not apply and the constitutional safeguards of due process have not yet been invoked. To a great extent, the most recent national commission on criminal justice supports Kittrie's argument. The National Advisory Commission on Criminal Justice Standards and Goals takes the basic position that the criminal justice system is incompetent to handle many of the problems that tradition decrees should be presented to it. The Commission recommends the increased use of diversionary tactics and the concomitant development of other institutions and processes to handle these social problem areas.[47]

Interpreting Kittrie's research and the Commission's recommendations broadly, we would conclude that American society is indeed in a state of flux, and that the principal values of our culture are rapidly changing. In this state of chronic change, as some have called it,[48] we would expect the traditional symbols of justice and fairness and law enforcement to be less important, and, consequently, the energy expended in criminal justice to be diminishing compared to energies expended by other systems of social control. By way of analogy, Leslie Wilkins interprets the last huge expenditures in criminal justice via the Omnibus Crime Bill and Safe Streets Act and the Law Enforcement Assistance Administration to be the death throes of a dinosaur. In other words, as a means of maintaining our values and our social order, the criminal justice system is approaching extinction.[49]

If this prediction is correct, several alternatives for the correctional system present themselves. One might be that the current agencies of corrections would simply fade away. Another might be that they would take on the dramatization of some new values such as the incarceration of an increasingly politically radical population that the state wants to control, not because of their guilt for traditional crimes but because they threaten the dominant political power. Another might be that correctional agencies, divested of their symbolic function, could finally take on a reeducation function in which the organizations could actually concentrate on the needs of individuals. There is evidence at this time to support the probability of any of these alternatives and others, but all of these alternatives in their ultimate delineation are beyond the scope of this text.

What we must deal with here is the correctional system—the design and analysis of correctional strategies as they are affected by these general criminal justice trends or by the prosecutorial tendency to select for criminal justice intervention those offenders who represent the line of least resistance.

THE INDIGENT DEFENDANT AND THE DEFENSE ATTORNEY

Throughout the 1960s the role of counsel in the criminal process expanded rapidly. The landmark case of *Gideon* v. *Wainwright* in

1963[50] provided for the assistance of counsel at trial and opened the door for similar provision at all critical stages of defense. Provision for counsel at the preliminary hearing,[51] at sentencing,[52] at line-up,[53] and at station house interrogations[54] followed in quick order. In addition, the *Gault* case applied the principles of the right of counsel and of provision of counsel to indigents in juvenile proceedings.[55] The importance of counsel in the view of the Court was underscored in that decision because of the inherent ideological battle over the treatment and punishment functions of the juvenile court. Fortas' opinion stated that a fair and orderly proceeding, such as that obtained through the presence of counsel, was a prerequisite for treatment.

While the implications for the rehabilitative consequences in- volved in provision of counsel were less clearly stated in the adult cases, there is little doubt that the court was attentive to the rising crime rate and the apparent lack of concern for offenders in the criminal justice process (particularly in the lower courts). The President's Crime Commission for example, pointedly criticized the quick hearings, careless sentencing practices, and shoddy jail conditions that characterized the misdemeanant process.[56] The Commission went on to suggest that a minor offender suffering through this disorder can very likely return to the system as a serious offender later on. And the Commission found it ironic that, comparatively, so much more money and time were spent in felony prosecutions when the social cost of misdemeanors and mistreating misdemeanants was probably as great.[57] Not long thereafter, the Supreme Court in *Argersinger* v. *Hamlin* interpreted *Gideon* to provide assistance of counsel to *all* offenders who are threatened with the possibility of incarceration.[58]

When we couple this kind of decision with the *dicta* about the lawyer's role in *Gideon* and the increasing interest in rehabilitation as a goal of punishment, it is reasonable to suspect that counsel is supposed to have a beneficial effect not only on the achievement of preconviction due process, but also on the effectiveness of correctional strategies.

There are strong theoretical assumptions in the behavioral sciences as well as legal reasons to support this possible dual outcome in the provision of counsel. Any person facing prosecution lives in crisis. His role in society, with his family, his image of himself—all face drastic changes. Those people who are most frequently prosecuted are facing this crisis without much of the educational, financial, and social support that other defendants have. They are also faced with the severest type of state intervention: jail before conviction and a greater possibility of prison after conviction. Unless they are provided with concerned and energetic counsel who can explain the process and predict the alternative outcomes of all the crucial decisions they must make, these defendants are very likely to face this stern test alone.

Even if they are guilty and will be convicted, the contribution made by counsel can be great, in terms of both sentencing outcome and additional social consequences.[59] But guilty or innocent, if the defendant can be accompanied through the labyrinth of prosecution by an educated and expert friend, the chances increase that prosecution and punishment can be an educative experience. For example, one of the most inefficient and ineffective aspects of the criminal justice process for the control of crime is the long hiatus between the crime and the ultimate outcome for the offender, resulting in the incapacity of the system to demonstrate to the offender that the punishment is a direct consequence of a specific instance of illegal behavior. There is evidence that some defendants do not even understand what crime they were sentenced for or, more broadly, why their behavior led to a particular period of incarceration.

Behavior modification research has demonstrated that the impact of negative or positive reinforcement for changing a particular behavior pattern is directly related to the immediacy with which the reinforcement follows the behavior.[60] While there is not much chance that the duration of prosecution can be reduced sufficiently to make this finding applicable in the physical sense, it is possible that concerned counsel could make this finding more applicable in the social sense. It could be, for example, part of the role of counsel to explain to the defendant the reasons for delay but also to impress on the defendant the legal connections between certain social behavior and the consequent punishment.

Of course, any of these possibilities require that counsel actually be perceived by the defendant as "his lawyer"—a helper whom he can trust and who is really working for the defendant rather than for the state. Unfortunately, there is considerable evidence from observers of court practices that this is decidedly not the case.

The lawyer as organization man

Many defendants, particularly in the lower courts, are indigent. *Gideon* and *Argersinger* state that, in cases where incarceration might be the outcome, the provision of counsel to indigents is a constitutional requirement. The administration of this constitutional requirement is left to the courts. There are three basic ways in which counsel is provided: (1) judicial assignment of lawyers from a list provided by the Bar, (2) legal aid lawyers salaried by private donations or some combination of public and private funds, and (3) a public defender operating out of a public office. Which of these three forms is used depends on the jurisdiction, but the most common form in big cities appears to be the public defender. In cities such as Los Angeles and Chicago, the public defender's office is large, with many assistants organized to handle cases in many branches of court. The advantages of this form include the size of the organization and the many resources for investigation and defense available to the public officials that are usually not available to privately assigned attorneys or to legal aid lawyers. Lawyers working in such an organization also gain considerable trial experience, and they have ongoing working relationships with the police, prosecutors, and judges that "outside" lawyers do not possess. Furthermore, large city defender offices afford better salaries for staff and can apparently attract more competent personnel.

There are many disadvantages, however. Two major drawbacks are that the public defender, like the public prosecutor, is usually overworked, and that the public defender, as a government employee, has considerable difficulty convincing defendants that he is really a friend of the defense rather than an officer of the court.

The defendant's perception of the public defender as a traitor to his cause is bolstered by the hypothesis that the same socialization factors influencing the prosecutor will influence the public defender. While the defender is a lawyer for the accused, he is also a member of the public bureaucracy. Like the prosecutor, his formal education in criminal matters is usually minimal. The career goals of the defender reach beyond the defender's office. The young defender may be looking for more remunerative employment with private counsel, with the prosecutor's office, or in other areas of public service. Perhaps most important of all, as Blumberg points out, the defender must maintain cooperative working relationships with the prosecutor, and he is not dependent on the outcome of his cases for his salary. For both reasons he is likely to be influenced by the prosecutor's and/or the judge's production goals which, as we have seen, refer to the number of cases processed rather than the way in which each defendant is treated.

The pressure that the defender feels to cooperate in meeting the prosecutorial and judicial production criteria are also likely to be found in the defender's office itself. The public defender's office is in business to handle the cases that no one else wants. His clients are bitter, confused, and distrustful. They are the type that the system in its entirety has focused on as most role-ready for the convict status. He is working with the people that society has differentially selected to carry the weight of the criminal justice drama. Thus the defender is under many pressures that make the individual defendant expendable for the maintenance of the criminal justice process.[61]

Perhaps it is not surprising then that when Jonathan Casper asked a Connecticut inmate whether he had received assistance of counsel, the inmate answered, "No, I had a public defender."[62] Supporting the interviews by Casper are some data collected by Duffee and Siegel in a New York State juvenile court[63] and by Bing and Rosenfeld in the Boston criminal courts.[64] Both studies discovered that indigent defendants with the assistance of appointed or public counsel were more frequently incarcerated than indigent defendants who waived their right to assistance. The Boston study did not control for the seriousness of the crime charged, but the New York study found that the relationship held even if crimes were classified according to seriousness. In other words, even delinquents charged with the most serious offenses fared better at disposition if they waived counsel rather than asking for representation.

These data suggest that the "work ethic" of the court, as Casper calls it, might co-opt the defender's defense function, regardless of how the defender himself acts. The judge in these cases evidently views the request for a lawyer as noncooperative behavior from defendants. Thus, if they are found guilty they are punished more severely than defendants who waive their right to defense and save the court time and money. And this sentencing differential operates over and above the common differential for pleading guilty as opposed to going to trial.

The organizational structure of the court, rather than the individual proclivities of prosecutors, judges, and defenders, should be seen as the basis of these outcomes. The entire structure of the pre-conviction system seems to operate antithetically to the needs of remedial social action. If case-processing is more important than decisions about individuals, the correctional process begins with the reception of offenders whose social direction is full speed ahead out of the social system. The preconviction process does not even apply the brakes to offenders who are traveling in the wrong direction on their own. Corrections becomes a catch basin for outcasts rather than a central point for the redistribution of social services.

The decline of the adversarial myth

Abraham Blumberg summarizes observations similar to these in his own study of the Manhattan criminal courts by lamenting the decline of the adversary system. He sees prosecutors in New York as fairly dedicated civil servants whose behavior is constricted by the work ethic. He sees the judge as a bureaucrat (to be discussed in the next section). He sees the defense lawyer, public or private, as a double agent—a mediator between the defendant and the prosecution—with the job of reducing the defendant's objections to pleading guilty. If these perceptions of role performance are true, none of them is congruent with the adversary model of justice. Whether they *should* be congruent with this model is, of course, a much bigger question.[65]

In the adversary model there is a purposefully constructed balance of advantage between the state and the accused. The judge is the neutral arbiter and the applier of precedent who maintains the balance. On either end of the seesaw are the defense counsel and the prosecutor, the first being the champion for the defendant and the second the champion for the state. Since the state champion has advantage of all state resources, investigatory skills, and information, the defense champion is given certain procedural safeguards that control the way in which the prosecutor applies his power. The purpose of the adversarial balance is the obtaining of valid information about guilt.[66]

This model, as we have seen, very probably does not apply in the great majority of cases. It remains important, however, because in the quasi-cooperative bureaucratic system, the major weapon of defense is the *threat* to use the adversary procedure if the deals offered by the prosecution are not satisfactory. Thus, as Blumberg states, the adversary system has not really disappeared so much as it has merged into the organizational operations of a highly complex bureaucracy. The guilty plea system is not a total disregard for adversary principles; rather, it is a bureaucratic administration of those principles. This makes the court organization fairly unusual. Most bureaucracies are based on the idea of legitimate authority and cooperation. The court bureaucracy (or more accurately, bureaucracies) is built upon the idea of power and conflict. Clearly, the bureaucratic procedures of the court would be sheer nonsense in a cooperative system. In many bureaucracies there is some agreement about what should be done. In the court there is little agreement about what should be done. Thus, there are in the court very strong social pressures to limit the way in which the disagreement will be resolved.

It appears that under this pressure, defense counsel loses the ability to behave as an adversary, a friend of the defendant, protecting his main interests during the process of state intervention. On the other hand, the defense attorney does not appear to develop the capacity to ameliorate the defendant's feelings toward society during the intervention. The defendants that Casper interviewed in prison, for example, spoke of public defenders as people completely swamped by work and uninterested in their clients' fate. Not only did counsel fail to protect, but essentially he failed to be the "agent-mediator" that Blumberg suggests, because the "contract" that the defense attorney works out between his client and the state is a very short-lived one. As soon as the defendant enters the correctional process he feels hoodwinked. He discovers that the "coming to agreement" on the charge or the sentence in return for the guilty plea does not help him in the long run. Not only is the defendant powerless to take up adversarial combat, but he is also powerless to negotiate an outcome that really is satisfactory to both sides. It would seem that if the criminal justice system is really changing from a drama about justice to a system of decisions about individuals, then it still has a long way to go. The old symbols may be decaying, but if prosecution is to be educational for the defendant, the skills and competencies that prosecutor and defense attorney should have are lacking. The merger of bureaucratic organization and adversarial process does not seem to bring either the state or the accused closer to correctional treatment.

THE TRIAL JUDGE AND THE COP-OUT

The guilty plea is a waiver of rights. It is a decision by the defendant, or the defendant and his attorney, that he can best protect his own interest or achieve his goals by cooperating with the needs of prosecution rather than objecting. The actual influence that the defendant gains over his fate by cooperating is probably slight. It would seem that the influence that the judge has over this process is even slighter.

The judge is, legally, the protector of constitutional standards. If the defendant pleads guilty and waives his rights, the judge must investigate the constitutionality of that waiver. The two major standards that the waiver process must meet are (1) the accuracy of the pleas and (2) its voluntariness. Voluntariness is usually broken down into (a) willingness (i.e., freedom from coercion) and (b) knowledgeability (i.e., awareness of consequences).

Donald Newman, who conducted the American Bar Association field study of the guilty plea process, suggests that the two components of the standard of voluntariness combined with the work ethic of plea bargaining make a constitutional waiver impossible. Newman points out that a plea cannot be considered voluntary unless the defendant is informed of his choices. However, Newman asks, if the information about sentencing differential is given to the defendant, how can the procedure be voluntary?[67] We can probably add that the judge's questioning about the accuracy of the plea is so quickly done that there is little guarantee of its accuracy.

There is much controversy over the role that the judge should play in plea negotiations. Whatever role he *should* play, it is certain that it should be a change from the present one. In most states, for example, the judge asks the defendant who is pleading guilty whether any promises have been given in return for the plea. If the defendant states that there have been promises, the plea, supposedly, will not be accepted. Therefore, the defendant is guided by counsel or by the prosecutor to lie—to say that the plea has been made without promises— so that the bargain can be kept. The defendant knows that the judge is aware of the lie. The judge knows that the defendant knows. And the defendant knows that the judge will sentence in accordance with the recommendation from the prosecutor—in accordance with the promises that have been made. In other states, the plea negotiation is much more in the open. Even if the negotiations are constitutionally not supposed to take place at all, the court is simply so overcrowded and the defenders and prosecutors so busy that negotiations are completed in open court.[68]

Whether the judge asks questions when he already knows the answers or simply watches the conclusion of negotiations from the bench, the judge's irrelevance to the outcome of the case is obvious to the defendant. According to Casper, the irrelevance of the judge to the process is the crowning irony in the system as far as the defendant is concerned. He expects the police and the prosecutor to work for what they achieve, because he knows that they are evaluated by solving and moving cases. The defendant even expects that the public defender will be too busy to help him. But he evidently does not expect the judge to sit back and accept the lies and perpetuate the hypocrisy.[69]

Several recent court and commission opinions would seem to have direct bearing on the future of guilty pleas, plea negotiations, and the judge's role in both. *North Carolina* v. *Alford*, the murder case discussed earlier in this chapter, clearly lends legitimacy to the negotiated plea. It was perfectly obvious that Alford was counting on a reduction in charge (and hence in maximum sentence) in return for pleading guilty. Despite the fact that Alford insisted he was innocent, the Supreme Court found that this situation met the constitutional standards of voluntariness and trustworthiness. The alternative would have been to insist on the prosecution of the first-degree murder charge, which Alford wanted to avoid. Certainly it would seem strange to uphold a defendant's rights against his wishes, particularly if he received the death penalty as a result. Rather than go down that road, the Supreme Court took a fairly realistic look at bargaining practices as they operate today and concluded that, within that framework, the plea negotiation is part of the voluntary decision to plead guilty. (Perhaps it would be more accurate to say that through the negotiation process, the defendant becomes more *willing* to plead?)

Two other important decisions about plea negotiation are those of the San Francisco Committee on Crime and the President's Commission on Crime. Both Commissions recommend that plea bargaining be brought out into the open, where it can be controlled, and that the judge should preside over such negotiations.[70] The Commissions suggest that this opening and formalizing of the procedure would limit the defendant's risk of striking a false bargain. The judge would not allow a prosecutor to claim as a "deal" or as a demonstration of leniency a practice that is really normal in the court. The judge would also gain more information about the bargain that is struck.

The National Advisory Commission on Criminal Justice Standards and Goals also suggests opening and formalizing the negotiation process in the short run, but they recommend abolishing the plea-bargaining process in the long run.[71] In making this recommendation the Advisory Commission takes a position contrary to those of recent court decisions and other commissions. They take this position because they can see no way in which negotiations about guilt can, in the long run, be reconciled with traditional American ideals about justice.

In quite another vein, a recent revision of the New York criminal code also attacks plea bargaining. The New York code is principally aimed at drug offenses but reclassifies all other felonies as well. It makes negotiation impossible, either because there is no reward for it, or because the negotiation itself falls under the code's definition of bribery, which is in itself a non-negotiable felony.[72]

Implementation of the Advisory Commission's recommendations or enforcement of the New York code would seem to require one of two adjustments from the criminal justice system. The first possibility would be the return of the adversary process and a tremendous increase in the amount of legal manpower needed. The second possibility is that the negotiation process would be driven further underground and further forward in the system, so that negotiation would take place before the prosecutor files the original charge. Either adjustment would change the face of the criminal justice system. The first would turn the courtroom back into a court, while the second would, in essence, switch all court decisions to the police station house.

Unless the Commission recommendations are implemented, or until the New York get-tough policy becomes popular in other states, one goal of court reorganization would seem to be to improve the negotiation process. All too frequently the judge has to make the decision either to remain impartial in the process (and thus lose control of the system and of information about the offender) or to gain some control over the system by accepting the traditional hypocritical position of "not knowing" about bargains but cooperating in achieving the bargained outcome. The recommendations of the President's Crime Commission and the San Francisco Committee would appear to ease this dilemma somewhat by making the judge's maintenance of control independent of his willingness to accept unconstitutional waivers. If the judge begins to participate more actively in the process, he will gain more power over its operations and outcomes; he will have more information about offenders; and perhaps most importantly, defendants will have more information about judges. Once again, the opportunity arises for the preconviction system to *itself* be corrective.

   If prosecution for a good many defendants (and most of those who will end up in prison or on probation) is really a series of steps in the negotiation of a plea, it is possible that the participating, inquiring, powerful judge can help to impress on the defendant the enormity of the outcome under question, stressing the fact that those negotiations deal with years in the defendant's life, and asking what is to become of that life. There is the suggestion in the works of Casper and Blumberg and others that if someone would demonstrate some concern for the defendant, the defendant also might take a different view of himself and of the system. He would, perhaps, be more prepared to do something with the time in prison for which he bargains. Perhaps that is the most ironic thing about the defendant's trip into the correctional arena in the present situation. Until the defendant actually goes through the correctional doors, people are more concerned with whether he will do time than what he will do with his time. When the judge accepts the guilty plea he is very frequently accepting the defendant as a member in a correctional organization. But people are so concerned with the fact of membership that no one is interested in the quality of it.

WHAT IS ONE'S "DAY IN COURT"?

This chapter gives a very brief overview of the preconviction process as it relates to corrections. We have tried to establish or to hypothesize connections among police, prosecutorial, defense, and judicial roles and the effectiveness of correctional strategies. It has long been assumed that there is a relationship between police activities and correctional activities, and between the court process and correctional activities; but no one has pursued these subjects with great vigor, and there is little in the way of reliable data about them.

To some extent, this chapter deals with a mixture of real and hypothesized effects and outcomes of the preconviction process. In some cases, such as the ultimate rate of incarceration for people awaiting trial in jail as compared with those out on bail, we know the impact of the preconviction process with some accuracy. In other cases we have had to rely on observer-participation material or simply on hypotheses drawn from a relevant body of theory. In all cases, we have tried to focus attention on the postconviction process that follows the phases we have been examining. But we have also emphasized that, in a much broader sense, the criminal justice process in its entirety, beginning with police intervention, can be conceived of as a *remedial* process, or as a correctional activity. From the time that the suspect becomes the subject of police attention in a particular case and thereby becomes a defendant, the initial decision to use a correctional strategy has been made. In this sense, the criminal justice system, from the point of arrest, is an institution built for tinkering with things and people that the primary institutions of society have botched. The things botched are generally intangibles—ideas, beliefs, and values that are not sufficiently supported or clarified in the normal functioning of a social system. At times the relevant social system may simply be one community. At other times it encompasses several communities, a city, a state, or the federation of states.

On this level, the operation of the criminal justice system can be seen as a corrective strategy for all major social institutions. It performs, we think, not simply political functions (as Parsons might have it)[73] or political and maintenance functions (as Katz and Kahn might have it),[74] or economic functions (as Marx might have it).[75] The criminal justice system functions in all these areas. If it is corrective, it can be seen as an institution for change in the social structure. It is a system of people whose interactions involve researching malfunctions in the daily order and coming to decisions about how to correct the disorder. We think that this is the sense in which several writers have suggested that "one's day in court" is symbolically everyone's day in court.

As Etzioni has argued recently, history is not a straight road, nor does it move in cycles. It is a shifting balance of many different cultural patterns and value systems that are always present in various degrees.[76] We are now at a point where these values and patterns are in a considerable degree of flux. As new dominant patterns emerge, one possibility is that the individual will be considerably more important, and the individual's capacity to switch values and roles over time will be seen as significantly more legitimate. If this trend does become dominant, then the criminal justice system may well become valued, not as an institution for the maintenance of one set of dominant values, but as an institution that has the power and authority to redistribute the resources and opportunities that allow individuals to attempt new behavior patterns. If this is to occur, then the individual offender's day in court can no longer be everyone's day—it must be *his* day. If this day is to arrive, then there must be much more systematic study of the way in which the decisions of many different officials finally do fit together and influence the course of events for any particular offender.

Traditional correctional agencies, at the tail end of the criminal process, are now very much affected by these shifting trends. Emphasis on the ancient goals of control, retribution, and deterrence appears to be waning and concern for the newer goals of individual and social change appears to be ascendant. The remaining chapters of this book deal with the influence of these trends on current correctional strategies and with the impact these changing correctional strategies will have on the entire criminal justice system and the broader social system.

NOTES

1. Donald Clemmer, *The Prison Community* (New York: Holt, Rinehart, and Winston, 1958).

2. Michael O'Neill, "The Role of the Police: Normative Role Expectations in a Metropolitan Police Department" (Dissertation prospectus, School of Criminal Justice, State University of New York, Albany, 1971).

3. On the importance of this area of discretionary decisions to the analysis of police behavior see James Q. Wilson, *Varieties of Police Behavior* (Cambridge: Harvard University Press, 1968), pp. 4–10.

4. Ibid., p. 10.

5. On this idea see Carl Werthman, "The Function of Social Definitions in the Development of Delinquent Careers," in President's Crime Commission, *Task Force Report: Juvenile Delinquency and Youth Crime* (Washington, D.C.: Government Printing Office, 1967), pp. 155–170.

6. Ibid.

7. Miranda v. Arizona 384 U.S. 436 (1966); and Terry v. Ohio 392 U.S. 1 (1968).

8. President's Crime Commission, *Task Force Report: Police* and *Task Force Report: Science and Technology* (Washington, D.C.: Government Printing Office, 1967); and Alfred Blumstein, "Systems Analysis and The Criminal Justice System," *Annals of the American Academy of Political and Social Science* 374 (November 1967): 92–100.

9. Jerome Skolnick, *Justice Without Trial* (New York: Wiley, 1967); and National Advisory Commission on Criminal Justice Standards and Goals, *Task Force Report on Police* (Washington, D.C.: Government Printing Office, 1974).

10. Lawrence Tiffany, Donald McIntyre, and Daniel Rotenberg, *Detection of Crime* (Boston: Little, Brown, 1967).

11. Dean C. Merrill, "Using the PROMIS Tracking System for Criminal Justice Evaluation," *Project Search Proceedings* (Sacramento: California Crime Technology Research Foundation, 1972), pp. 231–234.

12. John Griffiths, "Ideology in Criminal Procedure or a Third Model of the Process," *Yale Law Journal* 79, no. 3 (January 1970): 359–417.

13. Note 9, supra.

14. Note 3, supra.

15. *Task Force Report: Police*, note 8, supra, pp. 3–7.

16. Ibid., p. 18.

17. See Committee for Economic Development, *Education for the Urban Disadvantaged* (New York, 1971).

18. Skolnick, note 9, supra.

19. See Herman Goldstein, "Administrative Problems in Controlling the Exercise of Police Authority," *Journal of Criminal Law, Criminology and Police Science* 58 (1967): 160–170; and Egan Bittner, *The Functions of the Police in a Modern Society*, Public Health Service Publication, no. 2059 (Chevy Chase, Md.: National Institute of Mental Health, 1970), pp. 38–44.

20. Skolnick, note 9, supra, pp. 237–239; and Wilson, note 3, supra, p. 283.

21. On police antagonism to Civilian Review Boards see Algernon D. Black, *The People and the Police* (New York: McGraw-Hill, 1968).

22. On the problem of intangible goals and substitute measures of goal performance see W. Keith Warner and A. Eugene Havens, "Goal Displacement and the Intangibility of Organizational Goals," *Administrative Science Quarterly* 12, no. 4 (March 1968): 539–555.

23. Skolnick, note 9, supra, pp. 167–174.

24. Ibid., pp. 176–179.

25. For another kind of police evaluation more commensurate with the social science and order maintenance function see Jim Munro, *Administrative Behavior and Police Organization* (Cincinnati: Anderson, 1974).

26. On the prosecutorial discretion and its relation to organization see John Kaplan, "The Prosecutorial Discretion—A Comment," *Northwestern Law* 60 (1965): 174–193.

27. Amitai Etzioni, *Complex Organizations* (New York: Free Press, 1961), pp. 157–160.

28. Abraham Blumberg, *Criminal Justice* (Chicago: Quadrangle, 1970), pp. 44–46.

29. Monrad Paulson and Sanford Kadish, *Criminal Law and its Processes* (Boston: Little, Brown, 1962).

30. Herbert Packer, *Limits of the Criminal Sanction* (Stanford: Stanford University Press, 1968).

31. See, for example, Ibid., pp. 35–61.

32. See Emile Durkheim, *The Rules of the Sociological Method* (New York: Free Press, 1950), pp. 74–75.

33. On the idea of categorization and relationships to different treatment modes see Douglas Grant and Marguerite Grant, "A Group Dynamics Approach to Non-Conformity in the Navy," *Annals of the American Academy of Political and Social Science* 322 (March 1959): 126–155; and Marguerite Warren, "The Community Treatment Project: History and Prospects," *Law Enforcement Science and Technology* 1 (1967): 191–200.

34. The major work in guilty pleas is Donald J. Newman, *Conviction: The Determination of Guilt or Innocence Without Trial* (Boston: Little, Brown, 1966); and see Kaplan, note 26, supra.

35. For a good review of these systemic connections, see Remington et al., *Criminal Justice Administration* (Indianapolis: Bobbs-Merrill, 1969), pp. 3–47.

36. But on the differences between *legal* guilt, which is never contested in the guilty plea process, and guilt as understood by offenders, see Jonathan Casper, *American Criminal Justice* (Englewood Cliffs, N.J.: Prentice-Hall, 1970); and Newman, note 34, supra.

37. 400 U.S. 25 (1970).

38. John Kaplan, *Criminal Justice* (Mineola, N.Y.: Foundation Press, 1973), pp. 400–401.

39. President's Crime Commission, *Challenge of Crime in a Free Society* (Washington, D.C.: Government Printing Office, 1967), pp. 131–133; and Paul B. Wice, "Bail Reform in American Cities," *Criminal Law Bulletin* 9, no. 9 (November 1973): 770–797.

40. See Michael Katz, "Patterns of Arrest and the Dangers of Public Visibility," *Criminal Law Bulletin* 9, no. 4 (1973): 311–324.

41. See Blumberg, note 28, supra, pp. 105–106.

42. Casper, note 36, supra.

43. George Jackson, *Soledad Brother* (New York: Bantam Books, 1970).

44. Donald Cressey, *The Theft of the Nation* (New York: Harper and Row, 1969).

45. One of the best treatments of criminal justice as a symbolic drama of social values is Thurmond Arnold, "Law Enforcement—An Attempt at Social Dissection," *Yale Law Journal* 42 (1932): 1–30.

46. Nicholas Kittrie, *The Right to be Different* (Baltimore: Penguin Books, 1970).

47. Particularly The National Advisory Council on Criminal Justice Standards and Goals, *Report on Corrections* (Washington, Government Printing Office, 1974), pp. 73–98.

48. See F. E. Emery and E. L. Trist, "The Causal Texture of Organizational Environments," in F. E. Emery, ed., *Systems Thinking* (Baltimore: Penguin Books, 1969), pp. 241–257.

49. Leslie Wilkins, "Crime and Criminal Justice at the Turn of the Century" (Paper presented at the 77th Annual Meeting of the American Academy of Political and Social Science, Philadelphia, April 13, 1973).

50. 372 U.S. 335 (1963).

51. White v. Maryland 373 U.S. 59 (1963).

52. Mempa v. Rhay 389 U.S. 128 (1967).

53. U.S. v. Wade 388 U.S. 218 (1967).

54. Miranda v. Arizona 384 U.S. 436 (1966).

55. *In re* Gault 387 U.S. 1 (1967).

56. President's Crime Commission, *Task Force Report: Courts* (Washington, D.C.: Government Printing Office, 1967) pp. 30–34.

57. Ibid.

58. 92 S. Ct. 2006 (1972).

59. For a practical description of counsel's responsibilities at sentencing see Michael Feit, "Before Sentence is Pronounced," *Criminal Law Bulletin* 9, no. 2 (March 1973): 140–157; and the material in Kaplan, note 38, supra, pp. 465–475.

60. Ralph Schwitzgebel, "Limitations on the Coercive Treatment of Offenders," *Criminal Law Bulletin* 8, no. 4 (1972): 267–320.

61. Blumberg, note 28, supra, pp. 46–50.

62. Casper, note 36, supra, p. 101.

63. David Duffee and Larry Siegel, "The Organization Man: Legal Counsel in Juvenile Court," *Criminal Law Bulletin* 7, no. 6 (July–August 1971): 544–553.

64. Stephen Bing and S. Stephen Rosenfeld, *The Quality of Justice in the Lower Criminal Courts of Metropolitan Boston* (Boston: Governor's Committee on Law Enforcement and the Administration of Justice, 1970).

65. Blumberg, note 28, supra, pp. 95–116.

66. See Abraham Goldstein, "The State and the Accused: Balance of Advantage in Criminal Procedure," *Yale Law Journal* 69 (1960): 1149–1194.

67. Newman, note 34, supra, pp. 48–50.

68. See "I Have Nothing to do with Justice," *Life*, 12 March 1971, pp. 56–58.

69. Casper, note 36, supra, p. 144.

70. President's Crime Commission, *Task Force Report: The Courts* (Washington, D.C.: Government Printing Office, 1967), pp. 12–13; and San Francisco Committee on Crime, *Report on the Courts* 1970, pp. 54–59.

71. *Report on Courts* (Washington, D.C.: Government Printing Office, 1974), standard 3.1.

72. New York State Revised Criminal Code, 1973.

73. Talcott Parsons, *The Social System* (New York: Free Press, 1964), pp. 309–314.

74. Daniel Katz and Robert Kahn, *The Social Psychology of Organizations* (New York: Wiley, 1966), pp. 142–143.

75. David Gordon, "Capitalism, Class, and Crime in America," *Crime and Delinquency* 19, no. 2 (April 1973): 163–186.

76. Amitai Etzioni, *The Active Society* (New York: Free Press, 1970).

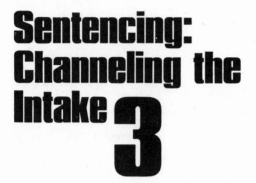

Sentencing: Channeling the Intake 3

GOALS OF THE JUDGE AT SENTENCING

In the past, the main goals of sentencing were vengeance, or retribution, and deterrence. The presuppositions of the classical school of criminology dominated the courts. These presuppositions stressed the moral responsibility of the criminal for his act and set forth the utilitarian concept of punishment, borrowing from the ancient law of retaliation, that the punishment must fit the crime. The classical school of criminology placed emphasis on the crime rather than the criminal and, following the philosophy of the classical school, legislative bodies enacted codes of punishment affixing a necessary and sufficient penalty for every crime.

Under the classical school judges were simply instruments for the application of the law. They had only to impose a "cook book" type of sentencing, similar in many respects to a cook following the directions of an authority in the field of culinary art. They gave little thought to what might have caused the criminal to act as he did or what means might be used to change the personality structure of the criminal so that he would act differently in the future as a result of being channeled through the criminal justice system. The penal codes of the various governmental bodies were assumed to be endowed with a particular magical power, enabling judges to locate the exact penalty that would fit the crime and deter the criminal. Things have not changed to a large degree over the years.

With the advent of the positive school of criminology, which emphasized rehabilitation rather than retribution, sentencing became more complex, and judges discovered that sentencing hearings could become long and involved. If the judge was to be concerned not only with the crime and the protection of society, but with the treatment of the criminal as well, such matters as the reasons behind the criminal act and the treatment that would alter the criminal's personality structure to make him a law-abiding citizen would have to be considered. The goals of sentencing were therefore expanded to include not only retribution and deterrence, but the treatment of the criminal as well. This, of course, gave rise to conflicts, since it is difficult to reconcile what is thought best for both society and the individual. Further, penal codes are not very flexible and sometimes demand a form of punishment that appears to be detrimental to the needs of a particular individual. In such cases, judges have to consider how to modify a sentence to meet the demands of the law and also provide for an intelligent treatment program for the individual criminal. According to the positive school of criminology, judges should attempt to provide for the welfare of the criminal without endangering the welfare of society. Judges have a difficult time determining how far they can go in providing for the welfare of the criminal without arousing the criticism of their fellow citizens that they are being too lenient and not sufficiently concerned with the protection of the community.

At the time of sentencing, the judge's hands are tied by codes passed by legislative bodies that determine, within rather stringent limits, what type of judgment can be pronounced in any particular case. Certain crimes, for example, are made punishable only by a sentence to state prison, even though the judge may realize that state prison would not provide the type of rehabilitation needed for the criminal and, further, that it is not needed for the protection of society. Even where the penal codes provide for more flexibility in the way of sentencing, the possible dispositions open to the judge in the adult courts are usually a fine, probation, jail, or prison; and many codes exclude a large number of offenses from the list of crimes for which judges may grant probation. Even with the most accurate and complete knowledge of the criminal's background and emotional needs, the judge can only pronounce judgment within the confines of the law; he cannot, by an order of the court, repeal the laws of the land. Every day the judge must face numerous criminals and pronounce judgment on them, and in each case he is expected to realize the major goals of sentencing as discussed above. In an effort to reconcile these goals he consults the penal codes, reads presentence reports prepared by probation officers, and obtains advice from prosecutors, defense counsel, and sometimes "experts" such as psychiatrists and psychologists. Much of the time this information is contradictory in nature. Whom is the judge to believe? How is the judge to resolve the conflict in the short time he has to pronounce judgment? How does the judge ultimately arrive at his decision when he discovers that none of the "experts" knows enough about human behavior to enable them to recommend the most effective sanction for the defendant?

Some scholars in the field of the administration of criminal justice claim that judges know nothing about sentencing and should not be allowed to pronounce judgment. But would any board of experts do a better job of sentencing than a judge? This subject will be discussed later in this chapter. A more detailed discussion of the major goals of sentencing is now in order.

Retribution and restitution

The judge must satisfy society's need for revenge and, at the same time, pronounce a judgment that would, as far as possible, restore matters to what they were before commission of the offense. In early times it was felt either that punishment was an end in itself or that a criminal act deserved punishment. No thought was given to reforming the criminal, and the ancient code of lex talionis (an eye for an eye) prevailed. The concept of retribution dominated the field of law for centuries and reached a possible culmination in Immanuel Kant's justification of punishment as an end in itself, as a categorical imperative or a priori truth (something that is true in an absolute sense independent of experience or scientific investigation).[1]

Acting within the confines of the philosophical presuppositions of the classical school of criminology, punishment was held to be appropriate for moral beings who were both free in spirit and possessed of an innate sense of what was right, but who still, through an act of reason and of free volition, intended and committed a wrong act. Such a school of thought set forth the doctrine that there are absolute "rights" and "wrongs" and that, somehow, any rational being knows and understands the difference between the two through an inborn moral sense. Since the concepts of right and wrong were taken as absolutes, and since man was free to choose to do right or wrong, it was impossible to justify a wrong act, and such an act therefore deserved punishment.

In discussing the retributive aspects of sentencing, one must be careful not to confuse it with the goal of protecting society from the danger that criminal behavior represents. It was, and largely still is, the belief of many individuals that the criminal should be punished for his act, whether or not the act endangered society. The conviction of criminals for "victimless" crimes is an example of the demand by legislative bodies for punishment of crimes which, in most cases, pose no real danger to the community.

Some individuals equate crime with sin and focus attention on crime as a moral issue. They identify the law of man with the law of God and feel that man must suffer for violating both the moral order of society and the commandments of God. Such thinkers appear to feel that they possess the one and only truth and have both the right to adjudge sins against God committed by other human beings and to anticipate the prerogative of God by imposing the requisite punishment.[2]

More likely, however, the cry for retributive punishment arises from a mechanism within human beings which provides an escape for their own hostilities and feelings of inadequacy. Since most individuals can't function in a role that enables them to satisfy these needs directly, the criminal justice system allows them a vicarious vehicle by which such needs can be realized. One wonders whether retribution must be maintained as a necessary goal of sentencing in order to prevent the destruction of defense mechanisms that maintain the status quo of a mass neurosis. Would the anxiety in man reach an unbearable peak if the mechanism of retribution was not open in such indirect and vicarious ways? Are we helping our fellow man when we sentence men to prison and death? Can we justify retributive punishment on such grounds alone, regardless of the detrimental effects such punishment may have on the criminal? Should the criminal be sacrificed for the mental health of society?

According to one argument for the preservation of retributive punishment as a major goal of sentencing, such punishment actually deters the criminal from repeating criminal acts in the future and deters the general population from committing their first offense. Studies are inconclusive, however, as to the deterrent effect of punishment. Since the deterrent effect of retributive punishment is not known, the main justification for retaining it as a goal of sentencing appears to go back to the need of individuals for revenge. As long as that need is part of human nature, retribution will continue as a goal of sentencing and must be dealt with.

Restitution has always been a problem. Some crimes appear to defy the concept of restitution. For example, if you were to fine or sentence a person to prison for the crimes of forcible rape, mayhem, child beating, manslaughter, or murder, what price would you extract for such offenses and what period of incarceration would be required? The victim hardly benefits from the punishment the criminal undergoes in the form of fines or imprisonment except, perhaps, through satisfaction of a deep-seated need for revenge. Victims are seldom compensated in the form of restitution for crimes against the person except, in rare cases, through compensation for medical expenses and time lost from work. In such crimes, restitution to society seems to prevail over restitution to the victim, and this restitution is measured by the amount of retributive punishment necessary to restore society, in some vague and indirect manner, to what it was prior to the commission of the crime. There are, therefore, certain crimes where the judge has a good deal of difficulty in determining what sentence to impose if he has only the goal of restitution in mind at the time of sentencing.

There are other types of criminal offenses, mostly crimes against property, for which restitution is more feasible, and matters can, to some extent, be restored to what they were before the crime was committed. For example, criminals who pass worthless checks and forge securities can be ordered to repay, as far as they are able, the amount of money lost to the victim. Such orders of restitution are not uncommon conditions of probation. In cases of burglary, the property damage resulting from "breaking and entering" a home or building can be taken into consideration, the value of the missing or "fenced" property that was never returned can be estimated, and a meaningful order of restitution can be delivered by the judge. In many property crimes, however, the perpetrator is poverty-stricken and has no source of income whatever, making it impossible for him to make restitution on any large claim. Even if placed on probation or ordered to jail with work release privileges, most criminals could, at best, make only partial restitution for their delinquent acts. Criminals sentenced to prison are seldom required to make restitution, because it is felt that the sentence alone somehow compensates society and the victim for his loss.

The concept of restitution is being reexamined in the criminal justice system today, and much thought is being directed toward finding more ways to adequately compensate victims directly through monetary means for crimes committed against them, whether they be crimes against property or the person. Moreover, attention is being paid to the rehabilitative potential of restitution and the application of this concept to correctional practice. Restitution made by the offender to victims of crimes within the jurisdiction of the criminal justice system is not to be confused with victim-compensation schemes operating within several states. The collection of damages by victims as a result of civil suits against offenders holds little rehabilitative potential for the offender and operates outside the criminal justice system. For restitution to achieve rehabilitative potential it must be meaningfully related to the damages suffered by the victim, the amount ordered must be made clear and specific to the offender, and a reasonable payment plan to the victim must be devised. The use of restitution as a correctional mechanism should further require the offender to engage in constructive acts that would lead to greater integration with society. The assumption must be made that individual offenders either possess or are able to acquire the necessary skills and abilities "to redress the wrongs done."[3]

The Minnesota Department of Corrections has established a program which attempts to compensate victims of crimes against property. The restitution program consists of the operation of a restitution house in which a selected group of inmates admitted to the Minnesota State Prison at Stillwater reside. Once selected for the program, the inmate meets his victim in the prison setting before he is released on parole. A contract is negotiated between the inmate and the victim under the guidance of a member of the restitution house staff, stipulating the amount of the restitution due and the manner in which it will be paid. The contract is reviewed by the parole board and becomes a "special condition of parole." Paroled inmates then live at the facility which has been located in a downtown YMCA. Inmates are required to pay a token amount for their room and board and must provide to their victim a monthly payment based on a percentage of their income.[4]

Several countries are attempting to emphasize restitution as a significant aspect of the sentencing process. For example, in Italy, labor performed in prison or under suspended sentence is combined with an obligation to make restitution out of earnings. Restitution is mandatory in Argentina, Colombia, Norway, and Sweden.

Deterrence

One of the major goals of the criminal justice system is to deter the individual citizen from the commission of crimes, or, if he is already convicted of a crime, from the repetition of such criminal behavior. Judges commonly justify a particular sentence they have pronounced by stating that they feel such a sentence will act as a deterrent both to the defendant and to society in general. Some judges feel that there is a positive relationship between the judgment pronounced and the deterrent effect of the penalty.

Many behavioral scientists have long assumed that criminal behavior was not controlled by legal sanctions and that judges were mistaken in the belief that the pronouncement of legal sanctions would deter individuals from the commission of crimes. Contemporary behavioral scientists, however, have challenged the assumption that legal sanctions do not deter and have "demonstrated" that under certain conditions behavior can be controlled by punishment.[5] In a criminal justice system where the punishment for a crime is relatively certain and where the punishment is closely paired with the commission of the crime in order for the criminal actor to associate the two, evidence indicates that punishment does deter. There is also some evidence supporting the belief held by most judges that there is a relationship between the severity of the punishment and deterrence in general. However, the relationship between the severity of punishment and deterrence does not appear to be consistent, but occasionally is significant in playing a deterrent role.[6]

Judges are probably correct in believing that sanctions do deter, but are wrong in believing that they deter under all conditions for all types of individuals. Much will depend on the certainty that the sanction will be applied for misbehavior; on the speed with which it is invoked; occasionally, on its degree of severity; on the complexity of the social system in which it is being applied; on the amount of investment the individual has in the social system; and on other variables as well.

Deterrence, then, is a complex issue which is still not clearly understood. The effectiveness of deterrence as a device for preventing and controlling crime is not known. The literature available concerning deterrence, for the most part, has little empirical or operational import, since there is a poverty of meaningful research in this area. Many assumptions are made about the value and effectiveness of deterrence, but the assumptions are of the philosophical sort set forth without any genuine attempts at verification. Proposals are being made for an increase in empirical research in this hitherto neglected area in order to expand our knowledge of deterrence as a mechanism of crime control and rehabilitation.

The judge faces problems when using deterrence as the basis for pronouncement of judgment. A criminal may be given a harsh sentence to provide an example for him as well as for others that the type of conduct he indulged in will no longer be tolerated. Normally the penalty would probably have been much more lenient if it were not felt by the judge that the time had come to "crack down" and let the individuals in the community know what to expect if they committed similar acts. In cases such as this, a criminal sanction is being imposed, not so much because of the crime committed, but rather to prevent future misbehavior. Louis P. Carney asks whether it is just to impose a penalty for behavior that may not occur in a future that has not yet taken place.[7] Is it ethical to use a defendant as an example to others and pronounce judgment on this basis?

Treatment

With the emergence of the positive school of criminology, judges attempted to individualize justice by having the sentence meet the needs of a particular defendant, rather than making the sentence fit the crime. Although limited by penal codes with respect to the types and degrees of dispositions possible, judges began to obtain further information about defendants, including prior criminal records and social, medical, and clinical histories, for the purpose of arriving at a sentence that would be of rehabilitative significance to the defendant. Experts in the field of criminal justice finally realized that a stress on rehabilitation would also pay dividends toward the goal of protecting society, on the basis that a rehabilitated criminal makes a good citizen and refrains from further criminal activity. Therefore, in addition to retribution and deterrence, judges must consider the treatment of the individual as one of their goals at the time of sentencing. Since little is really known about human behavior, and since prediction devices are still in their infancy, judges, like experts in the fields of social science, medicine, and psychiatry, have difficulty in determining just what kind of treatment plan would actually be rehabilitative.

Attempts are being made, at least, to take into consideration the needs of the individual criminal and the reasons why he committed a particular offense. But the treatment needs of some individuals cannot be met because of lack of the proper dispositions and lack of the necessary treatment facilities and personnel. Problems also arise in trying to reconcile treatment needs with the demand for retribution and the heavy value placed on deterrence. When the community demands that the individual be placed under maximum security, it is impossible to provide him with the program recommended for his rehabilitation and social growth. Since the protection of society is foremost in the judge's mind when delivering a judgment, the treatment needs of the defendant must always play a somewhat secondary role. There is every reason to believe, however, that society can still be protected by lighter and more humane sentences and that most criminals do not need the custody of a medium or maximum security prison. With this realization, more and more individuals convicted of crimes are being placed in programs where it is hoped that their treatment needs can be more adequately met.

Maintaining the preconviction process

Sentences are usually not impulsive judgments on the part of the judge during the sentencing hearing, especially in regard to serious crimes. In arriving at many sentences, much planning takes place in which various officers of the court and defense attorneys play a role. The entire concept of plea bargaining, for example, assumes that at the time for pronouncement of judgment, the judge will honor agreements made between prosecutors and defense attorneys. Plea bargaining avoids court backlogs by enabling courts to dispose of cases much more swiftly and inexpensively than would be the case if the majority of defendants were to demand either court or jury trials. The negotiated plea enables defendants to avoid severe sentences by pleading guilty to a lesser offense or by entering a plea of guilty to only one count of a criminal complaint listing multiple offenses. Even when innocent a defendant may plead guilty to a crime in order to avoid the possibility of a long prison sentence. The negotiated plea further provides an outlet for defendants to circumvent mandatory sentences prescribed by penal codes that prohibit judges from using discretion and shackles them to pronouncement of judgments that may be neither in the best interest of the defendant nor of society.

In spite of its faults, it appears that under our present system of criminal justice, plea bargaining is a necessary and sometimes beneficial device even though there are times when it is misused. It has a pragmatic purpose and it may have virtues that outweigh the evils it perpetrates. There have been proposals recognizing the negotiated plea as appropriate within our court system, and Chief Justice Burger has given approval to the practice of plea bargaining in a United States Supreme Court case.[8]

It is traditional for judges to ask the defendant at the time of sentencing whether or not promises have been made to him by any officer of the court to entice him to enter a plea of guilty, and the defendant is further reminded that the judge is not obligated to honor promises made by any court officer for the purpose of obtaining a plea of guilty. The defendant is made aware by the prosecutor that the plea bargaining agreement is not absolutely binding on the court and that there is always the possibility that the judge may pronounce judgment in a manner other than called for by the bargaining process. The defendant in entering into plea bargaining takes a gamble, but the odds are in his favor. The judge usually accepts the recommendations of the prosecutor under such circumstances, although he himself was not directly involved in the negotiated proceedings.

Avoiding the postconviction process

More and more, judges are making attempts to keep individuals convicted of crimes out of prisons and jails. Since many studies reveal that few criminals need institutionalization either for the protection of society or for their own rehabilitation, more use is being made of probation, parole, and community treatment centers. If incarceration appears necessary because it is required by the penal code or because other facilities are lacking in a particular jurisdiction, incarceration is often moderated by the application of work and educational release, allowing the inmate time in the community to earn a living or go to school. The role of the judge is then to decide which defendants are good risks for community treatment. The traditional sentence of thirty dollars or thirty days is no longer found in most of the lower courts of this country. Even in the higher courts, an increasing proportion of defendants convicted of felonies are being placed in community treatment programs, enabling them to remain in the community and avoid the stigma of a prison sentence. This is certainly a more humane way to treat an individual convicted of a crime, and studies reveal that society does not seem to suffer from a rise in crime rates as a result. In most cases, whether the criminal is treated harshly or leniently, the crime rate remains about the same, and little difference will be found in the recidivism rate of criminals once they are back in the free community.

THE SENTENCING HEARING

Information at sentencing—a critical evaluation

Before the rise of the "new penology," courts sentenced a defendant largely on the basis of the offense alone and neglected to obtain information concerning his family background, social history, and physical and emotional status. Sentencing followed the tenets of the classical school of criminology stressing the utilitarian concept that the punishment must fit the crime. Legal giants of the status of Blackstone advocated that criminals be treated harshly, but in an effort to save many of those convicted of crimes from being executed. It was discovered, however, that more information was needed at the time of sentencing than a mere indictment or complaint setting forth the crimes committed and the degrees thereof. With the advent of probation it was also necessary for judges to have information concerning the defendant that would enable them to determine whether or not he would be a good risk for community treatment. The need by courts for information for sentencing led to the development of the presentence report and investigation.

The primary function of the presentence report is to furnish the court with information that will help the judge understand the basic personality characteristics of the defendant, suggest a treatment plan that would provide for individual rehabilitation, and, at the same time, take into consideration the protection of the community. Such a report aids the court in pronouncing judgment on any given defendant, assists probation officers and workers of other interested agencies in developing a plan of rehabilitation, provides the treatment staff of correctional institutions with information that helps them in developing classification and treatment programs for new inmates, and helps parole boards to determine an inmate's eligibility for parole.

In many states the probation officer's presentence report is automatically forwarded to the correctional institution or diagnostic center to which the defendant is sentenced. Psychiatrists, psychologists, social workers, rehabilitational counselors, and other individuals concerned with rehabilitation find a well-constructed presentence report valuable in constructing a treatment program for any defendant. Presentence reports are never used for the purpose of deciding a defendant's guilt or innocence. Investigating probation officers are not permitted to question the court's verdict in regard to these matters, nor is the probation officer permitted to take it on himself to act as a court of appeals.

Presentence reports prepared by probation officers vary in quantity and quality according to the ability, knowledge, and insight of the probation officer who prepares them and the professional development of the probation department by which he is employed. A good report contains information in the following areas: present offense (the crime of which the defendant was convicted); prior offenses; social history (family background information, educational achievement, marital history, employment history and stability, military history, and present financial situation); medical history; clinical information of a psychiatric nature, if this is considered necessary; and comments by character references, witnesses, and other interested parties. After an examination of the data obtained during the investigation, the probation officer will write an evaluation and will usually set forth his recommendations to the court on how he believes the defendant should be sentenced. Some judges prefer that the probation officer not include recommendations in the report concerning sentencing. Other judges may prefer recommendations of either a general or specific nature. The format of the presentence report will vary, therefore, according to the preferences of the court regarding the amount and type of information that it should include.

Although it would appear that the information described above would prepare the way for impartial and scientific judgments at the time of sentencing, this is seldom the case. Sentences will vary according to the philosophy of the judge and the attitude and prejudice he has toward particular offenses, life styles, and racial and ethnic groups. Sex offenders, for example, may be treated with more severity in one court than another, although each judge may have available information of a similar quality and quantity. The pronouncement of a particular sentence may therefore depend more on the attitude of the judge than on the information provided to him in the presentence report.

To be sure, most judges are influenced by what they read in the presentence report. As a result, they adhere to the recommendations of the probation officer more often than not. This agreement is especially pronounced if the probation officer's recommendation is for a grant of probation. Cases arise, however, when the high correlation between final dispositions and recommendations for or against probation is due to the fact that the probation officer may construct his report and prescribe recommendations with the judge's prejudices and biases in mind, making it quite probable that the judge will be satisfied with what he reads and will not humiliate the probation officer in open court by raising vigorous objections. Can a report written primarily to appeal to a particular judge, rather than for the purpose of presenting an unbiased and impartial evaluation of the defendant, be considered of much value as a basis for establishing a program of custody and treatment? Perhaps this "game" between the court and the probation officer is played more frequently than we dare believe, and, if so, does anyone, outside of the defendant, really care?

There are other reasons for the high degree of agreement between the recommendations of probation officers and court dispositions. A probation department serving a particular court may observe especially high standards and provide the court with presentence reports of good quality and reliability. In such a case the judge will usually respect the recommendations made by the investigating officer because he feels that this officer has gained a more thorough knowledge of the defendant through the process of preparing the report. Other reasons for the high positive correlation between recommendations of presentence reports and judgments ordered by the courts are that probation officers and judges place emphasis on similar factors in arriving at a sentence alternative and that there may be many cases in which a recommendation either for prison or probation is obvious from the start.

The information finally incorporated in the presentence report is influenced by the biases and prejudices of the investigating officer and contains a great deal of hearsay obtained from interested parties such as friends, relatives, and character references. Much of the information in the report may go unverified because of lack of sufficient time for preparation or because of lack of zeal and genuine concern on the part of the investigator. In either case, nobody seems to be profoundly concerned, as the major emphasis is placed on getting some kind of report on the judge's desk by the time ordered.

In some instances, information from outdated reports or from juvenile reports that are supposed to remain confidential is carried over into the current report. The use of such information may dupe the judge into believing that the report reflects the defendant's present family, social, economic, medical, and emotional status, although it may actually bear little resemblance to the real person standing before the bench.

In order to make the presentence report a more meaningful document, information about the defendant's preconviction behavior should be included. All convicted offenders are subjected to a preconviction process consisting of apprehension and arrest; possible pre-plea or pretrial detention; numerous courtroom proceedings such as the initial arraignment, continuances for the purpose of submitting a plea, establishing a trial date, or presenting various legal motions; and the court or jury trial upon a plea of not guilty. During this period the defendant may be in contact with prosecuting attorneys, for the purpose of plea bargaining; with probation officers, if a pre-plea report is ordered; and with psychiatrists and psychologists, if psychiatric evaluations are ordered for the determination of sanity or to obtain information in order to establish possible mitigation. From the time of arrest to the time of conviction many weeks or even months may have elapsed. During this time the defendant may be incarcerated because of inability to make bail; or he may be allowed to remain in the community, on bail or by being released by the court on his own recognizance. In order to improve the diagnostic potential of the presentence report, information should be included concerning the defendant's preconviction behavior while either on bail or in custody.

Significant alteration of the defendant's behavior, either in the direction of reform or of further delinquency, can and does take place, including the commission of new criminal offenses. It is not uncommon to have a subheading in a presentence report for "subsequent offenses." While on bail the defendant's circumstances may also improve in regard to employment, family life, and emotional growth, indicating a different form of disposition than may have been indicated at the time of arrest. On the other hand, prolonged incarceration may have produced general deterioration, hostility, bitterness, and other negative feelings that should be included in the report in recommending a program of sanctions and treatment.

Even if the information presented to a particular judge is accurate and sufficient to provide the basis for an intelligent plan of action, there is no guarantee that the judge will actually read it. If he does, he may weigh the value of information according to his own priorities, giving family background and social history data little weight and placing prime emphasis on the arrest report and the defendant's prior record. This brings us back to where we began with Blackstone, but not for reasons as humane or honorable.

Judges are not provided with presentence services in all jurisdictions. Even in areas where such services are available to the courts, they are seldom used in connection with the disposition of misdemeanor offenses. In states where the use of presentence reports is optional, many defendants, even those convicted of serious felonies, are still sentenced on the basis of their prior criminal record and information found in the arrest report. In some states a presentence report is mandated by statute in regard to felony convictions. In New Jersey it is required by court rule.

Some states provide that their diagnostic centers, which are used for reception and classification of offenders sentenced to state prison, should also serve as presentence diagnostic clinics, furnishing information to courts on request as a basis for recommendations for sentencing. Courts wishing to take advantage of such an evaluation can, by law, refer a defendant to the department of corrections specifically for this purpose. Individuals referred for a presentence evaluation undergo essentially the same processing as inmates already sentenced to prison and awaiting assignment to a transfer institution. Once the report is completed, usually within 90 days but never more than 120 days, the offender is sent back to court for sentencing. This type of service is especially valuable to counties lacking a well-staffed and sophisticated probation department that is capable of producing a balanced, reliable presentence report. Sentencing judges are not obligated to follow the recommendations of the diagnostic staff, but judges do avail themselves of this service when they are not entirely satisfied with the sources of information available to them in their county. A judge may feel that a diagnostic center has a greater evaluative capability than a local probation department utilizing local adjunct referral services. Some judges make use of this service when they feel anxiety about making a decision and want to place the major responsibility of decision making on some source other than themselves.

Under a procedure employed by the federal system, the judge may impose the maximum term authorized for the offense and order the defendant to be placed in a diagnostic facility maintained by the United States Bureau of Prisons. A report is prepared by the diagnostic facility within three months suggesting a correctional program that the judge may employ at the time of sentencing. After reviewing the recommendations contained in the report submitted by the diagnostic facility, the judge may affirm the original sentence, reduce it, or grant probation.[9]

Disclosure

The policies of courts and probation departments differ concerning the disclosure of the presentence report to attorneys for the defense and to the defendants themselves. In California, for example, the law requires that the full presentence report must be made available to the court and the prosecuting and defense attorneys at least two days before the time fixed for the pronouncement of judgment. The law further provides that the report be filed with the clerk of the court as a record in the case at the time of sentencing, making the presentence report available as a public document.[10] Some counties in California—for example, Marin County—require that the investigating probation officer allow the defendant to read the presentence report in his presence before sentencing. This requirement sometimes causes a good deal of anxiety on the part of the investigating officer, especially if he is locked in an attorney's room with the defendant at the county jail and is recommending state prison; but it is thought to provide adequate due process to the defendant and to be conducive to more careful investigation and reliable reporting of facts on the part of the officer.

In the majority of states, however, and in the federal system, the presentence report is considered to be a confidential document and, at best, is only available to the defense on a limited basis according to the discretion of the judge. The United States District Court for the District of Maryland employs the interesting method of having the presentence report prepared in two parts. The bulk of the information is incorporated in a report that is made available to the defense counsel in chambers by the judge. A cover sheet containing the probation officer's recommendation, any confidential information, and any data which might injure the defendant's relationship with others is submitted separately. The cover sheet is not shown to defense counsel, although it is the judge's policy to discuss the information contained in this document with him.[11]

The majority of the judiciary and their probation staffs feel that the presentence report should not be made a public document and should be made available to the defense only at the court's discretion or as circumstances warrant; but many professional organizations are recommending policies to the contrary—for example, the American Bar Association in its *Standards Relating to Sentencing Alternatives and Procedures*, the American Law Institute in its

Model Penal Code, and the National Council on Crime and Delinquency in its *Model Sentencing Act*. These organizations recommend that the presentence report be made available to the defendant's attorney, and if he has no attorney, to the defendant himself, to give him the opportunity to reply to derogatory information in the report which adversely affects his interests. However, the abovementioned professional organizations recommend further that the court be permitted to withhold from disclosure parts of the presentence report which are not relevant to the defendant's chances of receiving a fair and proper sentence. Such information may include a diagnostic opinion which may disrupt a program of rehabilitation or sources of information which have been obtained on the promise of confidentiality.

The President's Crime Commission on Law Enforcement and the Administration of Justice recommends that in "the absence of compelling reasons for nondisclosure of special information, the defendant and his counsel should be permitted to examine the entire presentence report."[12] The Crime Commission appears to be especially concerned with "gossip" which finds its way into many presentence reports and which may have an adverse influence on the defendant if allowed to go unchallenged.

The Advisory Committee on the Federal Rules of Criminal Procedure has also recommended disclosure of the presentence report to the defense unless it is the court's opinion that the report contains information which, if disclosed, would be harmful to the defendant or other persons. In order to protect information the court believes harmful to the defendant or others, the Advisory Committee recommends that the court make available to the defense (in lieu of the presentence report) an oral statement or written summary of the background information contained in the report. This statement would be relied on in determining sentence and would further provide the defense with an opportunity to comment on the information.[13]

Those who argue in favor of disclosure feel that the defendant should have the opportunity to refute damaging information based on pure hearsay or to clarify statements that are inaccurate or exaggerated. Further, it is felt that the defendant will better be able to understand the reason for the court's disposition if he has had access to the presentence report and has been able to discuss the recommended disposition with his counsel and the investigating probation officer. Such an understanding by the defendant of the reasons behind the sentence ordered may help facilitate his rehabilitation process.

Those who maintain that the presentence report should not be released to the defendant and his attorney feel that the release of the information contained in such reports would "dry up" confidential sources of information, delay the sentencing process by allowing the defendant to question the probation officer in open court about his sources of information, reveal information that may damage the working relationship between the probation officer and the defendant, and possibly cause informants to be subjected to retribution at the hands of the defendant or lead to undue embarrassment for both parties.

According to William G. Zastrow, the Eastern District of Wisconsin has routinely made the presentence report available to defense counsel for many years, and such disclosure has not resulted in the problems anticipated by the critics of disclosure. On the contrary, sources of information did not dry up, the investigating probation officer became a better and more objective investigator as a result of disclosure, there was less confrontation between the defendant and the probation officer at the outset of probation, and in some cases, the disclosure helped the defendant to obtain knowledge concerning his strengths and weaknesses, making his rehabilitation more probable.[14]

Norm Larkins found that probation services in Alberta, Canada improved after introduction of the practice of making the presentence report available to the defense.[15] The courts placed a greater degree of reliance on presentence reports because of their improved degree of objectivity. This led the courts to request more reports and to grant probation to increasing numbers of people. It was also felt that such disclosure improved the relationship between the defendant and the probation officer by demonstrating to the defendant that someone was trying to understand his problems.

Role of the prosecutor

The prosecution is represented at all sentencing hearings by someone from the district attorney's or attorney general's office, depending on whether it is a State or Federal court. The prosecutor is usually asked by the judge to give his recommendation for sentencing. If plea bargaining has already taken place between the prosecutor and the attorney for the defense, both the defense and prosecution will agree on how the defendant should be sentenced. There are times when the prosecutor will arrive at a plea-bargaining agreement without sufficient knowledge about the defendant's background, which is later uncovered by the investigating probation officer. Such background information may indicate that a more severe sentence should be imposed rather than the one agreed to through the bargaining process, but the prosecutor will probably feel bound by the agreement he has already made with the defendant. When plea-bargaining agreements are arrived at in ignorance of information concerning a defendant's prior record and social history, justice has hardly been carried out either in behalf of the defendant or society, but the pragmatic considerations that govern the preconviction process are given priority over the welfare of the individual and the community.

Where no plea bargaining has taken place, some prosecutors usually argue for the more severe sanction. Other prosecutors, realizing the futility of severe sanctions in many cases, make recommendations that have the rehabilitation of the defendant in mind, even though the members of the community may view such a prosecutor as being "soft" on crime.

One major criticism of the prosecutor's role during the sentencing process is that, especially in jurisdictions with large criminal populations, the representative sent to court on behalf of the chief prosecutor's office is at times unprepared to present an intelligent argument. It is not uncommon to see the district attorney or his representative walk into court during the day set aside for sentencing, attempting to balance thirty or forty folders containing the records of defendants in his hands. He appears more like a magician trying out for a juggling routine on an amateur hour than an officer of the court. There are occasions when he has had time only to skim through the reports before entering the courtroom and has to read them before the judge calls each case. Judges are sometimes sympathetic in these matters and overlook the unpreparedness of the prosecutor because he realizes that most prosecutors are overworked. The question remains, however, does the defendant or society receive adequate justice when the prosecutor only gives cursory attention to a case?

Should the prosecution take any part in sentencing procedures? Some feel that the prosecutor's training does not provide him with the knowledge and experience necessary to make recommendations for a treatment plan for an individual convicted of a crime. Such critics would limit the prosecutor's role to the preconviction process. Others feel that the state should be represented in the sentencing process by the prosecutor's office in order to insure that the defendant is not treated too lightly and that the safety of the community receives adequate consideration. Under our present system of criminal justice it is most likely that the prosecutor will continue to be included in sentencing hearings.

The role of the defense counsel

Defendants are usually represented at sentencing either by counsel of their own selection or by a public defender or an attorney appointed by the court to represent the indigent. The Supreme Court has held that defendants have the right to defense counsel during sentencing and appeal.[16]

Before the time set for the pronouncement of judgment, the defense counsel may already have negotiated an agreement with the prosecutor's office in the form of a plea bargain. If no agreement has been reached, the defense counsel will present arguments for the most lenient sentence available for his client. During the time that elapses between conviction and sentencing, the defense counsel may also confer with members of the probation department regarding possibilities concerning sentencing.

When the defense counsel knows that his client needs treatment for narcotic addiction, alcoholism, or some emotional disturbance, a treatment program may be worked out in conjunction with the probation department and prosecutor's office before sentencing. During the preparation of a presentence report, it is not uncommon for the defense counsel to pay many visits to the prosecutor's office and to the probation department in order to obtain some agreement about his client's sentence.

Some states will provide defense counsel, upon request, with a "pre-plea" report prepared by the probation department. A pre-plea report is substantially the same as a presentence report, but it omits any reference to the present offense other than information provided by the arresting authorities. The probation officer makes a statement to the court indicating what he would recommend if the defendant were to be convicted of the offense with which he is charged. After obtaining a copy of this report, the defense counsel will virtually know the fate of his client if he "pleads him guilty" and will take action according to whether the recommendations of the probation officer are favorable or unfavorable. But reports of this type are rarely used even where the law provides for their preparation, because defense attorneys and judges alike are not aware of the availability of such reports, and because the courts are reluctant to burden the probation department with preparation of the reports.

ALTERNATIVES AT SENTENCING

Incarceration

Courts have traditionally used short- and long-term imprisonment as a sanction, to the exclusion of almost all other types of sanctions. To this day, institutionalization in some form is still the principal reaction to the commission of crime.[17] The judge employing this form of disposition may sentence someone to a straight jail or prison term, the length depending on the severity of the crime; or, in some jurisdictions, the judge may impose a jail sentence as a condition of probation. Once the sentence is pronounced by the court, the defendant is usually remanded to the custody of the county sheriff for execution of the sentence. Sentences may be definite or indeterminate and concurrent or consecutive.

DEFINITE AND INDETERMINATE SENTENCES

A definite sentence, also referred to as a fixed sentence, is for a stated number of years. An indeterminate sentence specifies a minimum and maximum number of years an inmate must serve. For all practical purposes, the indeterminate sentence is for the maximum number of years unless a parole board agrees to set a term of incarceration less than the maximum required by law. Confinement in a state institution for no less than three years nor more than twelve years is a form of indeterminate sentence. Under a definite or fixed sentence an inmate is not usually eligible for parole until he has served at least one-third of his sentence.

Indeterminate sentences were adopted in some states to make sentencing more flexible and to avoid forcing judges to impose a fixed number of years which a defendant must serve. In many respects, however, the indeterminate sentence takes sentencing out of the judge's jurisdiction and places it under the jurisdiction of "quasi-judicial authorities" such as parole boards. In some jurisdictions, once a defendant is sentenced by a judge to the term prescribed by law for a particular offense, the parole board determines, within the statutory limits prescribed for a particular crime, how long the defendant who is committed to a correctional institution will remain under the jurisdiction of the correctional system. The parole board will fix a minimum term for each prisoner and determine when the prisoner will be paroled. Under indeterminate sentencing procedures, parole boards become powerful bodies that engage in the process of "sentencing," although the term "sentencing" is never used in reference to the "fixing" of terms.[18]

In reality there is little difference between sentencing and term fixing. Only the participants are changed and the constitutional rights of the prisoner altered. Parole boards, unlike courts of law, function in closed hearings where prisoners have traditionally been denied counsel and access to their prison files. Parole boards are able to fix terms within statutory limits and at the same time "bypass a traditional limitation on judicial sentencing power."[19] Once a court of law imposes a sentence for a particular offense it cannot at a later point increase that sentence for any reason, including the prisoner's conduct in prison. However, a parole board, such as the Adult Authority in California, can fix a minimum term and then alter that minimum at its own discretion depending on whether it thinks the prisoner has conducted himself satisfactorily while in prison. Since administrative agencies such as parole boards are not judicial bodies according to the law, they are not, by definition, engaged in sentencing. But in practice, "term fixing" and "sentencing" amount to the same thing.[20]

If the indeterminate sentence is to be a workable dispositional and rehabilitative tool, data concerning the behavior of inmates must be capable of being accurately collected, meaningfully interpreted, and fed through predictive devices that would enable authorities concerned with sentencing and term fixing to predict, in a statistically significant manner, when an inmate will be receptive to parole. But at present, our lack of knowledge concerning human behavior prohibits us from manufacturing prediction devices that would meet these requirements. There is genuine doubt whether we shall ever obtain the necessary data concerning the intricacies of behavior to construct meaningful and accurate predictive devices. Even if we did increase our knowledge concerning human behavior, accurate predictions concerning success and failure on parole would also depend on such pre-release variables as conditions in the community in which the inmate is to be released, the reactions he will receive from his friends and loved ones once released, the state of the national economy, and more. Such factors are difficult, if not impossible, to measure. Where can judges and parole board members go for information that will help them improve their ability to make sound predictions concerning behavioral adjustment? At present it appears that every avenue they take in search of such knowledge results in a dead end.

The lack of adequate knowledge concerning human behavior is not the only reason why the indeterminate sentence fails as a rehabilitative tool. In order to prevent indeterminate sentence laws from functioning as they were originally meant to function, some judges impose a high minimum sentence in order to prevent parole boards from releasing an inmate at an early date. Imposing high minimums makes the indeterminate sentence in all practical respects a form of definite sentence, since the area of flexibility between the minimum and maximum term becomes negligible for the purposes of rehabilitation.

There has been much criticism of the indeterminate sentence. Many inmates on indeterminate sentences suffer from severe anxiety about when they will be released on parole. Some inmates would prefer fixed terms to a short term accompanied by this anxiety while they await a decision by the parole board. In states where the indeterminate sentence law is in effect, one of the major parole-related factors affecting inmate attitudes and behavior during incarceration is the indefiniteness of knowledge about the time of release. Further, in California, where the indeterminate sentence operates, inmates are serving longer periods of incarceration than in jurisdictions applying the definite sentence.

Another criticism of the indeterminante sentence law is that it contributes to hypocrisy among inmates. They pretend to conform to prison regulations; they participate in programs in which they have no interest or which they actually hold in contempt; and they pretend to acquire socially approved attitudes. This playing of the "time game" makes it difficult for parole boards to distinguish the sincere candidate for release from the "con artist" and significantly hinders meaningful communication between correctional officials and inmates.

It is of interest that there are no indeterminate sentences in Sweden because it is felt that inmates should know when they will be released from prison. Further, a recent Task Force to Study Violence, which was set up by the California State Department of Corrections, recommended that California's indeterminate sentence law be abolished because of the frustration it caused inmates by not giving them a firm parole date. The report asserted that such anxiety contributed considerably to violence within the prisons.

Louis P. Carney suggests that a reducible determinate sentence would be preferable to the indeterminate sentence. Under such a system the inmate would be given a fixed sentence and a goal-oriented program. As the inmate achieves the goals prescribed for him his sentence would be reduced according to a formula. Carney feels that this procedure would lessen the anxiety caused by the indeterminate sentence and yet retain the theoretical advantage of the indeterminate sentence, namely, the advantage of enabling the inmate to determine his release by his progress in rehabilitation. Such an approach would be impossible in jurisdictions where the fixed sentence is in effect.[21]

THE SPLIT SENTENCE

Under federal law, an alternative known as the "split sentence" is available.[22] Under this law, when the maximum punishment for an offense is more than six months imprisonment, the judge has the option of sentencing the defendant to a term of less than six months in jail and then placing him on probation to begin after he completes the period of incarceration. The probation period would run as long as the statutory limit of imprisonment permits. This degree of flexibility enables the court to meet the needs of the defendant more rationally than would straight incarceration in a jail or prison; and it helps to mitigate harsh punishment where it is felt that a severe sanction would serve no useful purpose.

CONCURRENT AND CONSECUTIVE SENTENCES

If a defendant is charged and convicted of more than one offense, he may receive either a concurrent or a consecutive sentence. Concurrent sentences run simultaneously and consecutive sentences run in sequence. During the plea-bargaining process a prosecutor may offer the defense counsel a recommendation of a concurrent sentence on three separate counts mentioned in the criminal complaint or indictment if, for some reason, he does not want to dismiss all the counts except one. For all practical purposes the defendant in such a case would end up serving no more than the maximum period of time specified for the offense carrying the longest prison sentence. For example, if the defendant were sentenced to prison on three counts, one carrying a seven-year maximum and the others a five-year maximum each, the defendant would serve no more than seven years in prison. All three counts would begin to run the day he was committed to prison, and by his seventh year he would have served all three of his sentences. If the same counts were ordered to run consecutively, the defendant could serve the maximum of seventeen years in prison.

When an inmate already on probation or in prison is convicted of a new offense, the judge must decide whether to sentence the inmate or probationer concurrently or consecutively on the new count. Some judges feel that all individuals serving time in prison should suffer the maximum penalty for any offense they commit while incarcerated and make it a blanket policy to order consecutive sentences for such inmates regardless of recommendations from probation officers to the contrary. Some judges will order a consecutive sentence if a defendant convicted of more than one offense demands a jury trial, and a concurrent sentence if he pleads guilty, thereby penalizing him for exercising his constitutional right to trial by court or jury.

Fines

Another alternative open to the judge at the time of pronouncement of judgment is the fine. A defendant may be sentenced to pay a fine directly or as a condition of either summary or supervised probation. Where allowed by the penal code, a judge may impose both a fine and incarceration for the same offense, with the result that the defendant suffers two different kinds of sanctions. It has been a tradition for judges to order incarceration for defendants who did not or could not pay the fine ordered. Imprisonment for nonpayment of fine has been common under our system of justice, and many short-term offenders have been placed in custody because they could not pay the amount demanded by the court. Traditionally, therefore, imprisonment for nonpayment of fines has fallen unequally on the indigent class. Most penal codes demand a fixed amount to be paid as a fine for a specific violation of the law. The amount may be of small consequence to a wealthy defendant but may result in a severe hardship on the defendant in the lower economic brackets.

More and more, the tradition of imposing an alternative sentence, such as jail, for the nonpayment of fine is being subjected to review. According to the *New Sentencing Standards* set forth by the American Bar Association, the court's response to nonpayment should not be an automatic "thirty dollars or thirty days" type of judgment. Instead, the effect of nonpayment of a fine should be determined after the fine has not been paid and after examination of the reasons for nonpayment. In California it is now unconstitutional to require a convicted indigent defendant, upon being sentenced to pay a fine and penalty assessment, to serve them out in confinement at a specified rate per day because he is unable to pay.[23]

Attempts are now made by the courts to take into consideration the inability of the poorer defendants to pay fines, which results in allowing defendants to pay fines on installments as a condition of probation. For those unable to pay a fine even under installment conditions, the judge may order a week-end jail sentence in order to moderate the effect of incarceration. Some judges substitute work done in behalf of the community for an unpaid fine.

Fines may have a deterrent effect if imposed in a reasonable manner and for a specific purpose. A fine is meant to result in some degree of financial hardship for the defendant, but not an unreasonable degree. For example, fines should never be imposed in a case where the defendant has already been ordered to pay restitution to a victim, or child support, if the imposition of the fine would interfere with the ability of the defendant to make the restitution or child support payments ordered. It is thought to be more important for the defendant to meet his obligations to his children or to an injured victim than to merely produce revenue for the state treasury.

Fines sometimes have a therapeutic effect when paid in installments as a condition of probation. In cases where the probation office serves to collect fines and restitution, the probation officer's role need not be limited to that of a collection agency. Visiting the probation officer's office on a monthly basis and paying a fine can serve to remind the probationer of his past act, and the probation officer can take this reporting opportunity to engage in supportive counseling.

In its *New Sentencing Standards*, the American Bar Association recommends that the legislature consider the feasibility of employing an index other than a dollar amount in cases where it might be appropriate in fixing the maximum fine for some offenses.[24]

> For example, a fine relative to the amount of gain might be appropriate in cases where the defendant has profited by his crime, or a fine relative to sales, profits, or net annual income might be appropriate in some cases, such as business or anti-trust offenses, in order to assure a reasonably even impact of the fine on defendants of varying means.

The question has arisen concerning who should receive the money raised by fines. In crimes where there is a victim, should the victim receive the fine, rather than the state? Some victims do receive restitution from criminal actions, but this is not always the case, especially where the defendant does not receive probation and where the offense is a crime against the person rather than property. Under the old Anglo-Saxon law known as "composition," the family of a murdered individual received compensation from the killer according to a complicated system of wergild ("man money") in which a compensatory value was ascribed to a murdered individual.[25] Also, under an old English procedure, any private person could bring a criminal action and recover the part of the fine that did not go to the crown.[26] Under our present system of criminal justice matters are reversed, and the victim receives no money paid to the state as a result of the imposition of a fine.

Probation

Defendants convicted of a crime may be placed on either supervised or summary probation by the court. Defendants convicted of felonies and serious misdemeanors are usually placed on supervised probation, for penal codes as a rule do not allow the granting of summary probation in felony cases. For lesser misdemeanors defendants may be granted summary probation under which they can serve their probationary period in the community without supervision.

SUSPENSION OF EXECUTION OR IMPOSITION OF SENTENCE

In the granting of probation the court may suspend either the execution or the imposition of sentence. When the execution of sentence is suspended the defendant is given a definite period of incarceration which he will have to serve if his probation should be revoked. As an example of suspending *execution* of a sentence, a court might order a defendant to serve 90 days in jail and then suspend sentence and place the defendant on probation. If the defendant's probation should be revoked, the court would have no alternative but to sentence the defendant to 90 days in jail. By suspending the execution of sentence the judge is forced to impose the fixed sentence if a revocation should become necessary.

But circumstances may change while the defendant is on probation, and if probation must be revoked, the original sentence of 90 days may no longer be appropriate. Perhaps a longer or shorter period of incarceration would be more in order. By suspending the *imposition* of sentence the judge can, if probation is revoked, sentence the defendant to any period of incarceration as long as it does not exceed the maximum prescribed by law. Since he is not limited to imposing a fixed amount of jail time, the judge can consider the defendant's current situation before ordering a period of incarceration.

In jurisdictions where the penal code provides for an alternative between a jail and prison sentence upon conviction of a particular crime, the distinction between the execution and imposition of sentence suspended becomes even more significant. For example, if a defendant is sentenced to state prison for the term prescribed by law and the execution of this sentence is suspended, the defendant stands convicted of a felony and must be sentenced to state prison if his probation is revoked. However, if the defendant is granted probation with the imposition of sentence suspended and the penal code allows for either a jail or prison sentence as a sanction, the judge may, upon revocation, sentence the defendant to a period of time in jail rather than state prison, thereby automatically reducing the conviction to a misdemeanor status.

Probation is increasingly being granted with the imposition of sentence suspended in both felony and misdemeanor cases, in order to give the court more flexibility in sentencing. The execution of sentence suspended is sometimes applied as a deterrent, in the hope that if the defendant knows exactly what sanction awaits him, he will be more apt to abide by the conditions of his probation.

There are serious felonies for which the penal code leaves no alternative but to impose a definite sentence and then order it suspended. For example, if the defendant is convicted of a felony for which only a state prison sentence is provided by the penal code, then it would make little difference whether the court suspended the imposition or the execution of sentence, since both would result in a prison sentence if the defendant were to have his probation revoked.

The distinction between execution and imposition of sentence suspended is most significant when the court is dealing with misdemeanors and with felonies which provide for the alternatives of a prison or a jail sentence.

REDUCTION OF A FELONY TO A MISDEMEANOR

California allows the judge to reduce a felony conviction to a misdemeanor at the time of sentencing if such a disposition is thought warranted by the court and by the parties present at the pronouncement of judgment. The penal code does not allow this type of automatic reduction in all cases but does permit such action in regard to many felonies. Such a provision enables the court to reduce a conviction without imposing a county jail sentence or without having to suspend the imposition of sentence and reduce the conviction at the time of expungement of record. The defendant receives the benefit of the court's action as soon after conviction as he can be sentenced.

JAIL AS A CONDITION OF PROBATION

In certain states, such as California, jail may be ordered as a condition of probation. For example, a defendant can be sentenced to the county jail for a period of four months with the execution of sentence suspended and be placed on supervised probation for a period of two years with a condition that he serve thirty days in the county jail. Once he has served the thirty days in jail he is free to return to the community under supervision but is still under a four-month suspended sentence, which could be imposed if probation is revoked. In jurisdictions where this is permissible, jail as a condition of probation is on a par with any other condition of probation, such as that of paying a fine or restitution and reporting as directed to the probation department. There are many authorities in the field of criminal justice, however, who feel that jail should never be imposed as a condition of probation because it violates the very nature and purpose of probation. But the fact remains that certain states allow such a disposition, and it is used quite frequently, especially in reference to short-term sentences. Some judges feel that such a disposition can be a genuine deterrent, since the defendant experiences a degree or "taste" of incarceration before being released in the community and can receive the services of a probation officer while incarcerated, since he is under probationary supervision.

For the most part, probation is in lieu of incarceration (except in those few states which require the defendant to serve a short period of time in jail before officially being placed on probation). It may be argued that the practices of having an offender serve time in jail before going on probation and ordering the offender to serve time in jail as a condition of probation more or less amount to the same thing. Some authorities feel, however, that by having an offender serve time in jail before being granted probation, the original meaning and purpose of probation is preserved. Probation is therefore, at least in a technical sense, not tainted with incarceration, as would be the case if jail were ordered as a condition of probation.

Jail as a condition of probation becomes important in certain felony cases, such as those mentioned above, in which the penal code offers only the alternative of state prison or probation and fails to provide for a jail term as an alternative to prison. Some offenders convicted of such felonies would not be placed on probation where the court feels that they should experience a considerable time in custody before being released in the community. By enabling the court to apply jail as a condition of probation, the offender can be placed on supervised probation under a suspended state prison term and still experience a good degree of incarceration (up to a year) as a condition of probation. During the offender's period of incarceration his progress can be observed by his supervising probation officer, and modifications of probation can take place in the form of work, educational release, or early release from custody. In jurisdictions where such a disposition is permitted, some offenders have been "saved" from serving long terms in state prison and have, as a result, been able to make a gradual adjustment to the free community. Although, in a sense, it might be inconsistent with the original meaning and function of probation, enabling a court to use jail as a condition of probation has some advantages.

CONDITIONS OF PROBATION

Most grants of probation carry with them common conditions to which the probationer must adhere. For example, all grants of supervised probation stipulate that the probationer must lead a law-abiding life, keep the probation officer informed of his whereabouts, and report to the probation officer as ordered. Special conditions of probation tailored to meet a probationer's specific physical or emotional needs and civil and legal obligations may be affixed to the probation contract, such as: seeking and maintaining steady employment; paying child support in such amounts and in such a manner as directed by the court; obtaining treatment for alcoholism or narcotic addiction; making restitution to victims; paying a fine to the state under an installment plan; maintaining psychiatric treatment for emotional problems; and engaging in family counseling in order to help overcome family problems that might be contributing to the probationer's delinquent behavior.

THE MODIFICATION AND REVOCATION OF PROBATION

Grants of probation can be modified or revoked. Conditions of probation such as those specifying a period of incarceration or psychiatric treatment are subject to periodic review by the court. As the probationer makes progress under supervision the probation officer may feel that the original conditions are no longer appropriate. As a result, he may request that the court modify these conditions by shortening the term of confinement originally ordered or by allowing the probationer to terminate psychiatric treatment. On the other hand, probation may be modified to provide for a more severe sanction for those not fulfilling the conditions of their probation, especially where a new offense of a minor nature has been committed. Modifications may include addition of incarceration as a condition of probation, lengthening the period of probation, or adding other special requirements as conditions of probation. The ability of the court to modify the conditions of probation enables the judge to review a probationer's progress during his period of supervision and alter treatment plans to meet his changing needs. It also enables the court to apply sanctions as conditions of probation and, at the same time, to retain the offender on probation when it is felt that supervised probation is still serving a valuable function.

If the probationer fails to cooperate with the probation officer and disregards the conditions of his probation, the court can revoke his probation. The reason for revocation may be the commission of a new criminal offense; or it may be a "technical violation"—failure to heed specific conditions of probation, such as reporting to the probation officer as directed, making child support payments, or moving from the area of jurisdiction without proper notification. Sometimes the real reasons for revocation are not made clear during the revocation process. For example, the probationer may have committed a new criminal offense and admitted this to his probation officer. However, in order to spare the state the expense of a new trial for the commission of the new offense (and to expedite matters, since it is usually a swift and easy process to revoke probation), the prosecutor is often willing to have the court revoke probation on technical grounds. He is willing to use revocation of probation as an alternative, especially if the penalty specified for the new offense is less than the sanction possible if a petition for revocation is granted.

This type of agreement among the officers of the court confuses the data concerning commission of new offenses by probationers while on probation and further misleads the public as to the genuine reasons for revocation; but, in most cases, it results in a sanction similar to that which the probationer would have received if he had been convicted and sentenced for a new offense.

To initiate revocation proceedings, the probation officer files a petition for revocation with the court, stating the reasons for the recommendation. A hearing is held in court on this petition and the defendant is given the opportunity to reply to the charges. Traditionally, defendants undergoing such action had no right to counsel, and the rules of evidence governing a criminal trial did not hold. In 1967, however, the Supreme Court ruled that a probationer is entitled to be represented by counsel during a revocation hearing, unless counsel is waived.[27] Such a ruling has made judges more reluctant to revoke probation on largely hearsay evidence and has provided the probationer the opportunity for a more adequate defense against unsound charges.

The penalty the defendant suffers from revocation of his probation will vary according to the suspended sentence he received when probation was granted. In most states, if the execution of a fixed term of incarceration has been suspended, the defendant will be ordered to serve the fixed term as a result of the revocation and will probably be given credit for time served in custody as a condition of probation. In the states of Illinois and New York, however, the sentence resulting from revocation of probation may extend to the maximum permissible by law for the offense, even though a fixed term of incarceration was pronounced in the original judgment.[28]

THE EXPUNGEMENT OF RECORD

Satisfactory completion of the terms of probation results in discharge of the defendant from probation. In certain states, such as California, the probationer may petition to have his record expunged as a result of a satisfactory discharge. The result of the expungement procedure is to wipe out, at least theoretically, the criminal conviction. For example, after the expungement of record, a former probationer could apply for a job and truthfully state that he has not been convicted of a crime. The expungement, in cases where the offense committed was a felony, would also reinstate all privileges the former probationer lost as a result of his conviction.

Even though in theory the expungement proceedings were meant to benefit the defendant, the practical results of such proceedings are not always very satisfactory. Prospective employers usually find out about former convictions, and it matters little to them whether or not the applicant has completed a period of probation satisfactorily. This is especially true if the former probationer applies for positions in the fields of education, law, or medicine, or in vocations which require that the employee be bonded or have a license to work. Further, in California, the expungement proceedings do not protect the former probationer in open court. If he is charged with a new criminal offense, the previous conviction will still be held against him. The expungement of record does, however, show the community that the former probationer made a satisfactory adjustment to supervised probation and tried to live a law-abiding life and adhere to a life style considered acceptable by community standards. Also in California, first offenders between the ages of eighteen and twenty-one who have been convicted by the adult courts and placed on probation may have their record sealed upon the satisfactory completion of their probationary period.

Probation without conviction

Deferred conviction is used in Maryland, Rhode Island, and Washington. Under this type of judgment, the court does not convict the defendant of a crime but places him on probation under such terms and conditions as are thought necessary. Upon satisfactory completion of the terms of probation the defendant is discharged without having suffered a conviction. Prosecutors have objected to this type of disposition because witnesses tend to disappear after the sentence, and, in general, the postponement handicaps the prosecution. The National Council on Crime and Delinquency, through its *Model Sentencing Act*, attempts to avoid this problem by recommending that the defendant be granted probation without judgment rather than without conviction. Such a recommendation would provide for the establishment of guilt by verdict or plea; but the judgment of guilt, instead of being entered at this point, would be deferred pending the outcome of the probation. Upon satisfactory completion of the terms of probation the defendant would be discharged without a court adjudication of guilt, and an order would be entered expunging the verdict or plea of guilty. If the defendant fails on probation, the court would enter the judgment of guilt and pronounce sentence. Such a recommendation allows the prosecution to finish its task but still protects the defendant from a criminal conviction if he completes a satisfactory period of probation.

Less common choices

In addition to the more popular types of dispositions such as incarceration, fines, and probation, the courts sometimes impose judgments combining certain aspects of those traditional dispositions and add a few innovations. With the contemporary stress on the significance of treatment as part of the sentencing process, courts, in some cases, attempt to provide a disposition which will meet the treatment needs of various defendants. This may result in permitting a defendant to live in a residential center such as Synanon in lieu of jail or prison, in order to help him solve his drug problem. Such a disposition would usually be ordered as a condition of probation, although the defendant would not be supervised by a probation officer.

The advent of community-based corrections has had a significant effect on the sentencing process by providing the courts with more than the traditional alternatives. More and more courts are sentencing defendants to partial confinement in jails, rehabilitation centers, community treatment centers, or prison farms, so that they can be released for a period of time in the community to engage in employment or attend school. Judges also order defendants to various types of halfway houses or clinics in the community where they may obtain help for various emotional problems, many resulting from alcoholism and narcotic addiction. Some of these commitments are made as conditions of probation, and some are pronounced as straight sentences with no commitment to an order of probation.

Civil commitments

In certain instances the question arises whether criminal proceedings should be suspended and civil proceedings initiated, in order to determine if the defendant is a sex psychopath, a narcotic addict, or is legally insane. In certain states, being convicted of a serious sex offense such as child molesting requires that the judge suspend criminal proceedings and initiate sex psychopath proceedings. Experts such as medical doctors and psychiatrists are then asked to submit written reports and testify in open court. Criminal proceedings might also be suspended if it is thought that the defendant is a chronic alcoholic and could best benefit from treatment in a state hospital under a civil commitment. In cases where criminal proceedings are suspended, such proceedings are reinstated when the defendant is either certified as "cured" or is determined to be uncooperative and unresponsive to treatment in a hospital setting. In many cases, as a result of the completion of a successful period of treatment, criminal proceedings may be dismissed altogether. In other cases, such as the commitment of alcoholics to state hospitals, criminal proceedings may be terminated at the time of commitment. In serious cases, such as sex psychopath cases, the judge will usually take the time the defendant has spent in the hospital into consideration; and after successful completion of treatment, the judge will place the defendant on supervised probation for a time usually specified by the penal code, with outpatient psychiatric treatment as a condition, rather than subject him to a further period of incarceration in a penal institution.

Being subjected to civil commitments rather than penal sanctions does not necessarily mean obtaining leniency. Most of the civil commitments are to special hospitals administered in much the same way as are prisons, except that the "treatment program" is oriented toward a specific problem area. In fact, a civil commitment might be the more severe in that the defendant is usually committed for an indefinite period of time and is not eligible for release without the approval of the director of the institution to which he is sent. There is no legal right to a review similar to a parole hearing and, in some prison-connected "hospitals," there is little meaningful periodic review of the defendant's case by the institutional staff. A sentence under such conditions could result in the offender remaining in custody for the rest of his life. However, most individuals sentenced under such commitments are usually released after a period of time and returned to society under some form of community supervision. Certain states provide for civil commitments that limit the length of time for which an inmate can be incarcerated, as in the program at the California Rehabilitation Center for narcotic addicts.

IMPROVING THE SENTENCING PROCESS

Sentencing councils

One of the major criticisms of the sentencing process, as it is carried out in our judicial system, is that different judges sentence differently, causing sentencing disparity. Because of such disparities found among judges, critics of our judicial system have stressed the lack of rationality in the sentencing process. Judges appear to be unequally influenced by such factors as the type of crime committed, the racial and ethnic background of the defendant, the defendant's particular life style, the socio-economic status of the defendant, and the defendant's general attitude and behavior while in the courtroom. Given the same facts, two judges may differ in a judgment to such an extent that one will grant probation with no severe sanctions as conditions, while another may order a straight period of incarceration. Not only do judges of different jurisdictions vary in their sentencing practices, but judges occupying the same court house within the same jurisdiction often place different weight on factors relevant to sentencing.

Differences in sentences are sometimes confused with disparity in sentencing. There may be *differences* among sentences of defendants committing similar crimes because the judge is trying to make the sentence fit the individual rather than the crime—a judicial philosophy adhered to by those concerned with the rehabilitation of offenders. For example, a defendant who has a long prior record and exhibits little interest in living a responsible life may receive a more severe sentence for an offense than a first offender who is convicted of a similar offense but whose participation in the offense appears to be situational and whose prior social history indicates a strong potential for reform. Differences in sentences, therefore, are not necessarily a result of arbitrary and capricious actions by the court. It is the present trend in the administration of criminal justice to foster the individualization of sentences and not aspire to uniform sentences for each offense and all offenders.

Disparity in sentencing occurs when defendants committing similar crimes and exhibiting similar characteristics receive dissimilar sentences, based on arbitrary and unreasonable grounds and the result of unjust and unacceptable judgments. It is to these practices of sentencing that most critics address themselves. In order that the judgment of an offender should not depend largely on the personality of the judge before whom the case is heard, methods are being proposed to reduce disparity among judges in the form of sentencing councils. In a sentencing council, several judges of a multi-judge court meet periodically to discuss dispositions of pending cases. The sentencing council fosters discussion of the application of sentencing alternatives and provides a vehicle for the emergence of uniform sentencing standards. Where sentencing councils are in operation, the judge to whom a case is assigned is still responsible for determining sentencing. It is hoped that the council will lead to more reasonable sentences by encouraging judges to state reasons for the disposition they propose.

Sentencing councils are now in effect in at least three United States District Courts.[29] Judges meet in panels, with presentence reports and other data relevant to arriving at sound judgments, and discuss the factors they believe significant in arriving at judgments. This pooling of knowledge and experience makes sentencing councils an educational experience. The major task of the sentencing council is not to end the complete disparity of sentences found among judges due to differences in ethical and judicial philosophy but to try to eliminate the excessive harshness or excessive leniency of the "unreasonable" sentence. It is hoped that sentencing councils will eventually promote the adoption of adequate standards which, if intelligently applied, will help eliminate or sharply reduce grossly inequitable sentences.

Sentencing conferences

Before sentencing, some judges hold a sentencing conference attended by the probation officer who prepared the presentence report and, if necessary, by representatives of the prosecution and defense.

At these conferences the judge discusses the presentence report and the recommendations made by the probation officer. If the judge raises objections to the recommendations, alterations may be made and new recommendations set forth. There are times when the judge needs clarification of the intent of a recommendation made by a probation officer in the presentence report. A discussion with the probation officer may produce the information the judge needs to bring about agreement between the prosecution and the defense. The investigating officer may also have failed to take into consideration certain aspects of the case that seem important to the judge. Such conferences help the parties concerned with sentencing understand each other and prevent time consuming arguments or attempts at clarification in open court. Judges and probation officers who engage in sentencing conferences feel that they are valuable if they are conducted on a democratic basis. Many prosecutors and defense counsels also welcome these conferences. If the conferences are held and the defense is not present, there are good grounds for the defense counsel to object that decisions that may significantly influence the welfare of his client are being made in the judge's chambers in his absence. Defense counsel should have the opportunity of being present at sentencing conferences in order to insure that the rights of his client are protected and to add information and insights that may be of value to all parties concerned.

Judicial institutes

Judicial sentencing institutes are held periodically to help train judges in correctional theories and practices and to provide them with information about current methods of rehabilitation and treatment in the correctional field. The federal government has provided institutes for judges of all the federal courts for many years, and some states also encourage their judges to attend such institutes.

The institutes consist of meetings in which problems pertinent to the sentencing process are discussed by trial judges, scholars, and other authorities in the fields of law enforcement and corrections. These problems may include disparity in sentencing, use of presentence reports, standards for commitment to correctional institutions, and policies relating to term setting and to determination by parole boards of parole eligibility.

Judicial institutes also provide judges with the opportunity to visit correctional institutions in order to become more familiar with their programs. In some institutes, trial judges, parole officers, and law enforcement personnel have actually been locked up in a maximum security prison for one day under realistic conditions, in an attempt to let them experience what prisoners are exposed to as a result of being incarcerated. Trial judges who never visit the institutions to which they sentence offenders harbor unrealistic beliefs about their effectiveness and value. Periodic visits to such institutions, especially in the form of an overnight stay, could alter a judge's opinion of their proper use as a sentencing alternative.

Appellate review of sentences

Another device which would contribute to reducing sentencing disparities and unifying the entire sentencing process is the appellate review of sentences. Traditionally in the United States there has been no right to review of sentences for defendants who feel that they have been sentenced unjustly, but many foreign nations require a written opinion detailing a sentence and the reasons for imposing it.

The laws of most states make no provision for a formal review by a higher court of sentences pronounced by a lower court. For the most part, in order for a sentence to be altered on appeal, it must violate the guarantees against cruel and unusual punishment as set forth in the Eighth Amendment to the Constitution. Many professionals in the field of the administration of justice advocate the establishment of an appellate procedure which would lead to a review of the sentence alone. Such a procedure would permit the modification of a sentence in accordance with statutory sentencing requirements, without first requiring the appellate court to send the entire case back for a new trial so that resentencing can take place after a second conviction. It is not uncommon for a convicted offender's appeal to be heard by an appellate court because of his dissatisfaction with the sentence, rather than because of any lack of due process during his trial. Professional associations such as the American Bar Association recommend appellate review of sentences as one method by which unjust sentences can be corrected and the disparity of sentencing reduced. It seems quite probable that judges would be more careful in pronouncing judgment if they knew that their sentences were subject to appeal.[30]

Toward a more meaningful sentencing process

Another stride in making sentences more meaningful would be the development of statutory standards embodying the purposes of sanctions and the criteria for the imposition of sentences.[31] The adoption of standards for sentencing might result in the training of lawyers for sentencing as well as for the determination of guilt and might further enable the attorneys for both the prosecution and the defense to prepare for sentencing as rationally as they do for trial.[32] The adoption of standards for sanctioning purposes and standards for sentencing would provide means by which courts could concentrate on the development of a correctional program "which is designed in terms of the impact of a sanction upon the life of the defendant within the community."[33] The court would receive evidence about behavioral changes, which would be used by all those parties participating in the sentencing process in developing rehabilitational programs for individual offenders.[34]

The *Model Penal Code* of the American Law Institute and the *Model Sentencing Act* drafted by the Council of Judges of the National Council on Crime and Delinquency contain sentencing criteria. Both the model penal code and the model sentencing act attempt to establish criteria identifying the persistent, habitual, or hardened criminal. The model penal code further establishes criteria for probation, listing eleven grounds for the granting of probation. The President's Commission on Law Enforcement and the Administration of Justice recommends that states reexamine the sentencing provisions of their penal codes in the direction of simplifying the grading of offenses and removing mandatory minimum prison terms, long maximum prison terms, and ineligibility for probation and parole.[35] The Commission feels that judges should be allowed to exercise their discretion in accordance with clearly stated standards.

In order to guarantee the proper and legal execution of a sentence within the total constitutional and statutory framework, Gerhard Mueller recommends the creation of a judicial monitoring system for all sentences involving institutionalization.[36] This would give courts the power to interfere with the discretion of correctional officials, a realm traditionally forbidden to court intervention. In their concern with prisoners' rights suits, courts are more and more ignoring the so-called "hands-off" doctrine. This doctrine can also be suspended to enable the courts to insure that a prison sentence calling for rehabilitation is being executed.

Sentencing clinics

There are those who feel that the power of sentencing should be taken from judges and given to boards of "experts" referred to as diagnostic or sentencing clinics or sentencing tribunals. Such clinics would be staffed by groups of persons skilled in the field of human behavior such as psychiatrists, psychologists, social workers, anthropologists, and sociologists. Individuals convicted of a crime would be subjected to diagnostic testing in a diagnostic center which would include medical examinations, psychiatric evaluations, and psychological testing. The staff of the clinic would also be provided with the offender's legal and social history. Those offenders suffering from mental and emotional disorders would be detected and placed in special institutions for treatment. Individuals considered to be dangerous would be isolated from the others and transferred to secure correctional institutions for an indefinite period. Offenders considered not to be dangerous but in need of a structured environment would be placed in community treatment centers, forestry camps or farms, and halfway houses. Other offenders would be placed on either supervised or summary probation in the community. The supporters of sentencing clinics feel that such clinics would make sentencing a science rather than an art.

Experience has shown that "experts" in the field of behavioral science do not at present have knowledge sufficient to make accurate predictions concerning human nature. Such a lack of knowledge is indicated by the fact that psychiatrists and psychologists disagree among themselves on what constitutes a proper diagnosis and treatment plan. Judges requesting psychiatric evaluations from more than one psychiatrist have often received two diametrically opposed diagnoses and two different recommendations concerning how the offender should be sentenced. Further, "experts" in the field of human behavior, like judges, assess the importance of factors relating to social adjustment largely through intuitive value judgments. Concepts of "maturity," "mental health," "delinquency," "maladjusted personality," and the like, are subject to value judgments and will vary according to the background, attitude, and training of the "expert" applying them. Recommendations made by sentencing clinics, therefore, would not be free of subjectivity. On the contrary, they would reflect the outlook and prejudices of every member of the clinical team. It does not appear that by placing sentencing under the province of a diagnostic clinic, disparity would disappear. On the contrary, since there is such a large room for conflicting value judgments concerning treatment and rehabilitation, it is quite conceivable that there would be even more disparity between decisions produced by different sentencing clinics than there are said to be between various judges at the present time. Further, it is also conceivable that the various members of one particular diagnostic team would disagree among themselves to such a degree concerning a diagnosis that the final recommendation of the clinic would at best be a compromise. This hardly seems scientific.

It has been said by some scholars in the field of administration of justice that judges know nothing about sentencing. Who does know anything about sentencing? Would a diagnostic clinic do a better job in predicting human behavior and disposing of individuals found guilty of a crime? Recommendations submitted to courts by some psychiatrists and psychologists acting as adjuncts in the sentencing process have been unrealistically harsh, and unrealistically lenient—indicating that behavioral scientists know little about sentencing. Should we consider their ignorance superior to the ignorance of a judge?

Sentencing as a science

At present, even with the use of prediction devices, sentencing is referred to as an "applied art" rather than a science. Sentencing and term fixing are said to be largely based on guesswork and hunches. Can we expect anything better in the future? Could sentencing become a science some day? Before the process of sentencing could even pretend to be a science, two things would be needed: accurate feedback concerning the positive and negative results of sentences and increased capability of the behavioral sciences to furnish information concerning the human personality, so that courts and term-fixing agencies can make meaningful choices among sentencing alternatives.

Courts now receive little reliable feedback concerning the impact of their sentences on the offender and on the community, and even where parole boards use prediction devices to distinguish recidivists from non-recidivists, this results in an improvement of only one percent over the personal judgment of an experienced parole board member.[37] It is doubtful whether certainty will ever be achieved in the prediction of human behavior, unless human beings become programmed through the extensive use of behavioral control techniques whose desirability is questionable. For some time to come, the use of prediction devices will probably be limited to reducing the likelihood that alternatives will be chosen which have doubtful prospects for success, in the hope that the offender will respond to an unexpected opportunity, such as a grant of probation where prison is clearly indicated.

Criticism of the sentencing process abounds, but efforts at meaningful reform, such as those mentioned in this chapter, are being made. However, much of the old system of sentencing will still grind on, due primarily to our ignorance of human behavior and to our inability to evaluate the data we already have on the comparative effectiveness of deterrence, retribution, incarceration, and community treatment.

NOTES

1. Louis P. Carney, *Introduction to Correctional Science* (New York: McGraw-Hill, 1974), p. 61.

2. Howard Jones, "Punishment and Social Values," in Tadeusz Grygier et al., eds., *Criminology in Transition: Essays in Honour of Herman Mannheim*, International Library of Criminology, Delinquency and Deviant Social Behavior, no. 14 (London: Tavistock Publications, 1965), pp. 6–7.

3. David Fogel et al., "Restitution in Criminal Justice: A Minnesota Experiment," *Criminal Law Bulletin* 8, no. 8 (October 1972): 682–683.

4. Ibid., pp. 681–691.

5. See Michael Geerken and Walter R. Gove, "Systems of Deterrence: Some Theoretical Considerations" (Paper prepared for the Study of Social Problems Conference, Montreal, August 1974).

6. Ibid.

7. Carney, note 1, supra, p. 65.

8. Donald J. Newman, "Role and Process in the Criminal Court," in Daniel Glaser, ed., *Handbook of Criminology* (Chicago: Rand McNally, College Division, 1974), p. 617. See also Santobello v. New York 404 U.S. 257, Dec. 20, 1971.

9. President's Crime Commission, *Task Force Report: Courts* (Washington, D.C.: Government Printing Office, 1967), pp. 18–21.

10. American Bar Association, *Sentencing Alternatives and Procedures*, "Presentence report: disclosure; general principles (Section 4.3)," Approved Draft, 1968.

11. President's Crime Commission, note 9, supra.

12. President's Crime Commission, *The Challenge of Crime in a Free Society* (Washington, D.C.: Government Printing Office, 1967), p. 145.

13. Federal Rules of Criminal Procedure for United States District Courts, Rule 32 (c) (1–2), 1970.

14. William G. Zastrow, "Disclosure of the Presentence Investigation," *Federal Probation* (December 1971): 20–22.

15. Norm Larkins, "Presentence Investigation Report Disclosure in Alberta," *Federal Probation* (December 1972).

16. Newman, note 8, supra, p. 612.

17. Gerhard O. W. Mueller, "Imprisonment and its Alternatives," in *A Program for Prison Reform, The Final Report*, Annual Chief Justice Earl Warren Conference on Advocacy in the United States, June 9–10, 1972, p. 38. Sponsored by the Roscoe Pound-American Trial Lawyers Foundation, Cambridge, Mass.

18. Caleb Foote, "The Sentencing Function," in *A Program for Prison Reform*, note 17, supra, pp. 19–23.

19. Ibid., p. 20.

20. Ibid., pp. 19–23.

21. Carney, note 1, supra, pp. 118–119.

22. Mueller, note 17, supra, pp. 37–38.

23. *In re* Antazo, 473 P.2d 999; 89 Cal. Rptr. 255, Sept. 3, 1970.

24. Ibid.

25. Carney, note 1, supra, p. 40.

26. Morris R. Cohen, "Moral Aspects of Punishment," in Leon Radzinowicz and Marvin E. Wolfgang, eds., *Crime and Justice: vol. 2, The Criminal in the Arms of the Law* (New York: Basic Books, 1971), p. 41.

27. Hazel B. Kerper, *Introduction to the Criminal Justice System* (St. Paul, Minn.: West Publishing, 1972), p. 352. See also Mempa v. Rhay, 389 U.S. 128 88 S. Ct. 254, 19 L. Ed 2d 336 (1967).

28. Ibid., p. 352.

29. President's Crime Commission, note 12, supra, p. 145.

30. Kerper, note 27, supra, pp. 341–342.

31. Mueller, note 17, supra, p. 43.

32. Ibid., p. 43.

33. Ibid., p. 43.

34. Ibid., p. 43.

35. President's Crime Commission, note 12, supra, p. 143.

36. Mueller, note 17, supra, p. 44.

37. David F. Greenberg, *Parole Recidivism and the Incapacitative Effects of Imprisonment* (Paper prepared for the Society for the Study of Social Problems Conference, Montreal, August 1974), p. 16.

Institutions 4

THE ORIGINS OF INSTITUTIONALIZATION

A new method of punishment and treatment emerges

The institutionalization of offenders, as we know it today, is of recent origin. Although the history of punishment can be traced back to primitive times, our criminal justice system is not even 200 years old. Many individuals feel that institutionalization is a necessary aspect of the administration of justice and has always been with us, but the history of punishment reveals that society worked quite recently without institutions and without an organized criminal justice system.

The innovation of the penitentiary was a product of the early nineteenth century in America. It emerged to replace other forms of punishment that were universally applied but were felt by the colonial reformers to be unusually cruel and degrading. At this time institutionalization as a vehicle of enlightenment and reform was not only predominant in the area of punishment, but it also prevailed in other areas such as mental health, the treatment of the poor, and education. In addition to the construction of prisons during the early nineteenth century, asylums, hospitals, schools, and almshouses were constructed as well. It appears that when one group of individuals is confined, other groups of people are also confined.[1]

The introduction of institutions such as penitentiaries was surrounded by hopes of reform. It was a massive effort by well-meaning men. They hoped, by the application of such a strategy, to cure all of

111

society's ills, not only in the area of criminality, but also in areas such as mental health, poverty, and education. One might use John Dewey's terminology here and say that institutionalization was a gigantic experiment in social engineering. Reform was the rhetoric of the period, and prisons were to be utopias of reform.

Recent trends in the field of the administration of criminal justice indicate that institutionalization as a correctional strategy might be becoming a thing of the past. Today there are significant moves away from institutionalization in the areas of corrections, mental health, and education. Have institutions worked as they were supposed to when originally conceived by our colonial fathers? If not, have we anything better to offer today in the field of corrections that hasn't already been tried in the past and found not to work?

Assumptions underlying correctional philosophies

To this very day the administration of criminal justice in the United States functions largely under the presuppositions concerning the nature of man and punishment set forth by the classical school of criminology. Classicism arose as a general revolt against the prevailing arbitrary and barbarous legal system found in eighteenth-century Europe.[2] Cesare Baccaria (1738–1794) was a reformer who took note of the prevailing conditions and helped to formulate the principles that now make up what is known as the classical school of criminology.[3]

One of the major assumptions made by classicism is that all men are responsible for their actions. Each man has not only a free will, but an inborn moral sense as well, that enables him to distinguish good from bad and right from wrong. If an individual does wrong, he does so knowingly and freely. He is responsible for his behavior and cannot shift the burden of his responsibility to the state, his family, his environment, or his physical and emotional makeup.

Another assumption of the classical school is that the purpose of punishment is to deter, and it can best deter if the punishment is proportional to the interests violated by the crime. A utilitarian system of punishment is proposed where each punishment set forth will fit the crime committed. The amount of punishment imposed on the criminal will be in proportion to the advantage he gained from committing the offense and the evil suffered by the victim and by the state. Under such a utilitarian system of punishment little or no emphasis was placed on reform or rehabilitation. A man had to pay a price to the state and his fellow man if he was convicted of a crime. Once he had paid his price he no longer had to harbor feelings of guilt for what he did, since he had undergone all that was expected of him by society.

Over a period of time early classicism was modified into what has come to be known as the neoclassical revision. Under neoclassicism the law takes into consideration mitigating circumstances such as the offender's social environment, mental state, and length of prior record. The criminal is still held to be responsible for his actions, however, and a major emphasis is still placed on the crime committed.

Later the positive school of criminology emerged, largely through the work of Cesare Lombroso (1836–1908), Enrico Ferri (1856–1928), and Raffaele Garofalo (1852–1934). The positive school of criminology placed emphasis on scientific method, empirical observation, and quantification and rejected the conception of the criminal as a free moral agent. The positive school saw crime as a product of biological, geographical, anthropological, psychological, and economic forces. Man's behavior, according to this interpretation, is a result of his environment and inheritance. The doctrine of "freedom of the will" held by the classical school gave way to a form of scientific determinism. With the adoption of these new principles, the focal point shifted from the crime itself to the criminal. The rhetoric of rehabilitation became fashionable in penology.

Both classical and positivistic theories of crime causation and treatment are theories of social control. They are on a par with other metaphysical theories about man and society. Although positivists stress the application of scientific method and support empirical research, many of their basic tenets rest on pure conjecture. The basic principles of the classical school were never considered as scientific hypotheses to be tested objectively in a value-free atmosphere. It may be that some aspects of the classical school are serving a useful purpose in the administration of criminal justice and are of some operational value. On the other hand, perhaps the widespread acceptance of classicism has hindered a truly scientific approach to criminology. This assumes, of course, that we can provide an adequate theory of human behavior and develop acceptable social controls through the method of science. Perhaps this is also an unwarranted assumption, especially when it is taken into consideration that ethics plays a predominant role in the development of any theory of punishment and treatment.

The early prisons were constructed and administered with the philosophy of the classical school of criminology in mind. It was only with the advent of the "new penology" that correctional administrators and paroling authorities took into consideration the principles of scientific positivism and placed emphasis on the individual offender rather than the crime.

Punishment prior to institutionalization

In the early American colonies, social order was maintained largely through a system of fines, banishment, and corporal punishment. Sometimes punishment was made severe for the sake of deterrence and retribution. Up to the end of the eighteenth century corporal punishment and exile were the basic patterns of punishment. Not until the time of the American Revolution did Western Civilization consider the substitution of imprisonment for corporal punishment.

The most widely employed type of corporal punishment was flogging. In fact, the whipping post was used in some states until recent years. For example, whippings took place at the state prison near Wilmington, Delaware in 1940, 1941, 1949, and 1952.[4] However, with the signing of the Revised Criminal Code bill by Governor Russell Peterson, Delaware has formally renounced use of the cat-o-nine-tails. Governor Peterson ordered the flogging post to be put away in the basement of the Delaware Correctional Center in 1969. The post had served as punishment for a variety of crimes including embezzling, wife beating, robbery, and larceny. In many cases floggings were carried out in view of the public as a general deterrent.

Did flogging deter? We have no way of knowing, since evaluative studies concerning methods of punishment were not a reality in colonial times. There have been strong opinions on the matter, however, and to this day some individuals, not entirely unsophisticated, feel that flogging might be a better deterrent to crime in certain instances than long periods of incarceration. Many experts in the field of corrections would claim to "abhor" flogging as a method of punishment and rehabilitation. One wonders, however, whether a few years of incarceration in one of our present correctional institutions is less cruel or more rehabilitative in nature. If given a choice between flogging and incarceration, one might speculate as to how many offenders would select flogging. Should convicted offenders be offered a choice in the type of punishment they receive?

Another method of corporal punishment adopted from Hammurabi's code of *lex talionis* consisted of mutilation.[5] In this instance punishment was to duplicate the injury originally performed. If the offender cut off the hand of another, he lost his hand. Mayhem was a common crime in some primitive societies and it is understandable why such a penalty was thought to be useful as a deterrent. Today mutilation is thought to be brutal, archaic, and of no rehabilitative value. We don't know if it would deter individuals from committing crimes. One can speculate about whether there would be as much burglary, stealing, forgery, or counterfeiting if the culprit were assured that after conviction he would surely and swiftly suffer the loss of a hand or two. Even if such a method of punishment were found to deter, it would probably be rejected on moral grounds. But in prescribing a sanction for a criminal offense, should we consider its morality as an instrument of punishment as well as its deterrent effectiveness? If so, is there any scientific way by which we can determine the morality of a method of punishment?

Still another widely used method of corporal punishment was branding. In late oriental and classical society branding was very common. Barnes and Teeters describe how branding was used in colonial societies.[6]

> Branding was frequent in American colonial jurisprudence and criminal procedure. In the East Jersey codes of 1668 and 1675 it was ordered, for example, that the first burglary offense was to be punished by branding a 'T' on the hand, while the second offense was to be punished by branding an 'R' on the forehead.

Would branding deter? At the present time there are those in the field of the administration of criminal justice who feel that chronic forgers and worthless check writers should undergo branding for identification and deterrent purposes. One major objection to branding as a method of punishment is its potential to hinder rehabilitation by ingraining the stigma of "criminal" on the person so treated.

Other modes of corporal punishment in the early American colonies were the stocks, the pillory, confinement in irons, and the ducking stool. The stocks, the pillory, and the ducking stool were largely employed for what was felt to be their psychological effectiveness as a deterrent. Offenders suffered such punishment in full view of the townspeople.

Exile or banishment to out-of-the-way places was a common form of punishment in most European countries. England had penal colonies in Australia and used the North American colonies as a dumping ground for debtors and criminals. The French banished criminals to French Guiana, Algiers, and New Caledonia. Czarist Russia transported criminals to Siberia, and the USSR continues this tradition. During the Fascist regime in Italy thousands of political prisoners were sent to islands off the coast of Sicily. Holland transported prisoners to the Dutch East Indies, Denmark sent prisoners to Greenland, and Portugal shipped prisoners to Africa and Brazil.[7]

The major argument used to support transportation was an economic one, i.e., that it would provide cheap labor to new countries; but transportation was found to be a nonproductive way of handling criminals. Transportation was also favored by some enlightened criminologists of the past, such as Lombroso and Garofalo, who viewed it as an effective deterrent.

Transportation of criminals on a major scale has never been employed by the United States or the Early American colonies. Expulsion was practiced by local communities during the colonial period, however. Townspeople took care of their own, but there was little concern for strangers. Since towns were physically isolated and geographic mobility was difficult, banishment was quite common. Interestingly enough, according to David J. Rothman,[8] banishment led to a major crime problem for the colonists. Some of those who were banished from local towns became road bandits and raided the townspeople when they left their communities.

On a limited scale, we still employ the practice in the United States of exiling members of organized crime. Italy has been the main country of exile for such offenders.

Capital punishment has been used since primitive times as a method of punishment. Primitive tribes used it primarily for the purpose of placating the gods. Later it came to be used as an instrument of revenge and as a deterrent to crime. It probably reached its zenith in England at the beginning of the nineteenth century. During this period the criminal code listed between 220 and 230 offenses to be punished by death.[9] The American colonies also practiced capital punishment, some in a milder form than others.[10]

Recent methods of capital punishment have been hanging, beheading, shooting, electrocution, and the use of lethal gas. In the past, however, the following methods were employed: drowning, stoning to death, burning at the stake, and mutilation. Hanging has been the most widely employed method of execution.

Many in the field of the administration of criminal justice feel that capital punishment is barbaric, unscientific, and a throwback to the medieval days of cruel and unusual torture. Others feel that capital punishment should continue to be used for its deterrent value. A recent U.S. Supreme Court ruling branded capital punishment as cruel and unusual punishment because of the inconsistent way in which it has been administered by the various states,[11] but there are several moves by state legislatures at the present time to reinstate it.

Does capital punishment deter? Numerous studies have been completed that are relevant to this question, but none shows conclusively that capital punishment does or does not deter. Those who argue for or against capital punishment have little scientific evidence to support their positions. Since the question appears to be incapable of solution on purely scientific grounds, it must be argued on the grounds of ethics, a subject which is hardly objective or value-free.

Theories of prison construction

HISTORICAL INFLUENCES

Perhaps the English reformer John Howard deserves the most credit for anticipating the penitentiary system.[12] He inspected many jails and prisons in Europe during the late eighteenth century, and made known to the public the sordid conditions he found. But he was impressed with the workhouse as an institution for housing young people. The workhouse movement began in the latter portion of the sixteenth century in England and on the Continent.[13] One of the first establishments was the Bridewell of London, which was set aside to cope with unruly elements who were menacing society. Two establishments of eighteenth-century Europe, however, appear to have had more influence in advancing the penitentiary idea, namely, the Hospice of San Michele for delinquent boys, erected by Pope Clement XI in Rome in 1704, and the Maison de Force, developed in Flanders in 1773, governed by Jean Jacques Philippe Vilain.

The Hospice of San Michele was built as a retreat for "wayward" boys in an effort to provide wholesome surroundings. Discipline and reformation were based on solitude and labor. The boys worked in a central hall during the day and observed the strict rule of silence. At night they were locked in their cells. They were forced to listen to the readings of religious tracts and were flogged for past mistakes and for infractions of institutional rules. In nearby Florence there existed during the same era a home for vagrants operated by Father Filippo Franci. As part of the discipline of this establishment boys were forced to wear hoods drawn over their faces, in order to prevent communication and avoid recognition. The rules governing these two institutions anticipated many ideas that became part of the penitentiary system in the United States 100 years later.

The Maison de Force was a workhouse primarily for the housing of beggars and vagrants. The philosophy of the institution was based on the work ethic, and productive work was a vital part of the program. In anticipating later penitentiary developments, a rudimentary classification of prisoners was provided. Felons were separated from misdemeanants and vagrants. Separate quarters for women and children, adequate medical care, and individual cells were also provided.

The basic ideas governing the workhouse model were incorporated in John Howard's classic *The State of Prisons*, which was published in 1777. At the time this book was published men interested in reform in Philadelphia were being influenced by reform philosophies from abroad propounded by such men as Bentham, Baccaria, Voltaire, Paine, Montesquieu, and David Hume. Incorporating the ideas set forth in John Howard's book and the writings of the philosophers of the Enlightenment, the Philadelphia reformers undertook the task of establishing a new penal code in protest against the severe Pennsylvania Penal Code of 1718. At the same time, they laid the groundwork for a new and untried method of punishment.

One of the major proponents of penal reform in Philadelphia was Dr. Benjamin Rush, a physician and surgeon, who was opposed to both corporal and capital punishment.[14] Dr. Rush also advocated the classification of prisoners for housing purposes, individual treatment of inmates according to their basic problems, and a system of prison labor. Most of his basic ideas were ignored in his day and were not put into operation until 150 years later.

On May 8, 1787, a reform group called *The Philadelphia Society for Alleviating the Miseries of Public Prisons,* later to become known as *The Pennsylvania Prison Society,* met in Philadelphia to discuss penal reform, with Dr. Rush present.[15] As a result of the work of this body of men an act was passed on April 5, 1790, which led to the construction of a block of cells in the Walnut Street Jail to be used primarily for solitary confinement of the more hardened criminals. This block of cells became the penitentiary for the Commonwealth of Pennsylvania and is referred to today as the birthplace of the American prison system.

THE EARLY PRISON SYSTEM IN THE UNITED STATES—1790–1830[16]

In addition to the Walnut Street Prison, a cellular prison, the model for which had been designed by Thomas Jefferson, was constructed in Richmond, Virginia between 1796 and 1800. New York opened the doors of the famous Newgate Prison in Greenwich Village on November 28, 1797. New Jersey completed its first prison in 1799, and Massachusetts established a maximum security prison at Charlestown in 1805.

These prisons used different methods of confinement. The New Jersey prison did not segregate prisoners according to sex, age, or mental state. Recidivists, first offenders, men and women, boys and girls, sane and insane, were imprisoned within the same walls. The Newgate Prison in New York was also built more to degrade prisoners than for reform and employed the congregate method of confinement. It was small and overcrowded. The one aspect that prisons had in common during this era was that they made no genuine provisions for reform. The prison could best be described as merely a custodial area in which some work was provided for the prisoners.

THE PENNSYLVANIA SYSTEM

Two models for prison discipline and construction dominated the prison scene from 1830–1870. These were the Pennsylvania and Auburn penal systems.[17] Eastern Penitentiary, built in Philadelphia and opened in 1829, is probably one of the most famous prisons in the United States from a historical perspective. It only recently closed its doors for the intake of state prisoners. It is famous because it institutionalized a unique penal philosophy of separate and solitary confinement referred to by penologists as the Pennsylvania System of prison discipline. The objective of this treatment was reform through expiation and repentance. It was felt by the Philadelphia reformers that reform could come only through individual contemplation in a state of physical and social isolation. The Philadelphia reformers had high hopes that such a philosophy would produce law-abiding and godlike citizens, and they engaged in this experiment with the optimism and eagerness of present day reform groups advocating the destruction of the penitentiaries and a return to community corrections.

In order to make such a philosophy of reformation operable, a unique type of prison construction was demanded. It was first necessary to keep all community influences away from the inmates so that they could spend their time in reflection on their evil deeds and sinful way of life. In order to achieve the privacy necessary for intimate contemplation of the self and God, a gigantic, thick wall was placed around Eastern State Penitentiary, not for the purpose of preventing escapes, but to keep community influences out of the prison. Later penal architects forgot the original purpose intended for prison walls and continued to construct them in order to prevent escapes and to more easily maintain internal order and control.

In addition to the giant wall, individual cells, each with its own small exercise yard, were constructed to house one and only one prisoner. Each yard was surrounded by a high wall, for it was important that no prisoner gain sight of his fellow inmate or communicate with him in any way. Discipline and treatment consisted of the prisoner's remaining in his cell at all times, except for the daily hour he was permitted to exercise alone in his yard. He was also given work to do, but he accomplished his work assignments inside his cell. The prisoner was allowed to see no one while in prison. He was blindfolded by a hood when he entered the prison and led to his solitary cell. The daily routine included work, exercise, and worship.[18]

Prison sentences tended to be longer than in most other countries, not for the protection of the community, but to allow time for the inmate to repent and become converted to God. The cruelty of long prison sentences still remains with us in the United States, but their original purpose has long been forgotten.

THE AUBURN SYSTEM

Another system of penal discipline, which was characterized as congregate and silent, emerged in the Auburn Prison. Located in Auburn, New York, it was constructed prior to Eastern Penitentiary. Under this system prisoners were permitted to work together in shops during the day under the strict rule of silence and were locked up in individual cells at night. In style of construction, the Auburn system adopted inside cell blocks, some of them five tiers high.[19] On either side, between the cell block and the walls, were narrow corridors running the entire length of the building. Any light or air that might penetrate the cells could only enter by the small and heavily barred windows built into the outer walls of the prison. The Auburn inside cell blocks served for years as a pattern for most state penitentiaries. The cells were very small—seven feet long, three feet six inches wide, and seven feet high.[20]

Discipline at Auburn was based on solitary confinement, the silent rule, and the lock step. An important phenomenon in the history of prison discipline,[21] the lock step was a form of close order shuffle in which prisoners moved in unison in single file, with downcast faces inclined to the right, each looking over the shoulder of the man in front. The purpose of the lock step was [not to prevent escapes, but] to keep the men from communicating when being transferred from their cells to work assignments or to the mess hall. It was also employed to degrade the inmate. Regular marching or military close order drill were not used because they helped to instill pride and dignity, and this would have been inconsistent with Warden Elam Lynd's philosophy that reform could not take place unless you first broke the spirit of the prisoner. In order to further degrade the prisoners, their heads were shaved and they wore stripes.

The Auburn system was adopted by most prison administrators in the United States; later, the Pennsylvania system served as a model for the construction of European institutions.

The failure of the models

PROBLEMS WITH THEORY

Both the Pennsylvania and Auburn systems of penal discipline were based on the assumption that the main purpose of the prison is to reform the inmate through expiation and penitence. The word "penitentiary" was originally an adjective meaning "in relation to penitence, or expressing penitence." It was soon discovered, however, that degrading prisoners and isolating them from their fellow man, for whatever reasons, led to the development of serious psychological problems. Instead of returning to society as reformed men, ready to take their places as independent and constructive members of the community as was envisioned, many prisoners went insane under the Pennsylvania system because of their complete solitude and isolation. Nor did the Auburn system serve as an instrument of reform and rehabilitation. It was learned that man could not be reformed by breaking his spirit, by isolating him from his fellow man and from the community at large, and by such forms of degradation as the lock step, shaved heads, and striped uniforms. Few prisoners came out of either of the systems' prisons better men than when they came in, and few were enlightened or came to follow in the footsteps of God. The theory behind America's first penitentiary system had failed to produce the results hoped for by the Philadelphia reformers, and most prisons, instead of being utopias of reform, degenerated into vehicles of punishment.

PROBLEMS WITH IMPLEMENTATION

It was not long before it was discovered that the Pennsylvania System could not implement its penal philosophy of separate and solitary confinement. The Eastern State Penitentiary soon became overcrowded and it was necessary to place two or more men to a cell. Even before overcrowding became a reality, prisoners had devised ingenious systems of communication by tapping out codes on water pipes. It was impossible to keep prisoners from communicating with one another under either the Auburn or Pennsylvania system.

The Pennsylvania system was also very expensive to implement. Money was not available to provide for the construction of new prisons that would continue to implement the philosophy of solitary confinement for every prisoner.

One of the major objectives of the Auburn system was to provide a work program through which a prison could pay for itself, and, by so doing, ingratiate itself with the taxpayer. The Protestant work ethic was consistent with the reform philosophy of the day, that the ideal prison kept its inmates profitably employed. Although work in prison was originally designed to be a mechanism of reform, some prison administrators emphasized it to the point where prisoners were worked like slaves and denied human comforts in an effort to make the prison self-supporting.[22] Under such conditions work was anything but a tool of reform, and the original idea behind the prison work program was lost in the desire to please the general public and gain political support.

The philosophy of reform through expiation, penitence, and hard work failed in theory and was impossible to implement in practice. The dream of the early Philadelphia reformers came to an enforced end.

THE POST-CIVIL WAR REFORM—1870–1900

From 1830 to 1870, many arguments were propounded concerning whether the Auburn or the Pennsylvania system was the best for universal adaptation. Penologists soon recognized these arguments to be futile and began to propose new models of prison discipline. One of these was the reformatory. The basic tenets underlying the reformatory movement were formulated at the first meeting of the National Prison Association (later to be known as the American Correctional Association) held in Cincinnati, Ohio on October 12, 1870, and commonly referred to as the Cincinnati Prison Congress.[23]

The Cincinnati Prison Congress of 1870

The Cincinnati Prison Congress, under the direction of Dr. Enoch Cobb Wines, adopted a set of principles which, among other things, opposed the doctrine of punishment, advocated a classification system for prisoners, argued for the indeterminate sentence and parole, promoted the cultivation of inmate self respect, and advocated vocational and academic training.[24] Even more revolutionary proposals resulting from the Congress were an appeal by the members for the establishment of a system for the collection of penal statistics and the advocacy of the centralization of management of state prisons.

Unfortunately, those who advocated the principles set forth at the Cincinnati Prison Congress were able to secure the introduction of these innovations only for the treatment of young, first offenders, housed in what were to become known as reformatories.

The reformatory movement

The first reformatory was constructed in Elmira, New York in 1876, with Zebulon R. Brockway appointed its first superintendent. The essential features of the reformatory movement were based on the principles proposed at the Cincinnati Prison Congress, such as the establishment of the indeterminate sentence; a classification and grading of prisoners' parole and release based on the marking system; and the adoption of such institutional programs as physical training, military discipline, routine education, and vocational training.[25]

The greatest advance of the reformatory system over the Pennsylvania and Auburn systems was its stress on rehabilitation rather than expiation and penitence. Another important gain was that the reformatory advocated education, especially vocational training. The major disadvantage of the reformatory movement from the beginning was that it remained limited to young offenders, usually between the ages of eighteen and twenty-five. Although it had been hoped by the reformers who attended the Cincinnati Prison Congress that their principles would be put into operation with adults as well as with the young offender, this was not to be the case until the rise of the "new penology" some seventy or more years later. The Auburn system of prison discipline, characterized by a form of "slave" labor, the rule of silence, and a smattering of corporal punishment, continued to dominate the treatment of the adult offender.

Since it was never applied to adult offenders, the reformatory concept was not given a fair chance to succeed. Even in the reformatories set aside for the youthful offender, hard-line penology, characterized by the placing of emphasis on security and control, dominated the philosophy of discipline. Reformatory administrators were expected to develop programs of rehabilitation in buildings that had been originally constructed for adults and were designed as maximum security fortresses. In this completely penal and punitive setting, an enlightened program of penology could not deliver the results which had originally been expected.

With the passing of time, most reformatories developed a form of discipline that was repressive in nature. In order to foster automatic obedience from inmates, military drill became an important aspect of the training program. Administrators paid lipservice to vocational and educational training, but such training as was provided never realized the ideals of the Cincinnati reformers. Most reformatories degenerated into conventional prisons for the young.

The Pennsylvania and Auburn prison systems failed in both theory and practice. The reformatory movement failed largely because the theoretical model it provided for the treatment of offenders was never properly or fully implemented. We can only speculate on the results that might have been achieved had the reformatory been given a reasonable chance to succeed.

The industrial prison—1900–1935

With the failure of the reformatory movement, penal institutions more or less stood still from 1900 to 1935. The only major change during this period was that the industrial prison replaced the older prison. Imprisonment during this period was substantially what it had been one hundred years earlier—a system of custody, punishment, and hard labor. Toward the end of this period, with the decline of prison industries, many prison programs reverted to mere custody and punishment. What little industry was left in the prisons turned into a vicious form of exploitation. Overcrowding was also prevalent and made any meaningful industrial program impossible. Education and vocational training were, for the most part, ignored. Finally, restrictive legislation on the part of the various states and the federal government strangled the industrial prison, which was finally revived with the advent of the contempory prison.

THE CONTEMPORARY PRISON

Changes in the purpose of the prison

Probably 1935 can be set aside as the year of the advent of "the new penology," when prison administrators and legislators began to implement some of the reform models proposed in Cincinnati in 1870. Even as far back as 1916, however, men such as Thomas Mott Osborn were anticipating contemporary correctional strategies. Osborn tried to train prison inmates in the duties and responsibilities of citizenship, through the establishment of the Mutual Welfare League at Auburn, Sing Sing, and the Naval Prison at Portsmouth, New Hampshire. His work led to the development of inmate self-government programs and inmate advisory groups in the prisons of today. Osborn also established the National Society of Penal Information, now the Osborn Association, functioning under the leadership of Austin H. MacCormick. The purpose of this organization is to supply information about prison programs and treatment throughout the United States and to offer advice on how to improve penal systems that do not meet satisfactory standards of operation and of treatment of prisoners. By exposing poor standards, brutality, and attitudes of indifference found in the penal institutions of the past, Osborn and his staff helped significantly to usher in the era of the contemporary prison.

The contemporary prison brought with it the reform models propounded by the "new penology" and was introduced with the same optimism and enthusiasm as had been manifested by the Philadelphia reformers at the birth of the first penitentiary. Progressive changes in the nature of physical plants, prison personnel, and treatment programs were advocated. Instead of stressing custody, security, and hard labor, the contemporary prison was to embody the ideal of rehabilitation and to design correctional programs to meet the individual needs of the offender. The rhetoric of rehabilitation again emerged on the scene, and it was believed that the contemporary prison would be administered in a manner consistent with such rhetoric.

One major change had to be brought about in the confinement of men: a system had to be devised that would allow prison administrators to relax their stress on internal control and security. Under former penal practices, dangerous and aggressive prisoners as well as passive and harmless inmates were confined within the same physical plant. It had been necessary, therefore, to construct each prison with the most dangerous inmate in mind. In order to alter this situation a system of security gradings was put into effect, making it possible to segregate and classify inmates according to custody and treatment needs. This concept revolutionized prison construction and led to the building of institutions classified as maximum close, medium, and minimum, according to their security capabilities. Security graduations led to the diversification of correctional programming, whereby inmates with a potential for rehabilitation were subjected to different treatment opportunities and custody provisions than were prisoners who appeared to have no capacity for reform.

Perhaps one of the best examples of a contemporary prison designed to embody the philosophy of the "new penology" is the California Institute for Men at Chino. This facility was opened in 1941 by Kenyon Scudder and a busload of inmates he had taken with him from San Quentin Prison. In place of concrete walls, a ten-foot cyclone fence surrounded the prison compound; there were gun towers, but they were not used; and there were no inside cell blocks. A new physical plant had emerged for the confinement of prisoners, less restrictive, more attractive, and, of course, less secure. Along with the new physical plant an attempt was made to provide programs that were oriented to rehabilitation and the individualized treatment of offenders. Perhaps this institution never realized many of its original goals, but at least it provided a more humane atmosphere in which to live. Although there was discipline at Chino, it was less cruel and repressive than the type found in the maximum security prison. Prisoners were allowed more freedom within the confines of the prison compound and there were provisions for more recreational programs.

Has the contemporary prison actually accomplished its objectives? Even though the contemporary prison has scrapped the restrictive and punitive methods common to nineteenth century penal institutions, there are those in the field of the administration of justice who feel that prisons today are run according to the same philosophy that dominated the old prison system, namely, a stress on custody and control and a concept of the inmate as dangerous to society. Has anything actually changed, or is the contemporary prison merely a streamlined type of regimentation and punishment?

Centralization of authority

Until recently there was little or no centralization of authority either in the federal prison system or in the systems operated by the various states. Prison administrators functioned independently and enjoyed almost complete autonomy. As a result, each prison, even those within the same state, was managed differently, depending largely on the personal biases and prejudices of the warden.

In the past prisons were operated as local enterprises and were governed by a board of trustees selected by the governor.[26] Board members were seldom experienced in the field of corrections and gave little of their time and thought to matters of prison management. The board and warden they appointed were concerned mainly with local problems surrounding the one institution under their jurisdiction. If the state had more than one penal institution within its system, no effort was made to coordinate the philosophy, programs, and policies of one institution with those of another. Further, no thought was given to the coordination of the prison system with other areas of the administration of criminal justice, such as juvenile training schools, probation, and parole.[27] The system was characterized by fragmentation and lack of common purpose, leaving the field of corrections with no uniform goals or philosophy.

A number of states still administer their correctional systems through boards. Some states have boards in charge of adult institutions and boards in charge of probation and parole. Under such a system administrative control is placed under the direction of several individuals. More recently, boards have been replaced by combining all institutions or agencies under a single administrator or by a separate and independent department of correctional services concerned with probation, parole, and institutions.[28] By placing the various aspects of corrections under a separate and independent department or under a larger state department such as the department of welfare, greater efficiency can be achieved, and the various services offered by the different agencies can be coordinated into a uniform and meaningful program for the treatment of offenders.

A system of penal facilities

Larger states and the federal government realized that they could not adequately process, house, secure, and provide programs of rehabilitation for all inmates in one type of correctional institution. Various types of facilities were required in order to satisfy the needs of a correctional service system providing for diverse programs of treatment and custody.

In order to provide a diverse custodial and treatment program for the inmates under its jurisdiction, the federal government, under the U.S. Bureau of Prisons, operates an integrated system of thirty-five facilities ranging from maximum security adult penitentiaries to youth and juvenile institutions and community treatment centers.[29] Upon entering a federal corrections institution, inmates are placed in a diagnostic unit which is separate from the general prison population. While in the diagnostic unit, the custody and treatment needs of the inmate are assessed and a treatment plan is developed. Assignments are then made in the hope of fulfilling the inmate's treatment needs.

Some of the smaller states still lack the facilities necessary for a multiple-facility program. Where institutions are lacking, various portions of one institution are sometimes partitioned in order to provide for the necessary gradations of security. Diversification of facilities is more desirable, however, in that different types of institutions can maintain independent correctional philosophies and goals depending on the purpose for which they were constructed within the larger system. When one institution attempts to provide for all types of security and treatment, seldom does any portion of the program gain any degree of excellence or genuine autonomy.

The county jail

THE JAIL AS A PROBLEM

A stay in a county jail is the most widely experienced form of confinement in the United States. For this reason alone the jail is an extremely significant institution. Although the jail affects the lives of millions of our people, most private citizens care little about its operation, and legislative bodies give it the lowest priority in the disbursement of funds. Many of our jails are old, unsanitary, and in poor structural condition. They neither lend themselves to the rehabilitation of the inmates they house nor provide for protection of the community from dangerous or disturbed offenders. Since little or no classification system is in operation in most of our local detention facilities, jail administrators can seldom distinguish the dangerous, violent, and escape-prone from the harmless and petty offender.

Overcrowding is common, especially in the jails of our larger cities. It is not unheard of to have fifty men confined in a drunk tank on a given weekend, sleeping on the floor in their own or their neighbors' vomit and urine. Since there is usually no supervision in the cell blocks of many detention facilities, especially during the late evening hours, vicious assaults and sexual perversions can take place, the victim sometimes being a young adult held overnight on a minor traffic violation.

Treatment programs are all but unheard of and custody personnel are usually poorly educated, untrained, and indifferent to their work. No attempt is made to segregate those detained for trial from those already sentenced for crimes, and, among those sentenced, genuine efforts are seldom made to segregate the felon from the misdemeanant or the normal from the emotionally disturbed. The jail, in most instances, serves no function other than to detain people. Most jails act as revolving-door institutions for vagrants and drunks and as a warehouse for juveniles when no juvenile detention facilities are available. For the most part, our treatment of the misdemeanant offender has shown little improvement since the opening of the Walnut Street Jail.

Jail management on the local county level is generally the responsibility of an elected official, usually a sheriff. Before assuming his duties as a jail administrator, a sheriff may have had no experience whatsoever with the governing of men. Because the sheriff has other responsibilities as a law enforcement officer, he often assigns the management of the jail to a subordinate, who also has no prior experience in custodial administration and knows little about human behavior. Jails are one of the few institutions in our society that are allowed to be administered by elected and untrained officials. One could hardly conceive of turning over the management of a hospital, mental health clinic, or public school to an elected official with no experience in these areas.

Some counties have altered this system in an effort to provide a better quality of correctional services. For example, in Bucks County, Pennsylvania, the director of the local Department of Corrections administers both the adult and juvenile detention facilities. In New York City, detention jails and institutions for misdemeanants are administered by a Department of Corrections, which is managed by a commissioner appointed by the mayor. In San Diego the sheriff runs the jail for pretrial detention; and a separate Department of County Camps, directed by an administrator who is appointed by the County Board of Supervisors, operates facilities for most sentenced inmates.

Even if a jail administrator is experienced to some degree in the field of corrections and has progressive ideas concerning reform and rehabilitation, he will have difficulty in obtaining funds from county and city governments. Without funds, the jail administrator is helpless to establish an effective custodial and treatment program. When one takes into consideration that the jail competes for funds with other community agencies and institutions, such as police departments, hospitals, public schools, and welfare departments, it is understandable why the jails are probably our most poorly funded community institutions.[30]

In 1968 Congress passed the Omnibus Crime Control and Safe Streets Act in response to a rapidly rising crime rate. As a result of this act, millions of dollars have been disbursed to states in order to fund anti-crime programs. The states, in turn, funnel this money into their local communities. Little money is actually disbursed for the purposes of improving jail plants or programs. Top priority for funding goes to innovative police projects, preventive programs in juvenile delinquency, projects for police cooperation and consolidation, purchase of modern police equipment for local departments, studies for redefining the correctional goals of the justice system, and projects for better police-community relations. When money is filtered to the county jail, it is seldom employed for the establishment of treatment programs or the hiring of competent personnel. For example, a local county jail in Pennsylvania recently received $200,000 for the improvement of its overall facility. Instead of being used to establish some meaningful jail program, the funds were channeled for the "renovation" and "reconstruction" of the physical plant. This consisted of replacing porcelain commodes with stainless steel fixtures and renewing the plumbing system. Any excess funds were appropriated for the purchase of riot gear for the custodial staff. This is interesting in that, to our knowledge, there has never been a riot at this particular jail.

Jail administrators have difficulty in attracting qualified men to act as custodial personnel or turnkeys. One reason for this situation is the extremely poor pay such a job offers. For example, during the year 1973, the average salary for a custodial worker in a local detention facility in Pennsylvania was approximately $5,300. Such low remuneration for a rather unpleasant task cannot be expected to attract well-qualified and motivated personnel. Nothing is expected of most jail custodians with respect to treatment and rehabilitation, and very few will ever receive inservice training to prepare them for their duties. Over half of all jails have no educational requirements for their jail personnel, and potential jail employees are rarely subjected to effective screening procedures before being hired.[31] Since screening procedures are not mandatory, some custodial officers come to their jobs suffering from a personality disturbance that manifests itself in highly authoritarian, prejudiced, and sadistic behavior. If jails are to be institutions of rehabilitation, local county governments must channel more of their money into the recruitment and training of more capable men and women for such positions as jail administrators, custodial officers, and rehabilitation specialists.

THE JAIL AS A PROMISE

Certain states are trying to do something in order to improve their quality of service to the misdemeanant offender. In Connecticut, Rhode Island, Delaware, and Puerto Rico, the local jails are no longer autonomous, but are operated by state institutions. In Maine, Massachusetts, and North Carolina, short-term misdemeanant offenders are being committed to houses of corrections, farms, and road camps, and the county jail is used only for prisoners detained for trial.[32] In San Diego County, California, a progressive honor camp program for sentenced misdemeanants is staffed by rehabilitative personnel who act as counselors and case managers.[33] A pilot program in Westchester County, New York, offers women a wide variety of courses ranging from methods of self-improvement to professional studies such as nursing.[34] A sophisticated educational program at the St. Paul Workhouse provides many inmates with the opportunity to earn high school diplomas and participate in vocational rehabilitational programs.[35]

Several county jails now employ such devices as work and educational release and provide special programs of treatment for the alcoholic and the narcotic addict. Instead of incarcerating alcoholics in county jails and contributing to the revolving-door syndrome, certain counties now use alternative methods for the processing of chronic drunks. In Los Angeles County, California, for example, three centers are operated by the County Department of Hospitals where social, medical, and psychological services are provided to alcoholics. Traditionally, such misdemeanants would have been housed at the Los Angeles County Jail without any type of treatment whatsoever.[36] Some states allow for the establishment of detoxification and treatment centers for alcoholics.

The jail does have possibilities as an institution in that it is an integral part of the local community structure. If these possibilities are to be realized, there must be more coordination between the jail and other agencies in the community, in order to provide expanded services in such areas as family service and counseling, treatment for the alcoholic and drug addict, vocational rehabilitation, and employment assistance and information. Badly needed are short-term programs to accommodate most misdemeanant offenders, who spend only thirty days or less in confinement. Many individuals experience their first period of incarceration in a county jail. Attempts should be made to provide help at this early stage before a recidivistic syndrome sets in. Special programs for young, first offenders should therefore be developed along with proper, segregated facilities. Expanded programs and facilities are needed for female offenders. Such facilities are now all but neglected in jail planning and construction.

Some communities are pooling their resources and establishing regional jails in order to provide adequate physical facilities and a treatment program supervised by competent personnel. Some states subsidize local jails, but most states accept no responsibility for their misdemeanant facilities. Some local communities refuse to accept state advice or help, and insist on maintaining complete autonomy over their institutions, even though they are incapable of operating their jails effectively. Many states provide jail inspection services, as does the federal government through the U.S. Bureau of Prisons. The advice given to local communities is frequently ignored, however, and there are seldom any penalties for noncompliance with state or federal standards, except, perhaps, the loss of revenue from housing federal prisoners.[37]

It is difficult to determine how to best administer a local jail system. Should the jail be managed by a local department of corrections headed by a director or commissioner? Should the local communities regionalize and share joint responsibility for their misdemeanant facilities? Or should the sheriff be given control over pretrial detention but not be involved in the custody or supervision of those sentenced for crimes? A general review of present organizational structures for local correctional services is needed in order to determine what kind of management is the most effective and at the same time least expensive.[38]

Richard A. McGee advocates that a state, a county, or a regional district within a state should establish the equivalent of a department of corrections. This department would be responsible for the management of all offenders under its jurisdiction, whether accused, convicted, incarcerated, or under community supervision. McGee states that under such a system, courts would relinquish administrative direction of probation services; jails and camps for adult offenders would be removed from the administrative direction of law enforcement agencies; there would be an end to the unrealistic dichotomy between youth and adult correctional services; and a system of financial assistance would be ensured, provided by state governments and the federal government to local jurisdictions and based on adherence to acceptable standards of jail maintenance and programming.[39]

In the processing of misdemeanant offenders, high priority should be given to methods by which more people can be kept from going to jail in the first place, such as the extended use of bail and release on own recognizance; a law permitting the collection of fines by installment; a greater use of supervised and summary probation; and the use of citations instead of jail bookings for certain cases at the time of arrest.

In order to ensure a jail service system that is operationally efficient and at the same time rehabilitative in nature, meaningful ways of evaluating the effectiveness of jail programs must be established. Evaluative studies in this area are sadly lacking. Universities and colleges could help provide these services.

PRISON ORGANIZATION

Prison selection and prison socialization

THE EFFECT OF THE PRECONVICTION PROCESS

Before being selected as a candidate for prison, all potential prisoners are subjected to a preconviction process consisting of apprehension and arrest; possible pre-plea or pretrial detention; and numerous courtroom proceedings, such as the initial arraignment; continuances for the purpose of submitting a plea; continuances for the presentation of various legal motions; continuances in regard to establishing a trial date; the court or jury trial upon a plea of not guilty; and the hearing for sentencing and pronouncement of judgment. During this period, contacts may be made with the prosecuting attorney for the purpose of plea bargaining; with probation officers if a presentence investigation is ordered; and with psychiatrists and psychologists if psychiatric evaluations are ordered for the determination of sanity or to obtain information in order to establish grounds for mitigation of sentence. From the time of arrest to the time of conviction many weeks or even months may elapse. It would be unrealistic to believe that individuals subjected to such a process would remain unaffected by the experience. A man enters prison with an image of the criminal justice system formed largely during this preconviction process.

The preconviction process will differ according to the accused's economic status, racial and ethnic background, length of prior criminal record, stability and type of life style, and degree of social and legal sophistication. It can be said with a high degree of reliability that selection for prison begins immediately after arrest, since it depends to a significant degree on whether the accused can post bail or meet the requirements of being released on his own recognizance. Those with the financial ability to post bail will avoid confinement in a local detention facility while awaiting the disposition of their case and will escape the emotional and physical trauma associated with such an experience. Such individuals, in addition to being able to keep their jobs and remain with their families, are more likely to obtain better legal representation; they are more apt to obtain an acquittal on the matters set forth in their criminal complaint or indictment; and, if convicted, they will probably suffer a milder sanction (such as probation or short-term detention) than their unfortunate counterparts who must remain in pretrial detention.[40] Minority groups and the poor are usually the people who fill our local detention facilities because of their inability to meet the financial requirements for release. This type of discrimination can only adversely affect the attitude of the accused toward the entire system of the administration of justice.

Whether released on bail or not, the accused will have been subjected to arrest and possible field or station interrogation. Arrest procedures can promote hostility and disrespect for authority if they are characterized by discourtesy, physical mistreatment, verbal abuse, and racial discrimination.

The experience of the accused with his own attorney, the prosecutor, and in the courtroom might further lead him to the conclusion that the criminal justice process is merely a game, and that his chances of winning depend not only on his financial, racial, and cultural background, but also on the degree to which he is subservient and cooperative with the officers of the court. He learns that he might have to make deals, even if he feels that he is innocent, in order to avoid a harsh sentence or even in order to be freed from a long period of pretrial detention.

The importance of the preconviction process should not be underestimated as a factor in determining possible selection for prison and in shaping the attitude of the accused toward the criminal justice system and authority in general. Depending on his experiences during his journey through the criminal justice continuum, he will enter prison anxious, but amenable to treatment; hostile, but willing to play the "time game" in order to obtain favorable reports and early release; or bitter, prejudiced, and ready to fight back at society and the judicial system responsible for his confinement.

DIAGNOSTIC CENTERS AND CLASSIFICATION

The functions of diagnostic centers are to receive new inmates and evaluate their custody, training, and treatment needs. The diagnostic classification movement, as it exists in many of our correctional systems, reflects the theory that criminal behavior is symptomatic of underlying mental or emotional conditions. Although the contributions of social factors to deviant modes of behavior are being given increasing consideration, they are still, for the most part, considered less important than psychological factors by the treatment personnel of our correctional institutions. This approach to the etiology of crime is based on the adoption of the medical model by "experts" in the field of corrections. This model, which is based on the aura of the magical powers of the physician, still influences treatment in our prisons and probation departments today. The medical model assumes that the criminal is ill and curable. It further assumes that psychiatrists, psychologists, social workers, and probation and parole officers have the ability and the knowledge of human behavior necessary to effect cures. Because it is believed that such "experts" are capable of curing deviant behavior, it is taken for granted that they must be given ultimate power in diagnosis and treatment to properly effect a cure. As a result of this myth of the curative powers of the expert in the fields of corrections, mental health, education, and social work, administrators of correctional institutions, especially those emphasizing diagnosis, classification, and medical treatment, have become all but completely autonomous and free from evaluation and review.

One of the most alarming results of the medical model is the construction of institutions for defective delinquents similar to the Patuxent Institution in Jessup, Maryland. This facility operates under an indeterminate sentence law which permits authorities to retain their inmates for the remainder of their lives, if it is felt by the experts that they meet the definition of a defective delinquent. A recent case reveals that an inmate, originally sentenced to prison for auto theft in 1958 under a maximum sentence of four years, is still imprisoned in this institution as a defective delinquent.[41] Such institutions have been referred to as model "Clockwork Orange" prisons advocating treatment methods found in Valery Tarsis' novel, *Ward 7*. Thus, the constitutional defective of Hooton and the criminal man of Lombroso is replaced by the defective delinquent.

Upon entering a diagnostic center a prisoner is first put through a reception and orientation program. He is assigned an institutional number, strip-searched, issued clothing, photographed, fingerprinted, screened for immediate security problems, and given a preliminary medical examination for detection of medical and psychological problems needing immediate attention.

After the required tasks of the reception process are completed the prisoner's orientation begins. During the orientation process he is usually provided with a rule book giving him information concerning the basic rules he must follow while in the center. He is also made familiar with the general operation of the center, and he receives information concerning visitation, correspondence, and programs that the center might offer.

The major task of the diagnostic center is to classify the inmate. Classification takes place in the areas of custodial management, training, and treatment. Custody status will be determined by the length of the prisoner's sentence, record of previous escapes, institutional record of previous commitments, adjustment during the reception period, capacity for violent and disruptive behavior, strength of family ties, and residential mobility.

Classification for training and treatment programs includes a consideration of such factors as work assignment possibilities, vocational and educational potentials and needs, medical rehabilitative requirements, religious preference, emotional stability and need for treatment, family stability and need for family case work, potential for transfer to community-based programs, recreational interests and potential, avocational interests and talents, and degrees of guidance and counseling needed.

In order to obtain the data necessary for the classification of prisoners in the above-mentioned categories the prisoners are interviewed by staff members such as a correctional counselor, a vocational/educational analyst, a psychometrist (for psychological testing and diagnosis), a physician, a chaplain, and a psychiatrist (if referral is made). The prisoners are also subjected to various tests measuring intelligence, basic educational achievement and grade level, vocational preference, and vocational aptitude.

Traditionally the findings of the staff are evaluated by a classification committee, representing staff members from the areas of treatment, custody, and administration. The classification committee will determine a custody and treatment program for each prisoner at the center and will recommend transfer to an institution where it is felt that the prescribed treatment plan can be realized. The inmate must accept the results of the classification committee whether he is in accord with them or not and has no means of appeal concerning the treatment program to which he is assigned. Attempts are being made to allow an inmate to appeal a program he feels to be unjust; but under present conditions he must go to a transfer institution to await reclassification and revision of his custody status and treatment program. This may take months, and there is no guarantee that the inmate's wants or needs will be reflected in the recommendations of the reclassification committee. Many inmates enter their transfer institution bitter and hostile over the assignment prescribed for them by the diagnostic center staff. Complaints center around such issues as not being given a sufficient voice in developing their own training and treatment program and of being given little time and consideration by most members of the staff with whom they come in contact.

Some correctional systems are experimenting with Mutual Agreement Programming, which gives the inmate the opportunity to supply inputs into his own institutional and parole training and treatment program. It is assumed that the inmate, by being involved in his own program model, will be more amenable to training and treatment and will probably show improved postrelease behavior as well. A mutual agreement program would involve a signed and completely understood set of expectations on the part of the institutional and parole personnel and the inmate himself. All parties to the agreement would have to agree on the treatment plan for an inmate and on the means by which the plan would be made operational. The value of mutual agreement programming is based on the treatment strategy that rewards received by an inmate must be contingent upon his behavior and achievements.

Problems with the diagnostic center model arose when it was discovered that the correctional system within which the diagnostic center operated could not implement the recommended treatment and training programs for such reasons as lack of adequate physical facilities, insufficient operating budgets, institutional overcrowding, failure to obtain modern vocational equipment that would enable inmates to acquire skills appropriate to the working world, and lack of professional personnel. Another factor that has retarded treatment programs in correctional institutions has been the indifference of custody and administration to such innovations and a lack of zeal on the part of the treatment staff themselves to initiate change. Failure to implement a treatment plan on the part of a transfer institution can produce feelings of antagonism on the part of inmates, who feel that the system has "let them down" by failing to keep promises.

One way to alleviate problems such as the inability of a correctional system to implement treatment and training programs prescribed by diagnostic centers is to appoint staff members in the capacity of Program Review Specialists. Program Review Specialists would review all classification reports and recommendations in order to determine whether they were capable of being implemented by the system. The specialists would also visit diagnostic centers to evaluate classification procedures; and they would visit all other institutions and community-based centers to study and evaluate reclassification procedures, programs available, space available, and atmosphere. They would be concerned with whether the original treatment and training plans developed at the diagnostic center were being carried out at the transfer institutions. Their task would be that of roaming inspectors or monitors for the administration.

THE INMATES' VIEW: PRISONIZATION

The adoption of the theory underlying the contemporary prison brought hopes of providing a penal system that would furnish treatment, training, recreational, and custody measures conducive to the physical, social, and emotional welfare, comfort, and well-being of the inmate. Although corporal punishment is not found in the contemporary prison to the degree it was in the past, the inmate still suffers from what sociologists refer to as the pains of imprisonment. It appears that these pains of imprisonment cannot be totally erased and that, to some degree, punishment will be an inherent aspect of total institutions regardless of how they are constructed, administered, supervised, or managed. The inmate regards any stay in prison as a painful experience, whatever the nature of the prison or the philosophy of the prison staff. The inmate might well agree with Richard R. Korn, who believes imprisonment to be a form of capital punishment, in that for the period of imprisonment all meaningful life processes for the inmate are lost.

Erving Goffman feels that in all total institutions such as prisons and asylums, inmates suffer loss of personal identity, become decultured, and undergo a process of modification characterized by abasement, degradation, and humiliation.[42] Total institutions foster the loss of identity and promote feelings of self-rejection on the part of the inmates they house, through programs designed to mold them into objects that can be fed into the administrative machinery. This molding and shaping of the inmate, either through the old techniques of corporal punishment and severe repression or through modern and highly sophisticated techniques of social control (under the guise of training and treatment), has as its real purpose, not the resocialization of the inmate, but the establishment of institutional control, making life easier for all members of the staff and administration. As we shall learn later, with the rise of prisoner awareness, these programming techniques are no longer working to the staff's advantage as well as they did in the past.

The pains of imprisonment, according to Gresham Sykes, are largely emotional and psychological.[43] The frustrations of being deprived of the satisfaction of such basic needs as self-esteem, liberty, security, love, and heterosexual relations tend to cause the personality of the inmate to disintegrate and lead to a process of dehumanization. Further, being confined and deprived of liberty weakens the inmate's link with his family and friends and promotes a form of moral rejection of the inmate by society. Feeling rejected by society at large, being isolated from his loved ones, and being forced to adapt to a social system designed, in many instances, to maintain the total power of his managers, the inmate tends to suffer from a syndrome called prisonization.

Much has been written about the effects of prisonization by Donald Clemmer and Gresham Sykes.[44] Clemmer believes that all inmates suffer from prisonization, but some to a greater degree than others.[45]

Prisonization is the result of incorporation by inmates of the norms, code, argot, dogma, and myths of the prison subculture, in an effort to cope with the pains of imprisonment.[46] In an attempt to regain a sense of self-worth and social recognition, inmates develop a society within a society which allows them to reject their rejectors rather than themselves.[47] Such a society is characterized by extreme authoritarianism and a system of social stratification according to status, functional roles, race, and nationality. An inmate hierarchical structure is therefore developed to help the inmate to cope with the lack of social mobility available, regardless of his talent or training, in a total institutional setting. To a large degree the inmate subculture is "a search for the symbols of status."[48]

One way to define social status and functional roles among the inmates is through the use of prison argot, or the development of a special vocabulary. Prison argot serves to order and classify experience within the prison in terms which deal with various aspects and problems of confinement.[49] Some prison argot refers to roles that are disapproved of by inmates and some refer to roles that inmates admire.

To a large degree, social status in prison is determined by the inmate's degree of self-determination. For example, an inmate who refuses to adhere to the custodian's concept of him and maintains a high degree of self-control and composure while still remaining oriented to the inmate code is called a *Right Guy*. He maintains a degree of dignity and never allows the custodians to strip him of his ability to control himself. He is the inmate who does his own time and is never subservient to the prison staff.[50] He will undertake risks and undergo punishment for the benefit of the prison community.[51] The *Right Guy* enjoys a high status among his fellow inmates.

On the other hand, the *Square John* is given a low status value in prison, since he adheres only superficially to the inmate code and will cooperate with the prison staff when it is to his advantage to do so. Many inmates in this category are situational offenders, who do not make crime their life vocation.

Other inmates who do not enjoy high esteem are: *Ball Busters* (the prison outlaw, who constantly antagonizes the prison staff and his fellow inmates by verbal abuse, physical assaults, and his unpredictability); *Punks* (inmates who become homosexuals while in prison either due to coercion or in order to obtain goods and services that are in short supply); and *Hipsters* (inmates who exhibit toughness only to those they are certain to subdue and are not nearly as brave as they make out to be).[52]

There is prison argot for such functional roles in the prison as: *Merchant* (sells stolen goods to other inmates at a profit); *Fag* (passive homosexual); *Gorilla* (uses violence to get what he wants); *Rat* (betrays his fellow inmates by giving information to the prison staff); *Wolf* (masculine and aggressive homosexual); *Tough* (the explosive inmate, who becomes violent and aggressive over a minor affront); and *Fish* (new inmate).[53]

Argot roles are not resorted to uniformly throughout the prison community by any one inmate. For example, an inmate may display one role in his cell block and another role in the industrial shop.[54] There can also be a shift of roles during an inmate's prison career.

In addition to the system of inmate social stratification as reflected in prison argot, there is also a strong tendency toward authoritarianism, and toward placing a dominant value on the possession and exercise of coercive power.[55] Since the inmates have been victims of the power of the judicial system and of the total authoritarian regime of imprisonment, they tend to regard the possession of power as the highest personal value.[56] The inmates' need for power and status will make unproductive all attempts by the prison staff to break down the authoritarian character of inmate relationships through increased programs of permissiveness and the granting of more personal privileges. As Korn and McCorkle have observed, the inmate social system wields much more authority over individual inmates than do the members of the prison staff. Inmate groups are capable of inflicting far more physical and psychological damage on their fellow inmates than any type of punishment the staff can administer. In fact, punishment by the staff may have a self-defeating purpose in that it may be regarded as a further source of status for the inmate.[57]

Although prisonization seems to occur in many inmates, the degree to which it dominates their values and goals differs according to the phase of their institutional career. There appears to be more conformity demonstrated by inmates during one phase of their incarceration than others. This phenomenon has led to the belief that the effects of prisonization are greatest during the middle of the inmates' stay in prison, at the point when they are farthest removed from the outside world, and least effective near the time of release.[58]

Such an assumption, however, should be entertained with caution. As the inmate begins to focus his attention on the free world and makes contacts with his friends, relatives, and prospective employers, the status given him by the inmate code often diminishes and becomes a less significant factor in his general outlook, making it appear that resocialization is genuinely taking place. However, when he recognizes the effect the stigma of being in prison has on how he is received in society, the inmate may realize that he has not obtained the status of a full citizen by being released from prison. In order to find a more supportive social environment, he may revert to acquaintances with other ex-offenders, which may result in his committing another crime, returning to prison, and reverting to the inmate code.[59] For this reason, more emphasis should be placed on the pre-release and early parole process.

Prisonization can vary from simply learning compliant roles or behavior to the internalization of the role behavior and a new conception of the self. Some inmates make few primary associations while in prison and do not allow the prison culture to be incorporated into their value system, except as they have to abide by it in making a surface adjustment to prison life. Membership in the prisonization process for such inmates is temporary and superficial.

The degree to which prisonization actually impedes resocialization is not known; it probably varies according to the correctional philosophy, program, and custodial plan experienced by the inmate. Clemmer and Sykes wrote about the maximum security prison, which was not geared toward resocialization in the first place. The general rule on the part of the inmates and prison staff alike at such institutions was "Do your own time." Such a rule, whether explicit or implicit in the formal structure of an institution, can hardly be conducive to the goals of resocialization. When one maintains, therefore, that prisonization impeded resocialization in Menard Reformatory (the institution mentioned in Clemmer's writings) or Trenton Prison (the institution which Sykes studied), one can question what possible resocialization goals were actually impeded. Even though the rhetoric of resocialization was used by the prison staff governing such institutions, it is highly questionable whether such rhetoric was ever implemented in practice or was ever intended to be implemented. Is prisonization really the product of the restraint kind of prison, and is the amount of staff/inmate conflict reduced in prisons that are more oriented toward treatment? Perhaps an inmate subculture is less needed in treatment-oriented institutions because the deprivations of incarceration are less severe and less universal.

In helping the inmate to cope with the pains of imprisonment brought about by the maximum security prisons of the past, prisonization may have had some positive effect. Investigators who stress the negative aspects of prisonization sometimes assume that attitudes considered by the staff to be negative in function are also of negative functional value for the emotional well-being of the inmate. Another assumption is that attitudes perceived as negative by the formal institutional staff are not conducive to resocialization.

It is difficult to conclude whether prisonization in a maximum security institution inhibits resocialization, since prisonization is really not in conflict with the operational goals of such prisons. Also open to question are the degree to which prisonization takes place in treatment-oriented institutions, and what negative effect such prisonization has, since there may be more attempts to reduce the pains of imprisonment through individualized treatment.

Some theorists, such as Garrity, question the belief held by many in the correctional field that the longer one remains in prison the greater the chances of prisonization, and, therefore, the poorer the chances of rehabilitation.[60] Garrity, using Schrag's typology,[61] studied 1,265 men released from two institutions, who had been on parole for at least one year. He found that the most stable type of offender was negatively affected by prolonged imprisonment, while those who were unstable were positively affected by it. As a result of his study he concluded that continued prison experience will increase the chance of successful adjustment for some inmates and that, therefore, prisons are not necessarily breeding grounds for crime for *all* types of offenders.

Activities of change and activities of order

CUSTODIAL FUNCTIONS

Historically, prisons and police organizations have copied military organizations and military terminology. In referring to the custodial function of prisons we still employ the terms "Captain," "Lieutenant," and "Sergeant." Terminology is gradually changing as prisons attempt to borrow a vocabulary more common to social agencies and mental hospitals. The change in the use of terminology is the result of changes in theory about the purpose and function of custody. For the most part, however, the custodial functions of most prisons are administered along militaristic lines. Custodians are usually dressed in military-style uniforms and are referred to as officers. The military salute is still retained by the custodians of some prisons as a means of greeting their superiors in rank. It is only recently that some prison administrators have allowed custodians to doff their uniforms in favor of street clothes.

Custodians have the responsibility of maintaining security and providing internal control. Accordingly they must exercise surveillance over the inmates—count them several times a day, search cells periodically for contraband and weapons, discreetly supervise their visitors, inspect the various aspects of the physical plant (bars, locks, windows, doors, etc.), control firearms and gas, inspect all vehicular traffic and supplies entering and leaving the institution, maintain control of all keys and continually check locking devices, have emergency plans ready for riot control, post riot procedures, and maintain gun towers.[62]

In order to maintain control over the inmates and have a smooth-running institution, more than rigid adherence to security measures is needed. Interpersonal relationships must be developed, no matter how shallow, and good morale must exist among the custodial staff and the inmates. In the past it was thought that prisons could be run effectively by arbitrary rules and hard work alone. Probably the most distinctive feature of the old prison system was the myth of the unparalleled power of the custodians. The custodians of the past did have some degree of autocratic power, and they exercised it through cruel and sadistic modes of corporal punishment; but it came to be more and more apparent that their power was more a fiction than a reality.

There are two major reasons why the concept of the absolute power of the custodian could never effectively be implemented. One reason is that custodians are human and are therefore corruptible. Borrowing from Sykes, Korn and McCorkle set forth three major ways through which the custodian can be corrupted, namely, friendship, reciprocity, and default.[63]

Since the surveillance of inmates requires personal interaction, there are pressures on the custodian to be accepted by the men he governs and, at the same time, to be loyal to the administration. From the inmates the custodian is "constantly exposed to a sort of moral blackmail in which the first signs of condemnation or estrangement are immediately countered by the inmates with the threat of ridicule or hostility."[64] In carrying out the orders of his superiors the custodian might be concerned about arousing ill feeling among the inmates. In the urge to be liked by the men he supervises, the custodian may overlook some rules and regulations he does not deem to be of much significance. To add to his feelings of ambivalence, his superiors, at times, reprimand him, show little appreciation for his hard work, and require him to carry out certain orders that appear incomprehensible to him. At the same time he is apt to find sympathy from the inmates, who can identify with the problems he faces in a bureaucracy run along militaristic lines since "they too claim to suffer from the unreasonable caprice of power."[65] The custodian may also have feelings of ambivalence in regard to the inmate he governs. He may disapprove of his criminal activities but at the same time admire his degree of prestige, notoriety, and wealth and feel somewhat gratified to associate with a famous member of organized crime.[66]

The custodian is further corrupted through reciprocity in that his superiors evaluate his performance in terms of how well he can maintain control and order in his particular cell block area. If his block area is poorly maintained by the inmates, and if disturbances occur, the custodian is felt to be lacking in ability and may be denied pay raises and promotions or even lose his job. He realizes that the absolute power he is supposed to maintain over his charges is a myth, and that he can't rely on threats and punishment to obtain inmate cooperation. In order to achieve a smooth-running cell block, therefore, the custodian may either ignore minor infractions of the rules or see to it that he never places himself in a position to discover them.[67]

A third mode of corruption is through default. In an effort to obtain more free time, because of indifference, or out of feelings that his authority is being largely diminished anyway, the custodian might delegate some of his duties to various inmates, such as making out reports, checking cells at the periodic count, and locking and unlocking doors. Such delegation of power violates the theory behind the traditional guard-inmate relationship, and the custodian becomes even less of a source of order and control. Delegation of power by a custodian also makes it difficult for the new custodian who will eventually take his place, since the inmates will resent giving up any power and privileges they have already obtained.[68]

The second major factor undermining the authority of custodians is that they must work in a state of continual tension and awareness of the possibility that the inmates may riot and gain control. While the inmates can relax and superficially adjust to the prison routine of the cell block, the custodian must constantly keep alert for the unexpected emergency and adhere to a rigid routine of surveillance. As a result of this enforced routine for the purpose of control and order the custodian may compromise, reaching a limit to the tolerance of tension, and not take his duties as seriously as he should. Such a compromise could, of course, lead to loss of control within a particular block area.[69]

Traditionally it has been difficult to recruit personnel for custodial tasks in prisons because of low pay, monotony of the work, lack of prestige in such a position, and the threat of danger, which is always present. Recruitment is accomplished in most states through civil service testing and selection. Although civil service selection is an improvement over the old political spoils system of recruiting prison personnel, civil service tests still do not properly screen and evaluate candidates for acceptable personality characteristics or adequately predict on-the-job performance. It is not unusual for a candidate to score high on his civil service examination but perform unsatisfactorily on the job. Many states and the federal government provide inservice training programs for their officers in order to provide for a more efficient quality of service.

At present there are ambivalent feelings about what the proper role of a custodian should be in a prison system. Traditionally he has been formally isolated from the treatment program areas and has been expected to concern himself exclusively with matters of control. This resulted in his being unable to fraternize with the inmates under his guidance or to become closely attached to them in any way which might lead to his becoming emotionally involved. Since, however, the custodian has more contact with and greater impact on the inmates than any other person on the prison staff, some administrators feel that he could provide a valuable service to certain aspects of the treatment program. In an effort to make the custodian's task more flexible and broader in scope, custodial officers have been used as liaison members of treatment teams at the U.S. Penitentiary at Lewisburg, Pennsylvania, and are allowed to conduct group counseling sessions at San Quentin Prison in California. To make the custodian's role appear less authoritarian and militaristic, some prisons allow custodians to wear street clothes on the job and encourage them to relax certain areas of surveillance.

Custodians could be employed as valuable resources on reception teams at diagnostic centers. In many ways, the custodian is the most strategically placed individual to observe the behavior and needs of inmates in such centers. He has daily face-to-face contact with the inmates and probably has a significant influence on what inmates believe about the prison system. The custodian's role during the reception process could be broadened to include such activities as conducting group sessions, reporting on such sessions, and compiling daily observation sheets on each inmate for later use by the classification committee. Giving the custodian such functions would promote morale among the custodians in general and help to end the dichotomy between treatment and custody personnel.

TREATMENT FUNCTIONS

Impediments to treatment

Although the purpose of treatment is to change the inmate and provide him with tools that he can use in the free world to make an adequate adjustment, problems arise as to how such a purpose can be achieved. One factor that hinders programs designed for inmate change and resocialization is that some inmates don't want to change. Such inmates feel that they can achieve more pleasure and prestige through a criminally oriented life style—even with the risk of periodic incarceration—than by allowing themselves to be assimilated into a social role involving limited enjoyment, monotonous work, and low community and peer group status. Such an attitude on the part of the inmate leads, in many cases, to the playing of the "time game" on the part of both staff and inmate.[70] The inmate communicates what the staff wants to hear, and the staff rewards the inmate by a favorable recommendation to the parole board. The parole board, in turn, likes to hear the rhetoric of personal reform produced by the time game and makes awards accordingly. The time game seems to satisfy everyone concerned and makes it possible for an inmate to progress through the treatment program of a prison completely unchanged in personality and, at the same time, be given the stamp of model prisoner. Everyone concerned knows that nothing has changed, nobody expected anything to change in the first place, and hardly anyone really cares. All that seems to matter is that the rhetoric is right.

Another factor that hinders the effectiveness of treatment programs is the assumption by the treatment staff that, because many inmates play the time game, all inmates are playing the game. After a staff member has been manipulated a few times, he becomes pessimistic, indifferent, and untrusting, regardless of his intentions when he entered the job. Such an attitude does serious injustice to the inmate who does have a genuine interest in change and desires a new life style. Not all inmates are "con artists" any more than all inmates are dangerous or escape risks. Being treated in a perfunctory manner by the members of the treatment staff, in spite of the fact that he voices a genuine need for help and guidance, leads an inmate to become frustrated and bitter.

The assumption that all inmates play the time game does make a staff member's task much easier, however. Knowing that all inmates are "out to con him" for a favorable report to the parole board or for a desirable assignment within the prison itself, the staff member can refrain from taking his job really seriously and, in turn, feels no pangs of conscience for putting in as little work as is necessary. "Why should I spend my time trying to help someone who really doesn't want to be helped?" becomes the philosophy of the day. This attitude results in the necessary papers being completed, case history folders being filed properly and kept up-to-date, and appointments being scheduled with no sincere belief that any of these tasks are going to make any real difference except to please superiors and produce a pay check.

Resocialization is also obstructed by the organizational structure of the prison itself, regardless of the treatment program maintained by a prison system. The attempt to merge the ideologies of punishment and reform in an institutional setting such as the prison leads to logical contradictions that seem to make genuine resocialization impossible.[71] In the first place the prison system allows for no social mobility on the part of inmates. This results in a society characterized by the mutually exclusive roles of captive and captor. Such a caste society leads to the adoption of the prison code described above, with its philosophy of remaining aloof from the staff, keeping cool, and doing your own time. Since there is no real chance for the inmate to change his status within the prison, such as becoming a counselor, teacher, or work supervisor, he must satisfy his need for power, status, and security through membership in the society of prisoners.[72]

If the organizational system is constructed to keep officials and inmates forever apart in their sharing of values and activities, can anyone ever take the resocialization or treatment function of a prison seriously?[73]

Some prison officials are either threatened by or opposed to prison reform, and make a sham of treatment by maintaining programs that are not really intended to resocialize inmates. Officials so threatened or opposed will argue from caution, which is expressed in the familiar jargon: "We just can't rush into these matters . . . we must go one step at a time." Meanwhile, conditions exist such as those in the Arkansas prison system, which Thomas O. Murton (former Superintendent of Arkansas State Prisons) found to be characterized by race discrimination and brutality, and which led Judge J. Smith Henley to declare the Arkansas prison system in violation of the U.S. Constitution.[74] Murton stated that officials applied such instruments of cruelty as clubs, whips, and the "Tucker Telephone." (This is an old-fashioned crank telephone with two loose wires; the wires are attached to sensitive parts of the body and the crank turned to generate electricity until the inmate has fainted.) Murton was dismissed as Superintendent of Arkansas State Prisons, partly because he dug up bodies of men he believed to have been inmates who were murdered and buried near a prison farm. Because of his findings, Murton has presented before the American Correctional Association, on at least three separate occasions, a resolution "condemning the killing of prison inmates and urging officials to render complete investigations." In every case the resolution failed to pass. One reason for the defeat of the resolution appears to be Austin MacCormick's contention that Murton had actually dug into a paupers' graveyard at the Cummins Prison Farm.[75] Having completed an intensive investigation of the Arkansas prison system, MacCormick is also considered knowledgeable concerning conditions that exist at Arkansas institutions. There has never been any agreement about whether Murton discovered the bodies of inmates or the remains of the poor, but his discovery seems to leave room for reasonable doubt.

Still another impediment to treatment is treatment itself. Although we have abandoned obvious methods of corporal punishment in our prisons, we have substituted methods called correctional strategies that are perhaps even more repressive in nature. In the name of behavioral control, treatment strategies which are designed to ruin a man's very mind or transform him into a kind of human vegetable are being advocated by members of the medical profession. Such repressive uses of the techniques available to modern science remind one of strategies applied for the purpose of human manipulation and control in Orwell's *1984* and Aldous Huxley's *Brave New World*. Two examples are cited here that should be a source of concern about the morality of applying certain forms of behavioral control.

In 1970, the California State Department of Corrections, looked upon as one of the most progressive in the country, considered, but did not accept, a proposal to control the "violent" inmate through the use of corrective brain surgery. Richard R. Korn believed the proposal to be an attack on convict resistance brought about by recent prisoner awareness.[76] There is sometimes no distinction between coercion and treatment, and when the two terms are equated in the minds of prison officials, we have returned to the days of the "treat 'em rough" school of penology, but on a more frightening and sophisticated level.

Another example of possible coercion through the application of medical science under the label of treatment is the use of the drug Prolixin. Reports indicate that prison officials at the California Mens Colony have created a new classification called "psychotic repression," meaning that the inmate is psychotic but is repressing the symptoms of his psychosis. Such a diagnosis warrants the administration of the drug Prolixin for control purposes (to undermine resistance and to quiet chronic complainers).[77] Gerald B. Walsh of the Legal Aid and Defender Society of Kansas City charged that Missouri officials inject prison inmates with Prolixin after making the clinical judgement that they are psychotic.[78] Walsh describes the effects of the drug as equivalent to a functional lobotomy. A prisoner at the Oregon State Penitentiary stated that he was forcibly restrained by being chained to a bed and given Prolixin. The purpose of the drug, from the inmate's point of view, was to turn him into a zombie in the manner in which McMurphy, the hero of Ken Kesey's *One Flew Over the Cuckoo's Nest*, was drained of his vigorous spirit through the use of the knife.[79] According to the manufacturer of the drug (E. R. Squibb and Sons of New York) the use of Prolixin may impair the mental and physical abilities required for driving a car or operating heavy machinery. It is also said to have side effects producing a persistent pseudoparkinsonian syndrome which may be irreversible. Other disorders that may be caused by the drug are blurred vision, glaucoma, paralysis, fecal impaction, nasal congestion, impotency in men, and skin disorders.[80]

Still another obstacle to treatment may be that the treatment program proves to be too effective. For example, an incentive program begun in 1971 at the Colorado State Reformatory was so successful that judges sent more and more individuals convicted of crimes to the institution. The increase in prison population caused security problems and handicapped the program by decreasing the amount of mobility the inmates could have. To cope with the problem, institutional personnel expanded the work release program and attempted to liberalize the parole system.[81]

Finally, one of the major functions of treatment in prisons is to promote change and resocialization. This assumes that the staff members are knowledgeable in matters of ethics and morality as well as in matters of medicine and therapy. Resocialization comes to mean the acceptance of values and life style approved by the staff members and the middle- and upper-class members of society. Deviance implies the rejection of society's clearly defined norms. To deviate from the norm, according to the medical model, is to be "sick" or "mentally ill." Such labels are referred to by Thomas Szasz as labels of rejection which replace the traditional dichotomy of good and evil with that of mental health and illness.[82] Any behavior that becomes annoying, improper, or unusual is called sick. Three dangers are implied in this common approach to the treatment of offenders. One danger is that by labeling an inmate as sick you are subjecting him to the rhetoric of rejection and placing on him a stigma of condemnation that will be difficult to overcome.[83] As Thomas Szasz states, "the chains removed from the insane by Pinel have been replaced by the chains of words."[84] Another danger is that implying that the inmate is sick allows him to evade his responsibilities and hide behind the label given him by the treatment staff. The third danger in using this pseudo-language of mental illness is the promotion of the belief that treatment staff members such as psychiatrists, psychologists, and social workers are somehow experts in the field of ethics and morality and can be entrusted to direct resocialization along areas most conducive to the welfare of the inmate and society. This assumption that the experts know best in all matters concerning the welfare of the inmate gives treatment staff members the power to impose their values on the inmate. If the inmate rejects such values and does not participate in programs promoting such values, he is labeled as unresponsive to treatment and unmanageable, which can result in long periods of incarceration and, in some cases, even corrective surgery or drug therapy.

Treatment strategies

Counseling strategies. Treatment strategies in penal institutions cover such areas as counseling and guidance, vocational training, education, arts and crafts, library services, recreation, inmate government and advisory councils, employment, and religious training. Ideally, treatment programs should be of a diverse nature and designed to meet the individual needs of the inmates. In the past and, to a large degree, at present, inmates have been exposed to basically similar strategies. Although the process of classification separated inmates from one another according to security and treatment needs, once separated they received basically the same type of treatment. The current trend, however, is to provide for diversification of treatment through the use of typologies.

The California Youth Authority attempted to introduce a strategy of diversification through classification by interpersonal maturity levels.[85] This classification was centered around the ways in which the delinquent saw himself and the world around him, especially in terms of emotions and motivations. The classification focused on the ward's ability to understand what was happening between himself and others, as well as among others. The typology identified seven successive states of interpersonal maturity characterized by psychological development. The stages ranged from the least mature, which resembled the interpersonal interactions of a newborn infant, to an ideal of social maturity seldom reached. It was assumed that each of the seven labels was defined by a crucial interpersonal problem which had to be solved before further progress toward maturity could occur. Each of the levels was, in turn, broken down into subtypes for even more specific identification and treatment. Staff members were assigned cases according to their ability to work with wards at various maturity levels. Some staff worked better with neurotics than with wards exhibiting psychopathic disturbances; such staff, therefore, were assigned a case load of wards whose delinquent behavior was believed to be the result of internal conflicts. The California system no longer officially uses this classification typology because the effort to make it operationally effective caused too many problems.

A recent trend in the area of counseling has been the adoption of *reality therapy* as a tool for initiating behavioral change. Traditional casework therapy was found to be largely ineffective with many inmates due to their basic lack of insight and their inability to verbalize. Further, such traditional therapeutic techniques took a long time and required knowledge and training beyond the scope of most institutional treatment staff members. The basic assumption of reality therapy is that everyone who needs psychiatric treatment is unable to fulfill his basic needs, namely, the need to love and be loved and the need to feel worthwhile to himself and to others.[86] The goal of reality therapy is to help inmates fulfill these two needs; and fulfilling these needs demands a therapeutic approach which concentrates on the problems facing the inmate here and now. The therapist will largely ignore the inmate's past and will not concern himself with unconscious material. The importance of past information is not denied, but the use of it in therapy is felt to be unnecessary in the process of helping an inmate learn to fulfill his needs. All inmates who are unable to fulfill their needs in a manner that is law-abiding and in a way that does not deprive others of the ability to fulfill their needs are labeled "irresponsible." Through therapy the inmate learns to fulfill his needs in a responsible and mature manner and, by so doing, avoids violating the law and personality disintegration.

Reality therapists are critical of the traditional labels of "psychotic," "neurotic," and "psychopathic" and believe that too much time and money is wasted on diagnostic studies. It is felt that these labels tend to categorize and stereotype inmates with harmful results. All inmates are given one classification—irresponsible. It is believed that responsibility can be learned at any age. According to reality therapy, we learn responsibility by being involved with responsible human beings. In many cases the inmate's parents have been irresponsible people and he grows up to be the same. The therapist must be a responsible individual himself, therefore, if he is to become emotionally involved with the inmate on a constructive level. Emotional involvement is encouraged to show the inmate there is someone who cares about him; but, at the same time, the therapist makes it clear that he will not allow himself to be manipulated. The therapist will show concern for the inmate but will never accept unrealistic excuses for antisocial behavior.

Also, according to reality therapy, the inmate will learn better ways to fulfill his needs within the confines of reality, even if this means participation in a therapeutic program he does not like or think will succeed. Forced therapy is therefore accepted as a legitimate strategy. Time is significant and concentration will be on accomplishing behavioral change as soon as possible. Unlike traditional therapeutic approaches, concepts of morality are dealt with in reality therapy, and the inmate is encouraged to accept the standards set forth by the society in which he lives. Once the inmate learns to satisfy his needs in a responsible manner, it is expected that he will discover a greater degree of happiness, love, and security apart from delinquent activities.

Guided group interaction is currently used as a therapeutic strategy in several juvenile institutions throughout the country and is also being attempted with adults. This therapeutic approach was first used during World War II by Lloyd McCorkle, who applied it at the Fort Knox Rehabilitation Center in an attempt to deal with military offenders on an other than individual basis. After the war ended, Lovell Bixby, as Director of the Department of Corrections for New Jersey, attempted guided group interaction at Highfields.[87] The use of this technique spread, and it has now probably reached its zenith.

It was found that many inmates and wards of juvenile institutions failed to respond to individual therapy and did not appear to benefit much from traditional modes of group psychotherapy where the major emphasis was on the treatment of the individual within the group. Guided group interaction attempts to promote the incorporation by the entire group of certain attitudes and values which, once accepted, will provide the motivation for behavioral change. It is assumed that the norms and conduct of delinquents are chiefly influenced and determined by their peer group. Thus, if the peer group as a whole is persuaded to change, the individual within the group will also alter his outlook and values. Emphasis is on the gradual incorporation by the group of a new set of norms that would be conducive to nondelinquent behavior.[88] Such an approach is helpful with adolescents, and it appears to be most effective with the aggressive gang boy from the urban slum. Children from middle-class socioeconomic environments do not seem to benefit as much. Aggressive boys who have become deeply committed to a criminal way of life also benefit little from this mode of treatment.

The group meeting is the vehicle through which guided group interaction is applied. Such meetings encourage responsibility and decision making on the part of members, and group members are generally allowed to speak with complete freedom about their reaction to institutional staff and programs. Daily interaction and group homogeneity are important if the technique is to accomplish its major goal. Groups are carefully structured, therefore, with respect to age, socioeconomic background, previous criminal record, intellectual competence, and racial background. For the most part, guided group interaction confronts the wards with the here-and-now realities of their lives. It is felt that when individuals are given an outlet for the expression of their hostility and frustration, aggressive behavior can be reduced and replaced by an attitude that will foster acceptable behavioral patterns.[89]

Still another therapeutic technique that is thought to be successful, especially with the nonverbal and impulsive inmate, is the *psychodrama*. During a psychodrama an inmate can act out past, immediate, or expected problem situations and obtain advice from the group with whom he participates. The inmate can also perform roles that conform to the norms of society in the presence of other inmates, who quickly detect whether he is conning the group or playing it straight. The psychodrama gives the inmate the opportunity to talk or act out his motivations in a controlled setting. It is felt that if the inmate is given the opportunity to act out destructive impulses during a group session, he may no longer have the need to carry them out in reality.

The California Youth Authority engaged in a research project to determine the effectiveness of *individual counseling* on an intensive basis—The Pilot Intensive Counseling Organization (PICO), started in 1955, at the Deuel Vocational Institution near Tracy. This is an adult prison, operated by the Department of Corrections, which, in the past, housed both Youth Authority wards and youthful prisoners sentenced to the Department of Corrections. By 1961, approximately 1,600 Youth Authority wards had been involved in this experiment. At the time of admission, the wards were classified by the clinical staff as being either amenable or nonamenable to treatment by individual counseling. Half of all the cases were then, independent of this classification, selected as control groups and placed in units with no special counseling staff. The other half were placed in treatment units where social workers, with a caseload of twenty-five inmates, provided individual counseling. Postrelease results showed dramatically less return to prison for those in the individually counseled units, who, on entering the institution, were classified as amenable to treatment, than for the amenable cases in the control group. For those who were also in the individually counseled units but on entering the institution were classified as not amenable to individual counseling treatment, there was a somewhat higher failure rate than for those placed in the control units.[90] It should be noted that CYA wards are no longer sent to the Deuel Vocational Institute, as it is a prison primarily built for adult offenders.

Behavioral modification is a current fad in the treatment of juveniles and adults alike. Behaviorism arose in reaction to the "Ghost in the Machine" myth advocated by Descartes, which separated mind from body and advocated introspection as a way of getting at the data of conscious activity. Man, according to the behaviorist, is subject to conditioning, and conditioning can become a source of both power and control. B. F. Skinner has promoted the behavioristic outlook in such books as *Walden II* and *Beyond Freedom and Dignity*. His philosophy centers around the belief that man's behavior is determined by his environment and that we must approach the study of man's behavior by using the same scientific strategies we use in physics and biology. Attention must be focused on the shifting of control from the autonomous man of existential philosophy to the observable environment. Skinner feels that we must go beyond the conception of freedom and dignity propounded by writers such as Dostoevsky and Sartre and look to the real causes of human behavior.

The trend toward a behavioristic explanation of the nature of man has led to the application of the therapy of behavioral modification or control. Such therapy can be found in various correctional institutions in the form of token economy ("good" behavior is rewarded by a token that can be spent for candy and other pleasures), programmed learning devices, the point system (good behavior is rewarded by giving the inmate points which may be applied to weekend passes, furloughs, better living accommodations, and more institutional privileges), electric shock, and the old technique of reward and punishment. Actually, behavior modification was first introduced into the correctional system in 1876, when it appeared at Elmira Reformatory in the form of the mark system. Instead of detaining a prisoner for a given term of years, a certain number of marks was charged against him, depending on the seriousness of the offense. Before the prisoner could be released, he had to redeem these marks by good conduct, labor, and study. This led to the philosophy that a man keeps the key to his own cell, as he could be released as speedily as he could remove the marks against him.

The major criticism of behavioral modification is that it could conceivably lead to the dehumanization of mankind and to the concentration of power in the hands of the controllers. How far human beings can be controlled by the techniques of science is not known. Dostoevsky felt that it would be impossible to design a culture in which man was completely controlled, because man will never accept the fact that he can be controlled. Does subjecting a man to scientific analysis, however, dehumanize him by failing to recognize the myth of the "self"? Does man lose his autonomy and freedom when science discovers the variables that control his behavior? Much would seem to depend upon how individuals in the world of science, such as psychiatrists, psychologists, and other therapists, apply the knowledge they have learned through empirical means. There is little doubt that behavior modification can be applied as an instrument of repression and punishment to satisfy the goals, biases, and prejudices of the controllers and to further gratify any sadistic tendencies they might have. The choice of whether to expand the application of behavioral control is, however, a question of ethics and not of science. Science can never tell us what type of society is preferable or what type of human being is desirable.

In addition to the programs mentioned above, correctional institutions provide treatment programs in the following areas: *drug abuse counseling* and *treatment, group counseling* involving all staff members, *alcohol abuse programs* such as Alcoholics Anonymous, *family counseling* and child care, and *recreational therapy*. Treatment programs should be continually updated to meet the current demands of the inmate and society.

Conjugal visitation and coeducational facilities. Conjugal visits have been allowed for more than sixty years at the Mississippi State Penitentiary in Parchman. It is felt that such visits have been a major reason why riots have not occurred in this institution. Conjugal visits allow a prisoner and his spouse intimacy for several hours to a few days for the purpose of continuing their sexual relationship and as a means of keeping the family together.[91] California has operated a family visiting project since April 17, 1971. The plan is currently operating statewide in all facilities. At San Quentin approximately sixty inmates are eligible for visits with their families or close relatives for either a nineteen- or forty-eight-hour period. For the nineteen-hour visits, a five-bedroom house outside the prison wall is used. Forty-eight-hour visits are held in a duplex next door.

Columbus Hopper suggests that conjugal visitation might reduce sexual assaults within prison; reduce homosexuality; release individual tensions, making the prison less subject to riots; enhance the self-esteem of the inmate; and help keep the family together as a functioning unit while one member is in prison.[92]

The separation of the sexes was once considered a necessary step in the successful development of the prison system. Now, however, consideration is being given to the establishment of coed jails and prisons. There seems to be nothing emotionally healthy or rehabilitative in segregating the sexes confined to penal institutions. Such separation leads to emotional problems and to the development of unhealthy sexual outlets and identifications that may permanently damage the inmate. The success presently attained by the expansion of conjugal visitation seems to indicate that the sexes can be housed together in the same physical plant area and allowed to fraternize, without producing any great problem of internal control or security.

To some degree, the concept of a coed prison can be found in Illinois, which has experimented with what is referred to as a "Synthetic Community."[93] The Illinois State Penitentiary at Vienna allows inmates to lead almost normal lives. The institution is con- structed around a town square. The area includes libraries, a movie theatre, a gymnasium, and a canteen. The facility houses adult men, women, and male youths in three separate but connecting wings. Visiting privileges are allowed between any two wings. There are no bars or high walls. The emphasis is on individualized treatment and the promotion of inmate responsibility. Inmates are made to feel that they are still a part of the community. Responsibility is encouraged on two levels—community involvement and individual activities such as getting up, eating, and going to assignments throughout the day. The ideal population for the facility is considered to be 300 to 500 prisoners. The Federal Bureau of Prisons also operates a coed prison—a coed facility for young adults eighteen to twenty-five years of age, opened in Pleasanton, California in 1974.

Education and vocational training.   A program of education should be provided by correctional institutions to meet the academic and vocational needs of inmates. These needs can be ascertained through interviews, performance scores on achievement and aptitude tests, and information obtained from the schools the inmate attended. To meet educational needs of inmates at all levels the institutions must have sufficient teaching personnel, the necessary equipment and supplies, the latest facilities for audio-visual and programmed in- struction, a functional educational plan, and an adequate budget, efficiently prepared and administered.[94] To say the least, most adult prisons do not provide for an adequate academic or vocational edu- cational program.

One major difficulty is in providing qualified teaching staff. Even with attractive salaries and benefits, recruitment of good personnel is difficult. Many teachers do not want to work in such repressive surroundings, and some are frightened to work among inmates. As a result, many of the teachers in correctional institutions are there because they were unable to find employment elsewhere, and they take little interest in their assignments. The indifference of the teach- ing staff short-changes the inmate and gives him little motivation to continue an educational program or take it seriously. Other prob- lems arise when teachers under contract with the local school dis- trict are assigned to the correctional institution as part of the public school system. In many instances such teachers associate little or not at all with other staff members of the institution. This makes it im- possible to coordinate efforts to help the inmate. Another difficulty is that the school is run as an autonomous plant apart from the other programs provided by the institution. Steps should be taken to absorb the educational program and personnel within the other program functions of the institution.

Programs to eradicate illiteracy are usually given preference in adult institutions, at the expense of programs for the more advanced inmate. Most adult prisons provide little classroom education beyond the eighth grade level. Some institutions allow the inmate to prepare for the G.E.D. examination. If he passes it he is considered to have the equivalent of a high school education and receives a certificate to that effect. A smaller number of institutions have a high school program through which the inmate can obtain a diploma issued by the public school district within the institution's jurisdiction.

Project Newgate is a significant program now in effect at a few institutions enabling inmates to attend colleges and universities. Preparation for university acceptance is accomplished at the penal institution largely through programmed learning devices. Institutions not having a Project Newgate program may provide college level courses at the institution itself taught by regular university or college faculty members. Some institutions without a program for higher education may allow inmates to take correspondence courses at their own expense. Others have education departments which offer a wide range of activities outside academic education, such as instruction in music, arts and crafts, dramatic art, and physical education.

Daniel Glaser believes that the field of correctional education needs a program of individualized, one-to-one instruction to meet the inmate's needs and to challenge and motivate him to go on.[95] As a means of providing such instruction, inmates could be trained to tutor other inmates. A program of individualized tutoring is in effect at the Draper Youth Center in Alabama. One of the purposes of this educational program is to change the social climate of the entire institution. Inmates who perform well in their studies are enlisted in a service corps to help other inmates and to develop programs to meet the needs of the wards in the institution. College interns from Auburn University are enlisted to work with the inmates as tutors.[96]

The Robert F. Kennedy Youth Center located in Morgantown, West Virginia employed behavioral modification techniques in a pilot project identified as CASE to motivate the youths to learn. Inmates were given a choice of how they were to occupy themselves. If they demonstrated the proper accomplishments and desired behavior, they were paid in points, which were equivalent to money. Misbehavior or indifference resulted in a fine of a number of points. They could use points to pay "rent" for an individual sleeping cubicle if they preferred it to the regular space assigned to them. They could also use points to purchase better meals than were usually served and buy a large assortment of goods from a commissary. The program was felt to be successful in motivating inmates to progress in academic level achievement.[97]

The New York State Department of Correctional Services hopes to open a new state college at which all of the students will be prison inmates. This will be a fully accredited, two-year college for men and women inmates and will be the first of its kind in the country. Except for a few inmates performing supportive and maintenance services, all other inmates will be full-time students. The tentative name of the institution is the State University Community College at Bedford Hills. Prisoners who become students at the college will have sentences ranging from one year to life, and will be eligible to participate in the program regardless of the offense for which they were convicted. Students will not be charged tuition and will be able to earn an Associate Degree. They will be guaranteed the right to transfer their credits in the State University system upon their release.

Although vocational training is provided to some degree in juvenile institutions, it is lacking in most adult prisons. Where such programs are found, many are irrelevant to the needs of today's labor market and have little interest for the inmate. Many programs employ instructional equipment that is outdated and provide training that could never be used in the job market.

There appears to be one exception to the general complaint that vocational rehabilitation programs in prisons are of no value—the animal psychology program offered at the California Men's Colony (Chino). This program has been in effect since 1970, when it was suggested by inmate Bob Jeffries and won the approval of the authorities. Inmates enrolled in the course learn such things as dog grooming and bird training. According to Morton Feinman, consultant clinical psychologist at Chino, the dog grooming program develops a sense of artistic accomplishment. He also feels that the bird training course develops a love of creatures on the part of inmates and fosters feelings of tenderness and discipline. One inmate actually turned down parole in order to complete his studies in the bird training course, and he is in line for a job that will enable him to travel to Europe as a professional bird trainer. The authorities state that upon release there is 100-percent job placement, as the men do excellent work and there is a large demand for their talents. The enrollment in the animal psychology course is usually forty inmates. This program has been awarded a subsidy by the United States Department of Health, Education, and Welfare.[98]

Both short- and long-term programs are needed in vocational

training, as well as imaginative programs such as the one described above. Short-term programs could include subjects such as guides for survival once released and consumer education, covering such materials as how to apply for jobs, how to talk to people in a social situation, how to use the telephone properly, how to cook, how to purchase medications, how to budget money, how to order a meal, how to write a check, and how to fix simple appliances. Job-oriented short-term programs could be provided in such areas as building maintenance, hotel and food management, clerical and secretarial training, and working in a service station.

Long-range vocational training programs in such subjects as dental and optical training are also needed; and when the inmate goes to a community-based center or is paroled, means should be made available to help him continue in such long-range programs through contacts with community vocational training centers and governmental agencies concerned with vocational rehabilitation.

Academic programs and vocational training should be coordinated to prepare inmates to meet the requirements for enrolling in such trade-oriented subjects as airplane mechanics, computer programming, and electronics. These vocational programs require the reading of technical manuals and the ability to perform mathematical calculations.

The use of trade advisory committees is also important in a prison vocational training program. Such committees are usually appointed by the director of a state correctional system. They meet periodically throughout the year to assist in providing meaningful work for inmates, and they help parolees to complete training started in prison. Attempts should also be made through a public relations effort to encourage the bonding of inmates and to provide them with any licenses they may need to practice their trade.

Employment.   In the early years of American prison development, prisoners were subjected to hard labor at little or no wages for the purposes of degrading them and providing a profit for the state. One way to break the spirit of the inmate was to impose work as a form of punishment. Most of the early prison administrators were in sympathy with the Protestant work ethic—the belief that work is the prime mover in producing good moral character and a closeness to God—and they felt that hard labor would eventually bring spiritual and material rewards. The late John D. Rockefeller, who also believed this, once remarked, "God gave me my money."[99] During the days of the early prison industries, and especially during the period of the industrial prison (1930–1935), the major emphasis was on the output of inmates with little or no thought given to working conditions or rehabilitation. Every effort was made to exploit the prisoner for a profit, and concentration was placed on the manufacturing of a few products. Since work was used as a vehicle of punishment, it was felt that the inmate should engage in unpleasant and unskilled work at the lowest wages, consistent with the philosophy that "the condition of the criminal should not be superior to that of the worst paid non-criminal."[100]

Prisoners first were employed, in the early nineteenth century, under the contract system. This system was devised to help meet the demand for cheap labor. Under this system manufacturers contracted with states for the products made by prisoners. The prison was responsible for housing and disciplining the inmates; and the manufacturer supervised the inmates on the job, supplied the machinery and other materials, and marketed the finished product. This system was replaced by the piece-price system under which the prison authorities supervised the prisoner on the job and the manufacturer furnished the raw materials.

During much of the same period in which the contract system was in use, the lease system was also applied. "Under this system prisoners were removed from institutions to engage in work outside. The employer or lessor paid the state a designated sum for the services of the prisoners, and the lessor assumed the responsibility of housing, feeding, and clothing them. He had exclusive use of the prisoners during the time the lease was in effect. Many leased prisoners worked in railroad construction, mining camps, and lumbering."[101]

Prison industries probably reached their peak under the public account system, which replaced the contract and piece-price systems. Under this system the state functioned as the manufacturer and assumed the expenses involved in producing and marketing the prison-made goods. The industrial prison used this system to advantage until 1930, when labor and industry alike became alarmed that prison industries might be a competitive threat on the open market. As a result of this mythical threat, the Federal government passed the Hawes-Cooper Act of 1929, which deprived prison-made goods of their interstate character and put them under the jurisdiction of state laws. In 1935, the Ashurst-Summers Act was passed by Congress prohibiting the transportation of prison-made goods into states forbidding their entry and requiring the labeling of such goods shipped in interstate commerce. These two laws strangled the prison industries and led to what is now referred to as the state-use system.

The state-use system restricts the sale of prison-made goods to departments and institutions of the state and its political subdivisions. It was hoped that government agencies and institutions would provide at least a fair market for prison-made goods, but such was not to be the case. Due to the unavailability of efficient and skilled workers and to the lack of any genuine incentive to do a good job, prison-made goods were sometimes inferior to the goods produced by private industry. In addition to being of inferior quality, they carried the stigma of being made in prison. For reasons such as these, prison industries under the state-use system have become a small-scale industrial operation.

Correctional industries probably offer the greatest possibility for the realization of economic profit on the part of the prison system. These industries could also play a significant role in the vocational training and resocialization of inmates. Improvement must be made, however, in many areas. At present, lack of opportunities for promotion results in low morale, indifference, inferior work, and lack of self-respect. Prisoners must have an incentive to work, and adequate financial remuneration should be given to those who are qualified and cooperative. The old philosophy of promoting a caste system between the inmate and his keepers must be broken down to facilitate social mobility and provide opportunities for inmates to be promoted while on prison jobs.

Attempts are being made to secure wages for inmate workers comparable to those paid to workers on the outside. It is felt that prisons should be humanized by giving inmates definite wage standards for their work. Legislation has been introduced in Congress that would allow prisoners in federal institutions to work for private industry at union wages. Such legislation would make it possible for private concerns to set up work facilities within prisons and employ inmate volunteers. Senator Charles Percy (R.-Ill.), who introduced the legislation, states that participating employers would also be encouraged to provide job training, counseling, and basic education. He also feels that such a program would enable inmates to return to the free world with marketable job skills, steady work habits, and an accumulation of cash to help them along after their release.[102] Minnesota has already passed legislation allowing for free enterprise in the prisons by establishing private industries in the prisons themselves. Such industries are permitted to sell and make anything and are no longer limited to state-use.

In order to provide for an adequate physical plant, trained and qualified supervisors, up-to-date, safe machinery, individualized work supervision and training, and incentive wages, private industry is needed in prison along with an end to legislation which imposes the state-use system. No matter how efficient, prison industries would be no more of a threat to private industry than work release. Under private industry prisoners would have an adequate market for their finished products and would also receive training that could be transferred to the free market once they are released on parole. In order for the staff and inmate to assess the appropriateness of training for a particular skill, updated labor information should be continually available. Inmates should know current qualifications for membership in various labor and trade unions, current requirements for bonding qualification, and the degree of discrimination in trade unions on racial and ethnic grounds.

Labor unions are now being developed among prisoners. The first labor union in the United States composed exclusively of prisoners was formed in the Green Haven State Prison in Stormville, New York.[103] Although inmates do not have the right to strike, and matters concerning vacation time and sick leave are not relevant, bargaining can be important in matters concerning wages, working conditions, job training, and fringe benefits. At Green Haven inmates were seeking to increase their daily wages, which were between twenty-five and fifty cents. Legal difficulties are involved in forming a prisoners' union. The authorities claim that it is illegal, and some labor lawyers feel that, since inmates work, they are entitled to collective bargaining rights under certain laws. It appears that the legitimacy of prisoners' unions will have to be determined in the courts.

Inmate self-government.   Although the trusty system now in effect in many jails and prisons throughout the United States cannot be called self-government in any sense, it did pave the way for the belief that inmates could be trusted to demonstrate some degree of responsibility. The trusty system probably originated in the Wethersfield, Connecticut prison in 1835, where Warden Amos Pilsbury developed a system of allowing certain inmates to go unguarded into the nearby town on errands. This practice eventually developed into the trusty system enabling inmates with records of good behavior to assume certain privileges and responsibilities.[104] Crude forms of self-government were found in the early Houses of Refuge in Boston and New York City. Children were promoted to various status grades through good behavior and were permitted to hold office and vote. In 1885, Warden Hiram Hatch of the Michigan Penitentiary at Jackson initiated what may be called the real forerunner of inmate self-government. He referred to this type of self-government as "The Mutual Aid League."[105] Although his experiment was short-lived it anticipated the famous experiment with inmate self-government devised by Thomas Mott Osborne in Auburn and Sing Sing prisons.

Thomas Mott Osborne became convinced that it was possible to rehabilitate inmates by entrusting them with various degrees of responsibility in the form of self-government. He felt that if inmates were allowed to participate in the duties and responsibilities of citizenship while in prison, they would be able to lead responsible lives in the free world. He started "The Mutual Welfare League" at Auburn, and then introduced it at Sing Sing and at the Naval Prison at Portsmouth, New Hampshire. Every inmate was eligible for membership in the League. Infractions of discipline were dealt with by a judiciary board consisting of five judges chosen by the delegates. An appeal from the board's decision was placed in the hands of the inmates and no guards were allowed to enter. Every aspect of institutional life was supervised by permanent standing committees. The foundation of a system of token money was set forth, but Osborne left the prison before it could be made operational. An employment bureau was set up by league members, and outdoor recreation, lecturers, and entertainment were provided.[106] Osborne described the League as a prison system not imposed arbitrarily by the prison authorities, but requested by the prisoners themselves. Osborne believed that the administration should have no control over the League's elections.

Osborne's system of self-government did not last. Prison authorities and the newspapers called it a form of coddling, and it had many inherent weaknesses as well. One major weakness of the system was that it applied to the nonreformable as well as to the reformable inmate. It is now felt that nonreformable inmates should be housed in a separate institution under the supervision of prison officials. Self-government appears to work best when limited to more reformable types. Some authorities in the field feel that even reformable types should go through a period of observation and supervision before becoming leaders in the self-government system.[107] Another weakness of the system was that some inmates used important offices for personal advantage and manipulated both the administration and their fellow prisoners.

Another famous system of self-government was established in the Norfolk Penal Colony in Massachusetts in 1927, under Superintendent Howard B. Gill. He established cooperative self-government as a practical means of helping to control escapes and contraband. The power of the government was later extended to having a voice in the nature of prison programs. It differed from Osborn's system in that it included all staff members of the institution except for the guards and watch officers. Committees were created to deal with different phases of inmate life, and each committee represented the inmates and the administration. Joint responsibility was the main theme of the plan. Inmates and staff worked together toward common goals. Since the staff was an integral part of the institutional government, the system was not dependent on the stability and honesty of an outstanding inmate leader as was Osborne's system. However, Gill was also criticized by the public press and was finally forced to leave and disband the experiment.[108]

Although self-government has never existed in prisons generally to the extent it did under Osborne and Gill, the concept of self-government is still alive in the form of inmate advisory councils in many of our contemporary correctional institutions. Such councils serve as a liaison between the administration and the inmate population. The primary purpose of advisory councils is not to have a role in the actual policy making of the institution, but to function in a manner providing for meaningful communications between the administration and the prisoners. Many inmates have expressed dissatisfaction with advisory groups because of their lack of actual power and because recommendations by such groups have been continually ignored by prison administrators. In 1970, in an attempt to obtain more decision-making power, the prisoners of the Washington State Penitentiary at Walla Walla formed a Resident Government Council (RGC) to replace their advisory council. Out of the Resident Government Council came numerous proposals and position papers. Some changes in the operation of the prison resulted from these efforts, but no single decision dealing with prison management has been made by the Council. Although the Resident Government Council has a broader influence in the institution than did the Inmate Advisory Group, it has never actually functioned as a governing body. There is hope, however, on the part of the inmates that the Council will begin to function as originally intended.[109]

Many superintendents and wardens want no part of inmate self-government because they feel that it has failed as a treatment device. Some of the wardens who reject self-government argue that agressive inmate types usually get elected to inmate councils and attempt to use their positions for personal gain. Others who reject inmate self-government feel that prisoners should not be permitted to give advice regarding the operation of institutions and should never be placed in positions over other inmates. Some wardens would be amenable to the advisory council concept, but only if such councils function in an advisory capacity and are not designed to assist in running the institution.[110]

Arguments in favor of inmate self-government center around the beliefs that an inmate can never be rehabilitated and act as a responsible citizen in the free community unless he is given responsibility within the prison itself, and that he must be able to make important decisions within the prison system if he is to live a responsible life on the outside, where he must make important decisions concerning himself and others in order to survive. It does not appear that the possibilities of inmate self-government as a rehabilitative force have been adequately tested in the prisons of the United States.

Sol Chaneles has advanced a novel idea for introducing self-government into the correctional system and providing inmates with the maximum degree of responsibility that is possible away from the free community. In an article proposing the substitution of rural communities for prisons,[111] Chaneles suggests that we find a way to get lawbreakers out of prisons and out of the cities and place them in communities where they can learn skills. In such communities, states Chaneles, prisoners would learn to handle free choice among realistic alternatives. In our present prison system the inmate has little responsibility and cannot exercise free choice. Chaneles believes that his proposed communities could serve as transitional communities or permanent settlements. He feels that the simplest and most practical way to establish transitional communities would be to convert some existing prisons into factories, schools, hospitals, and meeting places. In the vicinity of the converted prisons, houses, shops, and other community facilities could be built. In such communities the state, county, and township in which the community is located would provide services such as water, sewage, protective services, and recreation. The members of the community would exercise their own self-government. The prisons would provide the economic base for the townspeople, most of whom would be employed in the prison. Merging the prison with these communities, permitting the inmates to live outside the walls, and encouraging the expansion of industrial activity would, according to Chaneles, provide inmates with incentives to change their lives and help prison towns to grow economically.

Chaneles believes that self-governing transitional communities would eventually lead to the abolition of all laws that place unreasonable restrictions on the freedom of people who have been convicted of crimes. He also feels that transitional communities would eliminate many of the known causes of crime and delinquency by preventing a crowded physical environment, facilitating home ownership, providing stable and meaningful employment, and offering a sense of growth. He feels that crime in America is basically a problem of city life and that the solution is to get lawbreakers out of the city and out of the prisons which breed further crime.

MAINTENANCE FUNCTIONS

Maintenance in correctional institutions involves the use of inmate labor in activities relating to the care of prisoners and upkeep of the institution properties. Maintenance includes the preparation and serving of food; mechanical services (operation of power plants, refrigeration equipment, automotive repair shop); maintenance and repair of the institution's physical plant; storekeeping (receiving, storing, and issuing supplies, commissary operations); work in medical and dental departments (nurses, orderlies, and aides in laboratories); maintenance of grounds and gardens; and other tasks such as clerical work of a routine and nonconfidential nature, library work, and laundering and dry cleaning.[112] In the past many of the above-mentioned types of employment have been monotonous, dead-end jobs paying little or nothing in wages and providing the inmate with little training that could be transferred to the outside employment market. Where there is a poverty of counseling, educational, and work programs in an institution, inmates are assigned maintenance duties in abundance so that overloading of job assignments occurs. Many times four or five inmates are assigned a task that could be adequately accomplished by one or two of them. This practice is sometimes defended on the grounds that it is better for an inmate to have some type of work assignment than to serve his time in complete idleness. Such overloading of maintenance work assignments, however, leads to inferior job performance, waste and theft of materials, increasing loafing on the job, and a lowering of morale of inmates and staff, and it is detrimental to the emotional health of the inmate and to the security of the institution.[113]

Maintenance jobs should not be regarded as catchalls. Assignments to work of this nature should be made with care on the basis of recommendations made during the classification process. Maintenance programs should be coordinated with other phases of the institutional treatment program such as education and vocational training. There should also be continued institutional maintenance upgrading, i.e., industrial tasks such as floor polishing and electric and plumbing repair should be updated as much as possible to provide the inmate with job knowledge that can be transferred to the labor market. Training programs should be developed within the institution for such positions as job superintendent and food service supervisor, making maintenance tasks a part of the vocational training program.

RESULTS OF FRAGMENTATION AND ATTEMPTS AT MANAGEMENT

It might be said that the prison is destined to fail in most cases because it is asked to perform impossible tasks. We have already mentioned that it must perform activities of change and order such as custody, treatment, and maintenance, all of which appear in some respects to be incompatible with one another. Although these functions are not necessarily incompatible, the large institutions of today and the lack of administrative innovation leads to the fragmentation of the various tasks that the prison must perform. The results of this fragmentation make an overall treatment plan for any one inmate impossible. It also leads to divisions among staff members resulting in friction, hostility, misconceptions, and suspicions. Seldom do the members of the treatment and custody staffs communicate on anything but a superficial level, and, in many instances, the treatment staff itself is divided among those participating in counseling, vocational training, and academic education.

To add to the evils of fragmentation, the administrative staff in many instances remains aloof from other staff and fails to communicate to the staff as a whole a general policy governing what is expected of them and how the institution should operate. It is not uncommon for prison administrators to be unclear about what the general philosophy governing the institution is or should be, resulting in vague and conflicting goal expectations. This can cause anxiety in the staff, as the work behavior of employees is related to the harmony or conflict of their operational objectives with their personal goals. If the operational objectives are unclear and no attempt is made to see that they are harmonized with the worker's personal goals, conflicts arise, motivation is low, and job efficiency decreases.

Probably the most apparent conflict resulting from fragmentation is that between custodial and professional personnel. According to Charles McKendrick, professional staff members fail to see that the totalitarian structure of the prison community both limits and poses a challenge to professional services. The custodial and administrative personnel, on the other hand, fail to recognize the limitations placed on the professional staff by the totalitarian environment and expect the therapist to be successful despite the restrictions of the prison community. McKendrick further states that professional personnel fail to accommodate their techniques to the prison community, and custodial and administrative personnel fail to make the changes necessary for the full inclusion of rehabilitative programs.[114]

To make the dichotomy between custody and treatment personnel more pronounced, McKendrick states that professionally trained employees often underestimate the intelligence of custodial employees, who usually have less formal education; and custodial employees, in turn, often look upon the professional employee with suspicion.

According to Sykes, prison managers face impossible and inconsistent tasks.[115] One of these tasks is to provide custody. He must provide internal control and prevent escapes. Escape, especially from a maximum security institution, will arouse public opinion. One escape can destroy an administrator's position. As long as public opinion remains as it is today, custody will be of prime importance. The manager may realize that the unbalanced stress on custody hinders treatment and rehabilitation but feel unable to relax security measures. Along with preventing escapes the prison manager must preserve internal order. As we have already learned, this is difficult in prison, because the prison setting itself creates strong pressures toward behavior that would be deemed criminal and rebellious in the free community. With the advent of prisoner awareness the task of maintaining order becomes even more problematic.

Another task of the prison manager is that of prison self-maintenance and the duty of providing work for the inmates. However, this gives the prisoner freedom of movement and access to tools and machines that he can use for the purpose of engaging in assaults and escape. Also, it is very difficult to get the prisoner to work well when there is no motivation for him to do so. The prison administrator, then, has the responsibility of providing programs for reform in the atmosphere of a prison where the social order, fragmentation, and public expectations are not designed or geared for rehabilitation. Faced with the inconsistency of their tasks, many prison administrators remain indifferent to the treatment function of the prison, and their allegiance to the goal of rehabilitation tends to remain largely at the verbal level.

MOVES TOWARD INTEGRATION

There are trends in the correctional field to reduce fragmentation in institutions. Efforts have been made in the direction of establishing a more collaborative type of institution in which all staff members and inmates participate in the process of rehabilitation. Attempts are being made to reduce the sharp distinctions that now characterize prison employees and orient them all toward the common goal of treatment. Although the custodial officer's prime concern will be control and security for some time to come, steps are being taken to make him a meaningful part of a treatment team. The involvement of custodial workers on treatment teams enables them to feel that they have some input in an inmate's treatment program and thereby helps to reduce the psychological distance between them and the professional staff. Professional staff members, especially in juvenile institutions, are also being encouraged to participate in custodial activities enabling them to share in decisions concerning inmate and ward management. In juvenile institutions, for example, social workers are being moved into cottages so that they can share with the cottage parents the problems experienced by the residents. In this way, members of the professional staff also become better acquainted with the residents and can communicate with them on a more meaningful level.

Involving custodial personnel in group counseling with inmates also helps to break down some of the communication barriers isolating these two groups. Shared decision making on the part of both staff and inmates is being attempted, with a more serious revival of self-government and inmate advisory councils. Perhaps inmate self-government will never be very successful in contributing to the efficiency of institutional management, but it does have the advantage of bringing inmates and staff into collaborative interaction.

Further attempts are being made to develop a reception, planning, and release system which is closely tied together and serves as a complete delivery system, encouraging inmate participation in the development of individual programs and providing an appellate device by which an inmate can appeal a given program or program change. As mentioned earlier, reception teams consisting of treatment personnel, custodial staff, and inmates are being considered by some states for use in diagnostic centers. The purpose of this approach would be to provide for a collaborative effort in the establishment of a treatment program, taking into consideration not only the institutional needs of the offender, but his postinstitutional needs as well.

THE FUTURE OF PRISONS

The reduction of prison populations and decentralization

In the future, noninstitutional means will be used increasingly in processing those convicted of crimes. During the past fifteen years there has been much progress in overcoming stereotyped prison traditions through such strategies as work and educational release, community treatment centers, halfway houses, and extended prison furloughs. There is little doubt that the direction corrections is taking is toward the decentralized treatment of offenders in the community. Attempts are being made to keep offenders who are not dangerous out of traditional prisons by placing them on probation or in community-based programs. Means other than incarceration will be used in disposing of offenders convicted of "victimless crimes," political crimes (such as draft evasion), and conventional crimes of a nondangerous nature. For example, there will be a continual diversion from the criminal system of those who are convicted of "victimless crimes" involving alcoholism, narcotic addiction, prostitution, and compulsive gambling, because of the belief that individuals convicted of such offenses do not benefit in any way from incarceration in jails and prisons. Such individuals can be handled independently of imprisonment by the strategy of preadjudicative diversion. A pretrial intervention program is presently in operation in Dade County, Florida which provides for the supervision of those individuals subjected to the pre-adjudicative process.[116] There will also be an expansion of the use of such dispositional strategies as the imposition of fines, restitution, supervised and summary probation, and quasi-incarceration in such local establishments as boarding houses and small community correctional centers.

Most offenders fail to benefit from incarceration in the traditional type of prison and can be treated more effectively in the communities in which they reside. Local communities will become more and more responsible for the treatment and supervision of their residents. As large numbers of offenders are diverted from the traditional prisons, the fort-like prison will eventually become a thing of the past, since its continued operation would be highly unrealistic.

For those needing confinement in something other than an open community center, new prisons will gradually be constructed to house 200 or fewer inmates, but under unique conditions. Facilities will resemble normal residences and will include: separate rooms with modern security devices (no cells or bars); recreation facilities for all types of sports and hobbies; educational facilities with full access to educational services; work opportunities within the prison compound, preferably directed and managed by private industry, that are economically and socially viable; devices for inmate self-government; slf-supporting services such as a post exchange; and an integrated staff system exercising the team concept with ex-offenders making up part of the staff. Research will also be a primary function of prisons of the future. Since these facilities will be near communities, the staffs of colleges and universities will be able to assist in research projects and students will be able to use the prison as research laboratories.

According to Daniel Glaser, there will be many institutions of diverse custody levels, mostly within metropolitan areas. Because prisons will be small, there will be less emphasis on regimentation and more attempts at establishing personal relationships between staff members and inmates. A program of graduated release will be emphasized to give inmates the opportunity to solve their social and economic problems and to enable the prison staff to observe inmate behavior in the community for the purposes of determining good and bad risks for release on parole.[117]

Attempts have been made by certain states to close some of their existing institutions. In Massachusetts, juvenile training schools were phased out by the Department of Youth Services under the direction of Dr. Jerome Miller. Recommendations have also been made by study commissions and task force groups in states such as California and Wisconsin for the closing of many penal institutions. However, despite the fact that authorities in the field of corrections are advocating small, community-centered prisons, the Federal Bureau of Prisons has a ten-year plan that stipulates the building of three new correctional centers for youthful offenders in California; and the State of Ohio has recently opened a new maximum security institution at Lucasville, replacing the Ohio Penitentiary in Columbus, at a cost to the Ohio taxpayers exceeding $30,000,000.

The call for the maxi-max

Some correctional personnel are advocating the revival of what Barnes and Teeters referred to as the "treat 'em rough" school of penology. Alcatraz was an example of the maxi-max type of institution (super maximum security) built to house the "hopeless" criminal.[118] Alcatraz was created to be both a super-security institution and, at the same time, a scientific prison attempting to combine the complete isolation of dangerous criminals with as much humane treatment as possible.[119] Although no longer used as a prison, Alcatraz still stands as a monument to the philosophy that certain criminals can never be reformed and must be forever segregated from society under the most secure and repressive of conditions. Once Alcatraz was created, it was difficult for correctional officials to eliminate it and to admit that the super-maximum prison was not altogether a success. Alcatraz is a symbol of everything nonprogressive about penology, but the temptation persists to try a similar experiment under modified conditions. If constructed such prisons will, without doubt, become another dumping ground for problem inmates.

The maxi-max is already with us in the form of the adjustment center like the one at San Quentin Prison, where "problem" and "political" inmates such as the late George Jackson are housed under the most controlled of conditions. Adjustment centers are actually prisons within a prison, where super-maximum security is attempted with little or no regard to treatment or humane living conditions. Once confined to an adjustment center for disciplinary reasons, it is difficult for the inmate to regain his normal prison status. The very atmosphere of such centers promotes feelings of frustration, hostility, hopelessness, and psychic pain, leading to personality disturbances and to overt behavior that is diagnosed as unpredictable and dangerous. Further, once the system labels someone as dangerous, he is likely to live up to expectations. Some prisoners remain in such centers for most of their prison sentence. If and when such men are ever released, society can only expect the worst, and perhaps rightfully so.

The call for the maxi-max is partially a result of the prisoner awareness movement which threatens prison administrators and leads them to contemplate drastic solutions. Of course, there is some justification for wanting to isolate the dangerous prisoner from the remainder of the inmate population, so that custody and control measures can be relaxed for the majority of the inmate population. One danger of such a strategy is that means are not readily available at present for predicting who the dangerous inmate might be among others found in prison. The diagnosis of "dangerous" could be loosely applied to any inmate for a variety of reasons. There is little doubt, therefore, that the maxi-max will come to house inmates who do not meet the definition of dangerous offenders specified by the Model Sentencing Act, i.e., a dangerous offender is one who has committed a serious crime against a person and shows behavior of persistent assaultiveness based on serious mental disturbances or is an offender who is deeply involved in organized crime.[120] According to the Board of Directors of the National Council on Crime and Delinquency, the building of super-maximum security institutions would probably hinder the correctional progress by "intensifying the commingling of the small number of dangerous persons with nondangerous persons who then appear to be or become dangerous because of their maximum security environment."[121] Even if we could make accurate predictions as to which inmates are dangerous and nondangerous and be assured that the two groups would never be allowed to interact in a correctional setting, would the maxi-max type of institution still be desirable or serve any rehabilitative purpose? Do we need another Alcatraz and a reinstated allegiance to the concept of the "hopeless" criminal? It appears that even dangerous inmates could be handled by a more imaginative type of penal strategy that would allow for their possible growth and rehabilitation under secure conditions.

Radicalization of inmates

The prison has always been a place of violence, but reports indicate that there has been more violence within the prison during the past fifteen years than at any other time since the Reconstruction.[122] Recently the targets for violence have shifted to a large degree from the inmate to the staff. For example, eight staff members were murdered in the California prison system between January 1, 1970 and September 2, 1971. This was double the number murdered during the preceding seventeen years.[123]

Perhaps one reason for the increase in violence in the prisons of many states such as California is that many offenders who would formerly have been sentenced to prison are now receiving other types of sentences such as probation. As more nondangerous offenders are treated apart from prisons, the prison staff will have to find means of effectively managing and treating the hard-core and more rebellious inmate.

Some correctional administrators feel that the increase in violence is the result of recent court litigation compelling a de-emphasis on custody and control and providing the inmate with more individual rights. But it seems that the increase in prison violence cannot be effectively explained by the relaxation of custody and control, nor by the tendency to keep minor and nondangerous offenders under local supervision in the community. The trend toward a more violent society is prevalent in many areas. The wave of murders and kidnappings outside prisons indicates a growing discontent among the poor and minority groups, who feel that they have been cheated by society. Perhaps the aggressiveness of minority groups during the past few years can be traced to the frustration of expectations aroused by the great judicial and legislative victories of the civil rights movement. For these reasons and many others, minority groups have come to feel that there is no effective alternative to violence as a means of achieving what they want and moving the system. These frustrations are now being reflected in alienation and hostility toward the criminal justice system and the white society that controls it. The rallying cries resulting from such frustrations are such slogans as "Black Power" and "Power to the People." The failure of the law to bring equality to blacks has brought about a new mood, especially among the young blacks. Through such movements as the Black Muslims and the Black Panthers, self-esteem and enhanced racial pride are replacing apathy and submission to the system. As a result of this new found racial pride and ethnic awareness, riots and civil disturbances have taken place, not only in prisons, but in the streets of our cities as well.

Many minority group members feel that there is a double standard of justice in the United States and are especially resentful of the way in which they have been treated by law enforcement officers. For example, in almost every case where there was a riot in the summer of 1967, it was sparked by an act of police harrassment or police brutality. Attitudes toward the police as authority figures formed while young will carry over to other authority figures in the criminal justice system such as judges, probation officers, correctional officers, and correctional administrators. Such attitudes on the part of aggressive and determined inmates make the control of our temporary prisons a difficult, if not a hopeless task. Many blacks feel that they have always been oppressed by society and the establishment which controls it, and they feel that being sent to serve time in prison is the ultimate form of oppression. They see prisons, as they see all other aspects of American society, as dominated by white managers, white educational systems, white communication systems, and white law.[124]

This new radicalization among inmates has led to activities referred to by prison officials as revolutionary in nature. Unnecessary violence in prisons is said to be the tactic of the revolutionary inmate who is seeking to destroy the establishment. Prison officials tend to blame such radicalization on Maoist and Marxist literature smuggled into prisons and on such organizations as the Black Muslims and Black Panthers. Prison officials fail to realize that the radicalization of prisoners is the result of the way they have been treated both in and outside prison throughout their lifetime. A political awakening is not surprising in the least; the only remarkable thing about it is that it took so long to emerge. Keeping radical and revolutionary literature out of the prison isn't going to change matters significantly, nor is the further repression of inmates by placing them in adjustment centers or building maxi-max institutions for their incarceration.

It appears that prisoners of the new breed are here to stay and we must cope with this fact. Prisoners are no longer going to internalize their hostility, resulting in a syndrome of self-destruction, nor are they going to revive the traditional practice of directing all of it toward their fellow sufferers. The question remains whether it is possible to have prisons when neither the inmates nor the staff has any further confidence in their legitimacy. The lessons of the great riot at Attica indicated that prisons cannot be administered when they are no longer believed in and when the prisoners themselves withhold their compliance. There is always the possibility of more major riots. A more efficient guard staff may be able to prevent inmates from breaking out of prison, but it cannot stop them from taking over control. The question now appears to be "Can prisons survive the radicalization of inmates?"

Law as a lever of change

All of the riots experienced by prisons throughout their history did not accomplish the radical changes that have been obtained through recent laws governing prison administration and treatment. It has been a traditional practice for correctional officials to exercise almost a complete autonomy over the institutions they managed, making prisons in every respect similar to a totalitarian society. The power granted prison officials over the lives of the men they govern is inconsistent with our entire system of government. A great deal of discretion has always been left to prison officials to define the conditions of imprisonment. The courts' hands-off policy prevailed in regard to prison litigation until the 1960s. One major reason why the courts did not consider questions pertaining to the constitutional rights of prisoners was the belief that incarceration was considered to be a quasi-utopian movement during its early beginnings, and it did not occur to the founders of the prison system that such institutions might be administering cruel and unusual punishment.[125] The belief was that prison administrators were healers of the sick (the medical model concept of the causes of crime) and that they should be given time, without outside interference, to effect cures for their charges. Another reason why the courts ignored the plight of prisoners for so many years was the belief that inmates were dangerous individuals who should forfeit all rights upon imprisonment.

During the 1960s, the course of the courts and the hands-off doctrine gradually became modified. According to Rothman, Black Muslim agitation resulted in the first break in the hands-off doctrine.[126] Rothman states that in 1961, on their own initiative and assisted only by court-appointed counsel, the Muslims submitted writs demanding freedom to practice their religion.[127] This was the start of prison radicalization in regard to the approach of inmates to the courts. The docile inmates of the past never pressed their grievances in the courts to any degree nor compelled the courts to observe the prison at first hand. Later prisoners began to request relief from cruel and unusual punishment. Complaints were made concerning whipping in the prisons in Arkansas, and writs were submitted concerning the archaic conditions in the isolation cells of the California and New York prison systems. Activist lawyers, for a variety of reasons, not all altruistic, gradually took up the cause of the inmates and began to represent them in the courts. At the present time the suits filed in both state and federal courts number in the thousands. Suits range all the way from seeking monetary damages to challenges of the legality of the penitentiary system itself. Cases are too numerous to cite, but suffice it to say that through the lever of the law much change has taken place in the correctional system, resulting in the extension of inmate privileges and rights in the areas of correspondence, visitation, medical treatment, availability of law books, religious freedom, protection from cruel and unusual punishment, rights to tort action against prison officials for negligence, the right to vote, elimination of racial discrimination and segregation, and the right to have protection from assault by other inmates.

In certain cases judges have ruled entire prison systems to be unconstitutional. For example, in February 1970 Judge J. Smith Henley declared the Arkansas prison to be in violation of the U.S. Constitution, and on April 7, 1972 a three-judge panel ruled that the entire Philadelphia prison system violated prisoners' constitutional rights. As a result of court decisions proclaiming the rights of prisoners, the National Council on Crime and Delinquency adopted the Model Act for the Protection of Rights of Prisoners, commonly referred to as the Prisoner's Bill of Rights. In 1972 the United States Department of Justice created a new unit to deal with civil rights violations in prison and other institutions.

There has been some concern that correctional staff members and administrators will not be able to withstand the pressure brought about by protracted litigation. Some correctional officials worry about facing monetary suits amounting to millions of dollars. There are also complaints that the prison staff members will eventually have to spend the bulk of their time preparing for litigation rather than working with inmates toward rehabilitation. David Rothman fears that through litigation, prisoners might win the battle but lose the war. Litigation by aggressive attorneys, leading to the haphazard release of prisoners to the community or halfway houses, may have a negative effect on both the inmate and society. Rothman cites incidents of poor management in certain community treatment centers where "some keepers, it seems, are giving their charges breakfast and then locking them in all day; others are feeding them breakfast and locking them out all day."[128] Rothman worries that an accumulation of such tactics on the part of community correctional directors will possibly result in the consolidation of the centers into a central system where all the residents will be placed under one roof and managed by one administrator. This, of course, would be the revival of the prison all over again.

It is difficult to assess the value of the law as a means of producing prison change and bringing about a more humane and rehabilitative prison system. Judicial decisions alone seldom bring about large-scale reforms, but they do lead to administrative changes. Has correctional litigation encouraged or retarded administrative reform? Means should be taken to evaluate what has actually been accomplished by legal strategies.

EVALUATION OF PRISONS

Prison goals

The prison presents a parodox, since it is an institution with goals that appear to be irreconcilable. One of the goals of the prison is to reform and rehabilitate the inmates under its control. The rhetoric of reform is not new; there have been prison reformers for at least 100 years. There are many theories of reform, and each theory attracts a group of followers who project distant goals but forget to look back at the original problem.[129] The terms "reform" and "rehabilitation" are vague and mean different things to different people. When a prison administrator tells you that his major objective is the reform of inmates, he may refer to many activities ranging from painting the walls of cells to allowing a meaningful program of inmate self-government. To state that one goal of the prison is to reform is to project a highly ambiguous concept that can hardly be tested as to whether it is ever realized in practice. The major purpose of reform appears to be to alter the attitudes and behavior of inmates to the degree that they no longer commit criminal offenses once released to the free community.

A second goal of the prison is to provide retribution or punishment. Society feels that prisons should not be comfortable places enabling inmates to enjoy similar privileges that he would find on the outside. The principle of "less eligibility" as a guiding force in prison management is still probably more prevalent than one would like to believe, despite the reform rhetoric of many contemporary correctional policy statements. According to the principle of "less eligibility" the conditions of the convicted criminal should not be better than those of any other group in the community. Although the new penology has been instrumental in abolishing corporal punishment in prisons, the contemporary prison is still dominated largely by the philosophy of the past, pledging allegiance to what Barnes and Teeters refer to as "the convict bogey and jailing psychosis."[130] The general public and legislative officials have not really changed their views on incarceration since the days of the "treat-'em-rough" school of penology. They react to prison riots today largely as they did in the past and perceive the prison guard as playing the same role he did fifty years ago. There is little doubt that punishment is still thought to be a legitimate goal of the prison by the public at large and that such a goal has a submerged appeal to many correctional officials as well, in spite of the literature in professional journals advocating new methods of treatment.

A third goal of the prison is that of the protection of society from individuals who commit crimes. One way to protect a society from criminals is to isolate them from the community and lock them up in physical plants having the necessary security devices to insure that they do not escape and commit new crimes in the free world. Rehabilitation programs must be molded to fit the security requirements of the institution. Not only is the prison supposed to protect society by preventing escapes; it must also alter inmate attitudes and behavioral patterns so as to deter them from repeating crimes. After release, inmates supposedly will not return to prison but will lead law-abiding lives. Not only is the prison expected to deter the inmates already within its grasp; it is also expected that the very existence of such institutions should deter the normal citizen from indulging in criminal activity. By reforming its prisoners and deterring the general public from committing crimes, the prison has the implied goal of reducing crime rates.

Finally, the fourth goal of the prison is to provide for internal control within the prison itself. Riots are not tolerated by the public or by government officials. Matters of control have priority over matters of rehabilitation and treatment. Probably the maintenance of a smooth-running prison is the most important prison goal next to providing for the protection of society.

The above goals of reform, retribution, deterrence, control, and the protection of society from criminal and crime are supposed to be effectively realized through the institution of the prison. Since these various tasks appear to conflict in theory, one can speculate as to whether they can ever be made operational in practice.

Prison practice

It is the consensus among authorities in the field of corrections that the prison is an unqualified failure as an instrument for rehabilitation and for the protection of society. Robert Martinson, for example, says that he examined over 200 treatment programs in American prisons and that he was unable to find any evidence that a single one of them in any way reduced the recidivism of inmates subjected to their treatment.[131]

In regard to rehabilitation, studies indicate that the counseling and educational strategies presently being employed in American prisons make little difference in the inmate's behavior upon release. For example, after a three-year period adult inmates in the Washington State Penitentiary who had vocational training did no better on parole than those who did not participate in the program. Evaluative studies performed in both California and Wisconsin indicated that vocational training does not have any particular capability of reducing recidivism.[132] Daniel Glaser's study of men released from federal prisons found that those who had been exposed to education programs did worse on parole than those who had not.[133] A study from Milwaukee showed no rehabilitative effect resulting from a four-month program for jailed women consisting of education, grooming, child care, vocational guidance, and group counseling.

Types of institutions in which inmates are housed also seem to make no difference in regard to reform and recidivism. A California study concerning deterrence states that the most careful analyses of recidivism statistics for California, New York, and other large states showed no significant difference in recidivism rates in relation to the type of institution housing inmates whether they be of the maximum, medium, or minimum security types.

All treatment strategies used in prisons today have as their goal the reform of the criminal and the reduction of recidivism. An over-all evaluation of these programs indicates that the choice of one alternative disposition within the criminal justice system over another seems to make little difference as far as its effects on the inmate's rehabilitation are concerned. Most reports on treatment and rehabilitation experiments show no significant difference in outcome between treated groups and control groups. Those that do report some positive effects generally report small effects. In fact, some authorities in the correctional field feel that, instead of being rehabilitative, all correctional treatment programs are harmful and are increasing rather than decreasing the probability of re-cidivism.[134] The mythology surrounding the value of current treatment methods in the field of corrections is becoming more apparent. It appears that the prisons of America are not realizing their goal of reforming the criminal and reducing the crime rate.

Those members of the criminal justice system who call for more severe treatment in the belief that such treatment will deter also seem to be under a misconception. Inmates treated leniently seem to do no worse, and sometimes appear to do better, than those treated severely. Conversely, those reformers who believe that the more treatment-oriented the prison experience, the greater the chances for reform, are also mistaken. More lenient alternatives do not seem to reduce crime rates. It can be argued that since lenient methods of treatment seem to work as well as severe methods of repression, we ought to apply the lenient methods because they are cheaper and more humanistic.

In the section of this chapter on the radicalization of inmates, we learned that because of the phenomenon of prisoner awareness, the prison is no longer able to provide effective internal control over its subjects. The new breed of inmate threatens the existence of the entire prison as it exists today. No prison can maintain internal control without obtaining the explicit consent of the inmates to be controlled. Such consent is becoming harder and harder to obtain.

Perhaps the only goal the prison is successful in accomplishing is that of retribution. By being placed in prison, individuals are punished, if not physically, at least psychologically. The suffering of prisoners satisfies the emotional needs of many of the public, who seem to need a scapegoat for their own inadequacies and misdeeds. If punishment *per se* is the only demand the public makes on our prison system, then its objective is being realized. It is legitimate to ask whether or not the public would tolerate a prison system that refrains from making punishment one of its goals.

There is little relationship between institutional goals and practices. What prison officials say they do, therefore, is seldom what they do in reality. Although this is partially the result of their lack of genuine belief in the philosophy of reform, it is also, to a large degree, the result of the impossible task of achieving goals that cannot possibly be made operational because of their conflicting nature. Because of these conflicting goal expectations most prison administrators pay lip service to both treatment and punishment but in practice abandon almost all conditions conducive to effective treatment.[135]

NOTES

1. The universal application of institutionalization as a method of reform in the early nineteenth century American colonies was presented by David J. Rothman in a lecture at the *Workshop for Correctional Educators in Colleges and Universities*, Institute on Man and Science, Rensselaerville, New York, August 1–16, 1973. These ideas are also set forth in his book, *The Discovery of the Asylum: Social Order and Disorder in the New Republic* (Boston and Toronto: Little, Brown, 1971), pp. 13–20.

2. For a complete and interesting discussion of classical criminology and the positivist revolution the reader should consult Ian Taylor, Paul Walton, and Jock Young, *The New Criminology: For a Social Theory of Deviance* (London and Boston: Routledge and Kegan Paul, 1973), pp. 1–30.

3. Cesare Baccaria, *Trattato dei delitti e delle pene (Essay on Crimes and Punishments)*, published in 1764.

4. See Harry Elmer Barnes and Negley K. Teeters, *New Horizons in Criminology*, 2nd ed. (Englewood Cliffs, N.J.: Prentice-Hall, 1955), p. 343.

5. See Harry E. Barnes, *The Story of Punishment*, 2nd ed. (Montclair, N.J.: Patterson Smith, 1972), pp. 60–61.

6. Barnes and Teeters, note 4, supra, p. 345.

7. For an excellent summary of the history of transportation as practiced by European countries see Barnes, note 5, supra, pp. 68–92. For a realistic description of life in the penal colony of French Guiana see René Belbenoit, *Dry Guillotine* (New York: E. P. Dutton, 1938, or Bantam Books, 1971).

8. Rothman, lecture, note 1, supra.

9. Arthur Koestler, *Reflections on a Hanging* (New York: Macmillan, 1957), p. 7.

10. For a general discussion of the death penalty during American colonial times see Hugo A. Bedau, ed., *The Death Penalty in America: An Anthology* (Garden City, N.Y.: Anchor Books, Doubleday, 1964), pp. 1–32.

11. Furman v. Georgia, 408 U.S. 238 (1972).

12. A brief description of the work of John Howard can be found in Barnes and Teeters, note 4, supra, pp. 385–387; and in Barnes, note 5, supra, pp. 122–123.

13. For a more thorough explanation of the workhouse movement refer to Blake McKelvey, *American Prisons: A Study of American Social History Prior to 1915* (Montclair, N.J.: Patterson Smith, 1972), pp. 3–5; see also Barnes and Teeters, note 4, supra, pp. 382–385.

14. A more detailed description of Dr. Rush's accomplishments can be found in Barnes and Teeters, note 4, supra, pp. 390–391; Barnes, note 5, supra, p. 123; and Blake McKelvey, note 13, supra, p. 5.

15. See Barnes and Teeters, note 4, supra, p. 391.

16. A rather complete history of the early prison system in the United States during this period can be found in Blake McKelvey, note 13, supra, pp. 6–21; and Barnes and Teeters, note 4, supra, pp. 394–397.

17. For a detailed description of the Pennsylvania and Auburn systems of penal treatment see Rothman, *Discovery of the Asylum*, note 1, supra, pp. 79–108; Barnes and Teeters, note 4, supra, pp. 399–418; and Barnes, note 5, supra, pp. 124–148.

18. Barnes and Teeters, note 4, supra, p. 406.

19. Ibid., p. 407.

20. Ibid., p. 407.

21. Rothman, *Discovery of the Asylum*, note 1, supra, pp. 105–160.

22. Barnes and Teeters, note 4, supra, p. 412.

23. American Correctional Association, *Manual of Correctional Standards*, 2nd. ed. (Washington, D.C.: Government Printing Office, 1969), pp. 11–12.

24. Barnes and Teeters, note 4, supra, pp. 524–525.

25. For a more thorough historical explanation of the reformatory movement, see Barnes and Teeters, note 4, supra, pp. 519–554; McKelvey, note 13, supra, pp. 69–91; and Barnes, note 5, supra, pp. 144–148.

26. For an excellent discussion of current methods of correctional management see Garrett Heyns, "Patterns of Correction," *Crime and Delinquency* 13, no. 3 (July 1967): 421–431.

27. Ibid.

28. Ibid.

29. U.S. Bureau of Prisons, Annual Report—1969 (Washington, D.C.: Government Printing Office, 1969).

30. See Richard A. McGee, "Our Sick Jails," *Federal Probation* 35, no. 1 (March 1971): 3–8, as reprinted in Robert M. Carter, Daniel Glaser, and Leslie T. Wilkins, *Correctional Institutions* (New York: J. B. Lippincott, 1972), p. 95.

31. President's Crime Commission, "Local Adult Correctional Institutions and Jails," in *Task Force Report: Corrections* (Washington, D.C.: Government Printing Office, 1967), pp. 164–165.

32. Ibid., pp. 167–168.

33. Ibid., p. 167.

34. Ibid., p. 167.

35. Ibid., p. 167.

36. Louis B. Carney, *Introduction to Correctional Science* (New York: McGraw-Hill, 1974), pp. 263–264.

37. See President's Crime Commission, *Task Force Report: Corrections*, note 31, supra, pp. 79–80.

38. McGee, note 30, supra, p. 94.

39. Ibid., pp. 97–98.

40. Charles E. Ares, Anne Rankin, Herbert Sturz, "The Manhattan Bail Project: An Interim Report on the Use of Pre-Trial Parole," *New York University Law Review* 38 (January 1963) as reprinted in Leon Radzinowicz and Marvin E. Wolfgang, eds., *The Criminal in the Arms of the Law* (New York: Basic Books, 1971), pp. 430–440.

41. Donald P. Baker, "The Prisoner of Patuxent," *The Washington Post*, 24 March 1974, pp. C-1 and C-5.

42. Erving Goffman, *Asylums: Essays on the Social Situation of Mental Patients and Other Inmates* (Garden City, N. Y.: Anchor Books, Doubleday, 1961).

43. Gresham M. Sykes, *The Society of Captives: A Study of a Maximum Security Prison* (Princeton, N. J.: Princeton University Press, 1958), pp. 63–83.

44. Donald Clemmer, *The Prison Community* (New York: Holt, Rinehart and Winston, 1966).

45.   Stanton Wheeler, "Socialization in Correctional Communities," in Lawrence Hazelrigg, ed., *Prison within Society: A Reader in Penology* (Garden City, N. Y.: Anchor Books, Doubleday, 1969), p. 150.

46.   Ibid., p. 150.

47.   Lloyd W. McCorkle and Richard R. Korn, "Resocialization Within Walls," *Annals of the American Academy of Political and Social Science* 293 (May 1954): 88–98.

48.   Richard R. Korn and Lloyd W. McCorkle, *Criminology and Penology* (New York: Holt, Rinehart and Winston, 1959), p. 525.

49.   Sykes, note 43, supra, p. 85.

50.   Ibid., pp. 101–102.

51.   Korn and McCorkle, note 48, supra, p. 519.

52.   Sykes, note 43, supra, pp. 84–108.

53.   Ibid., pp. 84–108.

54.   Ibid., p. 106.

55.   Korn and McCorkle, note 48, supra, p. 527.

56.   Ibid., p. 525.

57.   Ibid., p. 526.

58.   Wheeler, note 45, supra, p. 169.

59.   Ibid., p. 173.

60.   Donald R. Cressey, ed., *The Prison: Studies in Institutional Organization and Change*, with Irving Goffman, Hohan Galtun, Richard McCleery, George Weber, Stanton Wheeler, Clarence Schrag, Donald Garrity, Daniel Glaser, and John Stratton (New York: Holt, Rinehart, and Winston, 1960).

61.   Clarence Schrag, "A Preliminary Criminal Typology," *Pacific Sociological Review* 4 (Spring 1961): 11–16.

62.   American Correctional Association, note 23, supra, pp. 366–367.

63.   Korn and McCorkle, note 48, supra, pp. 500–501. See also Sykes, note 43, supra, pp. 40–62; and Gresham M. Sykes, "The Corruption of Authority and Rehabilitation," *Social Forces* 34 (March 1956): 257–262.

64.   Korn and McCorkle, note 48, supra, p. 499.

65.   Ibid., p. 499.

66.   Ibid., p. 500.

67.   Ibid., pp. 500–501.

68.   Ibid., p. 501.

69.   Ibid., p. 498.

70.   See Anthony J. Manocchio and Jimmy Dunn, *The Time Game* (New York: Delta Books, Dell, 1970).

71.   LeMar T. Empey, "Introduction" to Manocchio and Dunn, note 70, supra, p. 27.

72.   Ibid., p. 24.

73.   Empey, "Implications: A Game with no Winners," in Manocchio and Dunn, note 70, supra, p. 244.

74.   The Murton Foundation for Criminal Justice, Inc., Minneapolis, Minn., *The Freeworld Times* 1, no. 1 (January 1972): 2 (hereafter cited as Murton Foundation).

75.   Ibid., 1, no. 8 (September–October 1972): 4.

76.   Ibid., 1, no. 1 (January 1972): 1.

77.   Ibid., 1, no. 2 (February 1972): 1.

78.   Ibid.

79.   Ibid., 1, no. 4 (April–May 1972): 7, 16.

80.   Ibid., 1, no. 2 (February 1972): 1, 12.

81.   Ibid., 1, no. 6 (July 1972): 5.

82.   Thomas S. Szasz, *Ideology and Insanity: Essays on the Psychiatric Dehumanization of Man* (Garden City, N. Y.: Anchor Books, Doubleday, 1970), p. 73.

83.   Ibid., p. 56.

84.   Ibid., p. 212.

85. Clyde Sullivan, Marguerite Q. Grant, and J. Douglas Grant, "The Development of Interpersonal Maturity Applications to Delinquency," *Psychiatry* 20, no. 4 (November 1957): 373–385.

86. William Glasser, *Reality Therapy: A New Approach to Psychiatry* (New York: Harper and Row, 1965).

87. Lloyd W. McCorkle, Albert Elias, and F. Lovell Bixby, *The Highfields Story* (New York: Henry Holt, 1958).

88. President's Crime Commission, *Task Force Report: Corrections*, note 31, supra, pp. 38–40.

89. Oliver J. Keller, Jr. and Benedict S. Alper, *Halfway Houses: Community Centered Correction and Treatment* (Lexington, Mass.: D.C. Heath, 1970), pp. 50–77.

90. Daniel Glaser, *The Effectiveness of a Prison and Parole System* (New York: Bobbs-Merrill, 1969), pp. 125–126.

91. Columbus Hopper, *Sex in Prison: The Mississippi Experiment with Conjugal Visiting* (Baton Rouge: Louisiana State University Press, 1969).

92. Ibid.

93. Murton Foundation, note 74, supra, 1, no. 7 (August 1972): 3.

94. American Correctional Association, note 23, supra, pp. 484–485.

95. Daniel Glaser, "The Effectiveness of Correctional Education," in Carter, Glaser and Wilkins, note 30, supra, p. 319.

96. President's Crime Commission, *Task Force Report: Corrections*, note 31, supra, p. 53.

97. Ibid., p. 53.

98. Murton Foundation, note 74, supra, 1, no. 9 (November 1972): 5.

99. As cited in Walter Lord, *The Good Years* (New York: Harper & Row, 1962), p. 63.

100. Elmer H. Johnson, *Crime, Correction and Society* (Homewood, Ill.: Dorsey Press, 1964), p. 558.

101. The American Correctional Association, note 23, supra, p. 394.

102. Murton Foundation, note 74, supra, 1, no. 7 (September–October 1972): 7.

103. Ibid., 1, no. 4 (April–May 1972): 1, 14.

104. Barnes and Teeters, note 4, supra, p. 688.

105. Ibid., p. 691.

106. Barnes and Teeters, note 4, supra, pp. 692–693.

107. Ibid., p. 694.

108. Ibid., p. 695–698.

109. Murton Foundation, note 74, supra, 1, no. 10 (December 1972): 4.

110. J. E. Baker, "Inmate Self-Government," *Journal of Criminal Law, Criminology and Police Science*, 55, no. 1 (1964): 39–67.

111. Sol Chaneles, "Open Prisons: Urban Convicts Can Turn Ghost Towns into Rural Communities," *Psychology Today* 7, no. 11 (April 1974): 30, 90.

112. American Correctional Association, note 23, supra, pp. 397, 398.

113. Ibid., p. 398.

114. Charles McKendrick, "Custody and Discipline," in Paul Tappan, *Contemporary Corrections* (New York: McGraw-Hill, 1951), pp. 159–160.

115. Sykes, note 43, supra, pp. 13–39.

116. Carney, note 36, supra, p. 366.

117. Daniel Glaser, "The Prison of the Future," in Carter, Glaser, and Wilkins, note 30, supra, pp. 428–432.

118. Barnes and Teeters, note 4, supra, pp. 452–458.

119. Ibid., p. 455.

120. Council of Judges, National Council on Crime and Delinquency, *Model Sentencing Act*, 2nd. ed., 1972.

121. Board of Directors, National Council on Crime and Delinquency, "The Nondangerous Offender Should Not Be Imprisoned: A Policy Statement," *Crime and Delinquency* 19, no. 4 (October 1973): 456.

122. Carney, note 36, supra, p. 172.

123. Ibid., p. 172.

124. Etheridge Knight, *Black Voices from Prison* (New York: Pathfinder Press, 1970), p. 9.

125. David J. Rothman, *Decarcerating Prisoners and Patients.* Mimeographed paper.

126. Ibid.

127. Ibid.

128. Ibid.

129. Murton Foundation, note 74, supra, 1, no. 1 (January 1972): 4.

130. Barnes and Teeters, note 4, supra, p. 577.

131. Murton Foundation, note 74, supra, 1, no. 8 (September–October, 1972): 9.

132. Robert M. Dickover, Verner, E. Maynard, and James A. Painter, "A Study of Vocational Training in the California Department of Corrections," *Research Report, No. 40* (Sacramento, Calif.: Research Division, Department of Corrections, January, 1971), p. 10.

133. Daniel Glaser, note 30, supra.

134. W. C. Bailey, "Correctional Treatment: An Analysis of One Hundred Correctional Outcome Studies," *Journal of Criminal Law, Criminology and Police Science* 57, no. 2 (1966): 153–160.

135. Edwin H. Sutherland and Donald R. Cressey, *Criminology*, rev. ed. (New York: J. P. Lippincott, 1970), pp. 498–499.

Probation

Probation is essentially a development of the twentieth century, but its origins can be traced to earlier devices used to humanize the criminal justice system which had developed under the common law of England. The harshness and severity of English criminal law led judges to search for innovations that would mitigate punishment. Because of the rigidity of English common law, the courts applied the principles of equity to the criminal law in order to allow flexibility and freedom for individual justice. Through the application of these principles of equity the rigid criminal law was modified by such devices as the benefit of clergy, judicial reprieve, recognizance, and provisional release on bail.

The English law brought to the American continent by the colonists embodied these devices for mitigation, but the spirit of the law called for severe and undiscriminating punishment. These two seemingly contradictory philosophies resulted in two parallel trends in the development of the criminal law of the United States: the trend toward leniency and humanization of the law as conceived at the Cincinnati Prison Congress in 1870; and the trend toward punishment in the form of severe prison sentences for major offenses—a trend that is still with us. Much of the disagreement in the field of corrections results from attempts at reconciling these different penal philosophies.

As has already been noted, institutionalization was first conceived by the early exponents of the prison system as a device to mitigate the cruel sanctions imposed by corporal and capital punishment. It was felt that through this new and revolutionary approach to the application of punishment the reform of the offender would become a reality and, at the same time, he would be in an environment free from the corruption of society and conducive to meditation and reflection, bringing about inner peace and harmony and closeness to God. Later, when it was realized that long term institutionalization failed to accomplish reform but, instead, served to promote that aspect of the criminal law which called for retribution, the rhetoric of reform turned progressively away from institutionalization in the direction of community supervision.

At the turn of the century probation and parole became a reality, but the results were disappointing. The rhetoric in favor of community supervision did not mitigate the penal system of the United States; instead, more and more individuals convicted of crimes were incarcerated and served longer periods of imprisonment in the United States than in most other countries. Prisons again placed major emphasis on custody and self-supporting industry at the inmate's expense. In the beginning, probation and parole were not uniformly received by the various states. Where they were implemented, they were usually placed in the hands of former law enforcement officers whose major concern was stringent supervision, leaving little leeway for the development of innovations conducive to rehabilitation. Again there was a significant lag between theory and practice just as there was during the reformatory era. Probation and parole did, however, pave the way for a more humane method of treatment and gradually became a necessary part of the correctional system because of prison overcrowding and the high cost of incarceration.

Again there is a call for reform involving community supervision, not only through such devices as probation and parole, but through community treatment centers, halfway houses, and work and educational release programs as well. The question arises whether we can expect a method of treatment to work in the future if it did not work in the past. And if we find that the strategy of community treatment is not living up to expectations, will this lead to new calls for institutionalization, and start the process all over again?

At present, studies attempting to evaluate the effectiveness of current programs in the area of community supervision are disappointing. Even though substitutes for incarceration are said to be cheaper and usually more humane, there is no empirical evidence that these new methods of community supervision are any more effective in preventing crime and reducing recidivism than are the old and more severe methods of punishment. Perhaps new and more sophisticated evaluative studies will be more encouraging. At any rate, the current trend in corrections is away from institutionalization, and it is to the history and practice of this current correctional strategy that this chapter will address itself.

ORIGINS OF PROBATION IN ENGLAND

Benefit of clergy

In an effort to allow members of the clergy to escape capital punishment and other severe sentences of the thirteenth century, a compromise was established with the church which permitted a member of the clergy who might be brought to trial in the King's Court to be subject only to the authority of the ecclesiastical courts. By such a compromise certain categories of offenders could claim exemption from punishment. In order to claim mitigation of punishment, the offender had to be able to read. Since the ability to read was usually restricted to the clergy this device to obtain mitigation and escape from capital punishment became known as "benefit of clergy."[1]

By the early eighteenth century every peer in the King's realm was granted the benefit of clergy regardless of sex, class, or ability to comprehend the written word. Until the late fifteenth century, however, the benefit of clergy gave an elite body of men the freedom to commit crimes such as murder with little risk of suffering any sanction, since murder was classified as a clergyable felony.[2] But the repeated use of this device by convicted criminals led to the practice of branding such offenders in open court with the symbol "M" for murderer and "T" for thief.[3]

Before the literacy test was discontinued as a basis of eligibility for the benefit of clergy, an attempt was made, through a devious practice of judicial connivance, to correct the gross injustice of restricting the device to those who could read. Clerks of courts, who reported to the judge concerning the offender's ability to read, often gave incorrect information. These false statements of the clerk would, at the judge's discretion, be accepted or rejected. In most cases the practice of the court was to accept false certificates of literacy without inquiry.[4] The actual test for literacy was frequently the use in court of a particular selection from the Psalms later known as the "neck-verse."[5]

There is little doubt that the plea of benefit of clergy became a common practice in England in the criminal proceedings of the eighteenth and early nineteenth centuries. It allowed many convicted offenders an avenue of escape from the severity of the English common law by reducing the number of executions and by enabling offenders to obtain a delay of sentence for the purpose of presenting arguments for a lesser punishment than otherwise might have been demanded by the law.[6] The benefit of clergy was abolished by statute in England in 1841. This form of clemency was brought to America by the colonists and was used until shortly after the Revolution.

Even though the benefit of clergy was a forerunner of probation, it is doubtful whether this device had any direct influence on the later development of the suspension of sentence or on any other more direct precursor of probation.[7]

Judicial reprieve

Under the English common law, new trials and appeals to another court were impossible. In order to permit the convicted offender to apply to the Crown for either an absolute or conditional pardon, the court would grant a temporary suspension of the imposition or the execution of sentence. This device was used in cases where the judge was not satisfied with the verdict; where he felt that the evidence was suspicious or the indictment was insufficiently supported; or where the felony involved was of small consequence and there were favorable circumstances surrounding the convicted offender's character.[8]

The device of judicial reprieve was practiced by the English courts in the seventeenth century in the form of reprieves granted to offenders under sentence of death on condition that they accept deportation. Transportation in connection with judicial reprieve was therefore another outlet for avoiding capital punishment. It is probable that this measure of mitigation was only meant to be a temporary stay of sentence, but it did lead, in some cases, to an abandonment of prosecution and to what is now referred to as an indefinite suspension of sentence. The American courts took note that in some cases where the strategy of judicial reprieve had been applied in English common law, the prosecution was dropped and the suspension was allowed to become permanent. This resulted in the practice by American courts of suspending a sentence indefinitely, under the pretense that such a power could be traced back to this early act of reprieve in the English courts and was therefore an inherent power derived from common law. The practice of suspending a sentence for an indefinite period of time by the courts was ultimately confirmed and regulated by statute in many states. Such a law was used to a large degree before the enactment of probation laws.

Recognizance and provisional release on bail

A measure of preventive justice has evolved which dates back to fourteenth-century England. Originally, this was a device which permitted an individual who was thought likely to have committed a criminal offense but was not yet convicted of a crime, or who was thought predisposed to commit crimes in the future, to be released after obligating himself to the court through a promise and sworn statement that he would conduct himself in a law-abiding manner and maintain good behavior. In order to benefit from this device sureties or bail were usually required, and the person who stood surety had both the power and duty to enforce the conditions of the offender's release. This principle of recognizance, or "binding-over," was later extended to individuals charged with a criminal offense and arraigned before the criminal courts. The English Criminal Law Consolidation Act of 1861 made such a device applicable to persons convicted of any felony not capital and further led to the development of the British probation service.[9] Using the device of recognizance, magistrates engaged in the practice of requesting volunteers to give advice and help to offenders discharged on recognizance and, by so doing, established a plan of supervision.[10] During the first half of the nineteenth century, it appears to have been a common practice in Massachusetts to apply this device in cases involving youthful and petty offenders.[11]

The practice of binding-over was used extensively, for example, by Judge Peter Oxenbridge Thacher while a magistrate in the Municipal Court of Boston. In the case of *Commonwealth v. Jerusha Chase* (1831), the defendant had been convicted after her plea of guilty for stealing from a dwelling house. Judge Thacher, by agreement with the prosecuting attorney, ordered that the indictment be "laid on file" upon entering into recognizance with sureties, with the obligation that the defendant appear before the court when summoned. This case was the first description of the process of "laying on file"—the unique Massachusetts term for suspending sentence under recognizance after a plea or verdict of guilty.[12] The order that a case be laid on file was not equivalent to a final judgment but left with the court the power to take action on the case at any time, upon motion of either party.[13] The defendant in the above-mentioned case later appeared in court for a new offense and was sentenced to the house of correction.[14] This case is important, since it laid the foundation for the enforcement of the conditions of probation. It entailed sentencing the defendant on the basis of revocation of a suspension after indictment for a second offense and the imposing of sentence on the original conviction.[15]

The strategy of releasing an offender on his own recognizance may be used with or without sureties. Conversely, the device of bail can be employed independently of releasing the defendant on his own recognizance. In both England and the United States, the device of bail has been used extensively, independently of recognizance. Whether or not an offender was released solely on bail, or on bail in conjunction with recognizance, the rudiments of probation were always present. Because of their financial interest in the conduct of their client, sureties would try to insure that provisionally released offenders behaved in a law-abiding manner through personal assistance and persuasion. Further, it became increasingly clear that the strategy of releasing offenders from custody under certain explicit conditions enforced by supervision of court advocates had strong rehabilitative value as a method of promoting good conduct and preventing crime. Such a strategy paved the way for a more professionally oriented extension of this process through supervised probation.

EARLY BACKGROUND OF PROBATION IN THE UNITED STATES

House of refuge

Together with the beginning of the formulation of ideas directed at individualized social treatment, especially in regard to children and youthful first offenders, mitigation began to appear early in the nineteenth century. Programs were initiated by English magistrates to save young offenders from penal incarceration and the stigma such a sanction entailed. Young offenders were bound over by the courts, to be brought back for sentencing if the conditions of their release were violated. Those who were released were assigned to the care and guardianship of their employers and parents. In addition to conditional release and community supervision, new institutions were developed, based on such "rehabilitative principles" as training and reform.[16]

In the United States efforts were made to counteract destructive economic and social forces conducive to juvenile delinquency by developing a new type of institution called the House of Refuge. The first house of refuge was opened in New York in 1825 under the management of Joseph Curtis. The groundwork for this institution had been laid by the dedicated members of the Society for the Reformation of Juvenile Delinquents, formerly known as the Society for the Prevention of Pauperism. The house of refuge was an institutional strategy employed to help prevent young people from committing criminal acts by subjecting them to a program of strict discipline based on religious and industrial training. The house of refuge no doubt had an impact on the reformatory movement of the post-Civil War era, but to what extent is not exactly known.

The house of refuge movement began as an attempt to help perpetuate an ideal society free from crime and delinquency. Eventually, however, the number of houses of refuge and reformatories increased throughout the United States, and many became overcrowded and poorly managed. Instead of being filled with youthful first offenders, many contained hardened recidivists. Custody became the major correctional strategy of these institutions, with the result that they resembled adult medium-security prisons. The house of refuge movement therefore came under attack from a group of people similar to those who had been responsible for founding it. Reformers proclaimed that such institutions were a breeding ground for crime and were a failure in preventing the spread of juvenile delinquency. It appeared that most of the boys taken into the houses of refuge graduated to an adult penal institution.[17] Nevertheless, the philosophy which surrounded the beginnings of the houses of refuge, with its stress on the prevention of crime and reform through methods other than penal incarceration, was a forerunner of contemporary strategies utilizing probation, parole, and the indeterminate sentence with built-in incentives for progress.

The reform movement

POST-CIVIL WAR RECONSTRUCTION

The aims of the post-Civil War reconstruction movement were to make the United States a unified nation and a great world power; slavery was to be destroyed once and for all, and the political liberties of all Americans were to be respected and preserved. There was much well-intended rhetoric, especially concerning the extension of civil rights to all the people regardless of race or ethnic background. Negro suffrage was a prime issue, and Negroes sought a program of social service financed by the state. Other movements became prominent, such as the Granger movement, which was an agency of agrarian protest calling for basic reforms of a social, cultural, and educational nature. The Grangers left their mark by persuading states to subject railroads to social controls and by launching the first major cooperative movement in the United States. The great Populist movement followed, demanding many political and economic reforms. Out of the many progressive movements emerged two major trends—the movement for social justice and the demand for political reform. Various groups concerned with social justice focused their attention on our treatment of the young, the poor, and the criminal offender.

This progressive era brought forth new philosophies for the treatment of offenders such as those set forth at the Cincinnati Prison Congress of 1870, which advocated such innovations as parole, the indeterminate sentence, a more judicious exercise of the pardoning power, a system for promoting inmate self-respect, and vocational and educational training. Also, reformers in the area of social work began to make their mark on the criminal justice system by establishing slum relief centers and settlement houses. Helping the progressive movement were the muckrakers, consisting of many talented and concerned journalists who dramatized the need for reform by exposing the many social injustices prevalent in the United States. The rhetoric for change in the direction of political, economic, and social justice was strong, and some of the rhetoric gradually became reality. For our purposes, the rhetoric laid the foundations for changes in the area of corrections that were not to be realized to any meaningful extent until many years later.

THE RISE OF SOCIAL WORK

The rise of social work in the latter part of the nineteenth century further paved the way for the development of probation. One significant step in this direction occurred in 1869 when the governor of Massachusetts appointed a visiting agent to the Board of State Charities, a public agency in the welfare field. The duties of the visiting agent included investigating and taking charge of delinquent children appearing before the court and, where possible, placing them in private homes or private agencies to avoid their being sent to state reformatory institutions. Soon after this practice was initiated the law required that a visiting agent attend almost all court hearings throughout the state involving juvenile delinquents. The visiting agent was referred to as the "friend" of the children accused of a crime. His primary duty was to act in behalf of the child and, at the same time, keep the protection of the community in mind. This type of placement was a kind of probation and continued in use for a number of years.[18]

The basic philosophy of social work, stressing the reform of the poor and unfortunate, set the pattern for the concept of the worthy defendant. The establishment by law of probation as a correctional strategy was motivated by techniques of social work, such as the provision of public assistance, supportive guidance, and supervision, performed by interested and dedicated workers, usually out of private agencies and charitable organizations.

THE CHILD SAVERS

During the 1880s and 1890s many middle-class intellectuals and professionals took an interest in the deprived conditions that appeared to them to influence the children of the lower socioeconomic classes. The feminist reformers in particular focused on the problems of the delinquent youth who lived in the cities. This group of women, commonly called the child savers, influenced program development in institutions and also influenced the way in which juvenile law was applied in the juvenile court. Child saving was predominantly a women's movement, since it was believed to be the business of women to regulate the welfare of children and to be the moral custodians of wayward youth. The women who took part in child saving were usually from the middle and upper classes and, before becoming involved in the movement, had played a more traditional female role. Their participation in the child-saving movement was conceived of as an extension of their housekeeping functions. These women were not militant in their ideas or behavior but were concerned individuals who formed societies on a volunteer basis for the purpose of learning more about the less privileged groups.[19]

The child savers were actually conservatives who hoped to preserve traditional institutions and parental authority, since the social trend at the time was in the opposite direction. Up to the time of the child-saving movement, control over youthful activities had been primarily informal in nature. The child savers hoped to extend governmental control over the young, making it possible to impose sanctions for wayward behavior and to reward dependent behavior, thereby prolonging the period in which a young person would remain an adolescent. Participation by adolescents in adult affairs was not accepted, and children were to be discouraged from engaging in the consumption of alcohol, smoking, reading or viewing pornographic material, and from frequenting dance halls and movies.

This prohibitionistic philosophy, coupled with the stress on dependency espoused by the child savers, became the basis for the juvenile court law in the United States. The juvenile court concept has always encouraged the court to act as a protective and understanding parent and, due to this concept, juvenile court judges were given a wide range of discretion in the application of sanctions.[20]

The importance of the child-saving movement for the establishment of probation is evident in the movement's preoccupation with removing adolescents from the criminal law process and the creation of special programs—both institutional and noninstitutional—for delinquent, dependent, and neglected children. There is little doubt that the movement led to some good through its encouragement and anticipation of reforms in treatment of the young. However, the movement was responsible for many evils as well, such as the antilegal trend of denying children the constitutional benefits of civil rights and procedural formalities granted to adult offenders; and the fostering of the belief that rural and middle-class values constituted morality, thereby automatically placing the label of "unsocialized," "maladjusted," and "pathological" on those who deviated from norms valued by the middle-class female. A further result of the child-saving movement that has proven detrimental to the treatment

and well-being of the young is the common practice of treating neglected, dependent, and delinquent children in a similar manner, as
if all could be classified as "wayward" in some mystical or
metaphysical sense.

THE IDEA OF THE WORTHY DEFENDANT

It became progressively clearer to the courts that individuals who
violate the law differ in basic personality characteristics. Further,
certain cases involved extenuating circumstances which impelled
the judge to favor a lenient sentence rather than impose a harsh
sanction. Both judges and private citizens alike began to feel that
certain individuals who commit crimes, such as the poor and the
very young, do so largely because of circumstances beyond their
control and are worthy of being given a second chance to lead a
constructive and law-abiding existence.

Before probation was legally established, some concerned members of the community began to practice a kind of informal supervision and initiated rudimentary forms of background investigation.
One such citizen was John Augustus, who is commonly referred to
as the "father" of probation in the United States. A bootmaker by
trade, he began as early as 1841 to take a special interest in poor
offenders and vagrant boys and persuaded the judge of the Boston
police court to release in his custody offenders who he felt were
reclaimable. He allowed many offenders to stay in his own home,
which became, for all practical purposes, a detention home for children and maladjusted women. He also placed children in foster
homes and helped raise funds to build an institution for destitute
children. Through kindness, supportive guidance, and belief in the
capacity for individuals to change, Augustus convinced the courts
that his strategy of reform could produce positive and permanent
results. He further convinced others in the community of the effectiveness of his correctional techniques and, as a result, many influential people gave him both moral and financial assistance.

Not only did Augustus set in motion the strategy of supportive
supervision, which has since been incorporated, with some refine-
ments, as a necessary ingredient of supervised probation; he also
originated in rudimentary form the preliminary social investigation.
In order to make a careful selection for voluntary supervision of
those offenders convicted of crimes, he would take into consideration their previous behavior, their age, and related environmental
factors that might be conducive to reform. John Augustus is especially significant as a pioneer in the field of probation in that he was
concerned with the application of the concept of the worthy defendant to adults as well as to children.

The Reverend George F. Haskins was also concerned with the

treatment of children. He made frequent visits to the courts to select neglected and delinquent boys for residence in the first Catholic home for delinquent boys in New England, called the House of the Angel Guardian, which he founded in 1851. Boys usually remained in the home for about a year under a program of supervision and training. On completion of their training the boys were released to relatives or placed in private homes.[21] His work made authorities aware of the need for probation as an official strategy, and his work was also influential in the development of the juvenile court.[22]

The Children's Aid Society and the Society of St. Vincent de Paul were influential in providing volunteer work for the courts. Rufus R. Cook was the first paid agent to work (on behalf of the Children's Aid Society) with children detained in the Suffolk County Jail. Before being appointed to this position he had engaged in extensive volunteer work with young people and not infrequently helped adults as well. His daily attendance at court for the purpose of rescuing children from jail commitment led to his being appointed the Chaplain of the Suffolk County Jail. His use of strategies similar to those employed by Augustus and his deep interest in the welfare of those offenders he thought worthy of help also establish him as a pioneer of probation.[23] In 1870 it is reported that Cook bailed from jail about 450 individuals of varying age groups, all of whom were placed on probation. Of these, Cook estimated that 87 percent made a good adjustment to outside supervision.[24]

The idea of the worthy defendant spread and was the prime factor in motivating private individuals and charitable organizations to plant the seeds of what were later to grow into the major correctional strategies of probation and parole. Such interest by private organizations in the welfare of the offender continued even after probation was made official by law.

Probation becomes law

The first probation law was passed by the Massachusetts State Legislature on April 26, 1878. Local rather than statewide in application, it was limited to providing a salaried probation officer for the courts of Suffolk County.[25] The act required the mayor of Boston to select a person suitable for the position of probation officer. The first probation officer appointed by the mayor was Henry C. Hemmenway, a police department lieutenant. After four months, Hemmenway was replaced as probation officer by Edward H. Savage, a former chief of police, who served many years in this position.[26] It is of interest to note that the first probation officers brought into the correctional field to implement the nonpunitive strategy called for by the philosophies of probation were former police officers. This was also the case with regard to parole. This tendency to appoint former law enforcement officials to controlling positions in the field of probation and parole suggests that the courts and governmental bodies considered it inappropriate and dangerous for probation officers to apply in reality the philosophical strategies of correctional reform. This failure during the beginnings of community supervision to narrow the gap between rhetoric and reality set back the progress of noninstitutionalized treatment of offenders for years to come.

Massachusetts passed a second law in 1891 requiring the criminal courts to appoint officers for the extension of probation. This law is significant in that it transferred the power to appoint probation officers from municipal authorities to the courts. Under this law, Hannah Todd, the first publicly salaried woman probation officer, was appointed by the Boston Municipal Court.[27] In 1898 Massachusetts became the first state to provide mandatory statewide salaried probation service and, at the discretion of the court, to make probation available to all persons charged with a criminal offense.[28]

The next two states to pass probation laws were Vermont and Rhode Island, in 1898. Vermont was the first state to adopt the county plan common to many states at the present time.[29] This plan paved the way for the decentralization of probationary services by giving each county the power to appoint its own probation officer and to establish its own standards of probation.

Rhode Island was responsible for the beginning of a completely state-administered system of probation service, which became effective in 1899. Under this law the Board of State Charities and Corrections was authorized to appoint a state probation officer, as well as additional probation officers to serve all the courts in the state.[30]

Although probation laws were gradually enacted by other states, the first federal probation law was not on the statute books until March 4, 1925, under the administration of President Calvin Coolidge.[31] By 1925 probation for juveniles also became available in every state, but it was not until 1956 that adult probation became a reality in all of the states.

The concept of therapeutic probation

Initially, probation was primarily a humanitarian strategy employed to enable offenders thought to be reclaimable by "friends" of the court to escape the corrupting effects of incarceration. Most of the supervision was provided by volunteer workers—ministers or other interested citizens who believed that many offenders were deprived and uneducated and needed support for the purpose of making a better adjustment to society. Beginning in the 1940s a new concept of probation emerged, proposing that probation should offer more than the mere suspension of sentence and the placement of an offender under the guidance of an untrained worker (who could at best supply supportive guidance based largely on surveillance, good will, and perhaps self-righteous moral zeal). Probation was no longer to be a mixture of surveillance and "fatherly" advice, but a legitimate treatment strategy employing techniques, such as professional casework, formerly applied only by trained social workers. The medical model prevailed as the panacea of corrections, resulting in labeling of offenders as "sick," "unsocialized," "emotionally maladjusted," and "mentally ill." This psychiatrically oriented approach to the causes of crime implies that some causative agent within the individual offender is responsible for his delinquent behavior and that it must be exposed and removed in order to allow the development of insight through therapeutic supervision by a trained person, which leads to a change in the offender's personality and conduct. This medical model has been under attack by experts in the correctional field for many years and is gradually being replaced by other models that are more sociologically oriented.

The development of supervision strategies necessary to make rehabilitation a reality required that probation officers be specially trained in counseling techniques similar to those employed in social work agencies. The larger and more financially capable probation departments began to hire college graduates as probation officers. At first it was felt that those trained in the various schools of social work would best be qualified to provide the therapeutic supervision necessary for constructive behavioral change. Now it is believed that correctional work is a highly specialized occupation requiring talents over and above those applied in a social work setting, and the former trend of fusing social work and corrections is being critically evaluated. The main point here, however, is that contemporary probation, stressing the need for professionally educated and trained workers, stems from the concept of probation as a therapeutic mechanism. The concept of therapeutic probation is still with us and dominates the philosophy of many probation departments.

THE INSTITUTION OF PROBATION

Various structures of probation

To a large degree adult probation services are state functions with a centralized administration; but in some large states, such as New York and California, probation is under various kinds of local administration. When administered locally, probation services may be directed by a judge or by an independent agency. The shift toward placing probation services under an independent authority within the local government is a result of the complexity of organization necessary to provide probation services to both juveniles and adults on a professional level. Such complex organizations require intensive administrative functions and full-time managers with specialized expertise. In some large counties probation has become so complex that juvenile and adult probation services are separate, with a separate manager for each, under the direction of a chief who coordinates the services. Such large and diverse organizations not only provide supervision services to probationers, but operate psychiatric clinics, juvenile detention homes and camps, and foster homes as well. In this section the various administrative structures for probation will be discussed in an attempt to analyze the advantages and disadvantages of each.

COURT ADMINISTRATION

Since 1891, when Massachusetts first placed probation services under the administration of the courts, this practice has been common throughout the United States. When probation services are under the direct administration of the court, these duties are usually assigned to the judge presiding over the juvenile court. In such cases the juvenile court judge appoints the chief probation officer and approves the appointment of other probation staff workers selected by the chief.

There are several arguments in support of the judicial administration of probation services. Supporters of such administration feel that if the court manages probation services, the judge will provide guidance to probation workers, support legislation favorable to the probation agency, keep informed about correctional alternatives in the county, and maintain an interest in feedback concerning the effectiveness of judicial dispositions ordering probation. It is further believed that judges may have more confidence in presentence reports and supervisory services provided by their own staff than they would have if such services were provided by an autonomous agency. Those who support the judicial control of probation also feel that in jurisdictions where such control is exercised judges may apply the strategy of pretrial diversion more than they would do otherwise because of their reluctance to transfer authority to other governmental agencies.[32]

Arguments against the judicial control of probation services focus on the judge's lack of training for directing such services and his inability to give enough time and attention to ensure that such services are being adequately provided. Placing probation services under the court may also mean that the probation staff, which is normally overworked, will be assigned such additional tasks as recommending for or against bail or release on own recognizance, issuing summonses, serving subpoenas, and engaging in other activities not directly related to probation.[33] When judges are their managers, probation workers may also feel obligated to orient their services in the direction of judicial approval instead of providing for the welfare of their clients. When probation services are administered by courts, therefore, the trend is to appoint court administrators to act in lieu of judges in presiding over probation matters.

EXECUTIVE ADMINISTRATION

Many local and state governments have established probation agencies under the executive rather than judicial branch of the government in an effort to promote organizational effectiveness, continuity of policy, and diversity of management according to specialization.[34] The move toward the administration of probation services under the executive branch of government has also been motivated by the belief that a probation agency should have an identity of its own, since it is a service-oriented body and not an adjudicatory or regulatory body. Since the orientation of a probation agency differs from that of a court, it is felt that such an agency should have a governmental base that is conducive to a greater degree of autonomy for its staff.

In order to give probation agencies more autonomy, some localities have adopted the practice of having citizens' groups or city or county officials appoint probation officers, while other counties have given such appointive power to a committee of judges. Where a committee of judges appoints a chief probation officer, the chief is allowed wide discretion in providing for the detailed administration of the agency, being responsible to the judges in matters pertaining only to broad policy.[35]

In localities where probation services are administered by an executive agency of the local or state government, the probation administrators appear to find no basis for some of the arguments set forth above in favor of judicial administration. Judges seem to trust well-managed probation agencies whether they are directed by courts or executive bodies. As a result, very close and satisfactory relationships have been formed between judges and probation staffs in these localities.[36]

Those who argue for the administration of probation by an autonomous executive agency feel that such administration would facilitate a more realistic allocation of probation services, encourage more interaction and administrative coordination with other agencies providing correctional and allied human services, promote the channeling of more funds for probation services on the part of both local and state legislative bodies, and provide an incentive for the removal of the judiciary from a role inappropriate to its basic constitutional function.[37]

STATE VS. LOCAL ADMINISTRATION

Probation services on the local level vary according to the financial resources of the local government, the support provided by the community, and the degree of professionalization of the probation staff. Within the same state, for example, one county may provide excellent probation services while another county may extend the bare minimum of services. Under a decentralized probation system, the probation agencies in the prosperous and metropolitan counties may flourish while the poorer and less populated counties lack the resources to provide qualified workers and adequate referral services. Centralization fosters a uniform level of probation services throughout a state and assures, to some degree, that equitable policies will be applied in making recommendations for or against probation. Decentralization, on the other hand, promotes wide variations in standards and policies, with the result that part of the state's population does not receive equitable consideration and treatment. In smaller localities judges are less likely to have adequate presentence reports on which to rely in pronouncing judgment, and defendants placed on probation suffer from the lack of meaningful supervision.

There are, however, some advantages in decentralizing probation services. Decentralization promotes a degree of support from local citizenry and agencies that is not usually forthcoming from highly bureaucratic state agencies. This lack of rigid bureaucracy can foster a healthy flexibility of services and standards not found on state levels. Decentralization also ensures that local agencies will tend to work together in attacking a particular problem, whether it be in the area of the administration of criminal justice or some other area. Employees of these local agencies tend to identify more with the community in which they work than do most state employees, and they are usually more knowledgeable about the localities in which they provide services. Once a defendant is placed on probation under a local agency, he is not forgotten by the community in which he lives but continues to receive local services and support— support that could be withdrawn if he were placed under the supervision of a state agency.

Large states which now provide decentralized services in the area of probation would have a difficult time providing the gigantic bureaucratic organization that would be necessary to centralize their services. There is always the danger that such an agency might be weak and ineffectual under improper political direction. If the leadership were strong and effective, however, a degree of continuity among all services provided in the area of corrections could be achieved, leading to meaningful coordination between probation services and services provided by institutions and parole.

States do have a responsibility to localities that provide correctional services under a decentralized system. Even though the state does not directly administer such services it can provide assistance to local agencies in the form of staff training and recruitment; it can insist on standards of consistency and fairness of policy among various local agencies; and it can provide the local agencies with subsidies based on improvement of local services in the form of treatment innovations. In the State of California, for example, the State Youth Authority has been authorized to pay up to $4,000 to each county for every adult and juvenile offender not committed to a state correctional institution. In order to be eligible for such a subsidy the local agency must ensure such improvements of probation services as the hiring of additional probation officers and the reduction of caseloads. Treatment innovations must also be demonstrated in the way of intensive supervision, especially in regard to high-risk cases. In New York, the state reimburses local communities up to 50 percent of the operating costs for probation programs if the local communities meet state staffing standards.[38] States also have the responsibility of providing referral services for local agencies, such as general consultants, diagnostic clinics, and noninstitutional placements in state-operated group homes and residential centers.[39]

The profession of probation

Can probation be called a profession in the sense that medicine, law, psychology, and engineering are considered professions? When one talks about the profession of probation, to what body of knowledge and skills is he referring? It is well known that many probation officers have had no special training in any aspect of the criminal justice system or in the behavioral sciences before being hired by probation departments. It is not uncommon to have probation officers begin work, with little or no inservice training, after obtaining degrees in English, Business Administration, Romance Languages, Philosophy, Sociology, History, Psychology, Political Science, Education, and Religion. Many probation officers have changed professions and have come into the field after serving as Catholic priests,

Protestant ministers, insurance salesmen, lawyers, retired army officers, and retired police officers. What skills and knowledge do individuals from these various backgrounds have in common that enable them to perform as probation officers? To make the issue even more confusing, some probation officers trained in fields unrelated to the criminal justice system or the behavioral sciences seem to function better on the job than do some probation officers with backgrounds in social work, criminology, police science, and correctional administration. Would people of such diverse backgrounds be able, with little or no inservice training, to work as medical doctors, constitutional lawyers, chemical engineers, clinical psychologists, botanists, or psychiatrists? Even with the training programs that some large probation departments provide for their newly hired personnel, it is difficult to believe that in six months an individual can be trained in any given profession. One can acquire special skills as a worker in six months, but can hardly obtain the necessary knowledge and skills necessary to practice a profession such as medicine or law. In this respect a probation officer might be compared to a paramedic who, through a short period of training, can acquire the skills necessary to engage in less complex medical tasks. Can we conclude that probation officers, like paramedics, are quasi-professionals in such areas as criminal justice and the behavioral sciences?

In order to ascertain whether or not probation can legitimately be called a profession it is best to reflect on just what probation officers do during the course of their employment. One task the probation officer must learn is that of preparing a presentence report. This report serves a diagnostic function, enabling judges to predict whether a defendant convicted of a crime would be a good risk for community supervision and treatment. Thus, probation officers function as diagnosticians. They have the responsibility of evaluating the human personality to provide a basis for making accurate predictions about human behavior and how such behavior is likely to respond to a variety of possible dispositions. Their decisions in this respect can make a significant difference in the life of the defendant being evaluated.

Probation officers also supervise cases assigned to them and administer probation programs ordered by the court. In the role of supervisor, probation officers are expected to provide surveillance and keep accurate records of the progress probationers make while on probation. In this role probation officers function as an arm of the court, keeping the court informed of the progress and delinquencies of probationers by periodically submitting petitions for the modification and revocation of probation.

One of the most important functions of a probation officer is to guide and help probationers toward a life style of noncriminality. This aspect of the probation officer's job is commonly referred to as treatment or rehabilitation. The probation officer is expected to change or modify attitudes and behavior through counseling techniques he has learned in the past. Such a role implies more than the term "supervision" usually connotes. A probation officer is more than a record keeper, surveillance officer, and case manager; he is a counselor and case worker as well, performing a role that is similar to roles performed by clinical psychologists and psychiatric social workers.

Diagnosing, supervising, and rehabilitating individuals assigned to him by the criminal courts account for most of the tasks performed by the probation officer. The function of a probation officer is therefore eclectic in nature, requiring the acquisition and application of skills from a wide variety of subject matter such as criminal law and procedure, psychology, sociology, biological science, political science, communications (writing and verbal skills), law enforcement, and corrections. Although many probation officers with little background in the above-mentioned subjects seem to perform satisfactorily on the job, the direction of the leaders in the field of probation is to continually require more academic learning and training in new job applicants on the line level. Their objective is to promote probation as a profession worthy of the same respect as is presently given to the many professions from which probation workers draw the foundations of their unique skills.

It is probably fair to say that in the past, professionalization in the field of probation was largely by fiat. Probation as a profession in the past can be compared to "fiat money," a form of paper currency made legal tender by law, although not backed by gold or silver and not necessarily redeemable in coin. This quasi-professional aspect of probation can best be found in an analysis of how probation officers view themselves and how professionals such as judges, psychologists, psychiatrists, sociologists, and lawyers view probation officers. As of this time in the history of probation, courts still do not consider probation officers "experts" in any subject matter, and behavioral scientists appear to view them as skilled workers who periodically need their consultation when matters in the area of diagnosis and supervision become complex. It is not uncommon to hear a judge in open court admonish a probation officer by reminding him that he is not a member of the bar and is not a practicing psychiatrist. Leaving the courtroom, a probation officer sometimes wonders what he really is. He feels that he is more than a skilled worker but hesitates to think of himself as a professional in the way in which a lawyer and psychiatrist consider themselves profession-al. Such feelings of probation officers lead, in some cases, to feelings of inferiority and produce defensive overreactions when their role as a "professional" is challenged.

There is little doubt that probation functions differently today from the way it did when the first probation laws were passed. Many probation departments now require their applicants for line posi-tions to have college degrees, sometimes on the advanced level, and to have already obtained some degree of skill in working with people; but can we refer to individuals possessing an eclectic pool of knowledge in the behavioral and social sciences as professional? The trend seems to be in this direction and is evidenced by colleges emerging on university campuses to train individuals in such sub-jects as community development and human services. Such fields require that graduates have knowledge and skills in a wide variety of areas instead of specializing in one area of study such as psychology or sociology. Such colleges have obtained professional status, and their graduates are gaining recognition as professionals with unique knowledge and special skills that can be applied in solving some of society's problems. Perhaps the social engineer that John Dewey once talked about is being born—a unique breed to be sure, and probation officers will appear to be more and more a part of this breed.

This expansion of the meaning of the term "professional" makes it seem possible that probation will eventually attain professional rec-ognition as an applied art, since skill in the area of human services is still more of an art than an exact science, whether it be practiced by psychologists, psychiatrists, social workers, or probation and parole officers. A probation officer will be expected in the future to have studied a diverse program of subject matter and to have attained some degree of operational proficiency before being allowed to prac-tice his "art." Since probation work is largely an art, the success of an officer will depend largely on his inherent personality charac-teristics and his ability to engage in meaningful interpersonal rela-tionships.

Organizational pressures for probation

ECONOMIC REASONS

Imprisonment has always been an expensive undertaking, and this is especially true today. It has been estimated that it costs ten to thir-teen times more to maintain a person in an institution than it does to supervise him on probation. In 1965, the average state expenditure to keep a youth in a state training school was $3,613. This figure does not include capital costs.[40] The national average per capita cost of institutionalization of adult felons in 1965 was $1,966.[41] Expenditures for corrections in the United States during 1965 totaled about $1 billion, and more than 40 percent of this amount ($454 million) was spent to operate institutions for adult offenders. Approximately $320 million was spent for all juvenile corrections during this period, with over two-thirds of that sum allocated for institutional treatment.[42] In New York, the cost of imprisonment in 1969 was eighteen times as high as probation per offender dealt with under each system, and in Massachusetts ten times as much.[43] Institutions are also expensive to build, and none of our state governments can easily undertake the construction of new correctional institutions. Even back in 1965, construction costs ran up to and beyond $20,000 per bed in a correctional institution.[44] Costs are now much higher than those quoted here, making it necessary for local and state governments to use alternatives to incarceration for the treatment of offenders. Probably the least expensive alternative is probation. An effort is therefore being made to utilize probation more frequently when such a disposition seems feasible and does not endanger the community.

Being at liberty, the individual placed on probation can also hold a job and pay his own way in the community. This affords big savings to the taxpayer, especially, who avoids the necessity of paying welfare costs for child support to families whose principal wage earner is incarcerated. In 1956, for example, 84,100 probationers in California paid, through their probation officers, $2,747,000 toward the support of their families and $902,000 in reparation and restitution.[45]

DISENCHANTMENT WITH INCARCERATION

As we have already discovered, the initial dreams of the founders of our prisons and reformatories were never realized, and institutionalization never achieved the goals expected of it when the first penitentiary was constructed in the United States. Numerous "fads" have surfaced for rehabilitating individuals convicted of crimes, and throughout the years the pendulum has swung back and forth between institutionalization and some form of community treatment. But the trend toward community treatment has never been stronger than at the present time (even though some disenchantment with the effectiveness of current noninstitutional programs is again leading some correctional experts to entertain fleeting visions of walls and bars). There are several reasons for the current disenchantment with institutionalization. Some of these reasons appear to have a basis in fact, and others seem to rest on gut-level feelings of a negative nature.

In addition to being costly enterprises, it has been discovered that institutions are not very efficient in rehabilitating the people under their control. There are still no studies giving completely reliable, realistic evaluations of the effectiveness of institutions as a correctional device; but the studies that are available so far are disheartening. The apparent destructive effects of the pains of imprisonment on many inmates have encouraged many interested in corrections to seek alternative methods of dealing with offenders. There is a gut-level feeling that many offenders who are subjected to the sterile and oppressive atmosphere of an institution, isolated from the community, and made to conform to meaningless rules and regulations, come back to society with far more personality maladjustments than when they entered. Although it is questionable whether correctional institutions are a breeding ground for crime for all individuals subjected to their care, there is a strong feeling that they do influence certain inmates to continue criminal careers. The pressure to find alternatives to prisons has led to the greater use of probation and has fostered the development of innovations, especially with regard to the supervision of high-risk cases. State subsidies to local probation departments are an indication of disenchantment with institutionalization, as is the trend toward decentralization of correctional services in many states.

THE PLEA-BARGAINING PROCESS

In the absence of probation, prosecutors and defense attorneys alike have little flexibility in negotiating a plea. If probation is not available, the only alternative to incarceration is the fine, which cannot be realistically bargained for in lieu of incarceration in serious offenses involving felony convictions. In order to provide an effective device for the negotiation of a plea, alternatives meaningful to the defendant and the State alike must be made available. Such alternatives must mitigate in some significant way the maximum sanction provided by law for the commission of a particular crime and, at the same time, provide for the protection of society and the rehabilitation of the offender. Probation provides a meaningful alternative to other legal sanctions and is therefore essential to the functioning of the negotiated plea process. Without probation, the preconviction process would undoubtedly suffer serious setbacks.

Plea bargaining can, however, have a detrimental effect on the probation officer's role as a quasi-judicial officer. Theoretically the probation officer is supposed to make sentencing recommendations to the court in accordance with his assessment of whether the defendant is a good risk for this type of disposition and whether it will be conducive to his rehabilitation. If, however, the prosecutor has already revealed to the probation officer that a particular plea has been negotiated with the defendant, the task of writing a presentence report may seem to be a futile exercise. Certainly plea bargaining diminishes the roles of both the judge and the probation officer in sentencing.

When the probation officer is aware that a plea has been negotiated, it would appear to be the best policy to make recommendations in accordance with his genuine feelings about what the proper disposition of a case should be, even though the judge may not accept his recommendation in open court because of the negotiated plea. At least, in this way, the probation officer's thoughts about how the defendant should have been sentenced if no plea bargaining had taken place become a matter of record. It should also be remembered that presentence reports are utilized by other agencies as well as the court, such as welfare departments, diagnostic centers, and mental health clinics, and that these reports should be written with the needs of such agencies in mind. The probation officer need not feel that he must agree with the prosecution or with the court in making his recommendations. It is often the case that, when probation officers exercise their own judgment in spite of judicial pressure or coercion from the prosecution, they are more respected by their own staff, by the court, and by the members of the community.

THE FUTURE OF PROBATION

Probation and research

Because of the lack of adequate funds, research in the area of probation has been limited. If probation is to emerge as a genuine profession, however, and if it is to improve its services to the community, research must be undertaken as the basis for improved standards of work. Most line officers are not trained in research methodology and have little time to engage in such activities, but they can make a genuine contribution to research by conducting full case investigations and maintaining careful records in order to make possible research by universities, consulting experts, and other research organizations. Many times a researcher attempting to evaluate the effectiveness of a particular aspect of a probation department's program becomes frustrated by the lack of accurate record keeping. The failure to keep reliable and extensive records can prohibit any attempt at meaningful research.

It would be ideal if more probation officers could engage in research or obtain training in formulating and evaluating research projects. Most probation departments have never attempted a self-evaluation concerning their efficiency and effectiveness. Lacking local funds to obtain such consultants as research specialists and analysts, self-evaluation is seldom attempted because few people engaged in probation are capable of such an undertaking. If probation is to advance to the status of a profession, its practitioners must become more sophisticated in research so that they can conduct meaningful evaluations of their own effectiveness.

Much of the research that has been attempted in the field of probation up to this time has revealed methodological uncertainties and equivocal results. Many times the original research design is too ambitious. Another problem has been the absence of a well-developed theoretical framework, resulting in lack of orientation and loss of efficiency. Sometimes the method and direction of a project are sought after the research is initiated. A vital problem for researchers in the area of probation is to identify and formulate clearly the problems to be solved without moving too rapidly from speculation to attempted experimentation.

If probation is to improve its services in the future, many questions must be answered in this area. We must attempt to analyze more painstakingly the impact of probation supervision, the factors that are present when officers make sentencing recommendations to the court (the "decision game"), the extent to which a violation index is a measure of success, the reliability of selection criteria for probation supervision, and the effects of varied intensities and types of supervision and caseload sizes. We must also attempt to discover what part of probation caseloads could function as well on a suspended sentence without any supervision.[46]

As Harold B. Bradley states: "correctional programs seem to survive or die by default."[47] There are few instances where we learn that a program was continued or terminated because careful evaluation found it to be strongly supportive or clearly nonsupportive of correctional goals. We seem to change programs without knowing whether the programs discarded were of any value or whether the innovations will be of any use. Change should not occur merely for the sake of change. Researchers in the field of probation must develop adequate means of quantifying the innovations developed and must evaluate them with regard to stated goals. In addition to quantifying and evaluating program innovations, there must be a continual preparedness to change presently accepted goals, and to change the means of attaining such goals if the present means do not appear adequate.

In order to engage in meaningful research each probation department should have available an agency that compiles and interprets statistical information. Each department should define the questions that it must answer for its operational purposes and for purposes of interpreting its program to others. The data needed to answer these questions should be gathered and fed into a statistical system that can render a meaningful interpretation of the information received. The American Correctional Association recommends that each state should establish a central correctional statistical system to obtain information from law enforcement agencies, courts, probation agencies, and other correctional agencies of the state and should further cooperate in an interchange of data with other states and federal agencies.[48]

In the future probation must serve two functions—operation evaluation and program innovation. Improvement in the development of rehabilitation techniques depends on the implementation of new programs which in turn depend on imaginative research performed to a greater degree by agencies themselves than by "outsiders" such as university faculty, consulting firms, and research institutes.[49]

Reorganization

CONSTITUTIONAL STANDARDS

The use of probation is significantly restricted at present by legal and constitutional barriers which make it difficult or impossible for the courts to use this treatment device in a way that is most conducive to the welfare of the state and the individual. Further, there is a need for continuing review of certain laws concerning due process in the arrest and seizure of probationers, the disclosure of the presentence report, and adequate representation at revocation hearings.

The criteria for granting probation should not depend on the type of offenses committed or the existence of a prior record. At the present time the laws of many states automatically exclude from probation individuals convicted of certain offenses, regardless of whether they might be good risks for this type of disposition. In such cases the court's hands are tied, and the defendant must suffer incarceration whether he is a danger to the community or not. According to the American Bar Association, courts should be able to grant probation according to the merits of each case after a careful examination of the nature and circumstances of the crime, the history and character of the offender, and the available dispositions in the form of institutionalization and community treatment.[50]

Judges should not be able to grant or deny probation on the basis of whether the defendant pleads guilty, pleads not guilty, or makes a motion to appeal. At present it is not uncommon to deny probation to a defendant who demands his right to a jury trial instead of pleading guilty to a particular offense—in effect, penalizing the defendant for exercising his constitutional rights.

In certain jurisdictions, for certain types of offenses (usually felonies and serious misdemeanors) the courts are prohibited by law from granting summary probation (probation without supervision). There are many occasions, especially with regard to situational offenders, where supervision is not appropriate and the necessity of imposing supervised probation places an unnecessary burden both on the probation department and on the offender. The American Bar Association recommends that the court not be required to attach a condition of supervision by the probation department if the court does not consider such a condition necessary.[51]

At present most penal codes allow a court to order probation in felony cases for the maximum period prescribed for incarceration. It is not uncommon for certain offenders to be placed on probation for a period of ten to twenty years. In certain instances, courts refuse to reduce the amount of time because of the nature of the offense alone, regardless of whether or not the offender is progressing well on probation and appears to be in no further need of supervision. Even though most offenders are placed on probation for a maximum of five years for a felony offense—a time maximum recommended by the American Bar Association,[52] such a standard is not always observed. It appears that in five years one would be able to ascertain whether or not an offender is capable of living a law-abiding life in the community or needs a different type of sanction. In some cases, after serving ten years of a twenty-year sentence on probation, the probationer is still required to write a letter to his probation officer on a monthly basis. This game that the probation officer and the probationer are required to play with each other should not be permitted.

Five years seems to be the maximum time that a probationer should be subject to supervision. The American Bar Association further recommends that the maximum time to be permitted for granting supervised probation in misdemeanor cases should be two years. Many states now have a three-year maximum, which can apply to misdemeanors such as disturbing the peace, where the maximum jail sentence may be only ninety days.

It is not uncommon to arrest probationers for the alleged violation of conditions of their probation without a warrant of arrest. It is sometimes felt by the probation officer, the police officer, and the court that probation excludes the probationer from the protection of the due process of law guaranteed by the Constitution. The American Bar Association recommends that arrests without a warrant should be permitted only when the violation involves the commission of another crime and when the normal standards for arrests without a warrant have otherwise been met. Other possible inequities of the probation system, such as standards pertaining to disclosure of presentence reports and revocation of probation, have already been discussed in Chapter 3 of this book.

In order for probation to be most effective and efficient, constitutional reorganization should be undertaken by the many states where legislative and judicial barriers now impede meaningful attempts at treatment.

THE RELATIONSHIP TO CORRECTIONAL OPERATIONS

Probation could probably work best if it were part of an integrated state-administered program which coordinates all aspects of the correctional process such as probation, institutions, and parole. Certain states have realized the advantage of integrating correctional services by combining all correctional agencies under a single administrator, or by placing them under a separate and independent department of correctional services concerned with probation, parole, and institutions. There is good reason to believe that this approach can achieve a more uniform and meaningful program for the rehabilitation of offenders and that it will facilitate the provision of equitable services to all parts of the state.

Uncoordinated efforts by isolated aspects of the correctional system lead in many cases to inefficiency and duplication of services and promote the misconception that the various agencies providing correctional services are isolated entities which can be studied and interpreted apart from one another. Corrections can only be adequately understood as a subsystem of the administration of criminal justice process and as a combined effort to rehabilitate offenders through the coordinated efforts of all vehicles such as probation, institutions, and parole.

Preconviction probation

STATION HOUSE PROBATION

In order to keep offenders out of the criminal justice process, police engage in diversion programs. In rural areas police sometimes use informal procedures aimed at avoiding arrest, especially in dealing with middle- and upper-class citizens. Such procedures include a reprimand, a referral of a juvenile to his family or another community agency, a requirement that restitution be made to the victim, or providing a kind of informal supervision with the goals of both prevention and treatment in mind. Recently, diversionary projects such as those provided by the Youth Service Bureau of the Pleasant Hill Police Department in California have introduced a variety of counseling programs, including family and school visits by bureau staff in place of the traditional methods of dealing with teenage lawbreakers.[53] Such bureaus may also provide special classes for girls exhibiting delinquent tendencies, classes in drug education, and police-youth rap sessions.[54] At the present time the Richmond, California Police Department is engaging in a Juvenile Diversion Program funded by the Law Enforcement Assistance Administration and aided by the California Youth Authority. Its purpose is to test the feasibility of direct help and counseling services provided by the police to youth involved in predelinquent and certain delinquent activities.[55] Formerly many of these services were provided by other agencies such as probation departments. The primary intent of such a program is to provide immediate intervention in order to prevent the lag that occurs between the time the youth comes to the attention of the police and the time he receives actual services after referral.

In Los Angeles County it was learned that the sheriff's department traditionally "counsels and releases" the least serious 55 percent of all juveniles arrested.[56] Informal diversion activities also apply to adult offenders, especially with regard to conflicts involving husband and wife, landlords and tenants, businessmen and customers, or management and labor. Alternatives to arrest in such cases may involve the initiation of informal procedures, such as a type of supervision, instead of official sanctions.

Major criticisms of police diversion activities in the form of supervision and counseling on an informal basis come from those who feel that the police have neither the time nor the training to provide such services at a professional level. The role of the police has been traditionally defined as that of detection of violations of the law and the apprehension of criminals. The provision of treatment appears to be seen as contradictory to the function of the police in society. An analysis of what police do when in the field, however, indicates that most of their time is actually spent in community-based work rather than in playing the game of "cops and robbers." It is true that most police officers are not trained in the behavioral sciences and are not adequately equipped to provide family crisis intervention and supportive help to victims. But inservice training programs for the police usually focus on the game of "cops and robbers," rather than providing meaningful instruction in community intervention and community relations that would help police to cope with the kinds of problems they confront most of the time. Preconviction probation at the station house level is ill-advised if practiced by departments which provide no training either in methods of selecting appropriate candidates for informal supervision or in adequate and meaningful supervisory techniques. Training programs in these areas, however, are being considered by the more sophisticated police departments. If these programs are implemented, they may serve a genuine preventive function by enabling the police to keep many juvenile and adult offenders out of the court and correctional machinery and free of the stigma of a criminal conviction.

VOLUNTARY PROBATION

In addition to police diversion programs there are also court-based diversion programs which are administered either directly by the court or by public and private agencies working in cooperation with the court. The purpose of court-based diversion programs is to provide the opportunity to treat behavior problems that appear to cause delinquent activity, apart from the formal adjudication and correctional process. Such programs minimize the use of coercive power and further prevent the stigma of a criminal conviction.[57] Court diversionary programs are also popular because they lessen the work load of the courts and the prosecutor's office by diverting cases from court and avoiding jury trials and all the possible motions and appeals that could result. There is little doubt that such diversion from the criminal justice system saves the taxpayers money. There are few studies to indicate the effectiveness of informal probation as a rehabilitative device. However, one evaluation of an informal probation project conducted by the Yolo County Probation Department located in Woodland, California, indicates that the selective use of informal probation presents no greater risk to the community, in terms of further official delinquency, than formal probation, even if such informal services are conducted over a shorter period of time.[58] Most of these diversion programs have built-in safety mechanisms by virtue of the fact that a participant in such a program must agree to abide by certain conditions, and violations can result in a different type of disposition for any given case.[59]

Some pretrial intervention projects operate by lodging no formal changes after an arrest has been made. The individual apprehended by the police is screened on the basis of a variety of criteria to determine whether he is eligible to participate in the diversion program. Many programs are limited to juveniles, first offenders, and nonviolent misdemeanors or felonies. If an individual meets the criteria necessary to participate in the program he must volunteer or consent to being subjected to this type of disposition. If he completes the program in a satisfactory manner the prosecutor will usually dispense with the case.[60]

Other pretrial intervention programs demand that formal charges be lodged, but further criminal proceedings are suspended pending the individual's satisfactory participation in the program. Successful completion of the program results in a request by the prosecution that charges be dropped.[61]

Pennsylvania has adopted a diversionary strategy referred to as "Accelerated Rehabilitational Disposition," which is intended to operate largely at the preconviction level. With the consent of the district attorney, the defendant, the defendant's counsel, and the court, an individual arrested by the police can be diverted from trial and conviction and can be either placed on summary probation (nonsupervised) or referred to the probation department for formal supervision. The defendant who agrees to participate in the program must abide by certain conditions, as do other offenders on probation. Probation departments sometimes submit a report to the court similar to a diagnostic or presentence report recommending for or against such a disposition. In other instances the offender might be placed on such a program without any recommendation from the probation department. The program is usually limited to first and nonviolent offenders. No offender is allowed to participate in the program more than once. If an offender does agree to participate in the program he must further agree to waive his right to a speedy trial if he violates the conditions of his probation. If he successfully completes the conditions of his probation and no indictment or information has been filed against him by the prosecutor, all matters pertaining to the case will be dismissed, and the offender can maintain that he has never been charged with the offense. If an indictment or information has been filed prior to his placement on informal probation, all charges will be dropped upon successful completion of the probationary period.[62]

In some jurisdictions preconviction probation may be used informally, i. e., in the absence of statute. In New York State, for example, probation officers are permitted to supervise offenders assigned to them by the courts during a period of adjournment before sentence or adjudication. These cases, as in Pennsylvania, receive the same treatment as the offenders placed on formal probation and are a part of the probation officer's caseload.[63]

EVALUATION OF PROBATION

Difficulties in measurement

It is difficult to measure the success of probation. There have been studies indicating that probation is a successful rehabilitative device. Ralph W. England, Jr. made an analysis of eleven studies, the results of which indicate a success rate of 60 to 90 percent.[64] An extensive study was performed in California which entailed a seven-year follow-up investigation of 11,636 adults granted probation during the period 1956 to 1958. It was ascertained that 72 percent of this group were considered successful in that their probation was not revoked.[65] These findings were not obtained under controlled conditions and were not supported by data that distinguished among the types of offenders who succeeded or the types of services that were rendered; but the success rate they indicate is relatively high, even if interpreted with a skeptical eye.[66]

One of the most famous studies attempting to evaluate the success of probation was the demonstration project conducted in Saginaw County, Michigan from 1957 to 1960. This project involved the state-administered adult probation service in Saginaw County. The major purpose of the project was to ascertain what could be accomplished by limiting caseloads to fifty units (one unit being awarded for every supervision case and five units for every presentence investigation), and by increasing the qualifications of the staff. Along with these changes the Saginaw court utilized probation more liberally than it had previously. An evaluation of the project indicates that the failure rate on probation during this experimental period was reduced despite the increased use of probation as a disposition. During the three years of the control period the failure rate was 32.2 percent as compared to the failure rate of 17.4 percent during the three-year experimental period.[67] Rigorous testing would be required to determine whether these figures can be interpreted at face value; however, they do indicate that offenders who would normally be incarcerated appear to succeed in the community under an intensive form of supervision.

Most probation departments assert that their success rates are high. A rough average of the reports of many probation departments during a number of different years shows that about 75 percent of their probationers succeed on probation.[68] Estimates of this sort, however, are surrounded by problems that make the results subject to suspicion. One problem is that the effects of probation on recidivism can never be fully established because there are so many factors other than probation supervision that influence abstention from crime. It seems impossible to isolate the degree to which probation supervision influenced the rehabilitation of any particular offender. Another problem is that most studies evaluating the success of probation fail to follow cases beyond the period of active supervision. The few studies that have used follow-up investigation, however, appear to show results similar to other studies in regard to success or failure.[69]

Still another problem in assessing the value of probation is that many departments do not maintain close enough contact with their probationers to find out what proportion of them become delinquent. This problem is compounded by the fact that the identification records of certain police departments are so restricted that they do not adequately supplement the knowledge of the probation officer.[70] The reason why some of the better probation departments show the smallest proportion of successes is possibly that they have more complete knowledge regarding the behavior of their probationers than do the departments which are doing their work in a less satisfactory manner.[71]

Perhaps it would be wise to take Sutherland's advice and not ask whether probation is a success or failure in a general sense, but attempt to ascertain what type of offenders succeed on probation and under what conditions probationers succeed.[72] Prediction devices have been developed and are gradually being improved in order to furnish us with such information. Up to this time prediction studies indicate that certain characteristics of probationers can be correlated significantly with failure on probation, such as whether the probationer has a prior criminal record, shows an irregular work pattern, has experienced previous institutional placement, comes from a family with a criminal history, shows a nomadic residence pattern, resides in a deteriorated or commercial area, and shows a history of alcohol or narcotic addiction. Prediction tables are still in their infancy, however, and in the area of probation they are not reliable or significant. It is questionable whether prediction devices will ever be 100 percent accurate, but they may be improved to the point of allowing us to make predictions that are significantly more accurate than predictions made on the basis of hunches and intuition alone.

Probation contrasted with prison

There have not been many studies comparing the success of probation with alternative methods of dealing with offenders such as prison. The few studies that have been completed indicate that probation is in general at least as effective (in terms of reconviction rates) as imprisonment.[73] For example, Leslie T. Wilkins found no significant difference in the reconviction rates (covering a three-year follow-up period) of a group of thirty-one offenders placed on probation by an English higher court, and a group of thirty-one individually matched controls placed in prisons and borstals.[74] A follow-up study of 5,274 adult male offenders was also undertaken in Wisconsin by Babst and Mannering in order to compare the success rates of incarceration to those of probation. During a two-year period, reconviction rates of those placed on probation compared with those sent to prison and paroled showed that the success rate of probation was about the same as that of imprisonment for recidivists and was significantly better for first offenders.[75]

Up to the present time research seems to indicate that institutional treatment is no more effective than treatment in the community on probation. If such studies are genuine indications of the effectiveness of these two treatment devices it would seem logical to select probation whenever possible, if for no other reasons than that it is more humane and costs a good deal less to administer.

There are strong feelings on the part of many correctional administrators that probation could be employed much more extensively than it is today without subjecting the community to danger. There is a gut-level feeling that an individual will maintain a self-image and a life style more conducive to responsible and constructive behavior if he is maintained in the community where he can support himself and his dependents, experience interpersonal relationships with his family and friends, and avoid the stigma and stultifying effects of incarceration. Whether these gut-level feelings can be substantiated through scientific research remains questionable, but research does indicate that we can apply the strategy of probation without fear that recidivism will increase to any appreciable extent.

More study is needed to determine the merits of probation as a treatment device. But there seems to be little reason to question the opinion held by many in the field of corrections that with proper selection of cases, qualified personnel, and adequate methods of supervision and management, probation is an effective and desirable way of dealing with a large number of offenders and could be expanded to encompass many offenders presently sentenced to prison.

NOTES

1. Charles Lionel Chute and Marjorie Bell, *Crime, Courts, and Probation* (New York: Macmillan, 1956), p. 12. See also Charles L. Newman, *Sourcebook on Probation, Parole, and Pardons* (Springfield, Ill.: Charles C. Thomas, 1968), p. 4.

2. Chute and Bell, note 1, supra, p. 14.

3. Ibid., p. 14.

4. Ibid., p. 13.

5. Ibid., pp. 12–13.

6. Ibid., p. 15.

7. Newman, note 1, supra, p. 4.

8. *Commentaries on the Laws of England, 1765–1769* (Albany, N. Y.: Banks and Co., 1900), p. 1041.

9. Chute and Bell, note 1, supra, p. 16.

10. Ibid. pp. 16–17.

11. Newman, note 1, supra, p. 6.

12. Chute and Bell, note 1, supra, pp. 33–35.

13. Newman, note 1, supra, p. 9.

14. *Reports of Criminal Cases Tried in the Municipal Court of the City of Boston before Peter Oxenbridge Thacher, Judge of that Court from 1823–1843*, edited by Horatio Woodman of the Suffolk Bar, Boston, 1845, pp. 267–270.

15. Chute and Bell, note 1, supra, p. 35.

16. Ibid., p. 22.

17. Robert S. Pickett, *House of Refuge: Origins of Juvenile Reform in New York State, 1815–1857* (Syracuse, N. Y.: Syracuse University Press, 1969), pp. 181–183.

18. Chute and Bell, note 1, supra, pp. 56–58.

19. Anothony Platt, "The Rise of the Child-Saving Movement: A Study in Social Policy and Correctional Reform," *Annals of the American Academy of Political and Social Science* 381 (January 1969): 25–28.

20. Ibid., pp. 27–30.

21. Chute and Bell, note 1, supra, p. 54.

22. Ibid., p. 54.

23. Ibid., pp. 54–55.

24. Ibid., p. 55.

25. Ibid., p. 59.

26. Ibid., pp. 60–61.

27. Ibid., p. 65.

28. Ibid., p. 66.

29. Ibid., pp. 67–70.

30. Ibid., pp. 70–71.

31. Ibid., p. 111.

32. National Advisory Commission on Criminal Justice Standards and Goals, *Report on Corrections* (Washington, D.C.: Government Printing Office, 1973).

33. Ibid.

34. President's Crime Commission *Task Force Report: Corrections* (Washington, D.C.: Government Printing Office, 1967), p. 35.

35. Ibid., p. 35.

36. Ibid., p. 35.

37. Ibid., p. 35.

38. National Advisory Commission on Criminal Justice Standards and Goals, note 32, supra.

39. President's Crime Commission, *Task Force Report: Corrections*, note 34, supra, p. 37.

40. Ibid., p. 28. See also President's Crime Commission, *The Challenge of Crime in a Free Society* (Washington, D.C.: Government Printing Office, 1967), p. 165.

41. President's Crime Commission, *Task Force Report: Corrections*, note 34, supra, p. 5.

42. Ibid., p. 5.

43. Edwin H. Sutherland and Donald R. Cressey, *Criminology*, 8th ed. (New York: J. P. Lippincott, 1970), p. 479.

44. President's Crime Commission, *Task Force Report: Corrections*, note 34, supra, p. 28.

45. Sutherland and Cressey, note 43, supra, p. 479.

46. Paul W. Tappan, *Crime, Justice, and Correction* (New York: McGraw-Hill, 1960), p. 584.

47. Harold B. Bradley, "Designing for Change: Problems of Planned Innovation in Corrections," *Annals of the American Academy of Political and Social Science* 381 (January 1969): 95.

48. The American Correctional Association, *Manual of Correctional Standards*, (Washington, D.C.: 1966, 4th Printing, 1969), p. 110.

218 *Probation*

49.   Stuart Adams, "Evaluative Research in Corrections: Status and Prospects," *Federal Probation* 38, no. 1 (March 1974): 18.

50.   American Bar Association, *Project on Standards for Criminal Justice*, Part I: "General Principles," Section 1.3: "Criteria for Granting Probation," Approved Draft, 1970.

51.   Ibid.

52.   Ibid.

53.   George G. Killinger and Paul F. Cromwell, Jr., *Corrections in the Community: Alternatives to Imprisonment* (St. Paul, Minn.: West Publishing, 1974), p. 30. A selected article, reprinted in the above volume, originally published by the National Advisory Commission on Criminal Justice Standards and Goals, *Report on Corrections* (Washington, D.C.: Government Printing Office, 1973).

54.   Ibid., p. 30.

55.   Ibid., p. 31.

56.   Ibid., p. 32.

57.   Ibid., p. 35.

58.   Peter S. Venezia, "Unofficial Probation: An Evaluation of Its Effectiveness," *Journal of Research in Crime and Delinquency* 9, no. 2 (July 1972): 149–170.

59.   Killinger and Cromwell, note 53, supra, p. 35.

60.   Ibid., p. 35.

61.   Ibid., pp. 35–36.

62.   Supreme Court of Pennsylvania, *Procedural Rules*.

63.   The New York Department of Correction, *Annual Report* (Albany, N. Y.: 1948), p. 120.

64.   President's Crime Commission, *Task Force Report: Corrections*, note 34, supra, p. 28.

65.   Ibid., p. 28.

66.   Ibid., p. 28.

67.   Paul W. Keve, *Imaginative Programming in Probation and Parole* (Minneapolis, Minn.: University of Minnesota Press, 1967), pp. 54–55.

68.   Sutherland and Cressey, note 43, supra, p. 477.

69.   Donald R. Taft and Ralph W. England, Jr., *Criminology*, 4th ed. (New York: Macmillan, 1964), p. 391.

70.   Sutherland and Cressey, note 43, supra, p. 477.

71.   Ibid., p. 477.

72.   Ibid., p. 478.

73.   R. F. Sparks, "Research on the Use and Effectiveness of Probation, Parole and Measures of After-Care," in a Council of Europe report on *The Practical Organization of Probation and After-Care Services*, Strasbourg, Council of Europe, 1968, as published in Leon Radzinowicz and Marvin E. Wolfgang, eds., *The Criminal in Confinement* (New York: Basic Books, 1971), p. 212.

74.   Ibid.

75.   Ibid.

Parole

Parole is similar to probation in that it is a form of community supervision, but it differs from probation in that it is a form of conditional release of an individual from a correctional institution after he has served a portion of his sentence. Although the supervision techniques applied by both probation and parole officers are somewhat similar, parolees are usually subject to more limitations on their freedom than are probationers. In some jurisdictions, parolees undergo a stringent form of supervision, which may involve more surveillance than would be the case with an individual on supervised probation.

THE ORIGINS OF PAROLE

History of parole

Although the concept of providing treatment in the form of counseling and guidance is relatively new, parole in the traditional sense can be traced back to a combination and extension of penal practices that have existed for many years.[1] Parole developed from various independent measures which include the transportation of criminals to America and Australia, the English and Irish Ticket-of-Leave, the conditional pardon, and various reforms that took place during the nineteenth century such as the modification of a fixed sentence through "good time" laws and the indeterminate sentence.[2]

TRANSPORTATION

During the early seventeenth century England began to transport criminals to the American colonies under a law passed in 1597 providing for the banishment of criminals or "rogues" who appeared to be dangerous.[3] There were two major reasons for applying transportation as a strategy. One factor that led the English government to favor transportation was the widespread unemployment in England at the time. The English labor market was overcrowded and taxes were high. Labor was also needed in the American colonies, and criminals could provide such labor without antagonizing certain groups in England who opposed colonization. The King therefore approved a plan to grant reprieves and stays of execution to the convicted felons, at first a group of prisoners convicted of robbery who were physically employable. In the beginning no conditions were imposed on those receiving pardons; but later, in order to prevent those pardoned from evading transportation or returning to England before their terms expired, it was found necessary to impose restrictions on the individuals who were granted pardons.

Another reason for accepting transportation as a strategy was to avoid the harsh and cruel English law stipulating capital punishment for a number of crimes. In cases wherein a death sentence had been imposed, a stay of execution was automatically granted until the King reviewed the recommendation of the judge in regard to transportation. Many prisoners died on the long voyage across the Atlantic, sometimes under inhuman conditions, and many died shortly after reaching the new world, but transportation did probably save many convicted offenders from certain execution.[4] After the revolutionary war, transportation to America ended, but the strategy was continued and criminals were sent instead to Australia. In many ways transportation was a harsh type of reprieve, but the alternative was often to hang by the neck until dead.

THE TICKET-OF-LEAVE

The English Penal Servitude Act of 1853 made it possible to grant a conditional release on Ticket-of-Leave to those prisoners who had served a specified length of time in prison. The amount of time that had to be served before becoming eligible for the Ticket-of-Leave depended on the length of the prisoner's sentence. The Ticket-of-Leave provided the prisoner with a license to be at large in specified areas under the control of the United Kingdom, and the conditions under which the Ticket-of-Leave was granted were specified on the license which every prisoner was supposed to carry with him at all times and present on demand. Some of the conditions the prisoner had to observe in order to prevent his license from being revoked were that he had to avoid any acts of misconduct, refrain from associating with notoriously bad characters and from leading an idle or dissolute life, and maintain a visible means of support.

It was assumed by the general public that the conditions imposed on the prisoners who participated in the Ticket-of-Leave program would be enforced. Such was not the case, however, and during the early part of the program no supervision was exercised over the men on leave, and crime in the United Kingdom increased. Prisoners on Ticket-of-Leave were blamed for most of the serious crimes committed, and the citizens demanded that the men be supervised or that the program be terminated. It appears that the British Home Office interpreted the law to mean that men placed on Ticket-of-Leave had, for all practical purposes, completed their sentences. As a result of public uproar, the services of the police were used for supervision. Later agents employed by Prisoner's Aid Societies were employed to supervise the released prisoners. These agents assisted prisoners in obtaining employment and finding shelter, provided a degree of surveillance for the purposes of enforcing the conditions of leave, made visits to prisoners having special problems, and explained the program to employers and helped obtain their cooperation.[5]

The Irish system of Ticket-of-Leave was put into use around 1855, after Sir William Crofton, one of the most influential pioneers of parole, became head of the Irish prison system. The Irish prison system became a model for the reformatory strategy in the United States because of its three-stage program of penal servitude. The second stage, later adopted in the reformatories of the United States, classified prisoners by marks obtained for good conduct and achievement in education and industry. Tickets-of-Leave were granted only to prisoners who gave evidence of definite achievement and change of attitude. Prisoners on Ticket-of-Leave were supervised entirely by the police in rural areas. In Dublin, they were supervised by a civilian employee who had the title of Inspector of Released Prisoners. The men were required to report at stated intervals, and field visits were made to their homes and places of employment. The Irish System of Ticket-of-Leave had the support of both the general populace and the prisoners.[6]

THE DEVELOPMENT OF PAROLE IN THE UNITED STATES

The beginning of the modification of a definite sentence in the United States took place in 1817, when New York State passed the "good time" law enabling inspectors of the prison to reduce a sentence in accordance with good behavior. Under "good time" laws a sentence is shortened by a definite schedule stipulated by statute and not by an authority outside the prison. It is a form of conditional release still employed in many institutions. Actually "good time" laws function as a form of institutional repression, often being held over the prisoner as a threat to assist the management in maintaining institutional control.[7]

Later interest developed in the modification of a fixed sentence through the indeterminate sentence and parole, an idea suggested by Philadelphia reformer Dr. Benjamin Rush as early as 1787. The first state parole law was enacted by Massachusetts in 1837. In 1868, Zebulon R. Brockway, influenced by the work of Sir Walter Crofton in Ireland, presented a bill to the Michigan legislature for the indeterminate sentence without any maximum or minimum, but it was defeated. Another effort to promote this penal strategy was made at the Cincinnati National Prison Association Conference in 1870, where papers were delivered by such men as Crofton and Brockway on the indeterminate sentence and the possibilities of parole.[8] Parole was adopted at the Elmira Reformatory under the management of Zebulon Brockway in 1876. To be considered for parole at Elmira an inmate had to maintain a good record of conduct for twelve months and, prior to release, was expected to submit suitable plans for permanent employment. Upon release, the parolee continued under the jurisdiction of the prison for an additional six months and was ordered to report to a guardian upon arrival at his place of employment. Although only three states had passed parole laws by 1880, parole as a correctional strategy gradually spread throughout the United States, and some form of parole legislation was passed in every state by 1945.

The theories of parole status

PAROLE AS A GRANTING OF MERCY

Parole is sometimes inaccurately associated with leniency or mercy. There is little question that courts do at times grant parole as an act of mercy, but such a reason for granting parole undermines the status of parole as a legitimate rehabilitative strategy. Mercy or sentiment should not be a criterion on which to base the selection of inmates for parole. If parole is to be efficiently administered, parolees must be selected in a manner guaranteeing that such a disposition will not, as far as can be predicted, endanger the community, and that the disposition will be administered in a manner that will enhance the parolee's rehabilitative potential. For many inmates being successful on parole is not an easy task, and some inmates would rather serve their maximum time and receive a straight discharge from prison. Parole requires that inmates demonstrate a responsible pattern of behavior once released and imposes various types of sanctions on those unable to fulfill the conditions of their parole. For some inmates, instead of being considered an act of mercy, parole is a difficult form of disposition to which to adjust.

In further consideration of parole as a favor or form of leniency, it should be realized that prisoners tend to serve as much time in prison in jurisdictions where parole is widely used as in those where it is used sparingly. In many jurisdictions, the use of the indeterminate sentence and parole does not actually decrease the amount of time a person serves in prison. Thus, the community is not placed in any unnecessary danger through the application of parole, and the inmate receives little in the way of leniency, since he may well serve as much or more time in prison before being released on parole as another will before being discharged. In such cases, parole is supposed to function as a safeguard for the community rather than as a form of mercy for the inmate.

PAROLE AS A RIGHT

Is parole a right to be granted to every inmate who is expected to return to society? Most authorities in the field of corrections feel that a prisoner does not have a right to parole; but the same authorities feel that most inmates, for their own growth and for the protection of the community, should experience parole supervision before being allowed complete freedom in society. Most state laws governing release on parole do not require parole boards to release every inmate on parole, thereby denying the status of parole as a right to be shared by all those incarcerated. However, except as prohibited by statute, an incarcerated man has the right to be considered for parole.

Differing from most state laws, the federal system does require the mandatory supervision of all inmates released from federal institutions before the expiration of their terms for having earned good time or other credits during imprisonment. Since almost all inmates in federal institutions receive good time credits, almost all federal prisoners will receive some type of supervision once released from prison, unless such supervision is waived by a parole authority as being unnecessary.[9] Under this system parole is more of a privilege or favor granted to society than a privilege provided the individual inmate, for its prime motivation is the protection of the community. To be sure, most inmates not released on parole would rather not be subjected to mandatory supervision and would certainly not consider such a measure a privilege.

PAROLE AS A CONTRACT

Parole may be considered as a contract between the agency granting parole and the recipient of such a disposition. Each parolee is required to sign a document setting forth rules that he must obey or be subjected to sanctions such as parole revocation. The document containing the orders of parole usually sets forth general rules that all parolees must follow and specific rules tailored to meet the needs of a particular individual. The parolee reads the document containing these rules and regulations, and, in addition, the parole officer explains the rules and their significance to the parolee.

There are those in the correctional field who feel that a parolee is successful if he abides by the conditions of his contract. If parole success is thought of in terms of only fulfilling the conditions of a contract, little need take place in the form of therapeutic progress toward genuine change in attitudes and basic life styles. If the supervising parole agent detects no overt behavior on the parolee's part that is in violation of his contract, he is recorded as a successful parole case. Certainly a contract does exist in the form of conditions of parole for all parolees, but parole should be thought of as more than abiding by the conditions of a particular set of rules and regulations, some of which are unnecessarily stringent and others more relevant to small children than grown adults.

PAROLE AS A THERAPEUTIC MEASURE

A popular concept of parole is that of a correctional strategy whose basic function is to reduce recidivism through a process of therapeutic movement. It is felt that parolees for the most part need more than surveillance to ascertain whether they are fulfilling their parole contract. They also need to undergo a process of change in their basic attitudes and life styles in order to live a more responsible, constructive, and happy life once discharged from the system. To bring about such a change necessitates supervision by qualified and interested personnel, who must function as therapists in addition to carrying out their duties as case managers and quasi-police officers. The emphasis today is on parole as a therapeutic strategy, and the goal is to reduce crime through treatment innovations capable of directing the behavior of parolees into law-abiding channels.

THE ORGANIZATION OF PAROLE

The parole board

THE ISSUE OF AUTONOMY

Parole boards determine when an inmate shall be released from prison on parole. In the early era of corrections there were special parole boards, each concerned with one institution. Such boards were usually composed of institutional staff members largely concerned with institutional needs and programs, and they tended to place institutional considerations before individual and community needs. The basis for decision making would rest upon such issues as overcrowding, the enforcement of relatively petty rules, or the desire to be rid of a problem case.[10] Under that system, institutional personnel had a high degree of autonomy, since institutions were largely removed from the scrutiny of an independent body. The institutional staff had almost complete autocratic power over the inmate, who was dependent on them not only for favorable treatment within the institution but also for his release on parole. This allowed the institutional staff to coerce the inmate with threats of denial of parole if he did not conform to their wishes.

It was eventually considered necessary to reform the field of parole by taking the control of release procedures away from men directly involved in the operation of penal institutions and placing this decision-making power under the jurisdiction of an independent authority. In the adult field, parole-releasing authority is no longer under the control of men directly involved in the operation of correctional institutions,[11] and the same is true of juvenile institutions in many states. California is a good example of a state where parole decisions concerning juveniles do not include the staff of training schools but are made by an independent board.

Where the parole board functions as an independent authority, board members are usually appointed by the governor of a state without any special consideration being given to their knowledge of the field of corrections. In certain instances this system has resulted in the appointment of board members largely on the basis of political affiliations, and new parole board members are appointed whenever there is a change in a state administration.[12] Although some highly competent individuals are appointed to such boards, many boards are composed of former law enforcement officers, attorneys, businessmen, opticians, and farmers. The states of Michigan and Wisconsin, in an attempt to avoid this type of situation, have adopted a "merit system" for the appointment of parole board members. Members are required to have a college degree in one of the behavioral sciences and experience in correctional work.[13]

Parole boards are allowed to develop their own procedures for obtaining information about the inmate being considered for parole. In some instances, decisions on whom to parole are made on the basis of intuitive hunches or cursory information about the offender. Inmates have been denied parole on the basis of the expressed disapproval of a chief of police, district attorney, or judge. Some inmates have been denied parole because of a particular religious bias on the part of a board member. For example, one inmate serving time for sodomy at a state correctional institution claimed that a parole board member questioned him about the Bible's pronouncements on homosexuality to test his attitude toward Western law and morality.[14] Such a basis for the denial of parole would seem to violate the potential parolee's right to freedom of religion.

Parole boards usually have access to the inmate file in making a decision, but, in many cases, such files are incomplete and are usually prepared by caseworkers who have relatively little opportunity to observe inmates. In a few states reports are prepared by professional clinical personnel, but this is the exception rather than the rule. Daniel Glaser feels that data should be provided to parole boards by staff members who have the most contact with inmates.[15] Some boards employ institutional parole officers who are assigned full time to penal institutions, and who make reports to the board concerning the progress of the inmates. Although parole prediction devices are available to parole boards, they are seldom used as a tool in the decision-making process.

Parole board hearings are generally short and simple and are conducted in a climate of relative secrecy. The inmate usually appears before one or two members of the board and is given the opportunity to state his own case. Most jurisdictions provide the inmate with no statutory rights in the parole consideration process, except in some instances where the inmate has a right to a personal appearance before the board. Traditionally inmates are denied the right to counsel at the parole hearing, although an attorney might submit written arguments on behalf of his client.[16] In all board hearings the inmate must make an affirmative case for parole, although the Model Penal Code recommends that the inmate should no longer have to assume the burden of proof in the determination of whether he should be granted or denied parole. It suggests that the board must release an inmate on parole when he is first eligible unless he fails to meet certain specified conditions.[17]

Parole boards also enjoyed complete autonomy in revoking the parole of anyone who was charged by his parole officer with violating the conditions of his parole. However, the power of parole boards to revoke parole was significantly modified by the Morrissey decision of the United States Supreme Court.[18] This decision gives the parolee the right to a pre-revocation hearing where he has procedural protections including the right to summon witnesses in his behalf. Written notice of the proceedings must also be given. Gradually the courts appear to be going in the direction of taking away some of the autonomy enjoyed by parole boards in order to provide inmates with adequate due process under the Fourteenth Amendment.

THE ISSUE OF CONTINUITY

The trend in the field of corrections is to consolidate all types of correctional services into distinctive departments of corrections that subsume both institutional and field service programs. Under such a system the parole board is composed of a decision-making authority organizationally situated in an overall department of corrections but possessing independent power.[19] This type of parole structure takes away some of the autonomy a parole board enjoys as a separate and independent authority and further establishes a high degree of continuity and coordination between parole decision making and other areas of corrections. By placing both institutional and field services under one department, parole boards become more sensitive to institutional programs and goals and can help rather than hinder the initiation of many innovations surfacing today in the area of community treatment and mutual agreement programming. This continuity in the area of institutional and field services is necessary if correctional programs are to provide meaningful treatment from the time inmates are received at diagnostic centers to their discharge from parole. Such coordination of services also diminishes conflicts between departments of correction and independent boards.

Parole supervision

THE ROLE OF THE PAROLE AGENT

When parole first became a reality the major emphasis of the parole agent was on making certain that the parolee was conforming to the conditions governing his release. Parole was mainly a surveillance device practiced by agents with little or no training in the behavioral sciences, who were concerned mainly with the law enforcement aspects of their job. As the concept of parole expanded, the role of the parole agent also changed. Gradually it became apparent that there is no real contradiction between the law enforcement component of parole supervision and the counseling and treatment components, if both are practiced to encourage therapeutic change. The protection of society depends not only on the assurance that the parolee under supervision adheres strictly to the conditions of his parole, but also on whether the parolee's attitudes and behavior are altered in the direction of a law-abiding and responsible life style. Society is protected as much, if not more, by efforts in the direction of treatment as it is by concern with enforcing the law. Parole agents therefore play dual roles in order to achieve their major goal of reducing recidivism through rehabilitating offenders. Although the role of enforcing the law through making arrests and submitting violation reports to supervisors seems on the surface to contradict the role of providing understanding and supportive guidance, such roles actually complement one another. Therapeutic change sometimes necessitates firmness and enforcement of rules as well as understanding, kindness, and concerned assistance.

In the area of treatment, parole agents should provide tangible assistance to their parolees in the form of help in obtaining jobs and secure housing. In this role the parole agent must be careful not to make the parolee overly dependent on him, but should provide assistance in a way that allows the parolee to show individual initiative and as much responsibility as he is able. Parole agents must also coordinate with other community agencies in providing needed services to their parolees by making meaningful and intelligent referrals. Further, parole agents are expected to provide counseling on an individual and group level that promotes therapeutic change. Depending on his background and training, a parole agent may employ such counseling techniques as reassurance and persuasion, as well as techniques conducive to meaningful interpersonal encounter; and these approaches require the ability to engage in effective communication and the capacity for nonpossessive acceptance, personal warmth, and empathy.

As mentioned above, parole agents must perform duties that are normally referred to as "policing," as well as tasks that are treatment-oriented. He must maintain the delicate balance between treatment and punishment with the realization that both are significant in the rehabilitation of the parolee.

To adequately perform his duties, a parole agent should develop the ability to listen effectively and to understand the meaning of what others are trying to convey; and he should be able to convey his own thoughts in a way that can be understood. In addition to communication skills, the parole agent should have at least an average degree of analytic ability and judgment in order to be able to select pertinent information, effectively evaluate alternatives, and make sound decisions on the basis of the data available.

One of the most important characteristics that a parole officer needs is the ability to be effective in interpersonal relationships. He must be sensitive to the problems of others and be able to detect problematic situations that have a significant bearing on his client's attitude and behavior. Further, he must be able to empathize with his parolees, be able to understand their point of view, and be flexible enough to tolerate various life styles. He must also be able to gain the respect of his clients to the degree that they will trust him but will also know that they cannot manipulate him.

In many instances parole agents do not fulfill these roles to the degree necessary for the provision of either adequate control or treatment. It is unfortunate that in many jurisdictions parole supervision is little more than nominal. It is the general rule rather than the exception that the supervision of a parolee consists solely of an office interview once or twice a month and the completion each month of a report. The information obtained during these office visits is seldom verified, and parole agents seldom go into the field to make home visits or visits to the parolee's place of employment.[20] Such cursory supervision renders little information about how a parolee is actually adjusting to the community. Although some cases need little or no supervision, others need rather intensive supervision, and it is in the areas where medium and maximum supervisory services are desirable that parole supervision is lacking.

There are a number of reasons for inadequate parole supervision, most of them not justifiable. It is much easier to conduct parole supervisory work from an office than to make field visits. Most parole agents can list a number of reasons why they are chained to their offices, but most of the excuses offered for their failure to go out into the field are usually rationalizations to avoid more work or difficult interpersonal encounters. Large caseloads are not generally an adequate excuse for failure to make field visits or to provide more intensive supervision where needed. If there is a strong desire to work, and if the agent organizes his caseload properly and plans his daily schedule so as to achieve maximum work efficiency, cases needing field supervision and intensive care can be given more attention in order to insure adequate control and some degree of therapeutic movement.

A parole agent may neglect his caseload out of indifference to his work because of continual frustration and failure. Being subjected to manipulation by the parolee who is primarily interested in playing the "time game" outside the institution turns some parole agents into cynical skeptics who come to believe that all parolees are insincere about their intentions of living a responsible and law-abiding life. Other parole agents with a strong need to be liked are emotionally frustrated by the indifference of many parolees toward them; as a result, they may either ignore or penalize certain parolees for not responding in a more positive manner.

Other reasons for providing inadequate supervision may be the employment of untrained parole personnel or insufficient parole agency budgets, making any attempt at meaningful supervision unrealistic. Although certain required duties in the form of paper work and seemingly trivial tasks take away from any activities of a more important nature, the average parole agent could probably accomplish more in the way of meaningful supervision if the desire to do so was strong enough, and if sufficient inservice training were provided.

THE CHARACTERISTICS OF FRONT-LINE ORGANIZATION

Before the establishment of a centralized parole supervision service, parole officers operated out of specific penal institutions and were responsible to the warden or superintendent of the institution. In furnishing services to parolees, parole officers had the task of covering the state. This organizational structure was found to be impractical since it promoted overlapping in authority and gave rise to duplication of expense in states having several institutions.[21]

Some smaller states have retained parole supervision as an adjunct of the institution because a centralized parole service cannot be economically justified; but supervision of parolees in the field today is most often supplied by a central office attached to a parole board or organized as a separate bureau.[22] In large state jurisdictions, parole officers usually work out of district offices which are controlled and budgeted from a central state office. If the state does not provide for district offices, parole officers are assigned certain territories and are directed from the state office.[23]

The traditional front-line organization assigns a specific caseload to each officer in the field. The organization takes on an administrative style similar to most large bureaucracies. The front-line workers are given specific and clearly defined tasks, and their supervisors periodically check their performance in order to ascertain whether the tasks are being properly carried out. In turn, the supervisors are responsible to middle managers who receive orders from a higher source.[24]

The rhetoric of the front-line organization is that of rehabilitation through supportive assistance, and the development of positive relationships between the parole officer and parolee. What often happens, however, is that field operations stress surveillance and the protection of the agency from outside criticism.[25] In front-line operations, stress is often placed on the number of contacts made by the parole officer and there seems to be little genuine concern for the quality of the supervision being received by the parolee. Since the major emphasis appears to be on control rather than treatment, a case is deemed successful if written reports indicate that the parolee is complying with the conditions of his parole. Parole officers are rated successful on the basis of the number of field contacts they make during a given period and the promptness with which they submit reports indicating compliance with agency policies.

The bureaucratic organizational structure of the front-line organization allocates power on the basis of a hierarchy of command, with the parolee on the lowest rung in the hierarchy and therefore the least powerful. The chain of command is usually rigid, standardized, and predictable; and it discourages innovations in field supervision and organizational structure that might alter the regimentation of the present administration.[26] Within this field organizational structure, parolees, who are the lowest element in the chain of command, are not encouraged to make major contributions toward setting their own objectives. Further, this organizational structure lacks the flexibility necessary for the realization of a high degree of individual autonomy within a broader policy-making organization. A rigid, hierarchical organizational structure tends to discourage individual change, which is said to be the primary goal of parole supervision, and promotes instead the goal of production and orderly task performance.[27]

CENTRALIZATION AND THE LOCATION OF AUTHORITY

Gradually parole organization is going in the direction of consolidation. Agencies that were formerly autonomous are being incorporated into expanding departments of correction. The linking of institutional and field services places institutions and parole under common administrative direction which can foster the innovation of programs that share common goals. Such common direction can make possible a model reception, planning, and release system in which the program planning and evaluation are coordinated from reception into the system to release from the system.

Consolidation can also provide steps to break down the communication gap between field workers and institutional counselors that is sometimes brought about by the rural-urban dichotomy. Traditionally, institutions have been located in rural areas far from urban centers, whereas field services have usually located their central offices in metropolitan areas. This geographic separation of two major aspects of correctional services can have harmful results. Institutional personnel recruited from rural areas have little understanding of life styles common to the city and the ghetto. On the other hand, field service personnel generally reside in urban areas and have difficulty in communicating with their institutional counterparts. Through consolidation of services, field workers and institutional counselors could participate in joint training sessions that would help to overcome this communications gap. Effective communications channels could be further developed through promotions from institutions to field services and vice versa.[28]

The structure of a centralized agency should be flexible, permitting a regional or branch organization to adhere to broad policies from above, but giving it the autonomy to deal with problems peculiar to its own geographic and cultural area. Institutional and field services could be regionalized and placed under common administrators in each area, who are responsible to the head office. Such regionalization under the direction of a centralized office would allow correctional personnel to become acquainted with the problems and resources available in their area and also to develop programs that are meaningful for individuals who share a common cultural heritage. A community-based thrust in correctional services, therefore, need not be lost by centralization of services. Centralization need not deteriorate into a hierarchy of impersonal and rigid organizational rules and regulations that make so many bureaucratic organizations efficiently ineffectual.

Probably the area where organizational structure is needed most is in juvenile parole. In some states there is no organized program of juvenile parole, and offenders released from state juvenile institutions are referred back to their local probation departments for supervision. Some states place released juvenile offenders under the supervision of child welfare workers; others provide aftercare services by utilizing the institutional staff of the training school where the juvenile was housed.

The trend in juvenile corrections is to establish statewide juvenile correctional services, embracing both institutions and field aftercare such as can be found in California, where the California Youth Authority provides parole services to juveniles released from its institutions. Under a coordinated service delivery system, it would be possible to incorporate aftercare services in programs for juveniles sent to institutions. This would prevent the termination of any given program simply because of discharge from an institution. In states unlike California, where there is no coordination between institutional and aftercare services, there is little or no relationship between treatment programs provided to juveniles in state institutions and the type of services they receive after being released.

THE INTERDEPENDENCE OF PAROLE AND INCARCERATION

Effects of parole on the incarceration period

The inmate's conduct and cooperation while in prison may depend on his postinstitutional expectations of success or failure on parole. Even if he has positive expectations, they may not be accurate or conducive to resocialization.

Negative postrelease expectations may result from imprisonment.[29] If the indeterminate sentence is in effect, uncertainty about his release date will make him anxious. He may anticipate having problems on parole such as difficulty in finding and holding a job; fear of nonacceptance by family and friends; harmful effects of being stigmatized as an "ex-con"; and inability to abide by the many rules governing parole. The inmate may feel that he will fail on parole regardless of what his situation will be in the free community, and this anxiety may be compounded by misinformation he obtains from other inmates concerning parole supervision and the problems he will face in society.

This situation can be partly alleviated through institutional programming providing accurate data to the inmate concerning job information; factors that may hinder or foster social acceptance by family members and by society as a whole; and full information governing parole rules and expectations. Prerelease programs should begin at the time of the inmate's initial reception and continue throughout his period of incarceration.

Training programs, especially in the realm of education and vocational training, should be directed toward minimizing false postrelease expectations (whether they be negative or positive) by preparing the inmate to meet the demands of the free world to the best of his ability. There is little doubt that the inmate is correct in his expectation that he will face a myriad of problems once released on parole; but his optimism about his ability to overcome these problems might be enhanced through better release planning. Better release planning might have other important effects. It could encourage good conduct while in prison, and it could give reliable clues about the inmate's chances of resocialization, in that his postrelease expectations would be realistic and accurate. To coordinate institutional treatment programs with postrelease strategies, the institutional parole staff should take an active part, not only in prerelease activities, but in the formulation of programs during the initial classification process and during reclassification reviews.

Steps are being taken in some jurisdictions to ease the postrelease process and thereby relieve some of the anxiety presently experienced by inmates concerning their ability to survive, especially during the early stages of parole supervision. California provides a loan fund in the form of meal tickets and, in certain cases, in the form of cash advances up to $75.00 for such needs as clothing and tools for employability. Meal tickets are provided in order to reduce the possibility that funds will be used for alcohol or narcotics. Pressure is not applied for loan reimbursement, since it is felt that the small loan appropriation will pay for itself if it prevents a parolee from violating his parole because he becomes economically desperate.[30]

The Louisiana Penitentiary has established an inmate lending fund composed of inmate contributions which are used to assist needy inmates in preparation for release. Such funds are used to a large degree for legal assistance, in order to remove detainers filed against the inmate's release.[31] The Massachusetts Parole Board helps needy parolees by providing them with outright grants rather than loans.[32] If a man released from prison in Great Britain is destitute but willing to work if given the opportunity, he can obtain unemployment insurance providing him with enough money to meet his presumed minimum needs.[33]

Effects of institutionalization on parole

There is little doubt that institutionalization affects the attitude of most people toward life and their ability to make an adequate adjustment in the free community. The experience might or might not be crippling, depending to a great extent on the individual himself and the time he served in institutions. Many inmates fear that their confinement will result in a loss of initiative that will hinder their success on parole, especially in the area of competing with others for the luxuries and necessities of life. In prison the basic needs of the inmate are satisfied with little or no effort on his part.[34] Most institutions treat inmates like infants, denying them any right to participate in formulation of the rules, regulations, and programs governing their daily lives. Those inmates who do demonstrate concern and initiative by attempting to behave responsibly and in a mature adult manner may suffer disciplinary action within the institution and possible denial of parole.

Being incarcerated also gives rise to feelings of inferiority in the inmate that carry over into parole supervision. These feelings affect his parole success by preventing him from assimilating the social role of a responsible citizen. Men behind bars begin to feel like caged animals in a zoo. Gradually their manhood and feelings of self-worth diminish; and these feelings cannot be fully reinstated through a brief, stepped-up prerelease planning program. This dehumanization process and fostering of infant-like dependence cannot easily be overcome by some inmates, even by progressive methods of parole supervision. When a man is broken both spiritually and physically, he cannot be expected to behave like a well-adjusted, happy, and responsible adult. He may, on the contrary, feel bitter, hostile, rejected, inadequate, and hold society in contempt.

Enlightened programs may be able to help diminish the negative effects of institutionalization by providing the inmate with educational and vocational training programs that are realistically oriented to the free world and to the current job market and by allowing him to participate in planning his own treatment program and in formulating the rules governing his life while incarcerated. There is a great need for programs that would enhance an inmate's feelings of self-worth and prepare him to take on responsibilities more appropriate for the adult world than for the world of a dependent child.

THE FUTURE OF PAROLE

The unification of services

Indications are that, in the future, institutional and community supervision will be linked within an organizational structure combining all correctional services in one administrative unit. The consolidation of probation, parole, and institutional services will result in a correctional continuum that will follow the offender throughout all phases of his correctional involvement. The artificial isolation of one phase of corrections from another, resulting in the fragmentation and duplication of services, competition for public funds, and political friction, will gradually diminish. As already mentioned, some centralized parole supervision units at present operate as divisions within a department of corrections. Some states also allow the centralized parole service to do both juvenile and adult probation work in counties which have no probation service in their courts. Movements toward the integration of services are becoming more pronounced.

The future will also yield to more collaborative administrative regimes in parole for the purpose of implementing reintegration programs involving other community agencies. Offenders will not be supervised by individual parole officers, as has been the tradition, but by teams involving parole officers, community volunteers, and paraprofessionals. Decisions concerning a parolee's status will not be made by a supervising parole officer acting alone, but by these teams, which will have collective responsibility for a group of parolees. Such teams will, in some cases, involve other interested parolees as well as the parolee affected by the decision.[35]

The reintegration model will involve work with other community agencies such as schools, mental health clinics, probation departments, police departments, and social welfare agencies. Parole officers will develop skills that promote cooperation, communication, and collaboration with other community representatives. The power formerly held by parole officials over parolees will be shared with others.

The reintegration model calling for the unification of community services employing the team concept of parole supervision is opposed to the traditional rehabilitational model, which employs professional caseworkers supervising individual caseloads, and to the police model, which stresses surveillance and control. It is an attempt to revitalize parole supervision, which, in many instances, has stagnated through regimentation within bureaucracies which have lost sight of their original mission.

Rational use of the distribution function

In order to make parole supervision more successful, means must be discovered to make caseload distribution more efficient and effective. Many times caseloads are assigned to parole agents at random with no special consideration given to the supervision needs of each case, or to the personality characteristics of the supervising agent. The size of caseloads varies from state to state. In 1965 a national survey showed caseloads ranging from 37 to 245 in states with mixed caseloads, and from 40 to 93 in states with separate caseloads.[36] During the same year adults released on parole throughout the nation were supervised in caseloads averaging 68, although 22 percent of parolees were being supervised in caseloads of more than 80. In many states parole officers, in addition to supervision, must conduct presentence investigations in probation cases and must also investigate release plans for parolees.[37]

There has been a trend in parole to attempt meaningful differentiation of caseloads in order to make caseload distribution more equitable and rational. Differentiation of caseloads by sex and age has been employed for many years without any empirical rationale to support this practice. Such rigid policies of caseload distribution can be unnecessarily expensive and dysfunctional in the area of treatment. Differentiation by sex, for example, ignores situations where the client may respond more quickly to a worker of the opposite sex. Segregating caseloads by sex also increases the cost of furnishing parole supervision, since such differentiation demands two parallel systems of agents covering the same territory. Caseloads have also been differentiated by race and religion. A trend today, in some metropolitan areas, is to distribute cases by matching minority group parolees with minority group parole agents. In certain cases such a policy may be necessary, especially during the early period of supervision. As a general policy, however, it lacks merit since it assumes that agents of various minority groups are incapable of working together regardless of their educational background and experience. Such an assumption, of course, is without any empirical foundation.

For years there has been a widely perpetuated myth in the field of corrections that the most effective way to differentiate caseloads is by size alone, and that the ideal caseload size is 50 parolees. This figure is not based on research involving the influence of caseload size on supervision results. It probably found its way into professional journals and textbooks through some chance remark at a professional meeting.

Extensive research has been devoted, however, to discovering whether caseload size influences correctional outcome. One of the most significant studies aimed at testing whether or not a reduction in caseload size will positively influence parole supervision was the Special Intensive Parole Unit Project of the California Division of Adult Parole. This project was divided into four separate phases and covered a period of 12 years. Phase I of the project showed that when caseloads were reduced to 15, and parolees were given intensive supervision during the first 90 days after release and then transferred to the standard 90-man caseloads for regular supervision, only slight reductions in parole violation rates occurred.[38] During Phase II of the project, intensive supervision was accorded caseloads of 30 over a six-month period before the parolees were reassigned to regular caseload supervision. Still no significant difference was detected with regard to postrelease infractions.[39]

Speculation then developed as to whether the intensive supervision provided in the first two phases of the SIPU Project had been ineffective because the agent-parolee relationship had been interrupted through reassignment. Such speculation led to Phase III of the project, during which 35-man caseloads were compared to 72-man caseloads over a period of one year. The initial findings showed that the men in the smaller caseloads performed significantly better than those released to regular caseloads. The results also indicated that the best results were obtained with medium-risk parolees rather than with the best or poorest risks.[40] These findings gave reason to believe that the effect of caseload size was not a simple function of numbers but the consequence of other factors as well.

In order to explore further the complexities suggested by the first three phases of the SIPU Project, a fourth phase was undertaken.[41] One part of this phase was devoted to a study of the interaction between parolee and parole agent types. Low-maturity parolees were matched with "external-approach" agents, and high-maturity parolees were matched with "internal-approach" agents. The sizes of the caseloads were reduced to 30 for some experiments and 15 for others. The caseload size for the control groups was maintained at 72 men. The findings of this phase indicated that the only variable that made a real difference in parole outcome was the amount of time the parole agent had to devote to supervision. Interaction between agent and parolee characteristics did not seem to make any difference in the outcome. It was further shown that the 15-man caseloads performed no better than the 30-man caseloads.

In 1965, the California Department of Corrections began another project called the Parole Work Unit Program.[42] The purpose of this project was to introduce new concepts into caseload management. Instead of focusing major attention on caseload numbers, as had been done in the SIPU projects, the major emphasis was on the time required by the parole agent to meet the special needs of the men in his caseload. Increased emphasis was therefore given to the supervision of each parolee with regard to his service needs, and to allow agents sufficient time to accomplish the tasks required of them. A classification system was built into the program that focused on parole service requirements. Three classes of parole supervision were distinguished: Special—for "difficult" cases; Regular—for "average" cases; and Conditional—for parolees requiring minimal supervision. For purposes of the project a parole agent's workload was defined as 120 units, after taking into consideration the time agents usually had to reserve for general field and office duties. A "special" parolee was regarded as requiring five units of time, a "regular" as requiring three units, and a "conditional" approximately one unit. A maximum supervision caseload would therefore contain 25 special cases, 40 regular cases, or 120 conditionals. Caseloads could be altered to permit some combination of the three above-mentioned types of cases.

The concepts mentioned above were applied to 6,000 parolees (about one-half of the total parole caseload of the Department of Corrections). The remaining 6,000 parolees were carried in the conventional 72-man caseloads. The findings showed that during the first six months of the program the Work Unit parolees performed no better than the conventional parolees. During the second six-month period, however, the Work Unit parolees out-performed the conventional parolees in several categories. They had less serious difficulties on parole and fewer new felony convictions. It should be noted that the Work Unit parolees and the parolees on conventional caseloads were comparable in personality characteristics, social history, and delinquent backgrounds.

The operational consequences of the findings in the SIPU III and IV Projects were that the California State Department of Corrections authorized staff increases that reduced caseloads to an average of 36 parolees across one-half of the Department's 12,000 parolee population.[43]

A rational distribution of workloads is not simple to obtain. Studies are still in progress in order to determine the most effective and efficient methods to supervise parolees. The future of parole with regard to successful supervision will depend a good deal on the flexibility allowed by agencies in their supervisory process, and on continued attempts to test innovations in supervisory techniques. Thought should also be given to early release of parolees who appear to do well in the community without much official supervision. If only minimal contact seems to be necessary in a given case, parole officials should have access to a procedure by which they can discharge the case from parole. There is little doubt that more inmates could be discharged outright from prison without having to be placed on parole supervision for the protection of society. As part of the task of making a rational use of work distribution, more thought should be given to reducing the number of men placed on parole.

The use of offenders and ex-offenders

Offenders and ex-offenders are a promising source of manpower for parole work, especially in the role of a paraprofessional assigned to assist an agent. It has recently been recognized that offenders may have a skill to offer that can be used in helping others. Prisoners have always been put to work in prisons doing maintenance tasks and providing manpower for prison industries. It is not uncommon for certain southern prisons to use inmates as correctional officers. However, experimental programs have recently been undertaken in which ex-offenders have been used as counselors on the assumption that they can be effective in producing therapeutic change in offenders.[44] Ex-offenders have also founded halfway houses and community programs directed at the rehabilitation of those who are presently a part of the correctional system.

There are sound reasons why offenders and ex-offenders may be helpful as workers in the correctional field. Meaningful communication between professionals and offenders, both on the juvenile and adult levels, has always been a problem. Professionals in the field of corrections enter their work with values formed by middle-class life styles which are foreign to many of the clients with whom they associate. Differences in life styles place cultural barriers between the client and the correctional worker. Such cultural barriers, in turn, foster a growing misunderstanding, distrust, and animosity between the worker and his client, which tend to minimize the effectiveness of any treatment strategy. To complicate the situation, many correctional workers have little tolerance for life styles differing from their own. They tend to believe that all people should be either encouraged or coerced to live a normal life, which, of course, is defined as a life devoted to the perpetuation of their own ethical, political, and social values. Failure to realize that society should allow for flexibility in life styles and diversity of values has crippled corrections as an instrument of rehabilitation. Engaging offenders and ex-offenders in the correctional field can help to open up needed avenues of communication. Having the ability to speak the language of the offender, the paraprofessional can also detect attempts at manipulation which significantly hinder meaningful communication and lead to the playing of the time game. The "ex-con," for example, can easily penetrate defense mechanisms exhibited by inmates and parolees that would bewilder many conventional workers.

Permitting offenders and ex-offenders to work in the field of corrections also contributes to the development of their own self-esteem and adjustment. Having been trusted to work with others they may see themselves as being improved. Such work can therefore act as an ego-building device and provide for a degree of social status for the paraprofessional.

Certain states already employ paraprofessionals in the field of corrections through such outlets as the Public Employment Program (PEP) and the New Careers Development Project. The PEP program came into being through the Emergency Employment Act passed by the United States Congress in 1971. The purpose of the program is to help overcome unemployment by providing financial assistance to public employers so that they can hire unemployed and under-employed individuals in temporary jobs. The program also provides for job training with the goal of developing new careers and the opportunity for advancement.[45]

The guidelines of the PEP program allow for financial assistance to those agencies in the criminal justice field which employ individuals for rehabilitation work in the area of corrections. This program has encouraged the use of paraprofessionals in the field of corrections and has resulted in the filling of a number of PEP positions in corrections with ex-offenders in several states, including California.

The New Careers Development Project is a field demonstration project sponsored by the National Institute of Mental Health. Its goal is to provide meaningful employment for the disadvantaged and ex-offenders in public service, including corrections.[46] As a result, a New Careers Development Project based at the California Medical Facility at Vacaville, California was set up to train selected inmates from various correctional institutions for eventual work in social service jobs. Unfortunately, interest in hiring the inmate trainees produced by this program was shown by governmental units other than correctional agencies.[47]

There are strong indications that more offenders and ex-offenders will be employed as new career personnel in decentralized probation offices and community treatment centers located in ghetto areas. These individuals are aware of the realities of such communities and are usually more capable than professional workers at effectively confronting certain problems peculiar to the ghetto area. The cities of Seattle, Washington and Austin, Texas have already undertaken programs that enlist citizens from the ghetto community as workers.

One of the major problems in attempting to bring offenders and ex-offenders into the correctional field as paraprofessionals is that most probation and parole agencies cannot hire a person with a felony record. A further obstacle is the resistance of correctional administrators to employing their own products. Laws and attitudes will have to be changed if more offenders and ex-offenders are to work in correctional agencies in the future. There is reason to believe that this potential work force would enhance the correctional field; however, at present there appear to be no studies that meaningfully evaluate the results of the paraprofessional's contribution to corrections.

EVALUATION OF PAROLE

Problems of measurement

It is difficult to evaluate the effectiveness of parole as a correctional strategy, because so many factors other than parole selection and supervision influence abstention from crime, and because the quality of parole changes with time and varies among jurisdictions. Beyond the parole officer's control are postrelease factors relating to a parolee's family stability, job situation, relationships with the opposite sex, and physical health, any of which might significantly influence the parolee's performance in the community in a positive or negative fashion. It is difficult, if not impossible, to measure the effectiveness of parole supervision against such postrelease factors, most of which cannot be predicted at the time of selection for parole. In many cases the parole agent has a legitimate concern about whether the variables surrounding a parolee's decision to live a responsible life style can be significantly correlated with how he (the parole officer) functioned in his attempts at both control and therapeutic change, or whether these variables depend on circumstances beyond his control. Did the parole agent make any difference in the postrelease adjustment of his parolee, or would the parolee have conducted himself as he did in the absence of parole supervision? Lack of convincing data assuring the parole agent that he is doing a "good job" can be a source of job frustration.

Factors making the effectiveness of parole even more difficult to measure are the variations found from state to state in supervision policies, staffing capabilities, criteria for revocation and selection, and violation-reporting procedures. Some states, for example, provide intensive supervision for their parolees, while other states offer such minimum supervision that the parolee is required only to submit written reports of his whereabouts and daily activities, which go unverified. In some states more parolees are returned to prison for technical violations than in others; and in some jurisdictions parole may be revoked on grounds of suspicion, even when there is reason to believe that the parolee has not been involved in criminal activity. There is little doubt that the high rate of return to prison on the part of certain parole agencies can be traced back to a situation created by the policies of the agency itself. This is indicated by the fact that approximately three-quarters of all male parolees returned to prison in 1970 were returned for behavior that is not forbidden to the general public, for suspicion of offenses where guilt was not proved in court, and for conviction for minor offenses which would normally not have resulted in a prison sentence had not the offender been on parole.[48]

Selection procedures also vary from state to state. Some states place only minimal risk cases on parole, in contrast with states which place most of the inmates released from their penal institutions on some type of parole supervision. Is the true effectiveness of a parole system to be found in a jurisdiction where the system must work with the more difficult cases? If so, do success rates accurately measure the effectiveness of parole as a treatment strategy in jurisdictions where this correctional device is limited to those who will probably do well once released from prison regardless of the aftercare services they receive?

Consideration must also be given to the fact that parole agents have considerable discretion in responding to technical violations and do at times manipulate reports on individual parolee behavior to achieve organizational objectives.

It is therefore difficult to compare the results of different parole systems having diverse policies and standards, in order to make a quantitative estimate, on a nationwide basis, of the value of parole in reducing recidivism. The situation shows even more complexity when it becomes evident that recidivism rates depend not only on postrelease variables affecting the individual parolee and policies adhered to by different parole agencies but also on such variables as the differences in the criminal populations in the many states with regard to their capacity for rehabilitation; the efficiency of police departments in detecting crime and making arrests; and policies of restricting probation to "good risks." For example, California tends to encourage the placing of all good risk cases on probation. As a result, California prisons are filled with more "hard-core" inmates, making success on parole less likely in California than in a state where the inmate population includes many "good risk" parole candidates.

Rates of success

Generally, success rates in reference to parole refer to behavior of parolees during the period of parole supervision that does not lead to revocation of their parole and their return to confinement in a correctional institution. Success rates vary from state to state because the parole policies and practices of states differ, and for other reasons already mentioned in this chapter. In an effort to cope with the variance in parole statistics, the National Uniform Parole Reports System has provided a document entitled *Uniform Parole Reports,* a publication of the National Probation and Parole Institutes of the National Council on Crime and Delinquency. Parole agencies on state and federal levels cooperate in sending to the Uniform Parole Report Center information concerning felony offenders, such as their age, sex, and prior record, in an effort to develop common terms to describe parolees, and common definitions of parole performance. As a result, comparison of parole performance from state to state is becoming more of a reality. Further, the information provided by the *Reports* can be used as an indicator of parole success on a nationwide level. By providing the basis for making reasonably valid generalizations or estimates about parole recidivism and the reasons for it, the *Reports* could reduce to a minimum the problems of interpreting data and coping with discrepancies in policy. One problem is, however, that some of the largest states report only a random sample of their parolees or report only on parolees released during certain months of the year. Consequently these states are under-represented in the *Uniform Parole Reports.*

An examination of the parole recidivism statistics from the *Uniform Parole Reports* of 1972 and 1973 reveal some interesting information. At the end of one year, 18.9 percent of the 25,602 inmates paroled in 1970 had been returned to prison,[49] and 27 percent of the 1969 male parolees had been returned to prison two years after release.[50] The figures for the recidivism rate given above for the two-year period following 1969 show that the recidivism rate declines substantially after the first year on parole. These findings would back up the belief of correctional administrators that the risk of recidivism is at its highest during the first year following release from prison.

The *Reports* also show that of the 18.9 percent of inmates paroled in 1970 and returned to prison, only 25 percent were returned with a new major conviction. The remainder of the parolees were returned as technical violators, the majority of whom were not even suspected of being involved in a new offense.[51] Further, if recidivism is defined as new known involvement in serious criminal activity, rather than as return to prison, the *Reports* show that the recidivism rate is only 5–8 percent for the first year after release, and less in subsequent years. Of those 5–8 percent returned to prison for a new major conviction, only 0.73 percent were returned for conviction or suspicion of a violent offense (homicide, manslaughter, forcible rape, and aggravated assault) and 1.1 percent were returned for potentially violent offenses (armed robbery and unarmed robbery). The other parolees were returned for nonviolent property crimes or violations of the drug laws.[52]

David F. Greenberg states that the low rate of recidivism shown by figures such as those given above is not to be thought of as the result of a highly effective parole system, because research on recidivism indicates that prisoners released without parole supervision recidivate with the same frequency as prisoners on parole.[53] Studies further reveal that the intensity of parole supervision does not appear to influence recidivism rates.[54]

The low recidivism rates might also be thought to result from successful rehabilitation programs within the prison itself, but this does not seem to be the case. Studies show that rehabilitation programs in prison have no measurable effect on recidivism.[55] Further, recidivism rates do not seem to be affected by the amount of time an individual serves in prison, causing one to question the common assumption that imprisonment increases the likelihood of future criminal activity.[56]

Greenberg also allows for the possibility that low recidivism rates for commission of serious crimes are due to the fact that official statistics seriously understate the amount of recidivism and that this understatement is due to the inability of the police to clear most such crimes through arrest, leaving the perpetrator to go undetected. The true rate of return to crime might be much higher than official statistics indicate.[57]

The *Uniform Parole Reports* do indicate that the assumptions that prisons are only schools for crime, and that parole recidivism rates are extremely high, might well be in error. Many politicians, civic leaders, and even those in the field of corrections make public statements to the effect that more than half the prisoners released from prison return convicted of a subsequent crime. Such statements are usually presented without reliable statistical information to support them, and they are sohetimes made for the purpose of generating interest and money in new institutional and noninstitutional treatment strategies or to provide ammunition for periodic "crime-busting" propaganda campaigns as a means to political advancement.

Perhaps we should reexamine the problem of recidivism more closely before committing ourselves to the time and money involved in correctional strategies that may prove ineffectual in changing rates of recidivism. Even those correctional administrators who estimate that only 10–15 percent of the inmate population present a threat of personal injury to the public may be overestimating their case. Parole statistics in this area do not seem to be as alarming as was once believed. The problem in corrections at present is to determine just what degree of success and failure on parole is a result of parole supervision and policy, methods of parole selection, and prison rehabilitational programs. It would be discouraging to learn that much of what is now being done in corrections is ineffective in producing meaningful change in the offenders within its sphere of influence. If such is the case, innovations in goals, attitudes, and correctional philosophies will have to emerge, replacing those that appear outdated and of little operational import.

NOTES

1. Edwin H. Sutherland and Donald R. Cressey, *Criminology*, 8th ed. (New York: J.P. Lippincott, 1970), p. 585.

2. New York State Division of Parole, *Manual for Parole Officers*, 1953, as reprinted in George G. Killinger and Paul F. Cromwell, Jr., *Corrections in the Community: Alternatives to Imprisonment* (St. Paul, Minn.: West Publishing, 1974), p. 400.

3. Killinger and Cromwell, note 2, supra, p. 400.

4. Ibid., p. 401.

5. Ibid. pp. 407–411.

6. Ibid., p. 414.

7. Harry Elmer Barnes and Negley K. Teeters, *New Horizons in Criminology*, 2nd ed. (Englewood Cliffs, N.J.: Prentice-Hall, 1951), p. 778.

8. Ibid., p. 781.

9. President's Crime Commission, *Task Force Report: Corrections* (Washington, D.C.: Government Printing Office, 1967), p. 63.

10. The National Advisory Commission on Criminal Justice Standards and Goals, *Report on Corrections*, 1973, as reprinted in Killinger and Cromwell, note 2, supra, p. 436.

11. Sutherland and Cressey, note 1, supra, p. 587.

12. President's Crime Commission, *Task Force Report: Corrections*, note 9, supra, p. 67.

13. Ibid., p. 67.

14. Murton Foundation, *The Freeworld Times* 1, no. 10 (December 1972): 5.

15. Daniel Glaser, *The Effectiveness of a Prison and Parole System* (Indianapolis: Bobbs-Merrill, 1969).

16. Hazel N. Kerper, *Introduction to the Criminal Justice System* (St. Paul, Minn.: West Publishing, 1972), p. 369.

17. American Law Institute, *Model Penal Code* (Philadelphia, 1962).

18. Morrissey v. Brewer, 408 U.S. 471, 33 L. Ed. 2d 484 (1972).

19. Killinger and Cromwell, note 2, supra, p. 437.

20. Terry A. Cromwell, "Supervision of Parole and Probation Iases," as prepared for Killinger and Cromwell, note 2, supra, pp. 501–502.

21. *15th Annual Report of the Pennsylvania Board of Parole* (Harrisburg: Board of Parole, Commonwealth of Pennsylvania, 1958), pp. 63–71.

22. Ibid.

23. Ibid.

24. The National Advisory Commission on Criminal Justice Standards and Goals, *Report on Corrections,* 1973, as reprinted in Killinger and Cromwell, note 2, supra, p. 465.

25. Ibid.

26. Ibid.

27. Ibid., p. 466.

28. Ibid., p. 463.

29. Richard Cloward, Donald Cressey, et al., *Theoretical Studies in Social Organization of the Prison* (New York: Social Science Research Council, 1960).

30. Daniel Glaser, note 15, supra, 271–272.

31. Ibid., p. 272.

32. Ibid.

33. Ibid., p. 274.

34. J. E. Baker, "Preparing Prisoners for Their Return to the Community," in Robert Carter, Daniel Glaser, and Leslie T. Wilkins, *Correctional Institutions* (New York: J. B. Lippincott, 1972), pp. 373–374.

35. The National Advisory Commission on Criminal Justice Standards and Goals, *Report on Corrections,* 1973, as reprinted in Killinger and Cromwell, note 2, supra, pp. 464–467.

36. President's Crime Commission, *Task Force Report: Corrections,* note 9, supra, p. 189.

37. Ibid., p. 70.

38. Division of Adult Parole, Adult Authority, *Special Intensive Parole Unit, Phase I: Fifteen-Man Caseload Study,* November 1956 (State of California).

39. Ibid., *Phase II: Thirty-Man Caseload Study,* December 1958 (State of California).

40. Joan Havel and Elaine Sulka, *Special Intensive Parole aunit, Phase III,* Research Report No. 3, California Department of Corrections, March 1962.

41. Joan Havel, *Special Intensive Parole Unit, Phase IV: The Parole Outcome Study,* Research Report No. 13, California Department of Corrections, September 1965.

42. California State Department of Corrections, *Parole Work Unit Program: An Evaluative Report,* December 1966.

43. Stuart Adams, "Some Findings from Correctional Caseload Research," *Federal Probation* 31, no. 4 (December 1967): 48–57.

44. President's Crime Commission, *Task Force Report: Corrections,* note 9, supra, p. 103.

45. Melvin T. Axilbund, "New Pep for Corrections," *American Journal of Corrections* 33, no. 5 (September–October 1971): 30 31.

46. Keith A. Stubblefield and Larry L. Dye, "Introducion," *Offenders as a Correctional Manpower Resource* (Washington, D.C.: Joint Commission on Correctional Manpower and Training, June 1968).

47. Paul W. Keve, *Imaginative Programming in Probation and Parole* (Minneapolis: University of Minnesota Press, 1967), pp. 217–219.

48. David F. Greenberg, *Parole Recidivism and the Incapacitative Effects of Im-*

prisonment (Paper prepared for the Society for the Study of Social Problems Conference, Montreal, August 1974), p. 9.

49.   National Probation and Parole Institutes of the National Council on Crime and Delinquency, *Uniform Parole Reports* (November 1972).

50.   Ibid., February 1973.

51.   Ibid., November 1972.

52.   Ibid.

53.   David F. Greenberg, note 48, supra, pp. 10–11. See also Research Division, Administrative Statistics Section, California Department of Corrections, *California Prisoners 1964–1966* (Sacramento, California, 1968); P.F.C. Mueller, *Advanced Release to Parole*, Research Report No. 20 (California Department of Corrections Research Division, Sacramento, California, 1965); Summary *Report* on New York Parole (Citizen's Inquiry on Parole and Criminal Justice, Inc., New York, 1974), p. 22.

54.   Greenberg, note 48, supra, p. 11.

55.   Ibid., p. 11.

56.   Ibid., p. 11. See also John E. Berecochea, Dorothy R. Jamen, and Walton A. Jones, *Time Served in Prison and Parole Outcome: An Experimental Study*, Research Report No. 49 (Sacramento: California Department of Corrections Research Division, 1973).

57.   Greenberg, note 48, supra, pp. 11 and 18.

Other Correctional Strategies on the Community Level 7

Corrections has more and more looked toward the community to assist the offender in his readjustment to society. At the community level, corrections involves both public and private agencies and employs many innovations directed at rehabilitation. Fines, imprisonment, probation, and parole cannot fill all the demands created by the wide variety of offenders who come to the attention of correctional agencies. Some offenders need close control and custody, and several correctional facilities are already available which were designed for that purpose. There are other offenders who require little or no control and custody, and problems may arise in finding meaningful correctional alternatives for this group.

Until recently, the only alternatives available to a judge were probation or incarceration. Probation might be ineffective in some cases because it provides neither sufficient structure nor adequate services for preventing the continuance of criminal behavior. On the other hand, incarceration is also inappropriate as a solution to many offenders' problems and may foster the development of more hardened criminality. For these and other reasons, correctional personnel have been experimenting with several types of residential and nonresidential strategies, in the hope of providing the "proper" program for each offender who becomes involved in the criminal justice system. Although there is no concrete evidence that any correctional strategy presently in operation is "the answer" to controlling crime and rehabilitating criminals, attempts are being made to find viable correctional alternatives to a system which has proven to be largely a failure. It is with these attempts at creative alternatives in the field of corrections that this chapter is concerned.

INSTITUTIONAL STRATEGIES AT THE COMMUNITY LEVEL

Work and educational release programs

HISTORICAL DEVELOPMENT OF WORK RELEASE

In 1913, the Huber Law was enacted by the Wisconsin state legislature, marking a milestone in the field of corrections. This was the first legislation in this country enabling local sheriffs to parole prisoners from the county jail during the day so that they could engage in gainful employment in the community. This parole technique has since been expanded and is now commonly referred to as work release. Its use has been hailed by many authorities in the correctional field as the most valuable rehabilitational tool since the advent of probation and parole.

As it is now applied, work release is a rehabilitational device permitting inmates of a local county jail, or a state or federal correctional facility, to leave their institutions in order to pursue regular employment in the community, while under the jurisdiction and supervision of correctional or law enforcement agencies. Recent legislation in some states allows prisoners, under existing work release laws, to further their academic or vocational education in public or private educational institutions in the community.

Until 1943, there was almost no application of the Huber law. In 1943 more extensive use of the law was made by Municipal Court Judge Oscar J. Schmiege of Outagamie County, Wisconsin. In order to meet the labor needs of the Second World War, Judge Schmiege initiated a day parole program under which almost anyone not dangerous to society could be regularly employed outside the jail and pay for his own keep. After the war, the law was largely forgotten until the 1950s when many states initiated work release legislation. The idea spread rapidly until today most states, the District of Columbia, and the federal government are offering some form of work release to confined prisoners.

ADVANTAGES OF WORK AND EDUCATIONAL RELEASE

The original impetus for expansion of the work release idea appears to have been the economic gain realized by the communities and governmental agencies adopting it. Once in practice, however, it was found that in addition to economic gains, work release provided a vehicle through which to keep families intact, preserve careers and jobs, and introduce previously untrained individuals to new vocational skills and responsible working habits. Work release was also felt to have a positive psychological effect on the prisoner. Persons committed to local jails and prisons face an unwholesome and monotonous existence, the effects of which do not automatically disappear upon release. In many cases a man comes out of jail or prison demoralized, lazy, hostile, and with little hope for the future. Work release can be a substantial morale builder, enabling men to make worthwhile use of their time by being constructively employed. In this way, consistent working habits are encouraged which help many prisoners to maintain their employment once released from jail or prison. By being regularly employed and by supporting their families unassisted, these individuals gain a degree of self-respect and community approval, which enable them to develop more satisfying self-concepts.

In Marin County, California, where the work release program is administered by the Chief Probation Officer, the families of work release participants benefit substantially from the program. Many prisoners with families in the community are allowed to eat their meals at home, spending an hour or so with their families during every working day. Such visits are important, for they allow the prisoner to be in immediate contact with his wife and children and help keep the family together as a unit. The children of such prisoners probably derive a sense of security from seeing their father in the household, and the identification that they previously established with their father is preserved. When released from jail, the father does not return to a strange or modified home environment but to one that he has been able to share during much of his incarceration. Because of this the family unit is more likely to continue functioning in a normal fashion. The federal government tries to provide the benefits of home visits through the unescorted furlough.[1]

The economic benefit found in work release is its prime selling point to communities and correctional administrators. Work release participants contribute toward their room and board, and money from their work release earnings may also be distributed among child support, fines, and restitution to victims.[2]

In addition to work release benefits, opportunities provided for educational release are most valuable in enabling prisoners to further their education whether it be academic or vocational. In many jurisdictions, if members of unions are on work or educational release, they are allowed to attend classes that are mandatory for continued union membership.

FACTORS THAT RESTRICT WORK RELEASE PROGRAMS

One major hindrance to work and educational programs is the restrictions placed on the selection of potential candidates. If full rehabilitative benefits are to be realized from work and educational release, there should be as few judicial or administrative exclusions as possible. The only cases that should be automatically excluded from work release are prisoners with prior escape records and prisoners who might be expected to do great bodily harm to others if released from prison. Experience has also affirmed that selection of candidates for work release on the county level can be made in a matter of hours. There are no grounds for restricting work release privileges to inmates who have received sentences of thirty days or over, or who have completed a good portion of a lengthy jail or prison sentence. Inmates sentenced to three days in jail for a vehicle code violation should be eligible for work release, for the obvious reason that they could lose their current jobs by being absent from work for the three-day period of incarceration. On the state and federal levels, means must be provided to allow recently confined inmates the privilege of work and educational release, instead of limiting participation to prisoners who are on the last six months or ninety days of their sentence.

THE FEDERAL GOVERNMENT'S WORK RELEASE PROGRAM.[3]

Inmates incarcerated in federal correctional institutions were given the potential of participating in work release programs with the passing of the Prisoner Rehabilitation Act, which was signed into law by President Johnson on September 10, 1965. The most significant provision of this law is the work release program.

The work release program provides that inmates of federal correctional institutions may be employed in nearby communities, returning to the institution at night. This program was enhanced on November 7, 1966, when the President signed the Manpower Development and Training Amendment authorizing the Secretary of Labor to develop and implement experimental training and educational projects for federal, state, and local inmates. Projects may include vocational, prevocational, basic and secondary education, job placement, and job counseling.

On January 1, 1967, work release was given added emphasis under a major reorganization of the Bureau of Prisons. A division of Community Services was created to administer work release and related programs.

Federal inmates must volunteer for work release. Full minimum custody is a prerequisite for eligibility. Work release is not authorized for offenders identified with large scale, organized criminal activity, or for inmates serving sentences for crimes of violence.

Work release is extended to an inmate only if it can be shown that there is a need for the opportunities and responsibilities which such a strategy provides, and if it is felt that the inmate will benefit from the experience. These matters are determined by a prison classification committee.

Each job offer is investigated to determine whether it is bona fide, is consistent with basic work release policies, and will adequately fulfill the institution's objectives for the inmate involved. Exploitation in any form is avoided. The compensation of work release inmates must be no less than that of comparable workers. They are not to be employed as strikebreakers. Work release jobs are not restricted to normal working hours. When suitable transportation can be arranged, there is no objection to shift work or overtime.

Work release prisoners share in the expenses connected with their employment. The inmate is outfitted with clothing suitable for the kind of work at which he will be employed. Inmates must purchase with their own funds all supplemental and replacement clothing. They also pay their share of transportation costs.

Inmates without funds may receive a cash advance, as authorized by the warden from commissary loan funds, up to $100.00. This money is used for the purchase of clothing and for payment of other necessary expenses until the first pay check is received. The inmate is required to make full reimbursement from subsequent earnings.

From its inception until the end of 1966, more than 2,000 prisoners participated in the work release program. Their earnings through December 31, 1966 totaled $2,147,000.00. Of this amount, $373,000 went to the inmates' dependent families; $203,000 went to the Federal government for the inmates' room and board; $303,000 was paid in federal, state, and local social security taxes; $575,000 was spent with merchants near the inmates' institutions; and the remainder was placed in inmates' saving accounts.

The release phase of the correctional continuum

COMMUNITY CENTER PROGRAMS

The community treatment center is largely the innovation of the federal government. Federal community centers first opened in 1961 in Los Angeles and New York. In Los Angeles, church property was rented by the government, and in New York, rooms in a Brooklyn YMCA were used for the housing of prisoners. At present there are federal community centers in such cities as Chicago, Detroit, Houston, Atlanta, Kansas City, Los Angeles, and Oakland.

Men are transferred from federal prisons to the community centers. Such centers may therefore be thought of as extensions of the prison. No federal prisoners are excluded from being considered for placement in such centers, except those connected with organized crime. Individuals coming under the Federal Youth Corrections Act can be sent directly to the centers upon sentencing. Prisoners are sent to centers located in areas where they have relatives and friends. A short time after arrival at a center the inmate is interviewed by a U.S. probation officer for future parole planning. It is felt that if the inmate forms a working relationship with the probation officer at the outset, this will facilitate a smooth transition from the center to parole supervision.

Federal community centers house approximately twenty-five men, most of them in their twenties and early thirties. There are few restrictions. During the week there is an eleven p.m. curfew, which is sometimes waived if a resident is watching a late movie on television. Inmates are free to leave the center at six a.m. If they have relatives or friends in the community they can obtain weekend passes. Even without passes, they can be away from the center on Saturdays and Sundays from six a.m. to midnight, and this time can be extended if they are on dates or attending special functions. Each center has a director, administrative assistant, caseworkers, and an employment placement officer. The centers also hire students as part-time personnel, who help manage the operation on weekends and also engage in research projects.[4]

The community center program idea spread, and many states have opened community treatment centers and prerelease centers. Usually the centers house prisoners who are on the last ninety days of their sentence, although there are exceptions to this rule. The centers depend largely on community resources for treatment and funding support. For example, wide use is made of such agencies as the Department of Employment, the Department of Social Services, the Department of Public Education, and the Department of Mental Hygiene. Staff members attempt to mobilize and coordinate community resources and involve the residents in community-based programs. In the more structured community treatment programs various types of counseling, educational, and vocational programs are available. Counseling services, for example, may focus on family problems, drug abuse and alcoholism, community awareness, and problems related to parole supervision.

One valuable treatment device incorporated in some community treatment centers is a community work training program. Many residents from the prison population must overcome various problems before they can obtain adequate employment in the community. Certain residents will not have the sophistication, training, and basic presence necessary to secure employment. Some residents will have difficulty in completing the simplest employment application and must be schooled in filling out job applications. Employment guidance specialists at the centers provide attention to those residents who need training in some marketable skill and instruction in how to compete for job opportunities in the open market.

Many centers have a house government program which encourages the residents to participate in self-government. "Out-count" programs are also available, in which a resident who has completed approximately half of his stay at a center can live outside the center at home with his family, or in his own room or apartment if he has no wife or family in the area. Residents living apart from the center maintain daily telephone contact with the staff and report to the center periodically during the week. The out-count program is another step in attempting to build the resources necessary for a self-sufficient life free of daily management by someone other than oneself. Various types of recreational and visitation programs are also available at the centers.

Credit unions have been established at such centers as the Brooke House (a Massachusetts halfway house for men coming out of correctional institutions and returning to Metropolitan Boston). Such credit unions open legitimate channels of finance to men who would otherwise not be eligible for loans or would be able to obtain them only at high interest rates.

The Community Correctional Center in Oakland, California, managed by the Department of Corrections, houses both parolees and the local State Parole Office in the same building, making parole officers available to the residents at all times.

PRISON FURLOUGHS

Furloughs from state and federal correctional institutions may be granted to inmates for such reasons as to visit and assist families in emergencies (such as critical illness or death), to interview prospective employers, and to aid the inmate in maintaining and strengthening family ties. Furloughs average from forty-eight to seventy-two hours, with some inmates in certain systems being allowed to remain away from prison for a week. It is becoming more and more common to allow inmates to have furloughs during major holidays such as Christmas.

There have been many criticisms of the furlough program by law enforcement officers, politicians, and members of the community. Although most inmates on furlough do not commit crimes and are not dangerous to the community, a few have engaged in criminal acts which were reported in the press and resulted in the termination of the furlough program in some jurisdictions. For example, in the state of Washington one inmate on furlough allegedly shot and killed a law enforcement officer. Up to that time 2,049 inmates had been released on furlough in Washington with only 2 percent, or 42, failing to return to the prison as directed. After the shooting of the police officer much pressure was placed on the Governor by law enforcement officers and prosecutors to have the program terminated. However, Governor Donald Evans insisted that the furlough program continue because he believed in its rehabilitative potential. The program was continued, but under new and more stringent regulations which excluded medium and maximum security inmates from furlough privileges.

California also experienced difficulty with its furlough program when an inmate from Chino shot a police officer to death. Two other deaths were also attributed to furloughed inmates. As a result, the seventy-two hour furlough program was temporarily halted in California.

In most states no such problems have arisen as a result of allowing furloughs to inmates. Most correctional administrators feel that the furlough program is of value as a rehabilitative tool in that it allows the inmate an opportunity to function in the community on his own for a period of time, thereby testing his ability to live away from a highly structured environment.

Halfway houses

Halfway houses were originally the creations of religious and private agencies and were limited mainly to the treatment of adult offenders. The early halfway houses did not appear to be considered as part of the correctional system, and many professionals during the 1880s held the founders of such houses in contempt. As early as 1864 a halfway house was opened in Boston for women released from institutions. During the latter part of the nineteenth century halfway houses were opened in New York City and Philadelphia. The early halfway house founders deserve a good deal of credit, for they not only pioneered an important community treatment strategy, but they also carried out their work in the face of public and official hostility and indifference.[5]

The early halfway houses did not have structured programs, and treatment was not an integral part of the service to residents. Their aim was to meet the basic needs of the offender so that he could survive and bridge the gap between institutionalization and the free community. The highly structured and treatment-oriented halfway houses of today have been in existence for only about ten years. Halfway houses were not accepted until fairly recently as a vital and necessary aspect of the correctional system. Because of its significance to corrections, the idea of the halfway house has been expanded to serve a diverse body of offenders, both juvenile and adult, through a wide variety of treatment and supportive programs.

Halfway houses serve many purposes as a correctional strategy. One major purpose is to provide supportive housing or shelter to individuals released from institutions who would otherwise have no place to live. This is an especially important function for overdue parolees—men who must remain in prison, although eligible for parole, because they have no job or suitable living arrangement available on the outside. Parole boards now allow inmates to be paroled to halfway houses, where they can live while they seek employment on their own initiative. Such houses also provide housing and programs for offenders who need more structure than probation can provide but who need not be confined in an adult correctional institution or a state juvenile training school. Certain halfway houses specialize in offering programs to narcotic addicts and alcoholics; others house individuals released on bail prior to the final disposition of their case, where bail might otherwise be denied because of the lack of a suitable living arrangement. Recently halfway houses have been used for the purpose of diverting the offender from the criminal justice system.

Halfway houses vary according to the type of individuals whom they house and treat. Some are highly structured, and some have little in the way of program. Although many do not have formal group or individual counseling programs, most do offer some kind of supportive assistance. Some halfway house programs, especially those attempting to treat narcotic addicts, employ guided group interaction techniques, including the encounter group therapy approach used by self-help groups such as Synanon. One significant development in the halfway house program is the use of offenders and ex-offenders as change agents.

It is of interest to observe that the early halfway houses were conceived and operated without help from professionals and that the current trend, also, is away from management of halfway programs by professional staff. More and more such programs are being conducted by private agencies under the direction of nonprofessionals and self-help groups. One sometimes wonders just to what degree the professional is really needed in the field of corrections and whether or not the field is recruiting most of its working personnel from the wrong source.

DRUG ABUSE PROGRAMS
Daytop Village

Daytop Village was originally a halfway house operated by the Kings County Probation Department in Brooklyn, New York, for convicted drug addicts on probation in the Second Judicial District. The program originated in October 1963 and was made possible through a grant of the National Institute of Mental Health.[6] It now operates as a private nonprofit foundation receiving funds from the New York State Narcotic Addiction Control Commission and is no longer restricted to probationers. The program operates out of three residential communities in the New York City area which have a total capacity of 550 patients.[7]

In addition to housing offenders convicted of crimes and placed on probation and parole, the Village also serves to divert individuals from the criminal justice process. There is no statutory provision for diversion, and the pre-adjudication diversion procedure is informal. A court liaison officer interviews individual candidates in order to evaluate their eligibility and willingness to be treated. If the person is felt to be a good candidate for admission to the program, his case is adjourned for a period of two months and he is placed in the Village on a kind of informal probation. Adjournment must be renewed every two months, and renewal is dependent on his progress in the program. After six to eight months of compliance with program requirements, the charges against these preconviction referrals are dismissed.

Daytop Village employs treatment techniques similar to those applied by Synanon, such as the use of encounter groups and the use of other addicts as change agents. Daily seminars are held on abstract subjects such as religion and philosophy. Reality therapy prevails, dealing with the here-and-now rather than focusing on the past. Residents go through three major program stages. During the first stage the resident is permitted no contact with family or friends and is supervised by an older and more mature resident who has already demonstrated a good degree of responsibility. During the second phase, the resident is permitted to accept employment on the outside but must return to the Village in the evening. He is expected to pay rent out of his earnings. During the final stage of the treatment program the resident returns to his family in the community, sometimes under formal supervision of a probation or parole officer. Whenever a problem arises he is encouraged to contact the Village to discuss it.

The Illinois Drug Abuse Program

The Illinois Drug Abuse Program was established in 1968 and is financed by the State Department of Mental Health. The major goal of the program is to help individuals who were once irresponsible and drug-addicted to lead productive and drug-free lives. The project utilizes a multimodality approach in an attempt to serve the diverse needs of patients and also to allow for program flexibility. Two multimodality residential centers are operated as part of the program in the Chicago area; these serve narcotic drug users, non-narcotic drug users, former users who have been detoxified by methadone, methadone-maintenance patients, and those now abstaining from drugs. Many staff workers are themselves former addicts.[8]

The program provides for group therapy, methadone maintenance, medical and social services in halfway houses and therapeutic communities; and treatment of users of amphetamines, barbiturates, and hallucinogenic drugs. Approximately 25 percent of the participants in the program have been referred from the criminal court. All agencies involved in the program have a structure and function which are defined by statute. There are statutory restrictions on the types of offenders who can participate in the program, depending on the nature of the crime committed. An individual is disqualified for treatment if he has been enrolled in a drug program on two previous occasions within any consecutive two-year period.

The program serves largely as a pre-adjudication diversionary device. An intake representative screens those arrested for drug use, and potential candidates are further interviewed and given medical examinations to detect signs of addiction. Candidates who are pre-adjudication cases and are accepted for the program because of their likelihood of rehabilitation are referred for a period of up to two years. The statute provides that treatment can be completed at any time during the two-year period. If the offender fails to adjust to the program or leaves without permission, the charges pending against him are reinstated. If he successfully completes a program of treatment, the charges against him are dropped without his having suffered a conviction. Some offenders are referred to the program as a condition of probation after having been convicted of a crime. The maximum term of treatment for these individuals is either five years or the length of their sentence on probation, whichever is less.

Detoxification centers

To help police officers divert homeless alcoholics from the criminal justice system, detoxification centers have been introduced in several metropolitan areas where the alcoholic is detained under a civil rather than criminal commitment. Such detoxification centers replace the police station and drunk tanks as initial detention units for alcoholics. Detoxification centers detain the patient until he is at least sober. The goal of these detoxification programs is not primarily to cure alcoholics but to divert nuisance cases from the jail and court and, at the same time, provide short-term care for alcoholics in need of treatment.

At the St. Louis detoxification center in the St. Louis Hospital, patients are given food and medical care, with optional counseling services available. Individuals arrested for public drunkenness in St. Louis have a choice between treatment at the center and criminal prosecution. Criminal proceedings are suspended against those who accept treatment pending the completion of the seven-day program.[9]

The District of Columbia operates a detoxification center program which is available to "walk-ins" and is mandatory for intoxicated persons apprehended by the police. These people may stay in the program for one to three days. Many are released after spending a day at the center receiving medical attention and food. Some remain for three days; and the more serious patients are referred to a sub-acute treatment unit of an alcoholism treatment hospital. Before the development of such centers in the District of Columbia, many alcoholics who were arrested were sentenced to jail for thirty days to "dry out."

Since 1967 the Vera Institute of Justice has operated a detoxification treatment program center in New York City referred to as the Manhattan Bowery Project. The program is supported by the New York State Department of Mental Hygiene and the New York City Community Mental Health Board. The program provides a three-day period of intensive care and treatment to homeless alcoholics in the Bowery area. A one- or two-day aftercare service is also provided which offers counseling and referral services and transportation to other agencies upon release. Seventy-five percent of the patients are recruited from the streets by a rescue team consisting of a recovered alcoholic and a plainclothes police officer who patrol the Bowery area and offer transportation to the center to persons severely intoxicated orin need of medical aid. Agency and self-referrals are also admitted, and all patients are admitted on a voluntary basis. After completing the three-day period at the center, many patients willingly accept referral services to other agencies for treatment of a longer duration.[10]

By routing public drunkenness offenders through detoxification centers rather than through the court machinery, the courts and jails in Washington D.C. and St. Louis have benefited from lower work loads. However, reports indicate that no police time is saved in these cities by the utilization of such centers, since the police are still responsible for keeping inebriates off the streets. The police do not fully support the centers and ignore many inebriates during their routine patrols. Both of the centers in St. Louis and Washington, D.C. are overcrowded and only the minimum amount of service is provided to patients.

In order to provide the alcoholic with treatment of a more lasting nature, detoxification centers should be supplemented by a network of coordinated aftercare services. This might begin with the mobilization of community resources. Such aftercare services could include Alcoholics Anonymous programs, outpatient centers, employment counseling, locally based missions similar to those of the Salvation Army, hospitals, and mental health agencies.

GENERAL PROGRAMS

Dismas House

Dismas House was founded by Father Clark in St. Louis in 1959. The opening of this particular halfway house helped to spread the halfway house movement throughout the United States. Dismas House serves ex-offenders, primarily, and is nondenominational and racially integrated. Since the Federal Bureau of Prisons uses this facility as a community treatment center, a large number of its admissions are received from the federal government. Dismas House has also been approved for the housing of parolees and of state prisoners who are eligible for community treatment. Most residents spend approximately eight weeks at the house and are provided with vocational and individual counseling by a professional staff. In order to further promote reintegration into the community, Dismas House offers a variety of social and recreational programs to the residents. Employed residents must pay something toward their room and board. Dismas House also allows ex-offenders to work in the house for pay even though they are not residents.[11]

The Austin MacCormick House

The Austin MacCormick House is located in San Francisco, California and provides services to parolees released from the California correctional institutions. Since San Quentin Prison is nearby, many former inmates of this institution come to the house for shelter and for help in securing employment. The program of the Austin Mac-Cormick House is unique in that it mixes offenders with individuals who have never violated the law. Some students from nearby colleges and universities interested in corrections live in the house with the parolees, so that the parolee can have someone to identify with who is not an ex-offender. It is felt that by mixing these two groups the parolees' experience of living in the house will be improved.

The Manhattan Project

The Manhattan Project is a combination of residential and nonresidential programs. It was opened in 1960 in Los Angeles, California. It serves sixty-five people, most of whom are occupants of five residences. The others participating in the project live elsewhere but engage in daily group discussions and seminars at the various centers located throughout the area. Some junior-high-school students also come together in their own group meetings at one of the residences. Over one-half of those in the program are under twenty-one years of age, and most individuals in the program have been in trouble with the law or have been referred because of narcotic drug use. The population consists of a wide variety of individuals including adult parolees, state or federal probationers, and psychiatric referrals. Some people "walk in" off the street requesting to be part of the program. Efforts are made to involve young people in the program by allowing them to participate on a voluntary basis in the group discussions and seminars conducted by the adults. The project also operates a twenty-four-hour emergency service in several city junior high and senior high schools. Teachers and counselors can refer young people to the director of the Manhattan Project for help.[12]

The project is managed by the residents themselves (after it was found that professional staff were unnecessary). Treatment is based on guided group interaction techniques common to the reality approach used in similar programs for narcotic offenders. The daily seminars encourage activities such as role playing and psychodrama. The participants move through several stages during their stay in the program. Newcomers are given little management responsibility and are allowed to leave the residence only to go to school or work. If they go shopping they must be accompanied by a more experienced member. Later, if a participant shows some degree of progress and responsibility, he is eligible to become a group leader or can conduct a seminar. The most experienced and responsible participants serve as department heads and sit in on board and executive meetings. They organize shopping expeditions for the newcomers and supervise the work of others lower down in the program hierarchy. Residents must contribute money to the program and are also expected to buy and prepare their own food.

Other residential strategies

HIGHFIELDS

Highfields was opened in 1950 as a small group home for boys on probation. The program is housed in the former Lindbergh estate near Hopewell, New Jersey. It is an important operation because it was the first residential program which applied to delinquent adolescents the techniques of guided group interaction which had been developed by Lloyd McCorkle at the Fort Knox Rehabilitation Center during the Second World War. The Highfields project was developed largely by the persuasion of Lovell Bixby,who, at the time, was Director of Corrections for the State of New Jersey. Since its inception, the Highfields program has been greatly expanded, and projects based on this approach exist on a residential and nonresidential level in many states, as well as in other countries such as Sweden and Australia.[13]

The Highfields program serves two major purposes. One purpose is to break down the highly selective communication between client and staff known as the "time game," a dishonest "con" game of no rehabilitative value, in which the offender tells the staff largely what the staff wants to hear. It is hoped that through the application of group interaction techniques in a controlled cultural setting, this handicap so prevalent in corrections will be overcome. The other purpose of the program is to keep boys out of youth institutions and prepare them for supervision on probation in the community.

The program is limited to twenty boys who live in the Lindbergh mansion. A main feature of the program is the free communication between clients and staff. The usual pattern of institutional rules is almost abandoned, and the boys receive little instruction from adults. The boys work during the day at a nearby mental institution and participate in discussion groups in the evening, using techniques of guided group interaction. It is felt that the boys themselves reflect the cultural pattern and values that their peers will identify with. Once some of the boys are won over to a responsible outlook on life, they try to win over their peers. The boys are therefore largely responsible for the treatment process and, to some extent, act as their own therapists. They are encouraged, when in groups, not only to talk about their own problems, but about the problems of the other boys as well. The atmosphere of the program is one of permissiveness and non-phoniness. Matters relating to discipline, furloughs, and release dates are discussed by the boys themselves. The entire program is oriented toward interaction with others. Distractions from this process are kept at a minimum, and boys are discouraged from isolating themselves from the group.[14]

FOSTER HOMES

In many instances juveniles are taken out of their own homes and placed in foster homes. Reasons for foster home placement may include the juvenile's inability to make a proper adjustment to his natural parents; the inability of his parents to care for him because of emotional or physical handicaps; and cruelty and neglect on the part of the parents. Foster care is provided for delinquent, dependent, and neglected children. Such services function under a wide variety of administrative patterns. In certain jurisdictions the juvenile court determines eligibility for foster home placement of the delinquent or neglected child and utilizes the local probation department for supervision. In such jurisdictions, the child may be housed in the local juvenile detention center until foster home placement is arranged. In other jurisdictions, foster care is not administered by the local court. Instead, referrals are made by the court to other public and private agencies for foster care placement. If the referrals are rejected, the judge has no alternative but to release the juvenile back to his own home, place him in a local detention facility, or commit him to a state or private institution. Where no state agency is designated as being responsible for institutions and foster home care, the program may be administered by the state welfare department.

Some private families volunteer their services to care for juveniles in a family setting and must meet certain qualifications. Although most volunteers try to provide satisfactory care for the children under their guidance, there are, unfortunately, those few who participate only for the money they receive from governmental agencies for the foster child's personal expenses. This money is then used by such foster parents to satisfy the needs of their own families, and the foster home children in their care are neglected emotionally and with regard to their basic needs for food and clothing. Since supervision of dependent foster home placements is generally lax, agencies are often ignorant of the neglect suffered by the children whom they have placed in such homes. Even if they were aware of such neglect, there are seldom other placements for these children except state institutions or local detention facilities.

Children in foster home placements are there through no fault of their own. However, they must face placement alternatives similar to those juveniles engaged in delinquent activity. A recent study of the population of the State Youth Development Centers in Pennsylvania showed that a large number of residents were dependent, rather than delinquent, children who had never been engaged in criminal activity.[15] Many children are in such institutions for lack of available foster home care.

The Detroit Foster Home Project was created to show that children who have lived in many homes and institutions and who are emotionally disturbed can be placed and treated successfully in highly reinforced foster homes. Various Detroit agencies refer boys between the ages of seven and thirteen to the project for placement. Such boys would have probably been denied foster home placement through the usual placement methods and standards. Under this program, considerable professional time is devoted to each child; and the services of psychiatrists, educators, and research personnel are used in an attempt to develop improved methods of foster home placement and care.[16]

GROUP HOMES FOR JUVENILES

One alternative to institutionalization or foster home care for the treatment of juveniles is the group home. There are several factors in favor of using such establishments. One is the recognition of the limitations of the traditional foster homes and institutions. Another factor is the increased number of adolescent disturbed and delinquent children who have special needs and require new resources. Many of the youth who are committed to large institutions for lack of other available placements would benefit from the small group atmosphere of the group home. Some adolescents cannot adjust to an institutional program where the rules are more rigid and the demands for conformity greater than in the group home. Some youths may need controls, but are confused by the multiple authority figures found in institutions, who, at times, express different ideas about what is acceptable behavior. Further, many young people find it difficult to adjust to the close, intimate relationship which is provided in foster home placement. Foster home placement may be traumatic for some young people who do not want anyone else to try to take the place of their parents and who will resist those who attempt such roles.

The group home provides structured rehabilitation for five to fifteen young people at one time. In this setting the juvenile can receive guidance in adjusting to the norms of society without being institutionally segregated from it. Group home parents can exercise authority and provide supportive help without threatening a young person with an intimate relationship such as would be the case with foster parents. Generally group homes are located in residential neighborhoods and are under the direction of a social worker who coordinates the activities of the various individuals involved in the program. The social worker may be responsible to an institutional director of social services or to the superintendent of a state training school. House parents live with the juveniles, and medical doctors, psychologists, and psychiatrists are available.

Group homes are usually administered by an agency or corporate group. The homes operated by agencies are usually staffed by employees of state training schools and serve the function of "halfway-out" houses for those released from state training schools or similar institutions. Agency-operated homes also cater to certain juveniles who fail on probation but appear not to need institutionalization; or to young people who have been paroled to the home directly from a reception or diagnostic center rather than transferred to a state training school. Such homes are sometimes referred to as "halfway-in" homes, as opposed to "halfway-out" homes, indicating that the resident has not been transferred to the home after a lengthy stay at a state training school. Contract group homes may be operated by an organization such as a church or civic group, or by private individuals. Such group homes are financed through a contract arrangement with a state agency. Agency-operated homes are usually more structured in their programming than are homes operated by a corporate group. Some agency-operated group homes have been compared to small institutions because of their highly programmed treatment techniques.[17]

Several states are utilizing group homes as a correctional strategy. In 1967 the Youth Commission of Minnesota reported using seven group homes under arrangements with the home operator or with an independent agency. The Wisconsin Division of Corrections was operating thirty-three group homes in 1966, with four to eight adolescents in each home. In both of those states the adolescents placed in the homes had been received on court commitment as candidates for institutional placement. Approximately one-fourth of the adolescents placed in group homes in Wisconsin had been released from institutions for placement in foster homes.[18] Pennsylvania is experimenting with two such homes in the Harrisburg area. Each home houses approximately fifteen adolescents who had been committed by the court to the State's Youth Development Center at Loysville. Research is being attempted to ascertain the effectiveness of the program.

A well known agency-operated group home program is the Silverlake experiment in Los Angeles. The program utilizes techniques common to such guided group interaction programs as are used in Highfields and Essexfield. An effort is made to create a nondelinquent culture and to involve offenders in decision making. The home is located in a middle-class neighborhood and houses twenty seriously delinquent boys ranging in age from sixteen to eighteen. The boys attend school daily and are expected to maintain the residence. The primary feature of the program is the daily group meeting, which fosters a collaborative inmate-staff decision-making process.[19] The goal of these efforts is to structure a social system in which emerging norms of a nondelinquent nature are developed and maintained.

In the Silverlake research study, personality changes have been reported based on comparison with a control group in a small, private correctional institution where there was a minimum of reliance on security and custody. The research found that both groups, the group home graduates and the institution releasees, had changed in a positive manner during treatment. Both groups became more trusting and also less alienated from persons and authority. It is of interest to learn that the boys who were released from the institution appeared to be less alienated than the Silverlake boys. This can possibly be explained by the fact that boys remain in treatment at the institution much longer than at Silverlake. The average boy's stay at the institution is 16.5 months as compared to a stay of 6.5 months at the Silverlake group home.[20]

The President's Commission on Law Enforcement and Administration of Justice feels that there may be more wisdom in placing young people in local foster and group homes than in committing them to state agencies for placement. Local placement could be carried out by the courts through associated probation and welfare services and would save the offender from the stigma of being committed to a state agency. Courts usually refer offenders to state-operated agencies because this is less expensive. However, more local placement could become a reality if states provided subsidy programs similar to the program established in California, which has reduced commitments to state-operated training schools and has further significantly improved community-based programs.[21]

NONRESIDENTIAL STRATEGIES

Volunteers in corrections

Many jurisdictions are now utilizing volunteers to help take a portion of the workload off the shoulders of probation and parole personnel. Such volunteers relieve the field officer of much routine work, freeing him for closer contact with his clients and coverage of his caseload. Volunteers also provide services for community treatment centers, halfway houses, drug abuse programs, alcohol-recovery houses, and traditional penal institutions. Aftercare and probation began with the use of volunteers; perhaps we are witnessing a trend back in that direction.

One of the more recent pioneer programs using volunteers was created by the Judge of Michigan's Royal Oak Municipal Court in 1959. Since the Municipal Court had no attached probation services at the time, and received no more than token service from the county probation department, he enlisted the help of his friends who were willing to supervise probationers. The program expanded until a sizable number of volunteers were employed in the field. Each volunteer carries one case at a time and does not assume an authoritative role. His role is to be a friend of the probationer and to provide supportive assistance in helping his client find employment and cope with basic practical matters. Both the volunteer and the probation officer see the client at least once a month. Volunteers are not assigned probationers who are dangerous or highly emotionally disturbed. The selection process for volunteers in the program is informal, and the volunteers are not paid for their work.[22]

Volunteers serve both juveniles and adults. They are an especially valuable source of manpower in those jurisdictions where a large number of offenders are released from institutions under no formal supervision. In North Carolina, for example, 79 percent of all persons released from the state prison system are released with no period of supervision and obtain no help in their attempt to make the difficult transition back to community life. To make some inroads on this problem, the North Carolina Department of Corrections trains community volunteers to assist released inmates in making necessary social and cultural adjustments to the community. Under this program each inmate is assigned a volunteer who serves the offender in a one-to-one relationship. The relationship begins in prison and continues after the inmate has been released.[23]

Many volunteer programs are being developed in which members of the community work directly with juveniles. In Oklahoma, the District Court of Oklahoma County received an action grant from the Law Enforcement Assistance Administration to finance a program providing volunteer juvenile probation counselors. In the first six months of operation, the program involved 60 volunteers and worked with 125 cases. The volunteers work on the average of three hours per week. The program provides for a salaried volunteer coordinator who not only supervises the program but helps plan innovations which might improve services. Response to the program has been favorable. Not only have the regular probation counselors benefited from the program through a caseload reduction, but the program also appears to be keeping juveniles from reappearing before the court on any new offense.[24]

In South Carolina, volunteers are utilized by the Department of Corrections to aid the Parole and Aftercare Section of the Youthful Offender Division. The program operates under an LEAA grant and provides volunteer supervision for seventeen- to twenty-one-year-old parolees over a two-year period. The volunteers are trained by and function under the supervision of professional parole counselors.[25]

Three of Utah's largest cities—Salt Lake City, Provo, and Ogden

—operate Misdemeanant Services Programs under LEAA grants. Each city utilizes a different approach in helping the misdemeanant offender and in attempting to keep him from graduating into the felony category. The Salt Lake City project recruits volunteers from the community to work with misdemeanant offenders on a one-to-one basis. The Provo project employs both students and professionals to work with offenders, individually and in groups. The program has operated since 1970, and there has been no problem in recruiting volunteers and professionals to participate.[26]

Volunteers are widely used in Europe, Australia, and Asia. In Perth, Australia the Child Welfare Department of Western Australia uses volunteers to help supervise delinquents placed on probation. Such workers are carefully screened and trained for their task. England has always employed a large number of volunteers in its after-care programs. Japan and Denmark also utilize this strategy in probation and parole.[27]

Attendance centers

Juveniles who fail on probation or require more intensive supervision than probation can offer but still do not need institutionalization are sometimes referred to "attendance" or "daycare" centers. Under the attendance center program the juvenile lives at home and participates in a school and counseling program. Such centers provide structured "in-house" programs, which differentiate them from programs using existing community services or outside employment. Juveniles are placed in these programs as a condition of probation or parole, and this placement serves as an alternative to institutional commitment.[28]

Attendance center programs are in operation in Philadelphia, Pennsylvania and San Mateo County, California. In Philadelphia the program operates out of the Philadelphia Youth Development Day Treatment Center and provides care for boys who are assigned to the program as a condition of probation. At the center the boys obtain vocational and academic training and engage in intensive group and individual counseling. While in the program the boys live at home and, by so doing, help reduce the commitment rate to institutions.[29]

The attendance center program in San Mateo County serves delinquent girls and is based on the philosophy that a child should be kept at home in her own community whenever possible. In addition to providing services to the girls, the program also encourages parental responsibility. Parents are required to pay a share of the child's expenses at the center and to help insure that the girls comply with the conditions of the program. The girls attend the center during the day for counseling and school classes and return home in the evening. They are supervised by probation officers with a caseload limited to twelve, which permits intensive supervisory services to both the child and her family. In many instances, parents are involved in group counseling sessions with the girl and her probation officer. Parents who have children participating in the program meet one night a week in a group at the attendance center to share their problems. When it is felt by the staff that a girl no longer needs placement at the center, aftercare services are provided both the child and her parents by the probation department. Research is presently being undertaken to determine the advantages of the attendance center program over the more traditional methods of dealing with delinquent girls.[30]

Drug programs

Numerous programs are available for the treatment of drug abuse at the nonresidential level. Since the goals, philosophy, and treatment techniques of the programs in this area are many and diverse, it will suffice to discuss only a few of the strategies closely related to corrections.

METHADONE MAINTENANCE

The treatment of heroin addicts through methadone maintenance began at the Rockefeller University Hospital in New York City in 1964, under the sponsorship of Drs. Vincent P. Dole and Marie Nyswander. Many heroin addicts on probation and parole are now participating in methadone maintenance programs throughout the country. The first phase of the program involves hospitalization and withdrawal from heroin. The patient is then started on daily doses of methadone which are gradually increased and are finally stabilized. Methadone is a synthetic opiate that is itself addictive. The drug removes the patient's craving for heroin, and a feeling of well-being usually follows its administration.

There are opposing views on the use of methadone. Those who favor its use believe that it can foster the adoption of responsible living patterns by enabling the former heroin addict to become reabsorbed into the community, to obtain regular employment, and to engage in healthier social outlets. Further, methadone maintenance patients are reported to stay out of criminal activity at a higher rate than addicts who are on probation and parole but not participating in the program.[31] Those opposed feel that, at most, the drug should only be used as a transitional agent with the eventual cessation of any drug administration. Critics feel that methadone maintenance deals only with the physical aspects of narcotic addiction and makes no provisions for the emotional problems surrounding addiction. Since addiction is felt to be a symptom rather than a basic cause of emotional maladjustment, the opponents of the program feel that methadone treats only the symptoms of the patient's problems and leaves his basic feelings of inadequacy untouched. Some critics state that methadone programs actually maintain addiction, with no serious treatment intent.

Recent research concerning the use of methadone is somewhat alarming, although much of it has not been fully substantiated. It is reported that unborn children have become addicted through the mother's use of methadone.[32] There are also reports of serious side effects and a large number of overdoses. It appears that further research must be encouraged in regard to the physical and emotional effects of methadone. It may be that such research will lead to the limitation of methadone use.

NARCOTICS TREATMENT ADMINISTRATION

The Narcotics Treatment Administration of the District of Columbia attempts to treat all addicts in the community, regardless of their previous criminal history and program failures. A desire to abstain from drugs is the only requirement for participation, and failure to respond to treatment does not result in automatic expulsion from the program. The program treats approximately 3,500 addicts in the District of Columbia, in twelve out-patient centers and four private contract facilities. Most treatment centers are located strategically in areas with high crime rates, although some are outside the core area, in neighborhoods where heroin use is not considered as severe a problem. Volunteers for the program are processed immediately and sent to a holding facility where they undergo methadone maintenance. During their stay at the holding facility a program of treatment is determined. Representatives from the Narcotics Treatment Administration also obtain participants by screening all defendants entering the Superior Court, for the purpose of identifying heroin users. Those considered eligible for the program are released on bail to the National Treatment Administration's Criminal Justice Intake Service. Each participant is given a medical examination and referred to a treatment facility nearest his home. While on bail the participants are subjected to urine surveillance tests to detect whether they are using heroin or other drugs. The program has separate facilities for adults and juveniles.[33]

The program utilizes a central computerized data bank which compiles information from all facilities for program evaluation. A study was made of the progress of 450 adult and 150 youth patients selected at random from May 1970 to November 1971. The study revealed that 46 percent of the adults were still in treatment after a period of eighteen months. Twenty-eight percent of the sample had been arrested within the study period and 27 percent of those still in treatment failed to meet one or more of the program's treatment goals. Nineteen percent were meeting all program goals which included abstinence from illegal drug use, maintaining regular employment or training, and no arrests. Of the 150 youth studied, 18 percent remained in the program for eighteen months, with only one percent satisying all treatment goals. Ninety-two percent were arrested within the study period and 12 percent of those treated failed to meet one or more program goals. There is no information regarding the dropouts from the program. The high degree of failure of participants in the program is blamed on inadequate planning and management.[34]

COOK COUNTY STATE'S ATTORNEY'S PROGRAM

The purpose of the Cook County State's Attorney's Program for the Prevention of Drug Abuse is to divert from prosecution first offenders charged with possession of small amounts of marijuana, stimulants, depressants, and hallucinogens. The program is operated on the basis of judicial and prosecutorial discretion rather than statute. Offenders accepted in the program must waive their right to a speedy trial, and the court continues the case for a period of two or three months to determine how the offender progresses under treatment. Those participating in the program attend five weekly group therapy sessions and must submit to urine testing. Removal from treatment can result from arrest, absence from group therapy sessions, or traces of opiates, amphetamines, or barbituates in the urine. Once removed, the offender is subject to prosecution or may be enrolled in a more intensive residential-type program. For those who successfully complete the program and refrain from further arrests, the State's Attorney moves to dismiss charges. It is reported that approximately 80 percent of the offenders participating in the program have been considered a success.[35]

Guided group interaction programs

Since guided group interaction originated at Highfields as a treatment strategy, this program has become popular in the field of corrections, in nonresidential as well as residential treatment settings. Many of the nonresidential programs, such as the Provo Experiment in Utah,[36] and the Essexfield Rehabilitation Project in New Jersey,[37] have based their program dynamics on those borrowed directly from

Highfields. Most of these programs provide short-term, group-oriented rehabilitation on a nonresidential basis as an alternative to placing delinquents in institutions. The underlying theory of such programs is that delinquent activity is the result of identification with a delinquent sub-culture sanctioned by the offender's peer group. The assumption surrounding the program is that most habitual delinquents are children from low-income families who have experienced only a limited opportunity for success through conventional channels. Membership in a delinquent system develops an alternative means for achieving goals which are emotionally, socially, and economically satisfying. In guided group interaction programs efforts are applied to promote peer group interaction that will result in the acceptance of nondelinquent life styles and values.

EVALUATION OF COMMUNITY STRATEGIES

Comparing the rehabilitative effectiveness of community strategies discussed in this chapter is difficult because of the large number of variables that must be taken into consideration. Programs vary according to goals, population, program, admission criteria, method of assignment, and the period of time selected for evaluating their effectiveness. To make matters more difficult for the evaluator, many of the program goals are unclear, and definitions of "success" differ.[38]

One major problem that surfaces in an attempt to determine the comparative effectiveness of various programs is that of accounting for in-program failures. Many individuals fail to complete a specific residential or nonresidential program because of arrest, absconding from the program, or being found unsuitable for the program by the staff. The usual criterion of success for measuring the effectiveness of a program is the recidivism rate of its graduates. A serious question arises as to whether the in-program terminations should also be counted as failures.[39]

In attempting to measure the effectiveness of any single program, problems also arise in the area of empirical research. Many research projects in the field of corrections depend on the principle of random assignment. In community programs, however, it is almost impossible to satisfy the requirements for carrying out research designs based on the random assignment of cases to experimental and control groups. For example, certain residential programs such as Highfields depend on judges for the assignment of residents. Judges will usually refuse to make random assignments to reformatories and halfway house programs for the sole purpose of evaluating the success rate of one as opposed to the other. Their refusal is based on the premise that such decisions should revolve around the offender's rehabilitative potential. There is little question that random assignment of cases by the courts to various types of treatment programs for the purposes of research would result in the unjust handling of certain offenders. Should an offender who shows potential for community residential or nonresidential programs be selected at random for reformatory treatment in order to satisfy the requirements of a research design? This appears to be a question of ethics that no amount of scientific investigation can settle. In most instances both courts and program staff personnel place treatment needs ahead of research needs.

Current research findings concerning the effectiveness of halfway house programs are not very encouraging. Those programs which admit seriously delinquent adolescents and maintain careful statistical procedures report a high in-program failure rate. For example, the Southfields project in Kentucky reported an in-program failure rate of 48 percent over its first four years of operation,[40] and Essexfield showed an in-program failure rate of 23 percent.[41] By comparing the success and failure rates of the Highfields graduates, in terms of those who had completed the program and those who entered but never finished, it was found that 63 percent of the graduates of Highfields were considered successful as compared to 47 percent of the Annandale Reformatory releases.[42] A similar study of the effectiveness of the Provo Experiment showed that Pinehill's residents were more successful than the control group of releasees at the Utah Industrial School, but not any more successful than boys who had been placed on supervised probation.[43]

Little attempt is made to measure the effectiveness of most community programs, especially those managed by private agencies. Even with adequate funds and a desire to engage in empirical research, many research designs used for evaluations fail to achieve legitimate random assignment to an experimental and to a control group, and are further handicapped by their use of very small samples. With such small samples, the conclusions obtained from such studies are tentative at best.

It seems that if one considers the research results presently available in the field of corrections, no single residential or nonresidential program can be rated as superior or inferior to any other. Although the failure rate of community programs seems high, there is no apparent reason to believe that the failure rate of those programs is any higher than the failure rate recorded for traditional institutions such as state training schools and adult prisons. If the failure rates of these two forms of correctional strategies are about the same, it would seem more logical to utilize community treatment whenever possible because of its lower cost to the taxpayer, and for the more humane type of environment it provides to its participants.

SPECIAL STRATEGIES

Self-help groups

Prisoners and parolees have played a leading role in organizing self-help groups throughout the United States. Today there are self-help groups such as the Fortune Society, Seven Step Foundation, Narcotics Symposium, the United Prisoners' Union, the Winners, Checks Anonymous, and the People's Association of New Jersey. Most of these groups are not radical. They function to help the inmate make a satisfactory adjustment to society and to promote ideas and activities that will foster a change in society itself. Prisoner self-help groups can trace their history to other self-help community groups such as Alcoholics Anonymous, Narcotics Anonymous, and Gamblers Anonymous.

The Fortune Society is based in New York and is under the direction of David Rothenberg, who gave up a theatrical career to help ex-offenders. The remaining members of the Society are ex-convicts. The Society prints a newsletter which is delivered throughout the United States and to many foreign countries. It offers practical assistance to ex-offenders and holds "rap" sessions at the center in New York. There are Friday afternoon seminars in which ex-offenders and students participate. Members attempt to make the community aware of the field of corrections by talking to civic groups and through appearing on radio and television.[44]

The People's Association is a self-help group of organized prisoners which has recently been formed in the state of New Jersey. The group claims that it is committed to preventive work with youth, and it hopes to be able to provide supportive services to inmates released from prison that will ease their reintegration into community life. The members try to cope with the fear, frustration, and apathy which surrounds the newly released prisoner and attempt to provide the education, motivation, and help necessary to deter him from returning to crime.[45]

ETHNIC SELF-HELP GROUPS[46]

Ethnic self-help groups are being formed which focus on individuals both in prison and on parole. This is a different type of self-help group than those formed along more traditional lines. Besides being based on a common ethnic identity, these groups are motivated by the war on poverty, the "new left," the youth revolt, and the recent civil rights movement, which is closely bound to political activism—especially in the area of promoting racial consciousness rather than integration.[47] The ethnic self-help groups appear to employ as a theoretical perspective the "conflict model of society," as opposed to the "order model of society" which is the traditional model underlying our present correctional system and most older self-help groups such as Alcoholics Anonymous.[48]

Ethnic self-help groups supplement agency services and are sometimes successful in recruiting volunteers from the community. Such groups have developed activities for inmates and parolees in the areas of ethnic education, legal aid, family counseling, and pre-parole classes.[49] These groups want to establish strong ties with minority communities which are involved in current social movements. Ethnic self-help groups are made up of volunteers who see themselves as "victims" of a "sick" society rather than patients in need of therapeutic assistance as advocated by the medical-clinical model, the philosophy of which still dominates correctional treatment programs. Such groups feel that society rather than the inmate needs treatment, and they are therefore involved in training their members to "become bastions of social change."[50] To put their philosophy into operation many of the graduates of these groups are now working "within the system" for such governmental agencies as probation departments, welfare departments, and youth agencies.

Two major problems of ethnic self-help groups are to avoid being "exploited" by revolutionary groups who have purposes in mind that are not in accord with the groups' philosophy and—for those groups still in prison—to prevent the correctional staff backlash that could result from the hostility of institutional staff members and parole officers who have little understanding of race relations and minority groups. White inmates who feel racial and ethnic prejudice also show animosity toward such groups, which could lead to racial conflicts within the prison.[51]

SYNANON[52]

Synanon is a famous residential self-help organization devoted mainly to drug abusers. The organization was established in Santa Monica, California by Charles E. Dederich in 1958. Synanon now has branches throughout California and in other states as well. Members of Synanon are volunteers who have been approved for admission by an indoctrination committee. No professionals are involved in the Synanon program, but they are permitted to visit the organization. The social organization of Synanon is family-structured, caste-oriented, and autocratic in nature. Newly admitted members must perform maintenance tasks as part of their responsibilities. The program attempts to promote self-reliance and self-awareness among its residents. Seminars are held in which discussions are encouraged on philosophical issues and current events. Members are taught how to express themselves to others in an intelligent manner, not just concerning their own problems, but on literary, philosophical, religious, social, and political subjects as well. No drugs of any sort are allowed in the organization and detoxification, if needed, is done "cold-turkey."

The major therapeutic device used by Synanon is the Synanon game, a type of group therapy patterned after guided group interaction. It is sometimes referred to as "gut-level" therapy or the "verbal haircut." Members of the group share their problems and experiences on an emotional rather than an intellectual level. During the sessions no rationalizations or pretenses are accepted. Such sessions are closely related to real-life problems and are conducted in a "goldfish-bowl" atmosphere.[53] The type of "time game" played with professionals by inmates in more traditional therapy sessions is not tolerated in Synanon.

There is no limit to how long a member can be a resident. Many seem to make it a way of life and remain with the organization. Synanon is in many respects a society within a society. However, its members interact with the community and manage Synanon business enterprises on the outside. Members who remain with Synanon have the opportunity for upward mobility in the hierarchy of command.

Major criticisms of Synanon focus around the organization's failure to release follow-up information concerning the success or failure of its residents and its reluctance to cooperate with professionals in the field, such as probation and parole personnel. Many probation and parole agencies are reluctant to send their clients to Synanon because of the total absorption of the residents by the organization. Another criticism of the organization comes from those who feel that Synanon produces a person who becomes entirely dependent upon the organization and is not really prepared to function apart from the structured social setting Synanon provides. How well those individuals perform once released from Synanon is not known, nor is any information available concerning in-program failures. Many members and non-members alike, however, feel that Synanon is one of the most valuable breakthroughs in corrections of the century.

Correctional ombudsman

The ombudsman idea can be traced back to Sweden, where the first office of ombudsman was created in 1809 to defend citizens from official wrongs. At the present time all Scandinavian countries employ ombudsmen, as do New Zealand, Canada, and Great Britain.[54] Ombudsmen in Scandinavian countries are usually appointed by the legislature and function as independent individuals with the responsibility of handling citizens' complaints against governmental agencies. Such ombudsmen have broad investigatory powers, and they are expected to make recommendations to help resolve complaints that they feel have merit. If an agency ignores a recommendation, the ombudsman is authorized to report directly to the legislature. The ombudsmen also have the authority to make their recommendations public so as to exert some pressure on agencies which fail to comply. Ombudsmen traditionally have had no power to enforce their recommendations, but act mainly as a grievance mechanism.[55]

Recently in the United States the ombudsman idea was introduced into the correctional field in an attempt to open avenues of communication for inmates. The hope was that such a grievance mechanism would resolve inmate problems, and by so doing, help prevent prison unrest and violence. Hawaii became the first state to appoint an ombudsman in 1967. The ombudsman was appointed by the state legislature and was authorized to accept complaints by prisoners against state agencies and officials. New York State's Division for Youth appointed four attorneys as ombudsmen within the Division's residential facilities in 1972. These ombudsmen investigate complaints concerning administrative action and policies and make recommendations to the director of the division. The Ohio Division of Correction appointed a chief ombudsman in June 1972, and he and two subordinates help to resolve inmate problems.[56]

Minnesota became the first state to appoint a correctional ombudsman who is independent of the state department of corrections. The appointment of Theartrice Williams as correctional ombudsman by Governor Wendell B. Anderson in April 1972 was made possible through LEAA funding. The proposal for the ombudsman experimental program was initiated by former Corrections Commissioner David Fogel.[57]

The trend is to extend the ombudsman idea to the entire criminal justice system in order to make it available to a person from the time of arrest throughout his stay in the system. Some inmates express dissatisfaction with the ombudsman system because of the ombudsman's lack of power to enforce recommendations. One hindrance to the system seems to be that all correctional ombudsmen in the United States depend for their tenure and pay on the very administration they are supposed to criticize. If the administration rejects his recommendations, the ombudsman has little recourse for further action.

FURTHER ATTEMPTS TO CHANGE THE SYSTEM

Ending the isolation of the system through citizen participation

It is possible that the final solution to the problem of criminality will be found in the community. It appears that no significant change in the criminal justice system will take place without citizen influence and citizen participation. It is becoming apparent that the "experts" and professionals in the field of corrections lack the means by which we can either reduce recidivism or rehabilitate offenders. The present system cannot function in a meaningful way as long as it remains isolated from the local community. Attempts are now being made to end this isolation and permit a greater interaction between the system and the community. It has been discovered that the community can be used as a change agent. As a result of this discovery, less faith is being placed in the traditional model for corrections based on the segregation of the offender. The pendulum has swung in the opposite direction since the days of the early reformers, who viewed the isolation of the criminal as necessary to ward off the evil influence of society. As we at first built high walls to keep society out of our prisons, we are now trying to find ways to tear down the walls in order to bring society back into contact with the offender. Not only does the end to isolation have a significant impact on the way in which offenders are treated; it also opens to the scrutiny of the public and the courts a system which has been favored by a "hands-off" policy and left to function in an atmosphere of almost complete autonomy.

There are many ways in which citizen participation can function to help change the criminal justice system. The use of volunteers in corrections, the employment of self-help groups, and ombudsmen have already been mentioned as sources of citizen participation. Citizens can also be represented to a greater degree than they are today in criminal justice planning groups, where decisions are made about how to improve and reform the system. At present the criminal justice planning groups are dominated by members of the criminal justice establishment and employees of state and local government. In order to assure an overall examination of the criminal justice system that will foster the establishment of legitimate priorities, as opposed to provincialism and vested interests, an expanded use of citizen participation is necessary.[58] Citizen participation on planning boards could also ensure that proposals calling for new citizen involvement with the system would be given adequate attention.[59]

Another way in which citizens can become involved in the criminal justice system is through the establishment of community coordinating councils, which enlist specialists and interested workers representing schools, police departments, courts of law, recreational agencies, public welfare departments, churches, libraries, and private welfare agencies. Such coordinating councils have been used in California to stimulate neighborhood concern for the welfare of children. The councils utilize the services and cooperation of all preventive agencies in fighting delinquency. Some councils have conducted studies, surveys, and conferences to discover the individual child, the groups of children, and the areas needing attention by public and private agencies.

The first coordinating council was established in California in 1919 through the efforts of August Vollmer, then Chief of Police of Berkeley, and Dr. Virgil Dickson, then Assistant Superintendent of Schools. The idea spread throughout the state until many large communities used the strategy as an alternative to the criminal justice system. In addition to promoting efforts to change social conditions and to make communities aware of problems surrounding delinquency, the councils have also worked closely with first offenders and predelinquents.[60]

Neighborhood alternatives are being utilized in attempts to change the criminal justice system, such as the community resource centers established in three San Francisco neighborhoods through California Council on Criminal Justice funding.[61] These centers provide neighborhood alternatives to arrest, detention, and imprisonment of juveniles. Each center has paid and volunteer workers from a particular neighborhood's ethnic and cultural group, who work with children in trouble. The centers provide children with legal services, group and individual counseling, supervision, recreation, training, and a wide variety of care, including foster homes and group homes.[62] One of the major goals of the program is to provide alternatives to the various processes of the criminal justice system,[63] and thereby to motivate the residents of black neighborhoods to accept major responsibility for the control and care of their predelinquent, delinquent, and dependent young people.

In addition to the programs mentioned above there are many other kinds of citizens' groups involved in the criminal justice system such as the National Chamber of Commerce and Junior Chamber of Commerce. The "JayCees," for example, have been pioneers in establishing many local prison chapters which work closely with inmates to help them with their problems. Other community groups that could be utilized in providing alternatives to corrections are the local bar associations and public defender agencies, local medical associations or societies, local educational associations, public welfare departments, and state vocational rehabilitation agencies.[64]

In the process of community interaction with corrections as a change agent, corrections has also interacted with the community in altering its views concerning the nature of offenders and how they ought to be treated. As members of the community visit institutions and listen to inmates, parolees, and ex-offenders, they become aware of an aspect of corrections formerly hidden from them. What they learn from listening to the inmate is quite different from what they have learned from newspapers, "crime-busting" politicians, television, movies, and correctional personnel, who are opposed to change because of vested interests in the system as it has existed in the past. Prisons were formerly but blurred shadows on the horizon to most people, and what occurred within the walls of any institution was of little public concern. Community involvement has placed a spotlight on the system which has brought to an end the system's complete isolation. The former autonomy of the correctional community has also been diminished by the U.S. Supreme Court's recognition that the Eighth Amendment of the Constitution, prohibiting cruel and unusual punishment, applies to inmates and parolees as well as to the average citizen.

Rechanneling of youthful offenders

Diversion of offenders has already been mentioned as an alternative to the criminal justice system. Methods of diversion such as "station house" and informal probation have already been mentioned as devices that are used to dispose of cases at the pre-adjudicatory level. In an effort to rechannel youthful offenders from the justice system, the President's Crime Commission in 1966 recommended the establishment of youth service bureaus which would act as central coordinators of all community services for young people. It was suggested that the prime function of such bureaus should be to provide services for the less seriously delinquent youth that were unavailable in a particular neighborhood or community.[65] When the President's Commission prepared its report, no empirical research or knowledge was available concerning whether it was desirable or necessary to establish such bureaus; but the idea became popular, and by 1972 a national survey identified 150 Youth Service Bureaus throughout the United States.[66] At present it is difficult to determine how many Youth Service Bureaus are in operation and how much it costs to maintain them with federal, state, local, and private funds. The National Council on Crime and Delinquency, in a further attempt to alleviate the juvenile courts' caseloads, proposed in 1967 that all cases be diverted from the juvenile court that could be handled more effectively through community programs.[67] In attempting to achieve this goal the Board of Trustees of the National Council on Crime and Delinquency made it a national priority in 1970 that the Youth Service Bureau should be used as the device by which children would be diverted from the courts.[68]

Another youth diversion strategy was developed by the Youth Development Delinquency Prevention Administration, which called in early 1970 for the establishment, on a nationwide basis, of comprehensive, integrated, community-based programs designed to meet the needs of all youth.[69] The strategy proposed by the YDDPA for prevention of juvenile delinquency is based on four program approaches: the application of behavior modification; developing new services and delivery systems to predelinquents and delinquents; improving institutional services to delinquents; and "developing programs that address themselves to the processes in communities that propel children into the juvenile justice system."[70] The YDDPA undertook to make such a nationwide strategy operational by establishing youth services systems. The systems offer comprehensive services to the community which are jointly planned and funded by local, state, and federal agencies, and which utilize YDDPA expertise. The strategy attempts to integrate services provided by the agencies funded under the youth service system. It is hoped that as a result of the establishment of nationwide youth service systems, the old system of fragmented services lacking in common goals and duplicating one another's efforts will gradually diminish. The objectives of this nationwide strategy are to provide more socially acceptable and meaningful roles for youth; to divert youth from the juvenile justice system into alternative programs; to reduce negative labeling; and to reduce youth-adult alienation.[71]

In an interesting article, Frederick W. Howlett states that movements such as the Youth Service Bureau concept and the Youth Services Systems strategy have evolved in a fashion similar to other child-centered movements in the United States. He notes that almost all such "child-saving" innovations have resulted in subjecting the child to more damaging effects and to further denial of constitutional rights than would otherwise have been the case.[72] Howlett suggests that the trend in treatment of juveniles has been to eagerly accept a "noncoercive intervention" policy without giving adequate consideration to the possible operational effects of such a policy.[73]

It seems that instead of decriminalizing children, the creation of the Juvenile Court in 1899 as a benevolent guardian of the child and the recent acceptance of the concept of "The Person in Need of Supervision" (PINS) have actually resulted in bringing more young people into the juvenile justice system, largely because of the all-encompassing definition of "delinquency" these concepts imply. As a result of the wide adoption of legislation making such concepts operational, the police, courts, and probation departments are eager to play the role of interested parents. With the zeal of a childless mother, they exercise jurisdiction over children on the basis of trivial complaints of parents, many of whom appear to want to rid themselves of the responsibility of raising their own children.[74]

The juvenile court was intended to act in the role of a fatherly benefactor, and children were not to be labeled criminals, but individuals in need of help and supervision. Thus, more and more juveniles were arrested and charged without any feeling in the community that they were being treated in a coercive manner. In a similar way, the philosophy inherent in the PINS concept has resulted in more nondelinquent children being committed to state training schools in certain jurisdictions than was the case previous to its adoption. For example, as a result of the passing of PINS legislation in New York State, more nondelinquent children were sent to state training schools than previously, and, during the period from 1966 to 1970, 80 percent of all female commitments to such schools were PINS children.[75]

In accord with Thomas Szasz's concept that the term "mental illness" generally refers to behavior deviation from some norm firmly implanted in society,[76] many child-service planners appear to regard children who deviate from well-established norms to be in need of treatment or supervision, even though such deviation might not be of the type that would be correctly labeled "delinquent." Many community leaders have little tolerance for life styles varying from their own and are always anxious to impose their values on others. This was the case during the child-saving movement, when the values of middle-class women were used as a standard to determine whether a child was to be brought to the attention of the authorities. In an attempt to minimize community intolerance of behavior that deviates from a cherished norm, Howlett suggests that society modify its concepts of deviance so that it can encompass behavior that is not in accordance with the life style of the middle class or the affluent. The fear expressed by Howlett is that strategies represented by the Youth Service Bureau may result, as did the child-saving movement, in actions that are well intended and administered in the name of humanitarianism but that produce results to the contrary. He asks whether we should place blind faith in child-service movements simply because of their intent as stated by correctional policy makers.[77] Many damaging programs have emerged in the field of corrections that were the products of humanitarian zeal, such as the prison system, the reformatory, and the civil commitment of offenders. Will the present youth-oriented movements in the field of corrections accommodate themselves to the acceptance of different norms and life styles, or will they promote their own ends by latching onto children who are not in need of their services?

It is not known at present whether the Youth Service Bureau movement is a success or failure. Reports indicate that the movement does not appear to be the nation's most popularly supported diversion effort.[78] The future of the Youth Service Bureau movement seems to be financially uncertain and the bureaus that survive are usually related to already established agencies. Many of those that seem to be having the most success are those related to such agencies as the police, probation, and the courts. Other bureaus are being incorporated with comprehensive youth service delivery systems. A national survey reports that 79 percent of the school age children for whom the bureaus provided services were either self-referred or referred by family or friends. The schools were responsible for 21 percent of the referrals and the police only 13 percent. Approximately 28 percent of the referrals were made for such behavior as incorrigibility, running away, not getting along, and school problems.[79] It is felt that meaningful evaluations should be made of the effectiveness of the Youth Service Bureau movement so as to determine whether it should be encouraged or abandoned.

Methods are being developed and refined for measuring the success with which the Youth Services Systems strategy is realizing its goal of providing integrated services to communities.

Producing change through conflict

Perhaps no other force is more pronounced in allowing for correctional and social change through reform rather than revolution than the gradual acceptance on the part of inmates, minorities, and the underprivileged of a new theoretical perspective which allows the American social system to be viewed quite differently from the way it has been seen in the past. Our social and penal systems have always maintained a vested interest in what theorists such as Ralph Dahrendorf call the "Order Model of Society."[80] This model is based on the assumption that every society is a well-integrated, relatively persistent, stable structure of elements based on a consensus of values and functioning in a context where every element in a society contributes to its maintenance as a system. Until the rise of the civil rights movement, stressing political awareness among minorities, and the beginnings of the "New Left," especially as exemplified by the youth revolts of the sixties, the Order Model of how society is structured was seldom questioned by professionals or the general public. It was learned, however, that this model could not accommodate the stresses, problems, and grievances brought to surface through current political and social movements.[81] The Order Model of Society permitted reform only along traditional lines of action and channeled thinking into certain patterns that did not appear appropriate for many ethnic and minority groups working for social change.

The "Conflict Model of Society" as developed by Ralph Dahrendorf, although not necessarily mutually exclusive from the Order Model, is based on assumptions that encourage its adherents to entertain different solutions from those who adopt the Order Model of Society. The Conflict Model of Society assumes that every society displays dissensus and is based on the coercion of some of its members by others. It further postulates that all societies are subject to change and that every element in a society contributes to its disintegration and change.[82]

Clarence Schrag outlined three basic revolutions that have taken place in the field of corrections: the substitution of the prison for corporal punishment; the development of the "new penology," with its stress on the therapeutic treatment of the offender through programs of education and counseling based on the principles of casework; and the contemporary approach to correctional change, focusing on society and the community as the patient, rather than on the offender, and stressing the idea that the community needs corrective action as well as the offender.[83] Milton Burdman has observed that the Order Model of Society as developed by Dahrendorf would account for the events leading to the first two revolutions in penology and that the current revolution, reflected in ethnic self-help groups and contemporary grievance mechanisms, has evolved through the acceptance of the Conflict Model of Society.[84]

It is not inconceivable that, as Milton Burdman suggests, if the Conflict Model of Society had not found its spokesmen through such contemporary correctional strategies as ethnic self-help groups, ombudsman programs, and newly developed grievance mechanisms, prisons would become breeding grounds for revolutionaries.[85] Many offenders, both imprisoned and on parole, demand change in the correctional system and in the social system as well. No longer can we isolate corrections from the community and promote strategies that focus only on one and ignore the other. Unless the present mechanisms for change promoted by those offenders who stress the need for changing the system rather than the individual are made operational to a greater extent than they are at the present time, correctional administrators may find it impossible to change those offenders who advocate change through revolution into men and women who will agree to change through reform.

One of the most interesting correctional strategies based on conflict theory is the current grievance mechanism established at the Karl Holton School in Stockton, California, an institution managed by the California Youth Authority, which houses young adults averaging nineteen years of age.[86] The grievance mechanism at the Karl Holton School differs from traditional methods of inmate-staff bargaining.[87]

Grievance mechanisms based on the ombudsman concept or on a formal multilevel appeal procedure have generally excluded inmates and line staff from participating in the grievance process. In both the ombudsman and multilevel appeal procedures, the primary focus is on the investigator or reviewing decision maker, who is in complete charge of investigating complaints and has total responsibility in formulating solutions.[88] Under the ombudsman system, inmate participation is limited to filing a complaint and, where the multilevel appeal process is in effect, the inmate is entitled only to an appearance at certain formal hearings.

In contrast, the Karl Holton School has developed the "mediation approach" to correctional grievances, in which inmates and staff work together to determine the merits of a particular complaint and to formulate solutions that are acceptable both to the general inmate population and to the staff.[89] The grievance mechanism goes into effect after it is found that the problem cannot be resolved informally. First, the inmate files a grievance with an inmate grievance clerk who has been elected to that position. The grievance goes to an inmate-staff committee, consisting of four voting members, two of whom are staff, and two are inmates elected by their peers. A nonvoting staff member acts as chairman of the committee.

The grievance must be heard and acted on by this committee within five days of receiving it, unless time is extended by the inmate. He has the option of appearing before the committee himself and calling witnesses in his behalf, or he can be represented by another inmate, a staff member, or an outside volunteer associated with the prison program.

A majority vote of the committee can decide grievances involving a living unit policy unless the grievant chooses to appeal. Grievances involving an institutional or departmental policy cannot be resolved by the committee alone. In such matters the committee recommends a course of action to the superintendent or the director of the department. The superintendent must also act on the grievance within five days.

The grievant can appeal to an independent review panel if he disagrees with the verdict of the superintendent or director. The independent review panel is made up of three members, one selected by the superintendent, one selected by the inmate (who may be another inmate, staff member, or outside volunteer), and a professional arbitrator selected by the first two.[90]

The procedure went into operation in September 1973, and by March 1974 it was in effect in all living units. The grievance procedure began with inmates being given advisory arbitration on all matters rather than binding arbitration. The system has acted on 277 grievances since August 1, 1974, and only ten percent were concerned with complaints against specific staff members. There were 139 grievances expressing dissatisfaction with living unit, institution, or departmental policy, and 107 grievances addressed to individual problems. Of the 277 grievances, sixty were settled informally after filing, but before the hearing. Thirty-nine were referred directly to the superintendent on an emergency basis. Twelve were withdrawn for various reasons, and the remaining 166 went to a first-level hearing before the inmate-staff committee on the grievant's living unit. In only twelve cases did the inmates and staff disagree on the disposition. Sixty-nine of the 166 first level decisions were appealed either to the superintendent or the director. Of the six cases going to the independent review panel, two were found in favor of the grievant and two claims were denied. In the other two cases the panel suggested that the parties find new solutions to their problems through an *ad hoc* committee structure. In the two cases where the panel found against the institution, the Youth Authority accepted the decision.[91]

Grievances at the Karl Holton School have revolved around such matters as medical care, visiting policy, telephone calls, hair and facial hair policy, work and room assignments, the searching of personal property, and the wearing of personal and state-issued clothing.[92] The most significant grievances are probably the six cases that went to outside review by the independent review panel. It was felt that this review provided the major impetus for the changes that have taken place as a result of the grievance strategy. This grievance mechanism is the first to permit an outside look at decisions made in a closed institution.[93]

Research undertaken by the Youth Authority indicates that the majority of Holton inmates were satisfied with the grievance mechanism, and the large majority of staff members found it necessary and useful. Some staff members felt that the mechanism should be expanded to consider staff complaints as well.[94] Based on the success of this strategy at the Karl Holton School, the California Youth Authority has decided to expand the application of these grievance procedures to all of its institutions, camps, and reception centers, and to develop and test models for parole regions and other community programs.[95]

NOTES

1. Robert Forest Fitch, *The Work Furlough Program in California* (Dissertation for the degree of Master of Criminology, University of California, Berkeley, California, 1967), pp. 21–66.

2. Ibid., p. 51.

3. U.S. Department of Justice, *Questions and Answers about Work Release; Questions and Answers about Unescorted Furloughs and Work Furlough Release,* January 27, 1967. See also: U.S. Attorney General's Office, *Progress Report on Work Release Program—Prisoner Rehabilitation Act of 1965,* September 12, 1966.

4. U.S. Bureau of Prisons, "Community Centered Correctional Programs," in *Trends in the Administration of Justice and Correctional Programs in the United States,* 1965, pp. 34–60. (Contents: Community Residential Centers, Community Diagnostic and Treatment Centers, and Work Release Programs.)

5. John M. McCartt and Thomas Mangogna, *Guidelines and Standards for Halfway Houses and Community Treatment Centers,* Department of Justice, Law Enforcement Assistance Administration Publication, May 1973, as reproduced in George G. Killinger and Paul F. Cromwell, Jr., *Corrections in the Community: Alternatives to Imprisonment* (St. Paul, Minn.; West Publishing, 1974), pp. 79–80.

6. Joseph A. Shelly and Alexander Bassin, "Daytop Lodge: Halfway House for Drug Addicts," *Federal Probation,* 28, no. 4 (December 1964): 46–54.

7. American Psychiatric Association and National Association for Mental Health, *The Treatment of Drug Abuse: Programs, Problems, Prospects* (Washington, D.C.: Joint Information Service, 1972), pp. 127–152.

8. Ibid., pp. 83–103, 242–244.

9. National Advisory Commission on Criminal Justice Standards and Goals, *Report on Corrections,* 1973, as reproduced in Killinger and Cromwell, note 5, supra, pp. 40–41.

10. Ibid., pp. 41–42.

11. Father Dismas Clark Foundation, "Dismas House," *Annual Report* (St. Louis).

12. Oliver J. Keller, Jr., and Benedict S. Alper, *Halfway Houses: Community-Centered Correction and Treatment* (Lexington, Mass.: D.C. Heath and Co., 1970), pp. 111–113.

13. Lloyd W. McCorkle, Albert Elias, and F. Lovell Bixby, *The Highfields Story* (New York: Henry Holt, 1958).

14. Ibid.

15. Daniel Katkin, Drew Hyman, and John Kramer, *Juvenile Justice: Love Them or Leave Them?* (Paper prepared for the Society for the Study of Social Problems, New York, August 1973).

16. The Detroit Foster Homes Project for the Merrill-Palmer Institute, *Current Project* (Project No. P487 in Information Center files).

17. E. Harlow, R. Weber, and L. T. Wilkins, "Community-Based Correctional Programs," *Crime and Delinquency Topics: A Monograph Series,* National Institute of Mental Health Center for Studies of Crime and Delinquency (Washington, D.C.: Government Printing Office, 1971), pp. 1–37.

18. President's Crime Commission, *Task Force Report: Corrections* (Washington, D.C.: Government Printing Office, 1967), p. 40.

19. Harlow, Weber, and Wilkins, note 17, supra.

20. Keller and Alper, note 12, supra, pp. 158–159.

21. President's Crime Commission, *Task Force Report: Corrections,* note 18, supra, p. 40.

22. Keve, Paul W., *Imaginative Programming in Probation and Parole* (Minneapolis: University of Minnesota Press, 1967), pp. 260–271.

23. Law Enforcement Assistance Administration, *3rd Annual Report* (Washington, D.C.: Government Printing Office, 1971), p. 209.

24. Ibid., p. 219.

25. Ibid., p. 233.

26. Ibid., p. 244.

27. Keve, note 22, supra, pp. 260–271.

28. Harlow, Weber, Wilkins, note 17, supra.

29. Ibid.

30. Ibid.

31. DuPont, Robert L., "How Corrections Can Beat the High Cost of Heroin Addiction," *Federal Probation* 35, no. 2 (June 1971): 43–50.

32. Milton G. Rector, "Heroin Maintenance: A Rational Approach," *Crime and Delinquency* 18, no. 3 (July 1972): 241.

33. National Advisory Commission on Criminal Justice Standards and Goals, *Report on Corrections*, 1973, as reprinted in Killinger and Cromwell, note 5, supra, pp. 47–49.

34. Ibid.

35. Ibid., pp. 45–46.

36. For a description of the Provo Experiment see: LaMar T. Empey and Jerome Rabow, "The Provo Experiment in Delinquency Rehabilitation," *American Sociological Review* 26 (October 1961). See also LaMar T. Empey, Maynard Erickson, and Max Scott, "The Provo Experiment: Evaluation of a Community Program," in *Correction in the Community: Alternatives to Incarceration*, Monograph No. 4 (Sacramento: Corrections Board, State of California, 1964), pp. 29–38.

37. More information concerning the Essexfields Project can be found in Albert Elias and Saul Pilnick, "The Essexfields Group Rehabilitation Project for Youthful Offenders," *Correction in the Community*, Ibid., pp. 51–57.

38. Keller and Alper, note 12, supra, p. 148.

39. Ibid., pp. 148–150.

40. *Southfields Residential Group Center, A Four Year Report* (Anchorage, Ky.: Southfields, March 1966), p. 31.

41. Richard M. Stephenson and Frank R. Scarpitti, *The Rehabilitation of Delinquent Boys: A Final Report Submitted to the Ford Foundation* (New Brunswick, N.J.: Rutgers, The State University, 1967), p.48.

42. Ashley H. Weeks, *Youthful Offenders at Highfields* (Ann Arbor, Mich.: University of Michigan Press, 1958), p. 42.

43. Keller and Alper, note 12, supra, p. 151.

44. Louis P. Carney, *Introduction to Correctional Science* (New York: McGraw-Hill, 1974), p. 396.

45. Ibid., p. 397.

46. The material for this section was largely taken from Milton Burdman, "Ethnic Self-Help Groups in Prison and on Parole," *Crime and Delinquency* 20, no. 2 (April 1974): 107–118.

47. Ibid., pp. 108–109.

48. Ibid., pp. 109–110.

49. Ibid., p. 111.

50. Ibid., pp. 115–116.

51. Ibid., pp. 116–117.

52. Information for this section was largely obtained from Lewis Yablonsky, *The Tunnel Back: Synanon* (New York: Macmillan, 1965); and Martin R. Haskell and Lewis Yablonsky, *Crime and Delinquency* (Chicago: Rand McNally, 1970), pp. 468–495.

53. Haskell and Yablonsky, note 52, supra, p. 489.

54. Walter Gellhorn, "The Ombudsman Concept in the United States," in Edgar A. Schuler, Thomas F. Hoult, Duane L. Gibson, and Wilbur R. Brookover, eds., *Readings in Sociology* (New York: Thomas T. Crowell, 1971), pp. 408–411.

55. Linda R. Singer and J. Michael Keating, "Prisoner Grievance Mechanisms,"

Crime and Delinquency 19, no. 3 (July 1973): 373.

56. Ibid., pp. 373–374.

57. Murton Foundation, *The Freeworld Times* 1, no. 4 (November 1972): 11.

58. Herbert S. Miller, "The Citizen's Role in Changing the Criminal Justice System," *Crime and Delinquency* 19, no. 3 (July 1973): 344–345.

59. Ibid., p. 345.

60. For further information concerning coordinating councils see Kenneth S. Beam, "The Coordinating Council Movement," 1935 *Yearbook*, pp. 200–213, and "Community Coordination for Prevention of Delinquency," 1936 *Yearbook*, pp. 89–115; and Kenyon J. Scudder, "The Coordinating Council at Work," 1936 *Yearbook*, pp. 67–77 (National Probation Association).

61. Law Enforcement Assistance Administration, note 5, supra, pp. 123–124.

62. Ibid.

63. Ibid.

64. Miller, note 58, supra, pp. 347–348.

65. President's Crime Commission, *The Challenge of Crime in a Free Society* (Washington, D.C.: Government Printing Office, 1967), p.83.

66. National Advisory Commission on Criminal Justice Standards and Goals, *Report on Corrections*, 1973, in Killinger and Cromwell, note 5, supra, p. 25.

67. National Council on Crime and Delinquency, "Goals and Recommendations," (New York, n.d.), p. 7.

68. National Council on Crime and Delinquency, "Minutes of the Meeting of the Executive Committee of the Board of Trustees, June 1970," mimeographed (New York), p. 4, as appears in Frederick W. Howlett, "Is the Youth Service Bureau All It's Cracked Up to Be?" *Crime and Delinquency* 19, no. 4 (October 1973): 486.

69. Robert J. Gemignani, "Youth Services Systems," *Federal Probation* 36, no. 4 (December 1972): 48.

70. Ibid., p. 49.

71. Ibid., pp. 52–53.

72. Howlett, note 68, supra, p. 486.

73. Ibid., p. 486.

74. Ibid., pp. 487–488.

75. Ibid., p. 489.

76. Thomas S. Szasz, *The Myth of Mental Illness* (New York: Bobbs-Merrill Reprint in the Social Sciences, 1961), p. 574.

77. Howlett, note 68, supra, p. 492.

78. National Advisory Commission on Criminal Justice Standards and Goals, *Report on Corrections*, 1973, in Killinger and Cromwell, note 5, supra, p. 25.

79. Ibid., p. 25.

80. The "Order Model of Society" was developed by Ralph Dahrendorf in *Class and Class Conflict in Industrial Society* (Stanford: Stanford University Press, 1959).

81. Ibid.

82. Ibid.

83. Clarence Schrag, "Contemporary Correction—An Analytical Model," (Paper prepared for the President's Crime Commission, 1966, and brought to our attention through Milton Burdman's article, "Ethnic Self-Help Groups," note 46, supra, pp. 109–110.

84. Burdman, note 46, supra, p. 110.

85. Ibid., pp. 115–116.

86. Michael Keating, Jr., "Preventive Mediation in Corrections," *Conflict*, published by the Institute for Mediation and Conflict Resolution, New York, 2, no. 1 (November, 1974). See also: George Nicolau, *Grievance Arbitration in a Prison: The Holton Experiment* (New York: Institution for Mediation and Conflict Resolution, 1974).

87. Nicolau, note 86, supra, p. 10.

88. Keating, note 86, supra.
89. Ibid.
90. Nicolau, note 86, supra, pp. 12–13.
91. Ibid., pp. 15–16.
92. Ibid., p. 17.
93. Ibid., p. 15.
94. Ibid., p. 15.
95. Keating, note 86, supra.

Predictions, Failures and the Examination of Correctional Policy 8

A STOCK-TAKING EXERCISE

We have described and analyzed to some extent the specific correctional strategies, how they developed, and where they are probably leading. It is now time to rethink that material, to assess the efficacy of any of these strategies, and to question the ethical bases of all of them.

This chapter and the next are an attempt to do those things by reviewing the responses of various groups who are influenced by correctional activity, by reviewing the available literature on the evaluation of correctional activity, and by integrating the myriad threads we have examined into a common cloth and examining the implications of the entirety.

Common sense evaluations of corrections

Too often in the criminal justice area, the common sense notions of the layman about what is working and what is not working are ignored. Evaluations of the effectiveness of correctional strategies and the value decisions about what kinds of effectiveness are needed are usually left to the professionals in the system or to the professionals in universities and private organizations. They assess current achievements and make decisions about redirection of strategies in the future, based on goals they have themselves postulated and on assessments of goal priorities which are biased by their own social station and point of view. Professional evaluations are indeed necessary, but too few of these strategies have been systematically studied, and, too often, outcomes are assumed rather than measured.

In the criminal justice area, the assessment by the common man about what is happening and what should happen is particularly relevant. According to professionally trained evaluators, very frequently the common sense assessment is made from a poor information base. The man on the street, the policeman, the offender, and the correctional officer, for example, all see bits and pieces of what is going on. Thus, subjective, on-the-spot evaluations by people without training in evaluation techniques and without access to more complete information are very likely to be biased, inaccurate assessments of what is right and what is wrong with any system.

The correctional system, however, is a social institution that supposedly serves a variety of people by punishing some, protecting others, reinforcing beliefs in legal or normal social behavior, obtaining jobs, and so on. It is an area of public administration where the thoughts and biases of the common man, in or out of the system, should be known and accommodated.

At the very least, if professional evaluators find that the layman's perception of the effectiveness of the system is different from their own, they should include in their assessment some recommendations for wider dissemination of information about what is going on, and for more widely dispersed educational programs that will demonstrate how data can be interpreted.This contact and exchange with the public becomes increasingly important as correctional services continue to be decentralized and to have an impact on a broader range of the population.

To some extent, the requirement that professional evaluations incorporate the perceptions of the uninformed man at the bottom is met in the behavioral sciences through questionnaire and interview results that are incorporated into evaluation and research reports. The summaries and interpretations of the collected data, however, are too infrequently fed back to respondents so that they may know what the final results were, and so that negative or positive reactions to the interpretations can be gauged. Social science information is gathered from many sources, but it is consumed by a much narrower band of the population.

A recent correctional survey conducted in an eastern state illustrates this point. One bureau of corrections recently contracted for a survey of public attitudes toward new prerelease and work release centers located in the community. Part of the survey involved measuring the objection of the public to this relocation of the offender population. The results of the survey were somewhat surprising. The public, it appeared, was strongly in favor of these community-based strategies but felt that the bureau of corrections had been ineffective or even inactive in this area. This discovery moved the bureau to hire a public relations expert who would be responsible for disseminating information about bureau activities, in the hope of taking advantage of the positive public attitude. While it is too early to tell what this maneuver will accomplish, it certainly suggests that the community-based program *had* been ineffective in capitalizing on the public support that was apparently available.

This kind of finding purports more, however, than the simple failure to accomplish as much as available resources would allow. It also suggests something about correctional policy in general. Under some correctional regimes, as we have seen, one apparent goal is to remain invisible—to cause no new waves in the community or in the public bureaucracy that might tend to constrict certain correctional alternatives that, inherently, involve certain risks. But this rather conservative orientation to correctional planning and program implementation is *itself* a constricting influence on the planning and programming activities. The "waves" created in the community are, in and of themselves, a fairly neutral phenomenon. They may be beneficial or detrimental to corrections, depending on how they are used by correctional managers. If managers avoid potential conflict situations, they are avoiding not only negative change outcomes but also positive change outcomes. Under this orientation, it is doubtful that "community-based" correctional programs are, in a social sense, really based within the community. These centers may be placed in cities instead of cornfields, but if the opportunity for interaction with the free community is avoided, then these centers really become small jail units rather than significantly different correctional experiences.

The validity of the layman's perspective in the criminal justice system, or in the work of social control activities, is a concept that goes back to ancient times. Socrates was evidently tried by 500 citizens, and the role of the *peer* in determining the facts and the moral value of an allegedly criminal act is of long standing. It would not be unreasonable to suggest that peer evaluation of correctional activity might be equally important.

This statement is ironic, perhaps, at a juncture in history where jury trials are infrequent and their efficacy, in the view of professionals, is doubtful. Frequently jury trials are waived by defense counsel, for example, because the lawyer would rather place his trust in the decision of a single judge. The jury selection process and the full jury trial slow down the criminal justice process tremendously, and many citizens now regard jury service as a nuisance rather than a duty.

It is also extremely difficult, in this increasingly diverse and complicated society, to define the term "peer." Should alcoholics charged with public intoxication be tried by other alcoholics? Or is every eligible citizen the peer of every other? The answer to both questions is probably no, and a workable concept of "peer" probably lies somewhere between these two extremes.

But even if we could tackle successfully such an elusive concept, another problem arises over the question, At what point should peer opinion enter the decision-making process? In the correctional area, perhaps the parole decision-making process is the most common and traditional point when peers are involved. The parole board in many states is still a body of citizens chosen by the governor to ensure that the common citizen's idea of a "redeemed" or "reformed" inmate has an influence upon who is released and when. However, there is a growing dissatisfaction in correctional circles with this application of "peer" review, because the common citizens appointed to parole boards to evaluate an inmate's progress are usually politically affiliated with the party in power, or are completely unaware of the significance of a prisoner's performance record in determining his success on parole. Thus, in some states there has been a move to a professional parole board consisting of psychologists, sociologists, psychiatrists, and the like, who are supposedly better equipped to evaluate an inmate's progress. This board membership pattern has not seemed to be much more satisfactory because appropriate individuals cannot be found; or the data to which they can apply their training in making the decision is deficient; or their point of view conflicts with the policies under which inmates have been treated; or their predictive skills are not terribly accurate anyway.

Another way of incorporating peer review and evaluation bypasses some of these problems by eliminating the reviewers from case-by-case decision making and elevating them to a position in which they have a voice in policy formulation. For example, the various state planning agencies with criminal justice planning functions frequently involve a set of regional councils that include business and political leaders and other representatives of the community. The professional staff of these planning agencies make recommendations to the planning councils, but the community representatives have some control over the kinds of plans that will be funded and implemented. Naturally these councils have some impact on correctional activities in a given region, but the concept of layman participation in correctional policy formulation and evaluation can also be carried out in a more direct fashion.

In some areas, for example, youth service bureaus and similar community correctional agencies are governed and partly run by volunteers. It is also a practice in areas where work release programs are well developed that citizens' councils aid correctional officials in directing work release policy, and in engineering community support in terms of locating or improving job opportunities.

On its most general theoretical level, the participation of common citizens in correctional activity is necessary because change in a system depends on increasing information in that system. For instance, on the human system level, there are reports that individuals isolated from other human beings from birth are totally incapable of acting like human beings. They are bereft of the information from their environment that enables people to change and mature. The need for information is equally necessary in a social system such as a correctional organization. The less information there is, the less variety there is and the less change is possible.

If correctional practices are governed solely by insiders (and by outside professionals with similar information) the kinds and quantity of information are limited and the chances of change restricted. The chances of directed change are even smaller. Thus, on the broadest level, theoretical and political concerns tend to merge, and correctional theory—a brand of change theory—appears to be essentially democratic in its implications. Hence conscious ignorance of the feelings, knowledge, and skills of the man in the street is a contradiction of correctional theory as commonly practiced by correctional professionals.

The liberal, the conservative, and the good life

Whether we speak of professional or lay assessments of correctional outcomes, a variable of considerable importance is the value placed on the kind of social life toward which correctional strategies are supposedly directed. In weighing what kind of social goals are valuable, we suspect that professionals and laymen are no different. Hardhats, truckers, school teachers, and researchers may enjoy or despise television, Monday night football, beer, Beethoven, and Johnny Cash. When we get right down to it, ultimate social goals are a matter of taste. Some tastes are legal, some are illegal, and persons whose values and culture are likely to influence their breaking the law are also unlikely to consult the law when they choose how to act. Two things about taste would seem to be certain. First, many more tastes are legal than illegal; but second, the number of tastes that may be legitimate is wider than the range of tastes of people who make and enforce the law.

Thus, one particularly knotty problem for correctional officials and offenders alike is that they must be able to accept and aid each other in pursuing tastes and goals that they personally do not like.

From the official's viewpoint, a major problem is separating the tastes of an offender that he does not like from his knowledge that the man with that taste is also a criminal. Officials must learn to be tolerant of life styles and values different from their own, and they must be able to distinguish within these styles and values possible kinds of behavior that they cannot condone. The offender, on the other hand, has the problem of recognizing in the official the possibility of help and understanding from a man whose values and life style he may dislike and distrust. Neither of these jobs is an easy one, and failing at either reduces the chances to implement correctional strategies and evaluate their impact. The consequences of behavior become confounded with matters of taste.

Rising in the 1960s and culminating in the Nixon-Agnew campaign of 1972, the major clash in taste appeared to be that of law 'n' order conservatism vs. an increasingly populist Kennedy liberalism. Both sides of that controversy were responsible for major landmarks in the rapid development of the criminal justice system. The crime commission convened by President Johnson was responsible for perhaps the greatest single study of criminal justice in history. One of the consequences of that study was the Omnibus Crime Bill and Safe Streets Act of 1968. Among other things, that Bill established the Law Enforcement Assistance Administration, most of whose expenditures have been controlled by the Nixon Administration.

But perhaps the greatest single impact of the conservative-liberal clash was the smashing victory for the law 'n' order platform in 1972, followed by Watergate and similar exposures in 1973 and 1974. It turned out that at least some of the politicians insisting on "getting tough" with criminals were themselves criminals. It is doubtful that any group will ever have such a battle standard again. Definitions of just what "the good life" is and what it takes to achieve it are likely to be more varied in the future.

The bad, the sick, and society

Ironically, the recommendations of the conservatives and the liberals for the treatment of offenders may not differ as much as the two groups might suppose. Furthermore, it is quite possible that inmates, given a choice between the strategies recommended by the conservatives and those recommended by the liberals, might form an odd coalition with the conservatives.

Traditionally it seems that conservative politicians, particularly those in the late 1960s and early 1970s who became the vocal mouthpieces of the "silent majority," favored more rigorous enforcement of the criminal law. For them this has usually meant a less rigorous enforcement of procedural law and an unbending faith in the moral value of retribution and the effectiveness of deterrence. The late legal scholar Herbert Packer suggested that this ideological camp supported the police and prosecutorial functions of the criminal process. They have not, until recent years, been terribly aware of or interested in the correctional process. This political camp supported stiffer legislated penalties, preventive detention for dangerous or recidivistic offenders, and more frequent use of incarceratory sentences.

Operationally, this camp has had much to do with structuring the preconviction system as it works today. It seems that formally limiting the discretion of prosecutors and judges has increased the use of informal, low-visibility discretion in the guilty plea process, and has emphasized the "work ethic" in the preconviction process. In any case, these political and operational forces have deemphasized the importance of correction, since, as we pointed out in Chapter 2, the work ethic and the guilty plea process are both based on ideas of retribution and deterrence which assume that control is accomplished at the point of conviction. The results of this conservative orientation have been the emphasis on clear and stiff penalties for an increasing range of acts defined as criminal, and the emphasis on prisons as the mode of punishment that deviants deserve.

Contrasted with this point of view is the liberal camp that has favored the judicial and correctional phases of the criminal justice process over the investigative and prosecutorial phases. This political group has advanced the decriminalization of many deviant acts such as alcoholism and drug use. Instead of depending on retribution and deterrence, the liberals have usually led the trend toward more "effective" social control strategies, such as emphasis on rehabilitative programs supposedly based on an understanding of the offender's problems; and the search for ways to manipulate the causal variables that might prevent crime and change criminals. A major consequence of this line of thought is the increasing use of civil rather than criminal remedies in social control problems. Alcoholism, delinquency, drug dependence, and other conditions that conservatives would punish, the liberals would try to understand and treat.

Thus, from the point of view of policy makers, these are two fundamentally opposed perspectives. The conservatives assume that offenders are bad and should be punished. The liberals assume that offenders are sick and should be treated. Regardless of what these two groups think, however, the views of the deviant as sinful or sick are not new assumptions. Badness and sickness throughout history have been rather common ways of perceiving the deviant, and they have implied similar strategies for social defense. The outcome for the deviant is frequently similar. Either he is incarcerated in a penal institution to atone for his sins, or he is incarcerated in a mental institution to be cured of his sickness. Regardless of the rationale, the deviance is located *within* the offender—in the condition of his bad character or in the condition of his malfunctioning psyche.

In certain cultures and at certain points of history it has not been to the offender's advantage to avoid one form of social reprisal more than the other. They were all equally noxious to him. Given, however, the rather liberal penchant of the founding fathers, there are certain advantages in the United States for the offender in being treated criminally rather than civilly. The Bill of Rights as it is constructed, and as it is still construed, constrains the manner in which criminal penalties can be legally applied. At this date the liberal strategy of quasi-medical intervention has not been similarly constrained. Thus, if Gerald Gault had been an adult when he made his bothersome phone call to his neighbor, he would have been subjected, at a maximum, to a short jail sentence. But as a juvenile under civil authority, he was sentenced to six years in a boys' training school.

The arguments for and against civil, rather than criminal, strategies of social control have been waged for some time now, and this controversy has finally entered the realm of traditional common law crimes. There are provisions in some states, for example, that "habitual" offenders may be sentenced to additional time over and above the penalty for their last crime. Moreover, some states have provided that these repeaters may be diagnosed as sociopaths or psychopaths and incarcerated in civil institutions for indefinite lengths of time. In the civil law provisions, the most frequent use of this intervention pattern has been against sexual offenders and narcotics offenders. But as we have seen, this quasi-medical strategy has also infiltrated certain correctional organizations such as California's, where indefinite sentences for felonies are the norm. In that state the actual sentencing decisions are made by the parole board, which can delay pronouncement of parole indefinitely until they are satisfied with the progress of the inmate.

Societies of ex-offenders, the Quakers, and other groups have opposed this tendency in corrections, arguing that the indefinite sentence and the rehabilitative ideology are subterfuges by which the state can maintain control of offenders as long as it chooses. Offenders such as George Jackson, for example, have argued that the conservative strategy of retribution and deterrence is better, because it is at least clear at the outset what the penalty for an offense will be and what the offender has to do to get out on parole. In other words, this conservative game is more easily understood and fought than the liberal game. In the quasi-medical game, the rules are much less clear to begin with and the offender is at a much greater disadvantage in abiding by or avoiding the rules.

In the ultimate analysis, radicals seem to prefer a conservative to a liberal opposition because the delineation of conflict is clearer and cooptation is less probable.

The third major group in this political battle of tastes is the radical group. From their perspective they argue that when crime prevention and rehabilitation are practiced on a retail basis—one offender at a time—this is not only a losing battle but a hypocritical one. Either the liberal or the conservative strategies result, finally, in the maintenance of the social structure at *status quo*. The really different explanation of crime, say the radicals, comes out of an understanding of the social structure itself. Crime is not caused by bad or sick men but by the nature of the social structure, which demands similar goal attainment of all men but limits the legitimate opportunities to only a few. Changes in the crime rate, radicals argue, will come about only if we stop focusing on the individual and his internal problems and begin to focus on the society and its interrelationships. There may be bad men and sick men, but crime as a social phenomenon and criminals as a group are adequately explained in terms of the sick or malfunctioning society. The concepts of individual badness and individual sickness keep social control strategies from focusing on the system itself.

RECIDIVISM AND THE CRIMINAL JUSTICE SYSTEM

About the most common evaluation measure of correctional effectiveness has been the variable of recidivism: the number of offenders returning to crime after one correctional experience (the correctional equivalent of the police clearance rate and the prosecutor's batting average). As a measure of productiveness, recidivism has not been very successful; but alternate criteria have not been very satisfactory either.

One difficulty with the recidivism criterion is that it has not been defined in the same way twice. One scholar suggests that the most satisfactory definition of recidivism is the number of people who return to crime, regardless of whether the crime is detected or the recidivist arrested. This definition does, of course, encompass all the events which the correctional system has not been able to prevent, but it is obviously a definition that cannot be measured. The measurable definition is the number of offenders who return to the same correctional system within a specified period of time. While much more measurable, this definition is unsatisfactory because it does not account for multiple offenses by a recidivist before he is apprehended, nor does it account for offenders who return to crime but are not caught.

Examination of past studies

Prediction, actuarial, or "experience" studies involve anticipating a certain result or outcome (the criterion) on the basis of another body of previously collected data. Perhaps the most familiar form of prediction studies are the actuarial tables by which insurance companies set the premium rate for a life insurance policy. Very simply, these tables classify people into different employment, age, medical and other groupings, and then rate the risk of death within the life of the policy for each of these groups. Naturally, premium price increases as the risk increases.

Prediction of outcomes based on known information is widely used in determining a course of action. For example, college admissions are based on prediction of academic success. (In some cases they are based on prediction of future alumnae contributions!) In some areas, police patrols are dispersed in relation to a prediction of crime frequency. Large restaurants and institutional cafeterias base food orders and preparation of quantities for particular meals on past information about customer consumption. Wall Street speculation and race track speculations are, for some investors, carefully weighed decisions about predicted outcome in relation to risk. Jeremy Bentham and other criminologists, as we have seen in Chapter 2, suggest that potential criminals decide the value of an illegal act in relation to the weight of the penalty and the probability of apprehension.

In general, there is little in the way of social interaction that is not based on a subjective prediction of alternatives. People anticipate what other people will do and act accordingly. In this type of prediction, which is made by most people many times a day, their information about past experiences is usually compacted and abbreviated in the form of cultural values which they take for granted. If people had to predict consciously every specific outcome in terms of particular knowledge about every particular incident, social interaction would crawl to a stop.

As social science has become more sophisticated about these everyday predictions, the theories of models and learning have emerged. Learning is a prediction process in which outcomes of past events are continually fed back into the present decision-making situation so that decisions about future outcomes become increasingly more accurate. Modeling theory summarizes the process of prediction in terms of the way people conceptualize future events and then act to achieve certain outcomes based on data about past outcomes in analogous situations.

In the criminal justice field, prediction has lagged for many reasons, which we will examine shortly. A major reason, of course, is that systematic data about transactions in the criminal justice system have not been collected. Nevertheless, we have seen the more or less subjective prediction process present in the bail decision, in various prosecutorial acts, in the sentencing decision, in various correctional classification processes, and in the parole decision.

Two major types of objective, data-based prediction processes related to corrections are (1) the prediction of criminality in different categories of the population at large and (2) the prediction of recidivism based on information about the previously incarcerated offender. By far the most important type so far, has been the prediction of recidivism.

Recidivism studies began in earnest in the 1920s. The first study of major significance was the work done by Burgess related to the implementation of the Illinois Indefinite Sentence Law.[1] The Burgess method was characterized by the inclusion of as many variables as possible and by the equal weighting of those variables significantly related to recidivism in the formation of the prediction tables. Sheldon and Eleanor Glueck, working around the same time, differed in their strategy. They gleaned as much data as possible about correlations to parole outcome, and then included in their prediction tables only the six strongest predictors.

The Gluecks' work has had a monumental impact on criminological research. They produced three different sets of material, one dealing with 500 adult male felons, one dealing with 1,000 juveniles, and one dealing with women prisoners.[2] Lately, their work has been soundly criticized for the inefficiency of their six variables (the last five are only 3 percent more helpful than the first item by itself); for the unequal periods at-risk to which their offenders were subjected; and, most importantly, for their suggestions that these prediction tables could form a basis for early intervention in the lives of precriminal or predelinquent persons prior to the commission of illegal acts.[3] Nevertheless, their work has attracted many other scholars to prediction work, and is responsible for the more frequent use of quantified data in criminal justice decisions.

Lloyd Ohlin, when he was an actuarial sociologist for the state of Illinois, was responsible for a major study in the 1950s. Ohlin followed Burgess in that he used some broad, subjective categories of "social type" and gave each variable equal weight in the prediction table. He followed the Gluecks' lead, however, in paring down the population of variables to include only the most highly correlated ones.[4]

There have been many other prediction studies of note, but perhaps the most widely recognized for its precision is the Mannheim and Wilkins study, *Prediction Methods in Relation to Borstal Training*.[5] This study examined boys released from the English Borstal schools (training schools) in 1946 to 1947. It is similar to the Glueck work in that the researchers studied many variables for relationship to outcome and then selected the most significant ones. They also used an unequal weighting system, scoring the positive or negative characteristics in relation to the proportion of their predictive strength. Unlike the Glueck studies, and similar to the Burgess and Ohlin studies, Mannheim and Wilkins used only the official record for their information. In doing so, the researchers had the advantage that the Borstal records are considerably more uniform and complete than files in American correctional systems.

While there are many similarities between this and the other studies, there are several differences that, in our opinion, place it above many other prediction attempts. Mannheim and Wilkins, for example, were very careful in maintaining equal periods at risk for their subjects. Frequently, researchers in this area have calculated the percentage of offenders recidivating from the total number of offenders in the original sample, despite the fact that some are already back in prison and no longer at risk. Or, looking in the other direction, many studies have calculated the percentage of failures for all subjects in a sample regardless of the fact that they have been released at different times. The Gluecks, for example, calculated failure from the time at which the formal sentences for their offenders expired. This technique ignored the fact that some had been released much earlier than others through parole or good time discharge.

Another major advance was that Mannheim and Wilkins actually carried out a prediction study based on their first round of research. This might seem surprising, since all of these studies are "prediction" studies. But the Gluecks, for example, in their study of 500 criminals' careers, did not use their prediction tables on a second sample in order to validate the utility of the predictive variables. In contrast, Wilkins and Mannheim studied the correlations between file data and outcome on one set of subjects and then drew a second sample on which to apply the prediction table. Periodically thereafter, the Borstal tables have been updated, variables being dropped or re-weighted as changes in the social system change the predictive strength of the selected variables.

A third major contribution, although conclusions were tentative, involves the work that these two men did with the middle-range or "average" risk cases. They scored boys within five risk categories. The best and worst risk groups, designated A, B, C, and D had chances of success of 7:1, 2:1, 1:2, and 1:7, respectively. These categories sandwiched an "x" group in the middle, having an average chance of success. It is in dealing with this group that almost all studies have proved inadequate. They could predict the best and worst risks, but the prediction equation proved inadequate to separating the successes from the failures in the middle group. The researchers handled this group in surprisingly simple fashion, considering the difficulty that this average group had given other researchers. Since the original prediction equation was of no help in separating sheep from wolves among this group (except that it *located* the group members), the solution was simply to use a second prediction equation! This second equation utilized information that had not been strong enough to enter the primary equation. But these variables helped in adjusting the original predictive score to make guesses about outcome in this group more meaningful than flipping a coin.[6]

This technique is so simple and normal to everyday experience that it was probably taken for granted by other researchers and therefore overlooked. Briefly, the principle used was simply one of separating out cases that are more certain from those that are less certain and then seeking out more information about the more uncertain cases in order to establish better guessing odds. We use the same technique on a more subjective basis every day, as in guessing which football teams will win, for example. We can guess the outcome fairly accurately when teams with a very strong roster and record meet teams with a very weak record and roster. But guessing becomes more difficult when apparently evenly-matched teams meet. Rather than flip a coin in these cases, effective prediction can be done by seeking more specific and less stable information. Rather than use data of past record and overall personnel strength, we seek, for example, data about injuries, or data about which team might be more "emotionally up" for a game. Similarly, when Mannheim and Wilkins found that the original seven variables merely indicated that certain boys had equal chances, they then added the less significant data of number of prison abscondings, number of misdemeanors, and type of training school to which the youth was sent.

While there are many other good research qualities that have elevated this study to its present classic status, one additional item is particularly important for our purposes. This one is that Mannheim and Wilkins investigated, at least in rudimentary form, the effect of the type of institution to which boys were sent. Most other studies have bypassed the prison experience itself as a factor contributing to release outcome. The most predictive variables have usually been items about past record, i.e., characteristics that offenders bring to the institution. The Borstal study, however, includes the examination of one institutional item—whether the Borstal school was open (boys were free to come and go) or closed (boys were incarcerated all the time). Mannheim and Wilkins discovered that open schools improved the chances of success not only for the best risk boys but also for the worst risk boys. Similarly, the closed institutions worsened the success chances of the best risk as well as the worst risk groups.

This finding, as simple as it is, may in the long run be as significant as all of the study's other methodological advances put together, because, as Wilkins writes:

it is in the assessment of what may be regarded as "reasonable allowance" for the "class of material" upon which different treatments operate that the prediction system may be of operational utility.[7]

In other words, it is the capability of the prediction study to classify offenders into treatment-relevant categories that enables us to establish the relative effectiveness of different treatments and to begin to make logical and systematic changes in the correctional system. Prediction studies have most utility in identifying the variables over which the correctional authority has some control. If prediction can do nothing but distinguish the risky from the not-so-risky at impact, it only helps administrators to know some of the things to avoid. But if prediction can identify variables that reduce or increase risk, it helps administrators to make decisions about what should be done. Thus, prediction becomes a planning and evaluation device.

Lack of correctional impact

One of the most disappointing outcomes of all the prediction work that has been conducted is its lack of effect on the ongoing correctional process. Regardless of the fact that prediction studies have demonstrated their validity in the assessment of outcome, available prediction tables have often been ignored by the administrators who are finally responsible for using this information. Parole boards are particularly notorious for ignoring statistically based predictions and substituting hunch and belief as the basis of their decisions. Prison administrators, too, have been slow to use objectively collected and analyzed data as the basis for decision making. Planning and programming continue at a snail's pace, on a trial and error basis or, worse, with a dependence on biased reports and first-hand perceptions of selected managerial aides who have only half the story and whose sources of information are uncontrolled and undocumented.

One reason for this rejection of information has been the sociopolitical climate of correctional decision making, in which the research information is perceived as irrelevant and thus as "noninformation." Researchers, too, must accept some of the responsibility for this perceived irrelevance of their work. Too often researchers have selected what should be studied on the basis of their own biases and goals rather than on the goals of the suggested user system. We have seen, for example, that a great deal of criminological thinking and research has been associated with the "classical school," whose basic assumptions and motivations conflict with the change-producing motives of the correctional phase of the criminal process. But equally damaging, much of the criminological research of the "positive school" has been based on academic notions in which the researcher is rewarded for finding causes for different types of individual crime behavior, regardless of the fact that the correctional system is politically, financially, and structurally incapable of dealing with many of these discovered "causes." Only lately has research focused on variables that are manipulable by the administrators in charge of offenders. More often than not, these variables are not characteristics of individual offenders, but characteristics of the system in which offenders are treated. The actions of many administrators are not directed by variables that classify offenders in relation to other offenders, or to free citizens, but by variables that classify offenders in relation to each other. Paradoxically, it is only as researchers divest themselves of their preoccupation with individual offenders that they can deliver information that will have an impact on offenders.

Researchers and managers are finally bridging the gaps between them. Research is more system-oriented, and managers are becoming more offender-oriented. Both trends have been generated by similar redefinitions of the correctional task and the correctional outcome. Applied, or operational research has freed itself from the structures of "pure science" by including man as both the scientist and the user of scientific research. Perhaps we can now look back on the separation of pure and applied science and decide that there never was much difference between them. Pure science, after all, has its uses, or it would not be carried on at all. Pure science has satisfied the needs of the scientists doing the research and of the organizations in which they worked.

Researchers have learned that there is nothing demeaning or unscientific about applying the results of their investigations to other peoples' needs; and managers have slowly come round to defining the type of correctional activity about which research data is needed. As corrections becomes proactive and the goals set for it are oriented to the future rather than the past, then predictions on a rigorous scientific basis become necessary. When corrections was rationalized as a meting out of justice, of deterrence, retribution, or whatever, then the abilities of scientists were not considered essential. The decisions about what should be done had already been made by police, judges, and legislatures. The correctional official was in business to ensure the durability of those decisions. But as corrections is increasingly seen as a public service, then correctional officials must gather data about how the job is being done and decide how it can be done better.

Another reason for the lack of impact of prediction studies is that correctional officials have usually harbored a dislike for statistics and for their use "against people." This dislike is found, not so much among officials of the traditional, retributive view, but on the contrary, among more progressive wardens who seek rehabilitation of offenders. They object, usually, not that statistics are irrelevant, but that their use is immoral. All individuals are unique, they say, and things that are unique cannot be classified.[8] Treatment decisions must be based on the individual's needs, not on the fact that he fits into some box in a statistical table.

Each offender is undoubtedly unique, but acknowledgment of his uniqueness does not help us to treat him. Even a psychoanalytic clinician treats individuals in terms of categories, or in terms of qualities in the person that he can recognize and describe because he has seen them before or read about them. His suggestions for cure or change are predictions; and all predictions are based on known, repeatable qualities or concepts—variables that have varied similarly in the past.

Thus, when a parole board member plays a hunch and votes to release an offender whom the actuarial table classifies as a bad risk, he is not being any more sensitive than the statistician is to the unique qualities of the individual offender. The parole board member's bet on release may or may not pay off. If it does pay off, he has been sensitive to a variable not included in the actuarial table, but which might have been included if another scientist, sensitive to other things, had constructed the table in the first place.

Thus, the refusal to use statistics cannot be rationally based on the insistence that uniqueness has been destroyed or ignored. If the statistically based decision is immoral, so too is the clinically based decision. Immorality would seem to enter into either type of decision when it is made for ulterior reasons, and when the statistical or clinical data have merely become a convenient rationale for acting with an ulterior motive.

A third reason for the lack of impact of recidivism studies is closely related to the first two. Some correctional officials claim that recidivism-related data are not used because it is not really within the province of the correctional organization to reduce recidivism. They point out, correctly, that recidivism is not simply a function of what happens to an offender in prison or on parole. Recidivism rates are influenced by a tremendous variety of variables, most of which are precorrectional. The offender's personality, his past family life, his previous arrest record, and so on, are not things for which correctional officials are in any way responsible. Furthermore, there are a host of other factors—parole employment, type of community released to, reaction of society to the convict stigma—that correctional officials also argue are beyond their responsibility.

This kind of objection, however, also indicates a misunderstanding of recidivism studies. The variables used to predict recidivism are not necessarily causal; they are merely the variables that are most constantly related to the fact of failure (or of success). Both the failure and the correlated predictors may be *caused* by some entirely different variable. It is quite possible that correctional officials might choose to intervene in a criminal career pattern by altering a few variables that have very little correlation with recidivism. Predicting recidivism only requires that we find variables that explain or account for the variability in a group recidivism rate. In order to change the chances of one individual returning to prison, we must select variables that are (1) accessible, (2) manipulable, (3) both accessible and manipulable within legal and ethical constraints. Such a variable may have very little direct relationship to recidivism prediction but may have everything in the world to do with reducing a recidivism rate. Thus, the objection of correctional officials that they cannot affect the recidivism rate is not really valid. It is true that many variables used to predict the occurrence of failure are not open to manipulation by correctional officials. But this is very different from saying that recidivism, as measured, is irrelevant to measuring correctional effectiveness.

Partitioning the recidivism rate

It becomes obvious, particularly when examining this last objection to the use of statistics, that one major reason for the lack of impact of recidivism studies is not that sufficient force is missing (some recidivism studies are very convincing) but that there is insufficient resistance or substance against which they must rest. Information is information only for particular purposes. When officials do not see change as their task, then recidivism studies are irrelevant because they contain no usable information. When correctional goals are in flux, there may be insufficient agreement among researchers and administrators about what data counts as information. Information is the reduction of uncertainty during the decision-making process. If correctional officials do not understand the function of uncertainty in making decisions, or if they are not making any decisions, then recidivism data is useless.

In the next section of this chapter, we will examine a model for the understanding of correctional goals. It is our aim that this discussion of goals, combined with the description of present correctional practices, will help to place within a coherent whole all of the programs and practices that make up modern correctional strategies. But we also see this discussion as a necessary lever by which to resolve some of the conflict about recidivism, effectiveness, and research utility.

As these goals are discussed, it should be remembered that administrators who claim little interest in "recidivism," or in any form of data-based evaluation, can probably not get off scot-free. It is true that many variables influence recidivism, and no one part of the correctional system is responsible for all of these variables. But the recidivism rate can be partitioned. For example, Mannheim and Wilkins separated the variance in the recidivism rate that was due to open or closed institutions from the variance that they attributed to preconviction risk characteristics. Given more data, we can partition the rate in any number of other ways, in order to determine what proportion of the recidivism rate is influenced by what stage of the criminal justice process, by which organization, and so on. Such statistical manipulations, however, are just as meaningless as the plaintive cries from officials that they "are not responsible for that part of the failure." The statistical variation can be partitioned for analytical purposes, but the parolee walking down a South Philadelphia alley looking for heroin is just as much a complete human being as the parolee in University Park studying for his master's degree. Neither of them can be partitioned.

Thus, while we can measure which kind of organization contributes how much to the overall success or failure rate, it would seem to make more sense to ask all the organizations with "partitioned" responsibilities to reorganize around the realities of the correctional process. As we examine the various correctional goals, then, it may be helpful to consider how each set of goals may or may not allow correctional officials to increase their cooperation with each other and with offenders, so that sooner or later we can get away from the bureaucratic diffusion of responsibility for success.

CORRECTIONAL POLICY

Common concerns of correctional administrators

As we look for a broad statement of correctional goals on which to base a reexamination of the utility of research findings and their implications for strategic correctional thinking, it is important to understand what kind of organizational goals we want to study. "Goal" is a very loose term that has been defined in many ways in the past. Charles Perrow, a major scholar in the field of organizational sociology, suggests four main groupings of organizational goals.[9]

1) We can understand goals as the official mandates of an organization. In this case, we should examine the legislative interest in setting up departments of correction or prisons or parole services, and so on. This goal statement is usually very vague and general, but purposely so. The legislative mandate has the purpose of *chartering* the organization . . . of giving it the authority to carry out its business. Thus, the statement, "the correctional department will be responsible for the care and treatment of offenders" makes sense on this level, because it is largely a symbolic, or support-gathering sentence, not a directive on how to proceed.

2) We can understand goals as the functions that an organization performs for an outside social group. For example, it has been postulated by Talcott Parsons that prisons serve an integrative function for society because they remove from circulation deviants who disrupt social processes. But this decision on function, or anyone else's decision on function, remains conjecture at this point in the development of social science. For example, George Jackson argued with vigor if not logic equal to Parsons, that the prisons serve an economic function by taking out of circulation dissenters to the present social distribution of rewards. Other people have argued that corrections perform a maintenance function for society by retraining offenders to take a more productive place in life. These issues are important, especially politically. But even if it were possible to settle such issues this would not, ipso facto, tell us how the organizations of correction work internally. Managers do not plan their day "to help society." They plan their day to meet particular people, to solve particular problems, and to go home in the evening.

3) We can also look at goals as the group commitments within the organization. We can ask managers what their goals are. We can also ask counselors, correctional officers, and inmates. The goals of each group are doubtless different. Some of these groups' goals are compatible and some are conflicting. But no one group's goals can be represented as the goals of the organization.

4) Lastly, Perrow suggests that we can look at goals as the "essential constraints built into the organization." That is, we can look at the organization's abilities to perform on a daily basis within the limits set by minimal standards of human decency, poor finances, changing politics, angry citizens, bewildered staff, and embittered inmates. We can look at actual operating programs and ask what the presence of one kind of training and the absence of another kind imply for the goals of the organization as a whole. It is this last organizational goal set that we want to concentrate on here, because it is basically this goal set of staff-offender structural relationships that would determine the immediate outcomes of the correctional experience in the life of the released offender. And it is these consequences that everyone now suspects corrections should play a part in improving.

One way of examining correctional policy is to inquire about the essential relationships in the organization. Since prison, parole, probation, and other organizations are "open systems" constantly interchanging different energies with a variety of environments, we suggest that the simplest set of essential relationships we can talk about are (1) correctional concern for the environment (primarily societal) and (2) correctional concern for internal relationships (ultimately with inmates).

Developing a model of correctional policy

Several recent studies, all using widely different methodology in different correctional agencies, conclude that concern about the community and concern about the individual offender are the two most important variables that make up the frame of reference within which policy is formulated. A recent parole study outlines the parole supervisor's concerns as (1) avoiding public and police criticism and (2) producing low returns to the prison.[10] In a recent probation study it is noted that:

> In probation and parole service there exists a contradiction between the agency-centered approach (the concern is the consequence of the clients' behavior) and the client-centered ap-

proach (the concern is actualizing the maximum self-potential of the individual).[11]

A recent juvenile study concludes that decision about disposition of the boys is made (1) in terms of the juvenile's needs and (2) in terms of protecting the community from the boy.[12] Cressey reaches the conclusion that the two major focal points of prison administration are concern for the individual inmate and concern for society in varying degrees.[13] On a slightly different tack, another prison study emphasizes the dichotomy between feelings and attitudes of organizational participants and the public behavior required for both.[14]

A rough and ready framework for policy formulation may then be drawn by using the two intersecting dimensions: concern about the community and concern about the individual offender.[15] (See Table 1.)

Table 1
FRAME OF REFERENCE IN POLICY FORMULATION

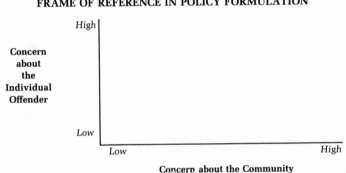

Concern about the Community

By dichotomizing the two dimensions, four possible policy complexes emerge:

CONSISTENTLY HIGH:	Simultaneous concern for individual and community
MIXED:	High concern for individual, low concern for community
MIXED:	High concern for community, low concern for individual
CONSISTENTLY LOW:	Simultaneous inattention to individual and community

The two dimensions may also be considered as polar ways of treating the system process—from a point of view in which the individual, organizational, and community goals are integrated, to a point of view in which the goals of individuals and the community are basically ignored and the goals of the organization are treated in isolation. (See Table 2.)

Table 2

THE VARIATIONS OF EMPHASIS IN POLICY CONSTRUCTION

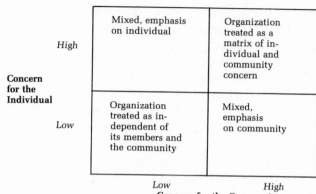

		Low	High
Concern for the Individual	High	Mixed, emphasis on individual	Organization treated as a matrix of individual and community concern
	Low	Organization treated as independent of its members and the community	Mixed, emphasis on community

Low   High
Concern for the Community

In Table 2, the policy makers' frames of reference are represented. In the top right-hand cell, policy is formulated on the basis that the organizational goals are most effectively met when the individual and the community goals are approached concomitantly. In the bottom left-hand cell, policy is formulated on the basis that the organizational goals can be achieved in isolation from the needs of offenders and the needs of the surrounding community. Between these two extremes are two types of "mixed policy." In the top left-hand cell is the policy that emphasizes the individual offender, but without a simultaneous concern for the needs of the community vis-à-vis the offender, or for the needs of the offender as they are modified by the individual's interaction with the community. In the bottom right-hand cell is a mixed policy that emphasizes the needs of the community, but without a simultaneous interest in the individual offender, or for the way in which community needs might be met in terms of the offender. To say that one policy emphasizes one concern at the expense of the other does not mean that the deemphasized concerns are totally ignored. Policies in which the organization is treated as independent must still allow for certain interactions with the community, namely, those directed at blocking influence from external sources. The policy which treats the organization as open to both community and individual influences must still allow for control and governance of interaction, namely, by channeling those interactions in ways that are conducive to productive activity. Between these two policies, there are the two mixed alternatives: (1) policy that treats the community as a given, or a machine, while accommodating the probabilistic nature of individual action; and (2) the policy that treats the individual as a given, or unchangeable, while acknowledging the problematic nature of community behavior.

Under the assumption that organizations and individuals do possess open system characteristics, the two mixed policy frameworks and the policy of isolation suffer from the following contradictions or misapprehensions.

1) *Policy of isolation:* that the organization and the environment are related in an unvarying fashion; that organizational arrangements are not altered by the goal-directed activity of persons who are arranged within the organization or by the changing demands of the community.
2) *Mixed policy with the emphasis on the individual offender:* that persons, once in the organization, are not affected by changes in the external environment; that the organization encloses its participants totally and can treat their needs regardless of different external demands that are made on the organization as it treats, or on the individual when he is released.
3) *Mixed policy with the emphasis on the community:* that the organization can effectively serve the community and be sensitive to community concerns about corrections without being sensitive to the needs and goals of offenders who eventually will be returned to the community.

These contradictions and mistakes about system relationships will, in these three cases, have the following uncontrolled results that administrators do not anticipate.

1) *Policy of isolation:* the organization will have difficulty adjusting to environmental change; it will not be able to handle new inputs (in terms of new kinds of offenders); outputs will be undirected (offenders will return to the community unchanged and will interact the same way as they did before). The internal organization will have to adjust to unacknowledged social systems within itself. Officials will have to accommodate informal inmate and staff norms without having official channels and planned alternatives by which to do so.
2) *Mixed policy with the emphasis on the individual offender:* the organization will have an inadequate basis for understanding characteristics of input; changes effected will be inadequate to withstand community influences on output; organization will grow cynical, blame organizational failure on community insensitivity.
3) *Mixed policy with the emphasis on the community:* the or-

ganization will have difficulty in changing individuals as the community desires, or difficulty in motivating inmates to deal with reactions of community. Although the organization will claim to serve the community, it will maintain low visibility of internal operations. It will ultimately call organizational failure a failure of individual inmates.

In any of these cases, considerable energy will be spent on maintaining the misconceptions, and less energy will be available for actual change processes.

In contrast with these three frames of reference, the policy of goal congruence would seem to be most effective if the goal of corrections does involve reduction of future illegal activity by offenders. Policy that treats organization as open to both the community and individual variation presents the greatest chance of effectiveness because it implies that the primary organizational task is that of achieving congruence between organizational and environmental processes and between organizational and subsystem processes. However, this trend toward high effectiveness, like the contrasting trends toward ineffectiveness, stipulates a considerable duration of organizational life. Sensitive to present realities, the policy of congruence must allow for the longer history and earlier evolution of the other three policy modalities.

Correctional organization cannot start new and fresh. In most cases, this means that a more open policy must accommodate personnel whose behavior is symptomatic of previous policy contradictions and communities that are habituated to stylized and limited interaction with correctional organizations. Hence the history of correctional organization places considerable pressure on organizations operating with an open policy to accept the tendency toward closure in one form or another. Persons and organizations are more acquainted with mixed and closed policies and will therefore respond to open policy as if it were overly demanding or surprisingly naive. Social systems built on the adjustments necessary to maintain contradictory policy can be so unequipped for open interaction that primary reactions to the open policy will tend toward rebellion rather than acceptance. The open organizational system that has been treated as though it were fragmented *becomes* less open and less integrated, and it will react to open policy as an oppression rather than as a return to a more natural state. While behavior in the open system will be affected by organizational reactions to previous closure, behavior in the mixed and closed systems will be affected by reaction to previous openness.

Motivation and control strategies in different policies

The specific policies of correctional organizations may be elaborated in terms of the control and motivation strategies administrators will use to structure the organization in order to implement the alternative policy concerns for community and offender. That is, the method by which organizational roles are mapped out and integrated is dependent on the system models used. As there seem to be four model complexes, organizational studies have identified four motivational patterns for the production of required behavior. These are:

(a) Legal compliance, the use of machine theory, that rules are sufficient
(b) The use of rewards or instrumental satisfactions, a modified machine theory of stimulus-response
(c) The use of internalized patterns of self-determination and self-expression
(d) The use of internalized values and development of self-concept [16]

These motivational patterns may be related to the policy frameworks in a consistent fashion. Legal compliance alone is likely to be considered sufficient for control of organizational behavior when the goal of that control is merely the minimum acceptable amount of work. What is really important in this situation is not the actual behavior itself but the demonstration through the rules that the organization and the people in it are adhering to orders, or, if they are not, that management has publicized the rules. Each level in the organization treats the one below it as a cog in a machine that ought to work properly because the rules of the position have been outlined. Likewise, the organization itself is treated as a cog in the social system, as if it cannot change or be changed since the rules have already been laid down.

The use of rewards or instrumental satisfactions (and the use of punishment or the denial of instrumental satisfactions) are frequently the motivational strategies in the organization when it is believed that the demands of the community require punitive treatment of offenders or when the goals of individuals in the organization are viewed as suspect and their participation in the organization requires coercive techniques of control. Individuals are controlled by making it more pleasant to cooperate with organizational goals than not to cooperate. Whether the organizational strategy is a prison or an oil firm, this kind of organizational strategy is frequently characterized by a strong paternalistic and moralistic tone: the organization can treat its members as it does because it serves a good purpose for society.

Patterns of self-determination and self-expression become a motivational strategy when the perceived importance of conformity to the community to organizational standards is decreased, and the perceived importance of individualized behavior patterns and goals is increased. The individual is encouraged to express his desires and to develop plans of action within the organization that will allow him to experiment with different feelings that he has about himself and the organization. The constraint is that the encouragement of individual freedom is limited by the confines of the organization. The organization is treated as *the* reality into which the individual must fit. It is assumed that fitting into that particular organizational reality enables one to fit into other realities.

In the last motivational strategy, that of internalized values and development of self-concept, the organizational constraint on self-expression and development are lifted. In this strategy, the organizational goals are seen to be congruent with the achievement of individual goals, rather than identical, conflicting, or greater than personal goals. What the individual will do for the organization varies with changing available tasks and individual skills and interest.

For a summary of these four patterns of motivation and their relationship to policy frames of reference, see Table 3.

Table 3

POLICY FRAMEWORKS AND MOTIVATIONAL PATTERNS

Concern for the Individual		Concern for Community	
		Low	High
High		Mixed, emphasis on individual The use of internalized patterns of self-determination	Goal-congruent The use of internalized values and self-concept
Low		Organization isolated legal compliance	Mixed, emphasis on community/use of rewards or instrumental satisfactions

In brief, the four policy modes now appear like this:

LOW CONCERN FOR INDIVIDUAL, LOW CONCERN FOR COMMUNITY: The organization is designed on paper to work on paper;

rules are written and naturally should be followed, both by organizational participants and outsiders. The organization is essentially at a loss when some do not comply, and force is the usual response. The organization is also at a loss to explain *why* rules should be followed. There is no positive, transferable value in so doing, because the behavior of offenders after release is an irrelevant criterion in formulating rules.

HIGH CONCERN FOR COMMUNITY, LOW CONCERN FOR INDIVIDUALS: The organization is established to serve the community, but its design does not include a component by which this service may be made desirable to participants. Dependency is on outside community values which may be different for different members or completely irrelevant to organizational participation. Roles are played in accordance with arbitrary rewards and punishments, in contradiction of the way roles are usually structured in the society supposedly served.

HIGH CONCERN FOR INDIVIDUAL, LOW CONCERN FOR COMMUNITY: The organization is designed to benefit members by presenting a stage on which they may be something other than they were before entry. Experimentation with different feelings and different social relationships offers some reward in the organization but does not take into account the environmental factors that did not accommodate this freedom on the outside. Hence, the rewards for new-found roles and feelings is not coupled directly to roles actually available previous to or following organizational membership.

HIGH CONCERN FOR COMMUNITY, HIGH CONCERN FOR THE INDIVIDUAL: The organization is designed to change participants' behavior toward patterns that can accommodate value systems of differing sorts. Organizational roles are geared toward the development of self-concept so that, after release, the individual may find status that is not dependent on any *one* way of behaving. Simultaneously, the organization is active in changing community structures that generated deviant responses and in opening new opportunities.

On this level, the policy modes refer to correctional organization in its entirety, and the motivational schemes that administrators use in managing offenders may have certain parallels in the management of staff. In the policy of organizational isolation, both staff and offenders are directed to keep interaction to a minimum. In the policy that emphasizes the individual, both staff and offender are directed to express themselves and to develop interpersonal relationships. In the policy that emphasizes the community, both staff and inmates are regulated by rewards and punishments in accord with what the community considers a good officer or offender. In the policy of goal congruence, both staff and offenders are directed to behave in accordance with how they see the world, and these perceptions are tested by offenders and staff in terms of the perceptions of others, and in terms of the behavioral consequences.

This fourfold policy classification may have implications for both staff and inmates, and may be equally applicable to other people-changing organizations. Verification of the general policy complex and the elaboration of policy in the specific activity of changing people is available in Herbert Kelman's extensive study of change strategies.[17]

Kelman's study lists three important variables that together determine the types of behavior change:

1) The basis for the importance of the induction of change
2) The source of the change agent's power
3) The manner of achieving prepotency of the induced response

In combining these variables, three change types emerge:

Compliance: The changee is deemed to have done something wrong that must be stopped. The change agent's power lies in his ability to manipulate rewards and punishments. Prepotency of the induced change is gained by continual surveillance. Since the new behavior in and of itself is of no value to the changee, he is not likely to continue in it unless he is watched.

Identification: The changee is perceived as immature or sick, as unable to form proper human relationships. The change agent wields power in terms of denying or developing a relationship which the changee desires. The changee identifies with the agent and changes his behavior in order to continue the relationship. The induced behavior will likely last as long as the relationship is salient.

Internalization: The change agent believes the past behavior of the changee has been learned as a way of resolving problems that the changee has met in the past. The change agent's power resides in his ability to show the changee other alternatives, or new opportunities that will more effectively resolve those problems. The new behavior is likely to be stable and long lasting because it has value independent of the change agent. The new pattern is internalized.

These change strategies may be substituted for the general motivational strategies represented in Table 3 with the following results. Kelman's change via *compliance* is a specification of motivation through the use of rewards and instrumental satisfactions. The correctional officer or correctional counselor in a prison with a policy emphasizing the community will frequently attempt to control the changee through compliance. Kelman's change via *identification* is a specific example of organizational motivation through the use of internalized patterns of self-determination. The offenders will be allowed considerable freedom to express themselves and develop their feelings, within the confines of the organization. Kelman's change via *internalization* is a specification of motivation through use of internalized values and self-concept. In this case, the offenders' views of themselves are recognized and respected and alternate means of achieving goals are presented and tested as substitutes for previous criminal methods. The fourth general strategy of motivation, that of *legal compliance,* has no analogy in Kelman's change typology because correctional organizations that depend on legal compliance or bureaucratic authority do not intend to change offenders. (See Table 4.)

Table 4

MODELS OF CORRECTIONAL POLICY

		Low Concern for the Community	High
Concern for the Individual	High	Rehabilitation identification strategy	Reintegration internalization strategy
	Low	Restraint Holding strategy	Reform Compliance strategy

Low   High
Concern for the Community

For the sake of expedience, these four correctional policies have been assigned the labels of Reintegration, Rehabilitation, Reform, and Restraint. These labels are a shorthand referral to the frame of reference and change strategy associated with each.

Restraint is the policy with low concern about the community and low concern for organizational participants. There is no change strategy involved. Corrections in this mode is a holding action or warehousing of offenders. In terms of traditional legislative and judicial goals for invoking the criminal sanction, this policy probably corresponds closely to the goal of retribution, in which the offender is sent off to prison as a punishment.

Reform is the policy with low concern for the participants and high concern for the community. The change strategy is one of compliance; people are molded into different behavior reactions according to a well-established set of rules, with rewards and punishments freely administered. In terms of traditional legislative and judicial goals, this policy probably corresponds most closely to the goals of specific and general deterrence. The correctional action is supposed to have future effects, such as deterring the offender from future crimes, and deterring others from following his criminal example. Safety of society (probably in the short run) is paramount.

Rehabilitation is the policy with high concern for participants and low concern for the community. The change strategy is one of identification; people change through a manipulation of intrapersonal and interpersonal relationships. This mode may be divided into 1) a milieu strategy wherein the social interaction is the dependent variable and 2) a clinical strategy wherein the individual personality is the dependent variable, and the social interaction is assumed to change contingent on successful internal manipulations. In terms of traditional legislative and judicial goals, this policy corresponds most closely to the goal of treatment or rehabilitation, as these goals have been borrowed loosely from psychiatry and social work. The society is seen as good, or functional, and the deviance is seen as a characteristic of individuals.

Reintegration is that policy with high concern for participants and high concern for the community. The change strategy is internalization; people change as they discover and test alternate behavior patterns congruent with their values and beliefs. This policy does not correspond to traditional legislative and judicial goals, because it treats criminal deviance as an interactive process that requires changes in both the individual and the system of justice and also in the external community. As such, it does correspond, however, to very recent legislative trends toward social reconstruction; and it corresponds to recent judicial trends, particularly in sentencing practices, where incarceration is viewed as a last resort, the usual correctional operations are viewed as failing, and the beneficent purposes of state intervention are viewed as suspect.

This model of correctional policy may be used in several different ways. Interestingly, it was implicitly used for many years as a training device in correctional manpower laboratories, before the major dimensions of the theory were clearly explicated, and before the relationships of organizational concerns, motivations, and change strategies were systematically delineated in the system model developed above. Professors Vincent O'Leary, Daniel Glaser, and others used the terms Restraint, Rehabilitation, Reform, and Reintegration to designate attitudinal and program orientation clusters in ongoing correctional systems before all the concepts were fitted into one model.[18] Furthermore, the methodology for measuring these concerns, and thus operationalizing the model for use in correctional planning and evaluation, took even longer. The first data using this model as a measure of organizational production goals were collected in 1969, and the questionnaire based on the model was published in 1970.[19]

This model is now being used in both training and research activities in a number of different programs in different correctional systems. Much of its success as a way of measuring organizational constraints must be attributed to the thousands of hours spent by hundreds of correctional personnel in discussing their operations, plans, and goals, and how all of these things fitted together or failed to function properly. Its success in summarizing all the correctional strategies we have described cannot totally be attributed to this inductive process, however. Its success is also a function of the fact that, unlike many other attempted syntheses of correctional strategy, this model is based on some apparently sound organizational and system theory whose major building block is the concept of homeostasis.

Homeostasis is the term used to designate the process by which an organization maintains its identity over time. The many different activities in the process of input-throughout-output form a complex relationship in which a system maintains its character over time by changing rather than by standing still. In an open system such as a prison or a parole organization, this equilibrium is achieved through constant variation of the internal components (such as management, staff, and offenders), and through a constant interchange between the organization and its sociophysical environment. The policy model summarizes the basic homeostatic states that are possible by relating the dimension of concern for the community with the dimension of concern for the individual in the organization. Depending on which homeostatic balance is achieved, the correctional organization will be more or less capable of achieving certain outcomes. Thus, the model, as we have described it, allows us to predict what kind of correctional strategies will be found in which kind of policy-directed correctional system, and also to predict what kind of impact or direction the common correctional programs and structural components will have. These predicted characteristics are summarized in Table 5. In this table, we have attempted to include most of the programs, such as work release, reception center diagnosis, and so on, that have been discussed in Chapters 3 through 7. We have also included most of the components that we have discussed, such as type of parole board memberships, type of prison staff, and so on.

Table 5

SUMMARY OF CORRECTIONAL STRATEGIES BASED ON THE CORRECTIONAL POLICY MODEL

Component or Program	Reintegration	Rehabilitation	Reform	Restraint
1) Change philosophy	Offender has learned crime as a solution to problems; more effective solutions are possible that are congruent with offender's value system.	Offender has committed crime as outgrowth of anti-social attitude and dysfunctional psychological developments. Offender needs to be changed internally so that he can adapt in suitable ways.	Offender has committed offense as direct result of disobedience to formally prescribed codes of conduct. This misconduct is willful, and this immoral stand should be punished.	Offender has committed crime in eyes of society and should be shown the negative consequences. He will not change unless he wants to, but he can be housed efficiently until he has served his time.
2) Change strategy	Internalization	Identification	Compliance	None, or maintenance of rules that have internal organizational benefit.
3) Sentencing policy	Light sentences, emphasis on controlling offender in community.	Indeterminate sentences in which judge passes on decision to therapeutic experts in correctional system. Use of additional sentences for dangerous offenders, or civil commitment of addicts, or offenders with other special needs.	Stiff sentences deter-mined by judge on basis of severity of the crime.	Sentence that satisfies the statutory requirements; judicial responsiveness to community desires is important.

4) Presentence investigation	Concentration on offender's social relationships in community, employment history, desires for other opportunities. Identification of offenders with good work records and social ties that should not be disrupted.	Concentration on diagnosis of internal problems, motivations for crime, familial history. Identification of offenders for probation not in need of continual staff support and care.	Concentration on past record aggravating or mitigating circumstance—demonstration of degree of guilt. Identification of offenders who are deserving.	Concentration on judicial and probation office requirements. Selection of good risks for probation who will not cause trouble.
5) Probation supervision	Advocacy of offender who needs help with employment, relocating residence, etc. Intervention in community relationships to promote offender goals legally.	Counseling of offenders on pressures of social demands, concern for developing offender's insight into problems.	Concentration on protecting community by policing probationers, enforcing probation requirements such as demand visitation.	Concentration on reducing "flak" from community. Adjusting probationer's behavior to meet staff needs.
6) Probation revocation	On full hearing about facts. Probationer with lawyer to challenge legality of revocation and its efficacy as a correctional strategy.	Clinical staff reviewing offender's problems in community decision as to whether stronger, more concentrated support needed to promote maturity, ability to adjust.	Pro forma hearing establishing probation officer's prima facie case, revocation of privilege for undeserving offenders.	Verification of rule breaking to justify imposition of originally suspended sentence.

7) Probation officer type	Community organizer skilled in advocacy techniques, use of ex-offenders and volunteers whose skills are integrated to maximize goal attainment.	Skilled therapist who combines rapport with individual case planning, establishing procedure for supporting emotional growth.	Skilled investigator able to deter law- or rule-breaking through firm but fair imposition of rewards, sanctions, or threat of them.	Trained organization man familiar with judge's desires, probation rules.
8) Jail facilities	Jails used as community centers for work release, study release, dialogue with community leaders, recruitment and coordination of volunteers.	Outpatient clinic for offenders in need of institutional stay before or during probation or parole period.	Place of punishment for minor offenders, emphasis on simple vocational skills, work release possible emphasis.	Place of restraint for minor offenders in accordance with statutory regulations.
9) Felony reception	Heavy dependence on coordination with probation staff reports and assessments; reception directly to community facilities wherever possible.	Heavy reliance on medical and psychological testing for diagnosis of need, psychological type, and suggestion of therapeutic program.	Major decisions based on security risk, vocational ability, and moral merit. Housing and work assignments major issue.	Major decisions based on system capacity—where will offender fit with least disruption and most contribution to institutional maintenance goals?
10) Prison types	Infrequent use of traditional custodial prisons, frequent use of small residential units based in or close to communities.	Large minimum security facilities usually isolated from community. Isolated to prevent inmate from being pressured by outside interests during intensive counseling phases.	Large maximum security prisons isolated from community to protect, and to provide visible symbol of regimentation.	Most common in large city jails and other traditional custodial units.

11) Prison staffing patterns	Small staff team with diverse backgrounds and complementary skills, use of ex-offender, volunteers, active participation by inmates in their own program and in aiding other inmates.	Bifurcation of custody and treatment functions. Guard force less militaristic but responsible for maintaining order. Professional treaters in management positions and in charge of inmate activities, milieu, and clinical arrangements.	Large custodial force, dependence on common officer to provide legal behavior and to enforce rules. Counselors in minority and out of power, provide staff services, aid in custody and regimentation by reducing inmate tensions. Emphasis on vocational skills among staff.	Primarily custodial, with less emphasis on inmate or staff regimentation. Maintenance of physical rather than social order.
12) Prison program	Varied, emphasis on vocational training. Active seeking of new opportunities for offenders to prerelease. Concentration on practical matters of reintegration.	Emphasis on various soft services, counseling in groups or individual emphasis on emotional support, self-expression, gaining insights.	Emphasis on regimented labor, gaining rudimentary skills, more sophisticated behavior modification a possibility.	Emphasis on busy work that will release tension. Hobbies, institutional repair and maintenance.
13) Preparation for release	Work release, study release, halfway houses, other means of actually introducing offender to community roles before parole.	Halfway houses, institutional prerelease, concentration on discussion of stigma, dealing with emotional pressures.	Release programs a reward for good institutional behavior. Maintenance of custody until man proves himself dependable.	No preparation that may disrupt routine.

14) Parole board decision	Review of institutional decisions and outcome, release as soon as possible. Emphasis on community parole plan.	Clinical staffing of offender's progress. Attention to change in attitudes, ability to relate and adjust.	Review of inmate institutional record, emphasis on obedience, worthiness for privilege of parole.	Review of community pressures, predictive of offender's non-troublesome status in community.
15) Parole board members	Mixed skills and background, inmate participation, or legal counsel.	Professional therapists and medical doctors.	Community leaders able to recognize productive citizens.	Political appointees sensitive to the climate of the times.
16) Parole supervision	Advocacy of offender's needs, acting as counsel to offender, helping to review goal accomplishment.	Therapist skilled in investigating emotional trouble, regression to former attitudes.	Investigator, surveillance to maintain viability of negative sanctions, community protection.	Bookkeeper, maintaining records on established parole regulations.
17) Use of volunteers	Frequently, seeking integration of skills and interests.	As aides to professionals or seeking outside professional group support.	Sometimes, seeking community business leaders' support.	Hardly ever, too risky and disruptive.
18) Attitude toward legal intervention	Invited, as aid to offender in challenging decisions and negotiating program.	Avoided, legal argument seen as conflicting with needs of therapy.	Avoided, offenders rights seen as lost at conviction.	Avoided, litigation does not contribute to smooth flow of operation.

19)	Relations to universities	Encouraged, particularly applied interdisciplinary research, increasing skill and competency range, opportunities for offenders.	Encouraged, for use of psychological and other clinical resources and consultant services. Research on offender personality types.	Approached cautiously, seeking management consultant help.	Avoided as disruptive.
20)	Evaluation	Data-based, democratic feedback process. Inside and outside evaluation for constant program modification.	Clinically based, emphasis on offender personality change, how to create effective therapy situations.	Belief-based, or action-based in terms of low crime rate, satisfaction of community norms.	Experience-based in terms of lack of negative repercussions, satisfaction of political support.

POLICY RELATIONSHIP TO THE IDEA OF FAILURE AND
SUCCESS

Now that we have taken a careful look at the variety of correctional policies that are logically possible within our theoretical assumptions, it is important to relate that goal's framework to the idea of correctional effectiveness. We have already looked at several arguments that militate against the use of recidivism data. We have also suggested that, statistically, the variations in the recidivism rate can be parcelled out in proportion to the influence of different contributing factors. But we have also suggested that this is a nonsensical exercise, since the actions in real life that produce the rate cannot be separated and fragmented arbitrarily to meet the needs of different organizational accounting and evaluation systems.

Occasionally, part of the objection to the use of such data in evaluation is not really due to the contamination of the data, but is a function of the different correctional policies in operation. While the fact of contaminated data is *true* under present policy, if prison administrators operated specifically to *alter* the community variables that militate against return, or were able to treat the variety of inmate problems in equally various ways, they would perceive the same recidivism statistics as uncontaminated. Since the mixed correctional policies attempt to change only certain aspects of their organization (inmates), only certain variables contributing to the recidivism rate are relevant. Since the reintegration policy attempts to change organization totally and to alter the community as well, more variables contributing to recidivism rates are relevant.

A preoccupation with refinement of measurements may, in actuality, be a symptom of ineffective policies. While the policy typology has been largely utilized as a classification of behavioral systems, the understanding of these policies as information systems may be helpful, particularly since the amount and quality of information is crucial to organizational change. The mixed policy evaluations reject recidivism rates because there is an implicit rejection of certain kinds of information. The mixed, open-to-community policy rejects all factors of individual difference in inmates. The mixed, open-to-individual policy rejects all factors of community influence. Publicly, evaluation under either policy is merely held in abeyance; administrators behave as if they would be willing to change when the information that they need is available. But *when* will information on community receptivity, independent of individual variations, become available? While administrators and researchers may treat the two sets of factors as independent, the actual behavior of individuals and organizations suggests that there are not *two* sets of factors that may be confounded, but *one* set of factors. That set of factors, relevant to the evaluation of reintegration policy, is a set of system interactions rather than a set of characteristics that may be separated.

While it may at first seem radical to suggest a change in policy rather than a change in measurement technique, it is no more radical than the transition in correctional policy by which any measurement of output became relevant to evaluation. Gross recidivism rate or rates of *some* potential refinement, were not always considered a measure of correctional failure. When no change, by any strategy, was intended by imprisonment, the return of punished offenders to prison was not relevant to the evaluation of the punishment. That is, under a policy of restraint, the offender and the community are both irrelevant to effective policy implementation.

There are, then, two polar cases of information utilization that are synonymous with the policies of the system model of correctional policy. The reintegration policy can use all information that comes to it in systematic fashion. The restraint policy limits information seeking and transmission as much as possible. Neither of these two uses of information is common. Most correctional policies in the United States are mixed and are sequentially open or closed to various parts of the organization. Hence, systematic information about the behavior of offenders as they return to the community is unusable in the evaluation of these policies. Coincidentally, managers with mixed policies now reject the measures of output that are available. While they may not *understand* that the kind of information they require to evaluate their programs is unavailable in the ways that they usually seek it, they *behave* as if the information they are seeking is unavailable in the ways they usually seek it.

What kinds of information should be sought to evaluate mixed correctional policies? It cannot be the kind of information where the contradictory portions of these policies will make it impossible to gather any information at all. The rehabilitation policy might be evaluated with information gathered about the institution itself. The prison atmosphere might be assessed as supporting or encouraging the kind of psychological readjustments that are wanted from the inmates. Behavior upon return to the community is irrelevant. Managers who seek to create a friendly supportive atmosphere do not want officers handcuffed by regulations and continually referring problems to superiors. The less the rehabilitation policy is directed at the manipulation of the group, and the more it is concerned with the psychoanalysis of individuals, the less relevant is any information about the atmosphere. Evaluation of completely individual change strategies should be made with information gathered by clinicians. The mass survey of changes in psychological insight in inmates where there is no behavioral index is not very consistent methodologically. There is nothing contradictory, in this policy, about the evaluation of an offender as successful who was treated for neurotic sex offenses, and who returns as the leader of an armed robbery gang. In this model, overt behavior is not important. The inmate's progress is measured by comparing one psychological state with a previous one. If the inmate gains some insight into reasons that made him behave as he did, some improvement is shown.

In the Reform policy, a different strategy for gaining information must be implemented. This policy, as an information system, is open to information about the community, but not about inmates as individuals. Information generated by individuals in the Reform model concerns what *rules* have been broken or obeyed, and the rules are applied uniformly to everyone. Success/failure of individual inmates is just as irrelevant in this system as in Rehabilitation. While evaluation of Rehabilitation proceeds from clinical assessment, evaluation of Reform should be done by political-economic assessment. The Reform organization is effective if it maintains a particular image that is of value to the community. It is not important what offenders actually do in prison or on parole, but it is very important what the public *thinks* they do.

Naturally, there is likely to be *some* convergence between the internal management of offenders and the image that correctional managers project. Nor is the idea in this policy to be dishonest; not at all. The Reform policy, like the Rehabilitation policy, merely arranges tasks into a list of priorities. In the Reform system visible maintenance of community norms and values within the correctional program is of first importance. Sensitivity to the needs of offenders is secondary. The information that is useful in this system exists on a number of levels. Good relationships with the governor and the legislature are important. The number of department-sponsored bills passed or the amount of budgetary allotment may be satisfactory indicators of the effectiveness of the organization. However, in building for governmental support, it may be advantageous to develop congenial relationships with local governments and with major newspapers. Thus, the number of services that the organization can perform for the local citizenry and the ratio of favorable to unfavorable reports about the system may be helpful evaluative indices. While individual offender behavior, in the aggregate, is not important, attention must be paid to symbolic exchanges between a single offender and the community. Anecdotes about praiseworthy or blameworthy actions by offenders may be collected, because these incidents are likely to be interpreted by the community to be characteristic of the entire system.

By classifying the kinds of information most relevant to the evaluation of each kind of program, it may also be possible to estimate the direction of the activity necessary to generate positive evaluations. In organizations that have only a secondary concern for the way offenders behave in the community, and hence do not want to be evaluated in terms of offender behavior, change-inducing activity must be deemphasized, and the organizational maintenance activity must be increased proportionately. In policies that require little outside interference, maintenance will be emphasized, management will develop an increasingly inward focus, and adaptation to the ouside world will become progressively impossible. Where behavior of offenders in the community is the primary concern, and hence where evaluation in terms of offender behavior is relevant, the change production activity must be emphasized; and the bureaucratic maintenance activity must be reduced, or made dependent on, the needs of the change activity. In the change-inducing organization, management develops an increasingly outward focus, and research activity becomes increasingly important (1) to measure achievement of change goals and (2) to assess needed alterations in change programs before alterations are demanded by outside leaders, such as legislators, who may not know the structural requirements of a change-producing organization.

In all cases, the organization must be arranged, and the interactions in the organization must be structured so that the policy to which the organization is committed can be carried out. Evaluations, in other words, must proceed in directions that are potentially achievable under the policy specified, and strategies for increased effectiveness must be manipulations of correctional subsystems possible under that policy. It makes no sense to evaluate a Restraint prison in terms of its recidivism rate; and it makes no sense to attempt to increase the effectiveness of a Reintegration parole office by instituting a new series of civil service regulations. Within these two parameters, change in correctional organization may probably be planned in a number of ways, according to a number of time schedules, none of which have been systematically attempted anywhere. Since the degrees of freedom in policy-chosen change is great, only general trends in organizational manipulation can be presented.

Effectiveness of a restraint policy

A correctional system administered under a policy of Restraint is effective only as long as it is in force. What happens to individual offenders is irrelevant, and what happens to the community that pays for a Restraint organization is also irrelevant. Since there is no goal of improving or changing offenders, or improving or changing the community, only those activities are engaged in that provide insurance against the destruction of the system. Management is successful if it prevents extreme forms of community revulsion, such as political attacks by reformists against the system for using violence to control offenders. The less the frequency and complexity of interactions with the community, the more effective is this correctional policy. Therefore, some Restraint managers may wish to elaborate a system of maintenance activities that will set the organization apart from other governmental agencies. A prison, for instance, may develop its own farm so that crops may be sold and profit used to reduce the need for state tax revenue. The same prison may also use inmate labor and expertise for maintenance of the physical building, since any upkeep and repair work that can be done by inmates reduces the need for outside contractors.

Advanced Restraint management may include experiments, in limited degrees, with officer or inmate governance. To the degree that management can make personnel and inmates attentive to formulation and ritual maintenance of their own or imposed behavioral codes, the less time these groups will have to think about goals that are relevant outside the organization. Heavy emphasis must be placed on status conceptualizations and on rigid adherence to prescribed roles if those levels of status are to be maintained. In general, the busier the inmates are, the less time they will have to challenge the assumptions of organizational isolation and independence under which the inmate roles are logical. The busier and less demanding the inmate population, the less physical activity will be required of officers. The dangerousness or distinctiveness of the inmate lot must be emphasized to officers. Officers must be rewarded for keeping inmates in place and must also be made to see that the usual amenities and courtesies applied to human interaction on the outside do not apply in prison. Hence, the increase in routine activities that delineate an internal caste-like separation of inmates and staff must be coupled with organizational activity that separates the prison, and the social system of the prison, from other types of organizations and social arrangements.[20]

Within the criminal justice system, Restraint is most effective that reduces court inspection of correctional operations and limits the possibility of drawing behavioral or legal analogies between penal and nonpenal situations. Corrections must be seen as independent and as following proper criminal justice procedures. An ideological and qualitative difference must be established between the status of suspect-defendant and the status of convict. For example, under a

Restraint policy, the *Mempa* v. *Rhay* decision introducing lawyers at probation revocation would be interpreted conservatively to apply only in cases where an actual sentence has not been announced and then suspended. It would not be interpreted to apply where conviction (including sentence) was complete, and it would certainly not carry over to cases of in-prison conduct or parole revocation decisions. Restraint management must carry to the courts the argument that all rights are lost with conviction. Management must also stress that legal interventions in correctional organization hamper security.

Effectiveness of a reform policy

Reform policy is effective to the degree that the system gains or maintains community support by satisfying feelings about danger and the need for deterrence. Activities that are not directed toward favorable community reaction are less important. The Reform policy is difficult to administer because there is no community consensus about what constitutes proper correctional activity. Since most of the money and political power is likely to be suburban and middle-class, the correctional image must be aimed at suburban middle-class groups. But current political developments make the administrator's decision about the proper image to maintain more difficult than it was a decade ago. The Reform system must project an image that ensures public safety at the same time that it satisfies the prevailing liberal desire that the state be humane to deviants. An effective Reform manager is very careful to assess the desires of particular audiences and to cast the image of the system accordingly. The Reform manager must be a good politician and never commit himself to one faction or another, unless that group happens to be a clear and enduring majority.

Production of change *is* important in Reform policy systems. There is a change strategy. However, it is a strategy that ignores differences among offenders. All offenders are assumed to be of a type, and the same kinds of activity are assumed to be change-inducive in all of them. All offenders, for example, are expected to learn a trade, or at least to put in a full day's work at an assigned prison job or parole employment. Keeping to rigid work routines should create habits of diligence and punctuality. In actuality, what the highly structured routine does for offenders is less important than what the community assumes it does, or should do. It is not important whether the offender fails after a Reform incarceration, as long as the failure can be attributed to the individual inmate. Thus, Reform management must play on community expectations of what they would appreciate if they were offenders—what kinds of lessons would the typical, law-abiding, middle-class citizen expect to learn as he imagines himself to be an inmate or parolee? Prison management can usually expect that the community, or the political power in the community, will attribute failure to individual inmates, as long as the prison is clean and orderly, and as long as the prison budget is obviously not squandered on luxuries, but is spent on providing opportunities for the underdog to work diligently at improving his lot. The same would be true of a Reform parole system. The correctional administrator must balance the image he presents between a lower limit where the system appears harsh and inhumane and an upper limit where offenders receive services that too many citizens might value for themselves.

Most of the activity in the Reform system must be guided by maintenance regulations, because it is more important to project an appearance of change activity than it is to produce changes in individual offenders. Hence, words such as "counseling" and "therapy" may be used to refer to particular parts of the work day, but counseling and therapy are usually valuable only if counselors are able to pacify offenders and make them feel satisfied with the rest of the correctional routine. Counselors are treated as part of custodial staff.

The maintenance of "show" programs is very important to the effectiveness of Reform policy. There may be a number of community groups, such as businessmen, women's clubs, church groups, who desire to be of service to the system or to the men supervised by it. This participation in correctional activity should be encouraged as precisely the kind of community effort by which offenders will be made to reform. Management must also be careful that such groups do not witness procedures that might be necessary for security (i.e., punishments for the breaking of rules, the reasons for which are clear to officials) but may look harsh to naive outsiders.

The same kinds of concerns should govern Reform interaction with the courts. The Reform system may not be totally opposed to court inspection and intervention in the correctional organization. The prison, for instance, should be careful that is never charged with cruel and unusual punishment. It is probably difficult for the layman to conceive of the Eighth Amendment as applying to anyone but criminals and deviants. It is the amendment that forbids kicking a man when he is down, and any correctional organization that was adjudged to have infringed on an inmate's Eighth Amendment rights could lose some political power. On the other hand, the Reform manager who opposes the application of the Sixth Amendment to prisoners might gain political support, even if he lost a court battle.

In dealing with constitutional issues, the Reform administrator has two goals. He must demonstrate that all his procedures are fair and aboveboard, and, simultaneously, he must limit the introduction of adversary procedures into adminstrative decisions. Lawyers for inmates are particularly dangerous, since they are trained to advocate their client's wishes rather than to mediate between sides, or to reconcile irate offenders to corrections procedures. The Reform administrator is most effective who can convince the court that offenders are afforded the protection of constitutional procedures, without resort to the procedures themselves.

Effectiveness of a rehabilitation policy

Rehabilitation policy, like Reform policy, includes a change strategy. Ironically, Rehabilitation and Reform are similar in that the change strategies involved are assumed to benefit all offenders. In the Rehabilitative system, all offenders may have slightly different problems, but all their problems are psychological (or medical). While energy is expended in the Rehabilitation system in order that offenders might change, most of the energy, as in Reform policy, is spent in the maintenance of the organization. The emphasis on organizational maintenance is logical if the assumption is accepted that all offenders have the same kind of problem.

If it is true that most offenders have psychological problems, maintaining the kind of organization that deals with psychological problems is all-important. It is particularly necessary that custodial staff know what categories of behavioral symptoms should signal referral to professional staff. The custodial staff must do nothing at all with offenders, or do nothing that retards the rehabilitative process. Hence, the officer and counseling or psychiatric roles must be clearly distinguished. Since it may be difficult to define the characteristics of the professional role that require professional qualifications and experience, the administration in a Rehabilitative prison is most likely to keep custodial and professional roles separate, by carefully defining the segments of the day in which the different roles will be performed. Each inmate may have a weekly appointment with a member of the counseling staff, or a period of the day will be set aside when any inmates who desire to do so may see the counseling staff.

In addition to separation in time, the counseling and custodial roles are likely to be separated in space. A particular building or complex of rooms may be set aside for counseling or treatment activity, and the rest of the prison may be the area of general custody. Inmates and staff are likely to act very differently in the treatment and custody areas. It is even likely, for example, that if officers participate in group therapy sessions, inmates will behave toward the participating officers differently from the way they behave when the same officers are out of the therapy space.

Rehabilitation policy that depends on other methods of role definition is likely to be less effective, unless the majority of staff are professionals or have sufficient education and orientation to understand the subtlety of the professional roles (as would be true of a Rehabilitation parole system). Even prisons where rehabilitation entails a milieu approach (i.e., where all staff are to contribute to a therapeutic climate) will need to set aside particular hours of the week and particular space in the prison for intensive analysis and interaction of some sort, or inmates may not be cognizant of any change attempts. While there may be some situations in which patients need not be aware that change-directed behavior is operating, inmates, as patients, are likely to interpret all staff behavior as part of punishment and therapy. Since inmates, like custodial staff, are not likely to be sophisticated enough to understand a positive definition of therapeutic practices (or may even be alarmed at the description of them), it is again advisable that differences between custodial and therapeutic treatment should be ritualistically separated. In the Rehabilitative prison, where the relationship between changee and change agent is the change inducive factor, a prerequisite to therapy is the willingness of the inmate to participate. The inmate may not be willing to participate in his own punishment, but he may be willing to participate in his own rehabilitation. Since inmates will equate successful rehabilitation with release from supervision, offenders may be willing to participate in therapy if it is sufficiently clear to them that the rehabilitative, or release-oriented, role and the punitive, or control-oriented, role are separate and do not conflict. Conflict may be reduced by the proper manipulations of symbols such as time, space, proper form of address to staff members, and staff members' attire.

The proper boundary activity for effective Rehabilitation policy involves isolating the system from most outside forces, while remaining open to outside therapists and researchers. Cooperation with outside professionals and professional organizations can be important to the therapeutic atmosphere. In order to attract professional collaboration, management must be careful that the organization is able to cooperate with changes in routine that professionals may make. Management must emphasize to staff, and staff to outsiders, that therapy is more important than security, or that the system that is effectively therapeutic need not be overly concerned about security. Offenders actively participating in their own rehabilitation are less likely to think of escape or other rule infractions than offenders who spend their time avoiding punishment and surveillance. Staff must be flexible enough to accommodate extra therapy sessions, longer than usual sessions, extra sessions for particular individuals, and the polite inquiries from clinicians about the behavior of inmates during the long hours of custody.

As there must be a clear distinction between punishment or control and the activity of therapy in order that internal interactions can be effective, there must be a rigid distinction between control and therapy in order to attract outside professionals or for purposes of interaction with the court. Potential outside professional or legal intervention must be carefully screened to prevent interventions that will suggest to offenders reasons other than psychological ones for their offender status. A lawyer's intervention, for example, that asks for proof of fact is not compatible with the inferential diagnoses of clinicians. It is necessary to guard against the intervention of sociologists who consider some offenders to have a healthy adjustment to deviant subcultures. While the Rehabilitation policy can withstand the introduction of some learning theory, such theory must be coupled to the conviction that as people learn to solve problems by nonnormal methods, or as they substitute illegal for legal opportunity paths, they *eventually* become psychologically imbalanced. Effective Rehabilitative policy hinges on the ability of administrators to demonstrate to insiders and outsiders alike that behavioral problems have internal origins, and that future behavioral problems are unavoidable unless the internal factors are sought out and dealt with.

Effectiveness of a reintegration policy

Effective Reintegration policy depends on the ability of the organization to accomplish specific tasks of change. It is the goal of this policy that offender X will not return to the system because he will find that he can fulfill his goals more adequately through legal behavior than he did in the past through illegal behavior. This policy requires both that community standards (legal behavior) be maintained and that individual needs (goals) be met.

The productive, change-inducing activity is the area requiring the greatest expenditure of energy. Offenders and staff must analyze what kinds of behavior are most likely to guarantee freedom from the criminal justice system in the future. It is likely that several avenues are available to each inmate, and correctional time should be used for testing the various opportunities available. Staff has the commitment *to develop* (rather than merely to find) the kind of opportunity in the community that will increase the offender's chances of successful return.

While status distinctions are very likely to be maintained in the organization, Reintegration policy is effective when differences in status are not stigmatizing. "Inmate" should not be negatively compared with "officers," or "parolee" negatively compared with citizen. Status that is ascribed is most easily stigmatized; hence, an effective Reintegration maintenance subsystem encourages the use of achieved rather than ascribed status. The emphasis on competence and status-by-achievement probably entails relationships of the trainer-trainee or researcher-assistant or colleague variety. Staff and offenders must develop roles in which they behave as much as possible like peers.

Since it is known that this kind of behavior is supported by small, semiautonomous work groups, the task in the Reintegration system is the development and continuation of a structure that supports productive small groups. Groups can amplify either negative or positive feelings about an organization and its management. To this date, most new career groups and other special small group projects in corrections have achieved positive, mutually supportive relationships within the groups, so that group goals were attained; but the group goals and the evaluation of those goals were never connected to the wider organization of the whole system. It is even likely that these small groups gained strength by being an out-group for the rest of the organization. The Reintegration system must direct itself toward goals that large numbers of staff and offenders may have in common. The goals and the skills necessary to achieve them must not be beyond the competence of the average official or the average inmate. While the goals in new career groups can usually be fairly specific, and to a degree formulated in accordance with the desires of the individuals in the group, the goals of Reintegration *organizations* must be expressed in such a way that offenders need not undergo a rigorous selection process, and new inmates are automatically included.

The production structure must always emphasize the congruence between personal goals of individuals and the organizational goals of the system. For example, if an officer's goal in correctional employment is to have a job that satisfies his intellectual and emotional needs and at the same time provides him with sufficient income, the Reintegrative goal of returning inmates to the community permanently must be accomplished so that the officer is satisfied and sufficiently reimbursed. The more expensive the physical facilities and upkeep of the plant, the less attention can be paid to personnel. The longer a particular inmate must stay in prison, the more it costs to house him and the greater the prison population. Hence, it is likely that officers will be satisfied with their jobs more of the time if the physical plant is small and uncomplicated, and if most offenders can spend a minimal amount of time in it. In this way, more time and money will be freed for individualized projects, and less money and time will be spent shepherding large numbers of men through repetitive routine. Officers must have sufficient interaction with superiors and with inmates to make their work interesting and intellectually demanding. The job should not become so rigid and routine that feelings about the job, or about particular people, must be suppressed.

The structure must also allow for congruence between offenders' goals and organizational goals. If the organizational goal is to reduce recidivism, the individual offender's goal of effecting his own release from supervision must be connected to the release of all other offenders. The desire for offenders to "do their own time" must be minimized. Offenders should find that the surest and most rapid route to release is participation in group activity where the aim is the release of other offenders.

The congruence between individual and group goals must also carry over to the outside. The organization should utilize the offender's unique informational resources about crime, deviant groups, and offender perceptions of the system. The offender's job, while in the system, is to provide information or suggest avenues of research that will be useful in reducing frequency of criminal behavior. Realistically, it is the offender's responsibility to widen the organizational boundaries. The organization should be deeply involved in the work of increasing the variety of places where offenders can go in the community. The Reintegration policy is effective to the degree that it becomes a sensing device in social system adaptation. The correctional system, as an organization with easy access to information about deviance and deviants, should be a prime organization in the restructuring of the larger social system.

THE ETHICS OF POLICY FORMULATION AND POLICY RESEARCH

Once policy is chosen, the game plan, the rules by which the organization should be judged, has also been chosen. The ethical questions that arise, or can be answered, are considerably different before and after the formulation of policy. Once goals have been chosen and made operational in a structural design, questions about those goals are inappropriate. An administrator cannot commit himself to a Rehabilitation policy and simultaneously ask if it is ethical to treat all offenders as if they were sick. An administrator cannot have doubts about the ethics of ignoring men's feelings and concomitantly enforce Reform policy. An administrator who believes he owes a service to either society or to offenders cannot administer a Restraint policy.

The time to ask ethical questions about policy per se is before it is implemented or at that point in an ongoing organization when policy is being reformulated. The administrator who enters an organization and endorses a policy that he personally dislikes is unlikely to be effective, and shortly becomes a moral liar. He acts as if people should suffer to achieve goals that he himself considers wrong. The administrator who says, "well, it isn't good, but it's all we have" is admitting personal, as well as organizational, failure because he has forsworn the development of alternatives.

It is unlikely that most administrators are so morally bankrupt. It is probably more often the case that the ethical implications of policy are never considered because the policy itself is never fully explained before it is implemented. What, for example, motivates administrators whose policy is reform and rehabilitation to search in vain for the proper recidivism statistics? Do they have a moral commitment in conflict with their policy? Have they ever considered that if they earnestly desire the type of evaluation in which the *number* of law-abiding offenders returned to society is relevant, then they may indeed care for offenders? They may favor a policy of reintegration without knowing it. On the other side of the coin, there may be modern, up-to-date administrators who have used the most technical and current language to describe the operation of their organization who would suddenly like to change their minds when the "wrong" evaluation measures appear. Perhaps they will say that "the goals of Reform are really all we can expect to achieve anyway." Hence administrators must also have an ethical commitment to the acceptance of goals and to the attempt to achieve them—pending failure as well as success.

It is in clarifying the appropriate time and place for various decisions that collaboration with academicians and researchers can be most helpful. University people and professional administrators are not so different from each other. If there are several academicians insisting that Reintegration is the policy most likely to be successful, there are as many administrators who arrive at the same decision. The researcher, particularly in the university setting, merely has the advantage of being separated from the daily grind of the system. He can sit back and mull over one concept in the same time that a warden or parole supervisor has made several decisions with immediate impact. Decisions as researchers conceive them, information that academicians feel to be relevant, differential effects as outside consultants weigh them—all are devoid of value when the administrator cannot implement the decisions, use the information, or accommodate the effects.

While researchers often talk about the relationship of theory, research, and practice, academicians tend to feel satisfied if a project born of theory has had a successful grant year. If, upon lapse of the grant, the effects of the project do not carry through, researchers can blame state or federal bureaucrats for not knowing a good thing when they see it. After a project is over, the attention of academicians is absorbed by the need to publish results and perhaps to correspond on a personal basis with researchers interested in the same kinds of projects. The assumption usually involved is: "concepts X, Y, and Z applied through structure-175 were successful in yielding Beta over a length of one year; therefore, it would work over 10 years, if the agency would only institute it." When academicians ignore the rejection of their project for permanent organizational adoption, or when they blame the administrators for the rejection, they are reacting much as administrators do to evaluation by recidivism rates. They have closed themselves off from relevant information generated by an inevitable interaction between researchers and practitioners. Practitioners do the same when they reject the inevitable interaction of individual and structural variables.

The researcher perhaps breaks no ethical contract by rejecting the acceptance and implementation of his findings as a valid criterion of the scientific accuracy of his study. Nevertheless, the researcher, who limits his thirst for empirical verification to segmented forays into the world of administrative practices, has implied something about the utility of his research program. There is a qualitative difference between the development of theories and brief research projects and the design of research so that such projects can be integrated permanently into organizational procedures. The researcher who states, "My project empirically tested and supported Theory X" should in all honesty add "in year 1902." What the project *definitely has not shown* is that Theory X concerns variables that are continually available for manipulation. If the concept of cause means anything within an open system theory, it has to do with the relative availability of variables to manipulation. A cause, an independent variable, is an item of information, an aspect of interaction, or a particular component of structure, that is accessible to variation at the hand of the researcher. *Surely the duration of availability to manipulation should be considered part of the criteria by which a variable is considered a cause.* Hence, the researcher whose theory is rejected for full implementation by administrators must revise his conclusions about cause.

For example, a researcher may write a grant to demonstrate the importance of stigma as a cause of staff-inmate conflict in a juvenile institution. For a year he personally oversees a program of action by which he assumes stigma is reduced. At the end of the year all people involved—inmates, staff, and researcher—agree that there is less social distance between inmates and staff than before the researcher began the program. The researcher writes a report that his hypothesis about stigma and inmate culture has been supported. After six months he revisits the prison and discovers that the inmate-staff conflict is as wide and unbridgeable as before. The warden explains that after the grant money ran out and the researcher left the institution, there was no one who could run the kind of program by which the staff-inmate conflict had been reduced. The warden may now feel hostile to the researcher who was responsible for all-round improved morale and living conditions for the short period of a year, after which the organization returned to normal. But worse, the organization returned to normal with a taste of what is better. Everyone in the prison, including the warden, is now demoralized. Perhaps after some further consideration, the warden writes a letter to the American Wardens Association that researchers are a serious security risk. Researchers are the cause of demoralization and staff-inmate conflict. Is the researcher right and the warden wrong?

Within their own perspectives they are both right, but neither one has participated at a level where researcher-administrator conflicts or staff-inmate conflicts can be resolved. The researcher has committed himself only to understanding something about stigma and inmate culture. The administrator has committed himself only to accommodating a one-year intrusion. Both have failed to understand that one-year intrusions are unlikely to yield anything of lasting value. The researcher still does not know how the variables he studied will interact under normal conditions. The administrator still does not know how to run his institution without feeling the constant threat of explosion.

The inevitable conclusion of systems research is that the long tradition of according superior status to pure research over applied research is based on illusory results. Much time and analysis have been spent on distinguishing pure research from action research, and on contrasting the processes of testing hypotheses and of making things work. But of what value are accepted hypotheses that are never incorporated in the daily running of the organization? Do researchers really understand the variables that produce an inmate culture if they cannot change that culture? Have they really changed it if it does not remain changed?

Only the researcher who ignores the administrative perspective can identify as causal variables phenomena that cannot be controlled by managers. The scientist *does* have the commitment to present conclusions that have been gathered through a logical, ordered, and reproducible plan of action. The scientist has a commitment to be self-conscious in his investigations and to be aware of the effect of his own behavior on his subject of study. Hence, the scientist whose research leads him to the conclusion that prison organization will only be more effective as administration acts openly with inmates has proven very little at all if he himself has not interacted openly with administrators, and if adminstrators cannot be open with inmates over an extended period of time.

Thus, the ideas of failure and success that we have investigated in this chapter are all relative to the ideological, prerational assumptions under which all social action and research begin. In the correctional area, it appears that we have been unable to measure achievement because we have never settled (or even discussed in very systematic fashion) what the goals were in the first place.

NOTES

1. Bruce, Burgess, and Harno, *The Working of the Indeterminate Sentence Law and the Parole System in Illinois* (Springfield, Ill.: State Board of Parole, 1928), Chapters 28 and 30.

2. Sheldon and Eleanor Glueck, *500 Criminal Careers* (New York: Alfred Knopf, 1930); *Criminal Careers in Retrospect* (New York: The Commonwealth Fund, 1943); *One Thousand Juvenile Delinquents* (Cambridge: Harvard University Press, 1934); *Five Hundred Delinquent Women* (New York: The Commonwealth Fund, 1940).

3. Leslie Wilkins, *The Evaluation of Penal Measures* (New York: Random House, 1969, pp. 66–68; Hermann Mannheim and Leslie Wilkins, *Prediction Methods in Relation to Borstal Training* (London: H.M.S.O., 1955). See references listed on pp. 274–275.

4. Lloyd Ohlin, *Selection for Parole, A Manual of Parole Prediction* (New York: Russell Sage, 1951).

5. Note 3, supra.

6. Ibid, pp. 153–157.

7. Ibid, p. 111.

8. See Wilkins, *The Evaluation of Penal Measures*, note 3, supra, pp. 25–26.

9. David Street, Robert Vinter, and Charles Perrow, *Organization for Treatment* (New York: The Free Press, 1966), p. 17.

10. John Irwin, *The Felon* (Englewood Cliffs, N.J.: Prentice-Hall, 1970), p. 158.

11. Robert P. Scheurnell, "Valuation and Decision Making in Correctional Social Work," *Issues in Criminology* 4, no. 2 (Fall 1969): 101–108.

12. Don Gottfredson, *Measuring Attitudes toward Juvenile Detention* (New York: National Council on Crime and Delinquency, 1968).

13. Donald Cressey, "Contradictory Directives in Complex Organizations: The Case of the Prison," *Administrative Science Quarterly* 4 (June 1959): 1–19.

14. Gresham M. Sykes, *The Society of Captives* (Princeton, N.J.: Princeton University Press, 1971).

15. The following discussion is taken from David Duffee, *Correctional Policy, Managerial Style and Social Climate in a Minimum Security Institution* (Unpublished Ph.D. dissertation, State University of New York, Albany, 1974), Chapter 4.

16. See Daniel Katz and Robert Kahn, *The Social Psychology of Organizations* (New York: Wiley, 1966), p. 341.

17. Herbert Kelman, "Compliance, Identification, and Internalization: Three Processes of Attitude Change," *Journal of Conflict Resolution* (April 1958): 51–60.

18.   See Vincent O'Leary and David Duffee, "Correctional Policy: A Classification Designed for Change," *Crime and Delinquency* 17, no. 4 (October 1971): 373–386; and references noted therein on p. 378.

19.   Vincent O'Leary, *The Correctional Policy Inventory* (Hackensack, N.J.: National Council on Crime and Delinquency, 1970).

20.   Erving Goffman, *Asylums* (Garden City, N.Y.: Doubleday, 1969) includes many examples of how managers of institutions may do this.

Self-Corrective Corrections: The Road from Fumbling to Designing 9

In Chapter 8 we discussed recidivism as a criterion variable in the analysis of correctional effectiveness, and we saw that this criterion is rationally usable only with regard to some correctional strategies and not others. In addition, we tried to bring most of the correctional strategies that have been discussed in the middle part of this text into a coherent whole, where the conflicts and similarities among them might be more easily visible. Then we sought to suggest briefly how each set of strategies might be more effectively implemented, within the game plan established by the assumptions on which each set of strategies is based. Lastly, we suggested in our concluding note that various ideas of success and failure are all relative, or are based in the long run on the likes and dislikes of certain people. Furthermore, we suggest that, while these likes and dislikes are irrational and not subject to scientific scrutiny and evaluation, the strategies within those broad ideological boundaries can be subjected to systematic evaluation. Consequently, administrators and the public at large cannot renege on the responsibility of evaluation by claiming that the right kind of data does not exist or cannot be found. Most frequently this claim implies that the goals and strategies generated by values and different tastes have not been fully and carefully anticipated, so that the most sensible form of evaluation cannot be structured; or it implies that there is such a fundamental conflict in the values influencing the organization that administrators (much like the uncommitted voter) decide that the safest evaluative action is no action at all.

In this chapter we want to go further than discussing the various differences that exist within the correctional system and the primary group of correctional strategists and decision makers. The lack of

345

evaluation appears to be a function of conflicting external interests and relationships more than it is a function of our inability to evaluate. A discussion of these broader outside interests and trends, therefore, would appear to be all-important in assessing the ability of correctional decision makers to formulate coherent and effective strategies, or to change the ones in operation in favor of new programs and processes.

There are many external sources of influence and constraint on the correctional system, and we obviously cannot deal with all of them. As persons primarily concerned with the application of organizational and criminological theory to the problems of criminal justice agencies, we are in all likelihood incompetent to deal with most of them. Indeed, we perceive this effect of criminal justice specialization to be one of the most debilitating factors in operational research about corrections and criminal justice in general. We pointed out early in this work that the systems analysis approach to criminal justice that began with the formation of the President's Crime Commission in 1965 has been a major impetus to change in this area. But, much like the strategies we have examined within four broad policy sets, this systems approach has also locked us into modes of inquiry and problem solution that concentrate on the internal organization. The vast amount of legislation and new administrative forms and funding patterns established in the last decade have done the same. The great number of new college and university programs in criminal justice popping up around the country will, if they last, perpetuate this trend.

This trend seems to have advantages over the long period of social and political neglect that preceded it, but as with other forms of specialization, a major part of the specialist's energies should be spent in the effort to integrate the specialization with the ever-changing social and cultural environment. Otherwise the new policies and strategies that are valid internally will be seen externally as scientific and administrative dinosaurs stalking their way to extinction. Even now, as the new crises of population explosion and resource scarcity become the most immediate challenges to social action, the primacy of criminal justice activity has diminished. It is possible that within a few years of publication, the urgency with which the authors prepared this volume may seem laughable as new cultures predominate and as new problems of survival are found more pressing.

These too pessimistic (or too optimistic—there is little difference) predictions behind us, they can serve an immediate purpose in several respects:

1) We reemphasize our introductory note in Chapter 1 that corrections, as we know it, is only one form of social control, and a relatively small one at that.

2) We suggest that some of the principles expounded in this volume are not limited to applications in corrections and criminal justice as we know them, or as they may become in the immediate future. The ideas of policy analysis, and of questioning the fundamental assumptions underlying strategies, are equally applicable to other social settings and social problems.

3) We hope that the preface to this chapter can serve as a rationale for the fairly unusual conclusions that grow out of the logic of the remainder of this chapter—that is, that corrections as a social institution should be "desystematized" or reorganized so that it can deal on a more fundamental level with "wholesale" social problems, rather than on a "retail" basis with people, themselves stigmatized as problems.

Thus the strategy of this concluding chapter is two-fold: (1) We will examine the most immediate environment of the correctional system (and the environment we are most competent to deal with), that of the larger criminal justice network. (2) We will then suggest new designs and operations in corrections that should enable that system to be more responsive and more useful to a second environment, that of the communities from which offenders come and to which they will return.

THE BATTLE MODEL OF CRIMINAL JUSTICE

A decade ago, in 1964, the late Herbert Packer published what was to become a seminal work on the foundations of criminal justice.[1] He later expanded this article into a book, *The Limits of the Criminal Sanction*.[2] This book was also rapidly adopted in criminal justice schools, and praised in academic circles, as the leading work on the nature of the criminal justice system, as a justification for deterrence, and as an appraisal of the reforms needed in the system so that it could more effectively deal with the areas of its special competence.

Packer's work was not really a bolt out of the blue. Rather it seemed to be the best treatment by a leading scholar of issues and trends that a variety of legal scholars had struggled with. Justice Frankfurter and Yale Kamisar, among others, had also recognized the "two models" that Packer isolated for study.[3] Whether the two poles or models were actually complete models of the criminal process has been questioned. A young Yale professor, for example, suggested that Packer was really dealing with ideologies—the value-sets or patterns of taste—that precede actual models and determine much of their structure.[4] For our purposes, so much the better, because it is the various ideologies at play in the criminal justice process that we want to investigate.

Packer suggested that two value poles underlie all the operations of the system itself—the "Crime Control Model" and the "Due Process Model." He suggested that neither model was dominant; that both affected the operations of all agencies of justice; and that it was through an understanding of the operational compromises of these two competing ideologies that we could understand why things happened as they did and could predict what might happen in the future.

The different characteristics of the two belief systems are contrasted in Table 1.

Table 1
A SUMMARY OF CHARACTERISTICS OF
PACKER'S TWO MODELS OF THE CRIMINAL PROCESS

	Crime Control	Due Process
1)	criminal justice process is positive guarantee of social freedom	criminal process is most severe social sanction to be used on free citizens
2)	criminal acts are major threat to social order	investigation and prosecution of crimes can lead to severe constriction of social freedoms
3)	to ensure social order we need high rates of apprehension and conviction	to ensure freedom we need to guarantee that procedures of apprehension and conviction are of high quality
4)	to achieve high rates we need a system that can process cases routinely with speed and finality of outcome	to ensure minimal abuse of coercive sanctions we must have highly visible decision process and means for review and challenge of outcomes
5)	speed can be gained through uniformity of procedures for all cases, and finality can be achieved through an informal, administrative decision-making process	to ensure visibility and care we must emphasize individuality of cases and high formality with a judicial decision-making process
6)	the best way of implementing above needs is through an "administrative" assembly line structure	the best way of implementing above safeguards is through adversary process, with continual checks and balances to provide obstacle course to flow of cases

7)	successful conclusion is achieved by an early screening-out of people who are innocent or unlikely to be convicted, and gaining quick and inexpensive convictions of the rest, with little opportunity for challenge	successful conclusion is full application of rights in adversary proceeding which is concerned with determining the *criminal* responsibility of the accused
8)	this conclusion rests on a presumption of guilt, which is a prediction of likely outcome of the case	this conclusion rests on a "presumption of innocence," which is a directive about how to proceed regardless of the probable outcome
9)	focal point of process is the guilty plea, which holds need for judicial fact-finding to a minimum	focal point is the trial, because adjudicative fact-finding is most accurate and fair
10)	reliability of the process is assured through high efficiency—processing cases as quickly and cheaply as possible, screening out weak cases prior to prosecution	reliability of the process is through quality control on each case; more efficiency can be oppressive in individual instance
11)	correction of errors through administrative controls; criminals should never be released because of mistaken procedure by officials	correction of errors through appeal; "self-corrective" mechanism applied on a case-by-case basis; release of offenders, as correction, deters official misbehavior in the future
12)	there is basic confidence in the agency action and in the representativeness of the government that structured the executive agencies	there is basic doubt about the efficacy of punishment applied through formal governmental mechanisms
13)	the validating authority in this process is legislative and statutory, where directives for action are set	the validating authority of this process is judicial and constitutional, where limits to allowable action are set

While Packer discussed these two poles as different models, John Griffiths' major article, dealing with the same area, argues that Packer was really describing one model in which there are two competing value systems. The model, said Griffiths, is one of Battle, because whether one upholds due process or crime control tactics, the goal of the process is conviction, rather than correction.[5] It might seem annoying that in 1968 Packer, a leading scholar, could talk about the "entirety of the criminal process" without once mentioning correction. (In Chapter 2, we discussed this typical "oversight" as a function of the retributive-deterrent philosophy.) Not surprising then is Packer's emphasis on general deterrence as the most reasonable and effective goal of the criminal process!

Whether we are looking at two models or one, the important point is, of course, that both sets of values are basically concerned with vanquishing the guilty party. Due Process adherents would make the road to exile a difficult one to travel, while the Crime Control proponents are more in favor of a major highway. But in either case, the interest in the *guilty* party stops at conviction. Packer is very clear on this point, in terms of the fairness that the Due Process model would extend to the defendant who is very probably guilty. He argues that the reason for treating such a man to all the rights and privileges of the innocent is not that even a guilty man is due such considerations, but, on the contrary, that even such a defendant in the Due Process model has a realistic legal chance of being proven legally (rather than factually) not guilty. Thus *every* man, no matter how weighty the facts arrayed against him, is due all considerations *until* the pronouncement of the judicial determination of guilt.[6] Given Packer's silence on punishment itself, one would assume that Due Process does not apply to corrections because the legal conviction has been pronounced, and hence the moral justification under the Due Process model for being fair and considerate is irrelevant: the battle has been won. Both Griffiths and Packer would agree that, regardless of what it is called, the strategy of battle is so dominant in the preconviction system, and in the general citizens' understanding of the preconviction system, that the consequences of this ideology permeate all of criminal justice operations.

The police and the Battle Model

In Chapter 2 we looked at police behavior and its relationship to corrections. We can now understand that behavior in terms of the battle tactics that are apparently the major structural influence in the police organization. As we have seen, one major result of operating as if in the midst of battle, is that no one knows what to do when victory is won. When the offender is caught, the game is over. Small wonder the police behave as if the battle is an unending struggle: the police, among other organizations, do not think of ways of ending it.

Many will say that it is the job of the police to catch the offender, not to end the battle; and that the police are not all of the criminal justice system. If it is a *system* of justice in which the efforts of different agencies are coordinated, then it can be someone else's function to end the battle, or to correct the offender.

The response to this line of thinking is available directly within the language of the preceding paragraph. *If* there is a coherent system of criminal justice, then *all* agencies or components within it must be working toward the same overall goal. If the goal of the system is conviction, or exile, then "corrections" is obviously a misnomer. What we want are more effective cages, or, perhaps in the near future, an intergalactic Australia where offenders can be shipped away, never to return. If, on the other hand, the goal of the system is the return to society of ex-offenders, then the police *cannot* go about their business as if it were a battle and expect their efforts to coordinate with the ultimate efforts of the system.

One difficulty is that the apprehension of offenders (whether for corrective or exile purposes) is, as we said before, only a small part of police business. The major part of police business may be defined as crime prevention, or order maintenance—but the battle has more visible rewards. A policeman may not be able to tell when he is successful in preventing a criminal occurrence, but he knows when he has caught a criminal. Thus he is more likely to seek the rewards for the small portion of the work than for the major portion of the work.

One might expect to find the battle tactic a more effective mode of operation when dealing with the police preventive function, and then be able to explain the battle approach to the apprehension function as a carryover from the preventive side of police activity. This, of course, is only true if we find that all crimes that have not yet been committed will be committed by potential criminals who are merely waiting for an opportunity to beat the police in order to become actual criminals. If this were the case, it might make sense to describe crime prevention as a battle, since indeed there would seem to be an enemy "out there" against whom the police should be maneuvering.

However, given our lack of data in this area, we can also suggest that the police preventive function might be explained as the effort of the police to ensure that no one becomes an enemy. The job would be to prevent free citizens from becoming *potential* offenders. Assuming that there is a difference between the potential offender's perception of a crime and the free citizen's perception of a crime, one would also assume that the police prevention strategies would have to differ. If there are a host of potential offenders waiting for a chance to steal, it might be rational to treat them as psychologically committed to the criminal action and thus to prevent crime through the use of threats (i.e., deterrence). But if crimes are not committed by a large group of potential offenders, already psychologically prepared to do the criminal act, then the threat strategy may be the *wrong* strategy. Because if, in reality, the police are approaching many citizens who are not potential criminals and threatening them as if they were, it might be a normal response to retaliate by becoming a potential criminal. In this case, the police are creating their own battles as they manufacture enemies out of the population at large. It is important to recognize that this second argument does not deny existence of potential criminals; rather, it suggests that people may acquire criminal status through a cycle of behavior in which police "preventive" tactics are a contributing factor.

The kinds of crimes and criminals that can be deterred and the business of crimes and criminals that should be handled some other way are matters with no simple yes/no answers. But we suggest that the Battle ideology supports simple yes/no answers. It seems not only to support solutions to some problems that do exist but also to suggest as solutions modes of action that are unrelated to the problem at hand (for example, arrest as a solution to crime prevention). For both reasons, we have doubts about the efficacy of the ideology for the accomplishment of normally accepted social goals by the police. What it does seem to do is to simplify for the policeman a job that would otherwise be complex and confusing. It reduces for him tremendous areas of doubt and uncertainty and replaces them with the "knowledge" that he is "doing right" because he is on the right side. But by "doing right" within this framework, he also reduces chances for change and for positive correction.

The courts and the Battle Model

Much of the court behavior that we discussed must also look familiar as behavior that is congruent with the values of the Battle model. It might appear at first glance that prosecution is dominated solely by the values of Crime Control, and that Due Process is very little in evidence. This, however, is not true to Packer's original analysis, nor is it really true to our previous description of the guilty plea system. We pointed out in Chapter 2 that court structure and operation are certainly not typical of bureaucracies—indeed, it makes little sense to try to understand court behavior by using a typical model of bureaucratic authority, structure, and process. The guilty-plea process has the characteristics of the Crime Control "administrative assembly line" as Packer would have it, but it is an assembly line whose operations at every stop-point are shaped by the Due Process standards, or the threat of their use. *Without* the threat of their use, in other words, the Crime Control values would be given an unfettered reign, and the process would look considerably different. The defendant would lose what little bargaining power he has, and the rate and perhaps the quality of the decisions would be considerably different.

Packer, for example, likens the Due Process model influence on the process to one of quality control. It would be possible, then, to suggest that the small number of cases that do go to trial are those cases selected off the assembly line for quality check. The fact that the Due Process checks are fully applied to that small number means that *all* cases are affected to some degree, because the actors cannot predict perfectly which cases will be checked and which will not.[7] Thus, the court process is, as a whole, a battle in which the agreed-upon end result is vanquishing the guilty. The disagreement concerns the tactics to be used.

We would suggest that (1) the application of the Battle model to the court process is as prevalent as the application of the Battle model to police operations; and (2) the effectiveness of the Battle model in the achievement of social policy is equally questionable in both areas. As many people have pointed out, winning the Battle does the victim no good; and, as other critics have suggested, the tactics used to win the Battle, as well as the Battle itself, explain why offenders do not feel guilty for their crime, and why they feel, after a period of punishment, that "society owes them." As John Casper implies over and over again during his interviews with Connecticut inmates, offenders might indeed reform if, during the criminal justice process some officials appeared to be concerned with the consequences of the crime for the victim and the offender. The criminal, suggests Casper, rejects the rightness of the punishment he receives because the state's official spokesmen have, by their behavior, implicitly rejected the significance of his acts before he does.[8] Just what kind of process *would* convince offenders of the rightness of action taken against them and enable officials to demonstrate the significance of the offender's acts, no one seems to be sure; but it would not seem to be a battle.

Corrections and the Battle Model

It is hard to talk about corrections in relation to the Battle model, because correction is not part of the Battle model. The Battle model ends with conviction, or, at the very latest, with the pronouncement of punishment. Never does it include a statement of what that punishment entails, or how it is to be meted out. Thus, as we said in the introduction to this chapter, what we are investigating here is an *external* influence on the correctional process. We were looking at one of the constraints that shapes the correctional process rather than at the thing itself. Battle tactics, fair or foul, simply have nothing to do with remedial action.[9]

Of course, it must be remembered that corrections never was part of the battle. When reformers in the 1790s were deciding what to do with convicted offenders rather than maim, ostracize, or restrain, they were not simply inventing a new punishment; they were ultimately suggesting a new criminal justice system. While we think the experiment was noble, we also think (with hindsight, of course) that it was rather silly. These men who wanted to redeem offenders should have known that they should have started elsewhere. Indeed, the models for construction of prisons came from men of utopian bent who would have redeemed society; and, within a system for redeeming society, the practice of redeeming individuals makes sense. Modern reformers of the criminal justice system, who have looked at the absurdity of the concept of "corrections" occurring after a battle, have realized this. People like Karl Menninger, Matthew Dumont, and Ramsey Clark speak about correcting social conditions before they lead to crimes by individuals. Otherwise we are caught in the illogical and maddening loop of fighting social problems by punishing those who have suffered the most.[10]

THE EFFECT ON CORRECTIONS OF THE PRECONVICTION BATTLE

When we call the present correctional situation absurd, we are *not* suggesting that nothing gets done within the system. On the contrary, we hope that we have demonstrated a great deal of what gets done, and that a considerable portion of it is valuable. But we also suggest that its accomplishments are, and perhaps always will be, the kind that Sisyphus experiences before the boulder begins to roll back again. Given the strength and endurance of the Battle model, new correctional strategies are strikingly effective in the short run, and gallingly ineffective in the long run. Something is wrong with the entire design, not of any particular correctional strategy, but of the entire way in which we try to be strategic. Four of the major drawbacks to our present strategic position are discussed below. Each would seem to be partly, if not totally, a consequence of the positioning of corrections in a system whose other agencies are concerned with winning wars.

Lack of information

Certainly the first major consequence is lack of information. In order for corrections to be effective, there must be a search for information about the dimensions of change. What are an individual's needs? What factors have promoted his choice of illegal behavior over legal behavior?

None of this kind of information is sought in the criminal justice process prior to conviction. What is worse, the workings of the preconviction system vis-a-vis the offender generally inhibits the flow of such information. Certainly the offender is much less willing to volunteer this type of information at the preconviction stage than he would have been immediately after the crime (or as some would have it, immediately before the crime!). Information is feedback about change, or a reduction of variability. If the offical is pitted in battle against the offender (and presumably he knows it) then we are in a zero-sum game. What one person gains, another loses. In this kind of game, to have all the information shared, as in a chess match, presumably favors the player with the most finesse and/or the most pieces. In the criminal justice system the state has the finesse and the pieces. Thus it is to the defendant's advantage to withhold information. So far as he can do that, he can keep the prosecution from the most adroit use of its skill or the most powerful deployment of its resources.

Once the offender is convicted, and particularly if he is sent to prison, then he has lost almost *all* power and finesse, and about the only advantage he has is the withholding of information; i.e., it is to the offender's advantage to withhold information as long as he is still playing (or thinks he is playing) a zero-sum game. About the only chance correctional officials have of achieving change is to convince the offender that the zero-sum rules no longer apply—that within the correctional game there are rules by which both sides can win. If both sides can win, then shared information is advantageous to both. We would suggest that the chances of convincing the offender that there has been a change in rules is exceedingly slight—when we (and he) consider that he has just scored zero on the previous game.

Social and physical isolation

An organization that cannot gather information is automatically isolated. Correctional systems which are structured to fit into a battle preconviction system will automatically be isolated and thus lose additional information. Since the goal of a successful battle is the exile of the guilty, the prison has basically been an isolated institution, and probation and parole officers are frequently isolated from the larger range of social services open to needy but "worthy" citizens; and offenders, wherever they are located, are socially isolated from other people.[11]

It is somewhat ironic that the inventors of Auburn Prison and Eastern State Penitentiary thought of isolation as a curative. But, of course, they did not expect the isolation of their design to result in a lack of information. Rather, they perceived isolation as a way of controlling information so that only the good information (e.g., the Bible) was received. What the reformers did not understand was that trying to control the variety of crime with the Bible was much like trying to control the variety of a football team by placing one man at the goal. It simply does not work.[12]

With hindsight, again, we can suggest now that the original reformers misinterpreted the function of the eighteenth-century community in the generation of crime, and that their strategy of isolation was related to that misinterpretation. The reformers were quite correct that most crime is urban, and that most criminals are slum dwellers influenced (as they would have had it) by the vice and corruption of the city. What these reformers did not seem to understand was that the social and physical milieu of most city-dwelling criminals is not one of *too much* information, but one of *too little* information. Urban poverty is tedium. Lack of education is a reduction, not an increase, in information. And the racial segregation that has always characterized the American city further reduces the experience of variety by the citizens who most often end up being corrected.

To eighteenth- and twentieth-century reformers alike, the jumble of the urban slum and the unfamiliarity of lower-class life styles have often seemed full of variety and complexity, simply because of their strangeness. Social and physical isolation were evidently considered to be the antidote for this "evil" variety. For some reason these reformers have infrequently suggested (much less placed into operation) a correctional system that desegregated rather than isolated, or a system that offered the offender the informational variety provided to the middle-class reformers, or the variety of ethnic or structural subcultures that could have been functional. The usual strategy has been to divest the deviant of any values that seem strange, but simultaneously to withhold from him the avenues of opportunity associated with the values that the reformers found familiar. Inevitably, offenders are supposed to turn out saints, instead of like the rest of us.[13]

Reaction to problems

As a result of the lack of information and the isolation suffered by the correctional system, probation, prison, and parole and other correctional agencies have a peculiar way of reacting to problems. Problems will occur in any organization. It is simply impossible to avoid faulty planning, faulty implementation, and faulty evaluation in any complex enterprise. But in many organizations, procedures are built in to account for problems, predict their occurrence, and plan for solutions. Many correctional organizations, in contrast, do not seem to be aware of problems until they reach crisis proportions. As the conflagrations become visible, management scurries around, putting out one fire and then another. Techniques of dealing with uncertainty and error seem to be lacking, and as long as managers' energies are continually pulled toward dealing with "routine urgencies," they probably will not develop those techniques.

Donald Cressey's series of papers on two west coast institutions provides some insights into the correctional problem-solving process.[14] He suggests that correctional organizations are frequently committed to an explanation of deviance or misbehavior by either staff or inmates as purposive nonconformity. Mistakes are treated as insubordination. While some deviant acts certainly are purposive rebellions, applying this motivational explanation to all behavioral or interpersonal problems reduces the willingness of staff and inmates to report trouble spots and disagreements before they become crises. If misbehavior is purposive, then the organizational reaction is usually punitive. Aware of the sanctions for causing (or even reporting) problems, many correctional personnel become apathetic, cynical, and evasive. The correctional climate, in other words, does not allow for preventive strategies or for cooperative problem solving.

Cressey suggests that another way of looking at deviance is that it is problem-solving behavior in which people are trying to do the best for themselves under difficult circumstances. He argues that once deviance is understood as nonpurposive, the reaction can be educative rather than punitive. If the correctional climate supported the quick and full report of errors and mistakes, information would be available to deal with problem situations before they become crises. A climate in which this negative feedback was actively sought and used for redirection, rather than for distribution of negative sanctions, would provide corrections with a climate conducive to systematic planning and evaluation.

Inability to change

This last consequence of the battle grows out of the way in which the Battle model reacts to problems. In organizations that react to problems after they occur instead of preparing for them beforehand, much less organizational energy can be devoted to change. Change in corrections has long been characterized as reactive rather than proactive. As such it happens in irregular and disconcerting fits and starts rather than as a regular and durable function of the organization.[15]

In agencies whose goals involve changing offenders, this inability to plan and implement systemic changes in the organizations themselves is a much more urgent problem than the inability to change in a manufacturing plant might be. For instance, Street, Vinter, and Perrow classify correctional institutions among "people-changing" organizations along with schools, churches, and the Salvation Army. Then they proceed to describe certain core characteristics of people-changing organizations:

a) certain change techniques are ruled out because the "material is human rather than non-human";
b) people are self-activating, and their cooperation in the change process must be gained;
c) because they are people, there is a strain between the individualizing of the change process and the routinization of the bureaucracy;
d) people-changing work is hard to evaluate;
e) therefore, belief systems about change are very influential in structuring the organization;
f) because belief systems conflict, outside groups are very interested in the activity of the organization, which is careful to keep the public (and conflict) at a distance.[16]

While these characteristics do seem to describe a great many of the correctional organizations we have studied (field work as well as institutional work), the sequence of these characteristics also describes why many such organizations have a great deal of difficulty in changing people and themselves.

a) they lack information;
b) they are isolated;
c) they react to problems out of beliefs rather than from information;
d) they have difficulty in changing.

We would suggest that a more neutral description for these organizations is "people-processing organizations." Sometimes they change people and sometimes they do not. When they do, sometimes the change can be attributed to the organization and sometimes it cannot. When organizations *do* change people and the change *is* caused by institutional strategies, it seems likely to us that the organization in question has a characteristic that Street, Vinter, and Perrow do *not* mention. And that would be that the organization itself is continually changing! The reason for this conclusion is that the "unit of production" or the "change material" in such an organization is not the people, but the way in which people in the organization (staff or offenders) interact. And the interaction of people *is the structure of the organization. Thus we hypothesize that most effective change organizations are effective in constantly changing themselves.*

REDESIGNING CORRECTIONS

If it is correct that an organization is effective in changing the behavior of offenders to the extent that the organization is effective in changing itself, then corrections, to be effective at correcting, needs to be redesigned. By redesigned, we mean much more than re-planned.

The difference between planning and designing

A great deal of planning activity goes on in corrections, and it is increasing constantly. Planning occurs within institutions and field agencies, in centralized headquarters units, in state planning agencies, and in the work of national institutes and commissions. But very little design activity takes place. By "plan" we mean the laying out of steps by which to reach specific goals. By "design" we mean the fundamental shape of the enterprise, the basic assumptions under which it operates, and the basic frame of reference within which specific goals make sense.[17] Henry Ford planned a particular automobile, but he also designed a special mode of travel. The design of a motorized conveyance was manifested in the Model T, but had many other manifestations as well.

Planning should occur after design work has been completed. One of the leading experts on correctional organization and change, Harold Bradley, has lamented that a tremendous amount of careful planning effort in corrections has gone to waste because no one bothered to design the broad outline of goals that the plans are to implement. He gives the example of a novel institutional program in California that was planned down to the last detail. It was not implemented because the planners merely accepted traditional correctional designs rather than making sure that the designs were congruent with their plans.[18] The specific plans entailed a new, small institutional program that was to provide intensive treatment and early release for offenders. But in the plan, the usual characteristics of correctional management and staffing patterns had been accepted. The traditional paramilitary design had been incorporated in a plan with nontraditional goals. The planners had not stopped to consider whether a uniformed guard force and regular eight-hour shifts would be compatible with the new goals of intensive treatment and early release.

This is just one example of how new programs frequently fail because they incorporate dysfunctional aspects of designs that the programs themselves are trying to correct. Perhaps the biggest example of this contradiction between good planning and poor design is the way major structural components of corrections have been tacked onto each other without much regard for whether the pieces can possibly form a coherent system. Parole programs, for example, were tacked onto the usual prison programs in the 1870s. No one bothered to inquire whether parole, which is based on the assumption that deviance can be treated within the community where deviance was generated, could be integrated with prison operations, which were based on the assumption that deviance could only be treated by isolating the deviant from the community where the deviance had been generated.[19]

Designing for goals that can change

When retribution was socially acceptable as a goal of the criminal sanction, correctional agencies were less pressed to be institutions of control (or institutions of change). For example, when the prison manager was the chief keeper, he was responsible for keeping the castoffs of a social control process that had already been completed. Retribution is a reflexive process that looks back to an act already completed. It is morally right to punish the morally wrong. In that situation, the warden was not responsible for the future behavior of inmates or for any effects that his prison had on that behavior.[20]

At present, society seems to desire not only that something go into the correctional system, but also that something different comes out of that system. Faced by this demand, the correctional officials must not sit on the lid but take the top off and stir the contents in the pot.

In order to accomplish goals when the use of the criminal sanction is forward-looking, the manager must perceive his role as different from that of chief keeper. Processing, rather than keeping, people requires of the manager new ways of relating to people, whether they be staff or inmates, and new ways of putting these people together. Or, to state it more precisely, the chief keeper's problem was one of separating people (making prisoners and society independent), while the contemporary officials' problem is one of integrating people (making offenders and society interdependent).

In a sense, then, the keeper had no goal to achieve, or needed no production or change subsystem. He was in charge of maintaining a stable structure and was responsible for environmental activity that was supposed to keep community and prison from influencing each other. Since it does not make much sense to talk about a system that is not productive, it makes more sense to treat a retributive correctional program as a component of another, larger system, whose productive activity is supported by the stability given it by the retributive organization. The political system of society may be such a system and could be used to explain, for example, why keepers were political appointees.

Contemporary officials, in contrast, are definitely saddled with a production goal, although they may not have developed the techniques by which to achieve it. One of their difficulties, as we have seen, is that the prison has usually adopted the environmental and maintenance structures that were effective in the retributive organization.

The correctional policies of Restraint, Reform, and Rehabilitation, it was argued in Chapter 8, all have basic inconsistencies that will have dysfunctional consequences when organizations are built upon them. It may be possible to understand these policies as rationalizations for the continued utilization of these outmoded structures. New support structures could be generated by the tasks of people-processing, but the outlines of these tasks remain vague when they must be invented in organizations where restrictions on change are very strong.

Faced with this dilemma, the correctional manager has begun to turn to researchers for consultation. Perhaps it is this search for information more than anything else that identifies the qualitative shift in correctional organizations. It is through this search for information that the manager takes on the role required for system management. It is in terms of gathering and analyzing information about the organization that the manager can compare output with goals and react to the difference.

INEFFECTIVE CHANGE ATTEMPTS

Many attempts to improve corrections, to make it more capable of changing offenders' behavior, are too recent to warrant anything but very tentative evaluations. There are some change attempts, however, that have been instituted frequently enough that we can attempt to analyze why they have been ineffective. Based on this analysis, predictions can be made about the effectiveness of more recent, but similar, change attempts.

As the comparison between the goal achievement of earlier and later correctional organizations indicates, many characteristics of correctional organizations can change without altering the perceptions of offenders about their conditions. The salaries of correctional workers relative to the general financial distribution in society can increase; the educational requirements for correctional staff can increase; the physical living conditions for inmates can improve; the frequency of parole can increase; or correctional policy can change from Restraint to Rehabilitation, without changing the inmates' understanding of their condition as prisoners or their understanding of the intentions of staff.

Some of the contrasts in this comparison of correctional policy are drastic enough to lead one to conclude that effective change is impossible. Inmates respond to incarceration as such an overwhelmingly negative experience that variations in the nature of incarceration can elicit no distinctive responses. Nevertheless, change is not impossible. Inmates *do* distinguish between hard time and easy time, or good time and bad time. Moreover, even inmates as resolutely opposed to the present regime as the late George Jackson believe in the possibility of a correctional experience that would be beneficial to the inmates from the inmates' point of view.[21] Furthermore, while the programmatic change between, say, 1850 and 1970 was considerable, it seems unlikely that design differences were very great. A policy change might bring some changes such as those that we have listed; but unless the policy change is mediated by changes in the information system, the basic control of the situation will not change, and the internal conditions of the organizations will remain about the same.

We can call this kind of change ineffective because it is incomplete. If only one aspect of the basic design changes, the correctional improvements actually resemble a name-changing process in which the basic structure of the thing renamed has remained unchanged. There would seem to be two basic reasons for the incompleteness of the attempted change. Either officials have not understood the interdependence of the parts of the design, or they have been unable to achieve such interdependence.

We have covered in some detail the failure to understand the interdependence. Part of the failure may be due to the newness of the idea of system management. This new concept of management is delineated over time. It is a developmental, evolutionary process. If, as Emery and Trist have suggested, the "causal texture" of organizations has evolved to a new stage of "turbulence," or chronic change, correctional officials lack role models on which to base their behavior.[22]

In support of this evolutionary assumption, a general history of the humanities and philosophy is relevant. The traditions of Western philosophy and social thought have emphasized analysis considerably more than synthesis. In the literary realm, for example, the social system model constructed by William Blake was long regarded as "visionary" and "apocalyptic" rather than as a realistic appraisal of urbanization, industrialism, and capitalism. Western religions have traditionally focused on salvation of individual souls rather than on the reorganization of the social structure. Constrained by these broad trends that retarded synthetic and integrative approaches to the resolution of social problems, the role of system management is part of a cultural revolution. It may take considerable time for a prison manager, for example, to begin thinking of his role as one of integrating an organization rather than balancing its separate parts.

If a manager does understand the need for redesigning, then a major problem of fulfilling the design is the number of secondary reactions that occur in a system that has traditionally been treated as an aggregate of parts. For example, correctional officers have for years been managed on the basis that their custody function can be isolated from "treatment" of the inmate. They learn, therefore, to react in certain ways to managers and inmates. They will tend to reject suggestions that they should interact socially with inmates because increased social interaction, while necessary to people-processing, is detrimental to guarding.

The manager's initial attempts at increasing the frequency and complexity of staff-inmate interaction will meet with resistance, even if these overtures are made through managerial behavior congruent with more democratic decision making and greater use of discretion at lower organizational levels. These changes in behavior will be contradictory to well-established methods of officer evaluation and threatening to the officers' perception of their role.

It has been contended that unionization of the guard force can be attributed to the autocratic managerial behavior that was compatible with retributive goals. Nevertheless, the initial reaction to the democratic behavior that is compatible with people-processing goals may well be a strengthening of unionization around such issues as specifications of the custodial position and fairness of evaluation. It has also been demonstrated that inmates will react similarly to the new request that they be interactants in an organization, rather than captives in a larger social conspiracy. Inmates accustomed to being evaluated in terms of "keeping in line" will react to the changing managerial role as a new ploy in that conspiracy. Thus, even a manager who understands his role as one of system management will have considerable difficulties with his role performance.[23]

These trends may highlight the reasons why many efforts to change correctional policy are ineffective. Some recent change attempts that seem to conform to these broad trends and may also be ineffective are the following:[24]

1) *Higher educational requirements for correctional personnel, particularly for officers.* There is little evidence in studies conducted so far that the amount of formal education correlates with any particular correctional behavior. There is some evidence that, as officers receive college-level training, their commitment to the job decreases. Higher educational requirements themselves would not seem to influence behavior in the desired directions. There must first be some decisions about organizational design, about the goals to be achieved through that design. Then we might begin thinking about the educational prerequisites of people expected to interact in that design. At present, much of this design activity seems to be bypassed in the rush to educate personnel. Improvements in individuals may not bring improvements in organization.

2) *Increased inservice training.* Several states have opened training academies for their correctional personnel. Many of the same problems that pertain to higher educational requirements pertain here. The training academy usually runs a one- or two-week session for all entering personnel, or for all working personnel, as they can be relieved from duty. The actual training and curriculum resemble lower-level college courses, with an emphasis on one- or two-hour guest lectures by relevant state officials. There is little opportunity for the examination of the training information under actual working conditions.[25] Other than the fact that personnel can be required to attend inservice training more easily than they can be required to attend an outside college, the value of this form of training is rather doubtful.

3) *Training conferences and training laboratories.* A setting that usually does offer new information in ways that promote adoption of the information by the trainees is the conference or laboratory setting. Lecturing in this setting is usually held to a minimum. Questionnaires, simulations, and seminars on problems suggested by the work situation are used to help the trainee examine his own operating assumptions and compare his ideas with those of his peers. In this training there is considerable value in an atmosphere that is remote from the pressures of daily work. Competent trainers can also provide a valuable experience in group process. On the negative side, it would seem difficult to schedule these training experiences at regular intervals, and it is usually difficult or impossible for

the trainers to follow up the behavior of trainees back on the job. A related difficulty is that the expense of these conferences and the need to keep the organizations running during a conference prevents training all members of the organization or all members of a work unit at the same time.

4) *Inmate governments.* Recently, there have been some experiments with elected inmate councils or governing bodies that make some important decisions about inmate welfare. This kind of approach to increased inmate responsibility may tend to highlight the caste-like separations between staff and inmates.

A variety of other innovations aimed at the improvement of correctional organizations could also be mentioned, but these four are sufficient as examples. While there are considerable differences in aim, and probably in outcome, of these change attempts, they would all appear to address the secondary reactions to fragmented organizational life. As such, they may mask difficulties in the basic organizational design by legitimating the perception by staff and inmates that problems in prison life lie within an individual or in a certain set of individuals, rather than in the way in which these people interact.

THE STRUCTURE OF A LEARNING SYSTEM

In contrast with these kinds of change strategies, the strategy implied by organizational theory and research involves rebuilding the organization rather than adding pieces as new problems appear. Rebuilding should begin with the development of new models of organizations that have a more logical relationship to the kinds of goals correctional organizations are now trying to achieve. It is obvious that once such models are constructed, a major problem is one of implementation. In order to implement a new model, existing structures and personnel will have to be changed rather than discarded. Thus the models that are developed should include methods of transition from the existing organizational structures to the new ones.

We have concluded in Chapter 8 that existing structures and policies emphasize maintenance activity and deemphasize change activity. The performance of certain specified roles in the organization has been substituted for behaving in ways that achieve a desirable external output. The existing environmental activities lower the visibility of internal operations by demanding autonomy from external influence, so that custody precautions or professional relationships are not disrupted. The existing environmental subsystem also questions the legitimacy of, and devalues the reliability of, external validation measures such as recidivism rates.

These activities are not conscious efforts by correctional administrators to avoid evaluation of their procedures. Rather, they are a functional statement that the fragmented organization cannot withstand much external influence. The tremendous amount of energy that goes into maintaining an unhealthy organization requires that the organization take a defensive stance toward the environment. Since productive techniques of correctional change require an increase in the flow of information and resources between the organization and the environment, maintenance of a rigid social structure obviously decreases the ability to develop productive techniques of change that might withstand an external validation process. The existing structure might be summarized as a vicious cycle from low goal attainment to a defensive organizational posture to the inability to develop the kind of environmental relationships that could improve goal attainment.

While this is a vicious cycle, it is also a rather stable one. Violence within prisons and occasional riots demonstrate the dysfunctional aspects of the cycle on the institutional level only when it reaches extreme proportions. But the information about internal violence and about riots usually feeds back into the system in a way that validates the felt need for high overt control and limits attention to the dynamics of change.

In other words, this vicious structural cycle is a homeostatic process: the system responds to changes in input by returning the system to its original operating state. For example, inmate and officer roles in the Trenton prison studied by Sykes formed a homeostatic system. Each party had negotiated with the other a state of interaction in which both sides were satisfied, although that state was "corrupt" in the perception of managers.[26]

In a correctional model that emphasizes production rather than maintenance, the manager must use, rather than ignore, the process of homeostasis. Organizational goals and organizational structure must utilize the tendency of human participants to be interactive, rather than utilize organizational authority to keep such interactions from occurring. A manager who accommodates the principles of homeostasis in his organization will increase the capacity of his organization to facilitate interaction. However, this manager would want not only to facilitate interaction, but also to select from a variety of interactions those that are most likely to have desired outcomes. He would want to have many of these interactions programmed or planned, so that he could predict outcomes and rechannel interactions that are leading away from program goals. He also needs structures that can react to new problems to which responses have not been programmed, so that an effective search can begin for new paths of action.

One could say that, under this kind of management, organizational change and organizational control are synonymous. The organization is under control to the degree that it is free to change internally in order to meet any specific problems that arise. This kind of organization could be called a "learning system" because it responds to newly presented problems in terms of past experience with similar problems, or it begins to study a novel problem by applying processes of problem solution that have been effective in the past. As the organization continues to confront problems, its store of usable information increases. An ongoing evaluation process weeds out programs that no longer seem usable.

In the correctional area, this kind of system might be approximated if the correctional ideal, "treat each inmate as an individual," became a structural principle rather than grist for a cynic's mill. Internally, such a prison would have to provide for the inmate an organizational structure that reacts to his definition of his problems. Externally, such a prison would have to provide for the community an organizational structure based on the community definition of the inmate as a problem. Or, to state these requirements another way, the prison must serve two client demands simultaneously, one from the community and one from the inmate. These problems are probably not the same, but they are obviously related and may be reciprocal. For example, the inmate's problem may be lack of a job or lack of the training needed to obtain a job. The community problem may be its inability to provide jobs, or to provide the training for them, or to handle the people who have neither jobs nor training for them.

If the problems presented by either client were even that simple, the correctional task would be relatively easy. A major confounding factor in the presentation of problems of either client is that both clients have reduced the problem-solving alternative through coercive actions (commission of a crime and prosecution) long before service from the correctional organization is demanded. Thus, a major correctional task is the redefinition of the problems to lower the coercive constraints for each client, prior to selecting channels of action.

If this is the general pattern for the construction of a change-productive correctional organization, the key structural principles should involve: 1) goal definition, or identification of problems, and 2) information flow, or accuracy and frequency of communication. The internal organizational structure suggested by these two points is one of small, fairly autonomous teams who have large, centrally stored resources available upon which to draw as the team members define problems. The structural relationship to the environment suggested is one of small, geographically dispersed units, located close to the source of the original problem identification by both clients, but linked to other units by a central information system that can facilitate the learning process in all units.

The staff of these small units should probably have backgrounds and skills that are very mixed. The mix should change in relation to the kind of community and individual problems that are brought to that particular unit. Although it may not always be the case, the variety of problems brought to any particular unit should be smaller than the range of resources that can be called upon for solutions.

In order to facilitate the accuracy of information, the communication within units should be democratic. Anyone who has the information or other kinds of resources that have bearing on the solution of a problem might be part of staff for the solution of that problem. In other words, each unit should have very flexible boundaries. Members of the community (volunteers or consultants) should be sought and included in unit operations for the duration of particular projects.

There would seem to be two major prerequisites to this kind of communication and flexibility of structure. The team members must be skilled in problem-directed communication rather than in communication that is protective, defensive, or built around hidden agendas. If boundaries are to be flexible, legal restrictions on the physical movement of staff or clients should not be excessive.

In order to increase the accuracy of problem definitions, as little activity as possible should intervene between the presentation of the clients' problems and the response of correctional units. The larger the distance between occurrence of problems and correctional response, the more work must be done by the unit to redefine the problem in its orginal terms. If too long a time has intervened, this redefinition becomes impossible because both clients have undergone significant change. Ideally, these units would be preconviction problem-solving centers dispersed throughout a community in proportion to frequency and type of problem presented in different parts of the community.

Behind these small units should be an information network with centralized storage. This center would constantly monitor the activity in any of the action units in order to provide feedback to the units, based on information about similar activity in the past. Furthermore, the central data analysis center must coordinate the problem-solving activity of all the units. In order to carry out this coordinating activity, the center must be able to synthesize data on all problems in terms of patterns that are presented. By focusing on *patterns* of problems, this central agency will be able to predict specific problems before units are confronted with them, and it will acquire the information it needs to develop new problem-solving strategies. In addition, the central information agency can treat these patterns *themselves* as problems and begin problem solution on higher governmental and organizational levels. For example, it is on this higher level that problems of impoverished individuals can be related to the economic structure of the entire community.

UNRESOLVED PROBLEMS OF IMPLEMENTATION

One issue that is beyond the scope of this text is the strategy of change required to move from our present organizational structures to the new model. It is considerably easier to build a model that would increase the probability of goal achievement than it is to suggest how we can move from an existing model to a new one. However, we can suggest some guidelines from which a systematic strategy might emerge.

Organizational climates seem healthier when staff perceive management as more democratic and when the correctional policy demonstrates more concern for needs of inmates.[27] It would seem likely that present structures can be changed to emphasize these two aspects of management when decision making is decentralized and when goal attainment is openly discussed with staff and offenders. This trend may be encouraged when the correctional agency staff is organized into small work teams which are allowed to decide their own roles for the duration of particular tasks. Teams might be staffed differently depending on the range of problems that will be brought to them, but, as a general principle, it would seem beneficial if the staff members were heterogeneous in skills and interests. In this way, the teams might avoid the identification of staff with like groups of staff, and instead, emphasize identification with the problems to be solved. As staff members become competent team members, teams might be enlarged to include offenders as problem-solvers.

Management must take a risk in beginning the team-building process. Managers must turn over some authority to these groups in order that the teams may define problems and define their roles in solving the problems. The manager has to take the risk that men who have been closely supervised and have shown little initiative and creativity will behave differently when the situation is changed. The men who begin the teams must take the risk that the manager will not undercut their assumption of responsibility and use of discretion. Outside intervention may be helpful in this process, as it has proven helpful in reports of several correctional organizational development programs.[28]

Teams within the agencies must be coordinated, just as units in a community need to be coordinated. If each team is working successfully internally, the possibility remains that they will conflict as they compete in the organization for scarce resources and for different uses of the same information. Careful attention must be given to the system of interrelationships between teams and the way in which the accomplishment of their individual goals will contribute to the overall goals of the organization.

If correctional systems can make the shift from centralized to decentralized decision making, and from goal definition by the top of the organization to goal definition by work teams, then the manager becomes a coordinator. Just how far the manager of an existing correctional agency can go in this direction is not known. It would seem likely, however, that there are limitations on the decentralization of power within present probation, prison, and parole enterprises, beyond the obvious one that inmates have been convicted and are being coerced to remain under supervision. The correctional manager will have his parameters set for him by external agents much more than would be true for the community-based units described in the new model. He cannot be simply a coordinator but must approach the work teams with much of policy decided and a considerable number of problems already defined. He can probably take a consultative role, but it is not known at what point between the autocratic role and the coordinator's role he will find a viable balance for his organization.

If correctional organizations do become more democratic internally, they will also need to become more integrated with the surrounding community. Prison or parole work groups, for example, will eventually work on problems that carry the team out of the prison, or out of traditional parole responsibilities, and into the community activities that have not been touched by corrections before. One example of this process would be if a small team of staff members accompanied a group of inmates from prison to a halfway house setting, and then to parole supervision. Another way of accomplishing this interchange would be to have organizationally stable teams work on the problems that cross the usual agency barriers, such as creating suitable employment opportunities, or in other ways acting as advocates for prisoners. Concomitantly, these teams should also begin the task of helping to solve community problems.

As the community perceives corrections as a resource in some areas, it may be more willing to extend aid to other areas.

This process of restructuring may be valuable in its own right, depending on the goals of specific agencies; but it probably makes more sense to reorganize present correctional structures in this way if this retooling process is a transition to the new correctional model. If the aim of restructuring is the implementation of the new model that we have described, the restructuring process might be seen as a large retraining program; but it would actually be much more valuable than that. This transition stage would not only serve as a retraining period but as a testing period, in which everyone concerned could study different kinds of staff-offender team combinations and different kinds of corrections-community interactions. The new model could be modified in terms of an ongoing evaluation of the transition period.

There are some factors that are very likely to retard this change process and, therefore, deserve considerably more study in relation to organizational change in correctional agencies. Many of these factors may be invisible now and will only emerge when the actual change process begins. Some other difficulties, however, can probably be predicted.

The unions to which some correctional officials belong are likely to offer some resistance to change. The growth of the unions has been built partly around union success in objecting to particular demands of the fragmented organization, especially the demands on its uniformed civil service members. The union may react to organizational change as a threat, if the changes are sweeping enough to undercut the organizational facts of life within which the union has found its strength. The nature of the union as an organization and the peculiar legal restrictions on unions of government workers should be studied.

In addition, the trend toward unionization of inmates should be studied. The new model, and the transition to the new model, would seem to address through structural change many of the problems that a union of inmates would address as grievances. However, even if there is no inmate union where such change takes place, there may be social forces among inmates that could generate a union, and could also generate objections to change in the prison organization.

In studying either staff or inmate unions, research should include the study of the functions a union could serve if correctional structure changes. While much union activity focuses on objections to certain demands of the work organization, the union might also serve other functions in relationship to the new correctional model, such as how a union of first-line workers can organize to suggest additional changes in practice.

A second source of objection may come from the new political activities of minority groups. The issue may be similar to the one with the unions: changes in the present structure of corrections may do harm to the maintenance structure of other organizations even if the change in the agencies is in the directions preferred by these organizations. Militant black politics, for example, may need the traditional prison as something against which to rally. If this rallying point is taken away, these political groups may feel a lack of power, rather than a victory for their ideological position.

A likely complaint by such political groups, or, for that matter, by officer or inmate unions, will be that the new changes are just additional ploys by the establishment to fool the underdog and gain his cooperation. The ethical issue raised by this kind of complaint is a complex and far-reaching one: the difficulty in differentiating the engulfing and confining supersystem from an enabling and facilitating one. The dilemma has frequently been pointed out that rehabilitation is brainwashing. There are many ways to mask the coerciveness of "helping activity." The mask may even fool the "helper." Similarly, if organizational change techniques really become effective, there may be little more than the razor's edge separating changes that are socially beneficial from vast plots of political sabotage. Increased effectiveness in social system change will increase the chances of detrimental as well as beneficial change.

The only way in which this problem has been addressed in this work has been through the discussion of the smaller, but similar, problem of the relationship between the researcher and the administrator. This relationship itself deserves considerably more study. More effective ways must be found for these two types of people to communicate if the transition between models is to be successful. If a new model of corrections is to be implemented, then it is likely that a correctional administrator will have to be a researcher. It will be his task to gather information about community organization, and to make decisions based on that information so that communities are less frequently disrupted by the process of change.

There are obviously many other issues such as local-state-federal governmental relations, alternative funding methods, and the relationship between funding continuity and the effectiveness of program, that should be investigated for their effect on planned change in corrections. Perhaps two of the most important issues are the adaptability of the proposed change strategies to different kinds of agencies, and the effect of this kind of change on the other components in the criminal justice system.

One might question, for example, whether the data collected on organizational change in corrections and the new correctional model that we have based on that data would be as valid for a maximum security prison as they are for a minimum security prison or a parole enterprise. Obviously, there is no way of answering such a question without attempting the same kind of research in maximum security prisons. Some data collected by Duffee and others suggests that the general system model is equally applicable in maximum security prisons. That is to say, the behavior in present maximum security prisons can be predicted by using the general systems model.[29]

That maximum security prisons might be described in the same way, however, does not mean that maximum security prisons are equally open to change. It is probably much more likely that change-productive teams can be built in small institutions and field organizations than in maximum security prisons. It is much easier to carry on research in a minimum security prison, for example, than in more secure ones. It may also be more likely that the people in minimum security prisons see more reason to change. Some of the differences between types of correctional organizations have not been emphasized in this text, because they have not been relevant to the portrayal of general correctional strategies. Some of these differences, such as size of the population and dangerousness of the population, are going to make a difference *to somebody* when the issue becomes one of organizational change.

If the thoroughgoing change represented by the new model is desired, then one way of beginning change in maximum security prisons would be to phase them out slowly after the more flexible agencies have obtained some experience in the methods of change. If we can think of one level of a correctional system slowly changing over to a community-based system with many preconviction activities, it might be possible to time the transition so that maximum security prisons really need not change. Rather than change, the maximum security prison, its personnel, and inmates might be gradually transferred to less secure facilities and field agencies after the community-based system was already operational.

Lastly, we can also anticipate some mind-boggling problems in police and court organizations when these agencies have to adjust to the new correctional model. The majority of correctional work would be handled by community units on a preconviction basis in order to avoid redefinition of the problem that would occur if there were intermediate processing by other agencies. Police organizations would need, in this case, to act as referral agencies to the correctional units; and criminal prosecution would be replaced in many instances by informal, preconviction adjustments. *The kind of* correctional center suggested by this research is a social welfare center, if we could learn to understand welfare as a quality of life rather than a method of income. Community units would be problem adjustment centers, particularly for an urban population. It is unclear what kind of postconviction alternatives might be needed to back up such a system. But it is clear that the primary function of the new correctional model would be to retain people in the community rather than to take them out.

The basic function of such a system, if one function can be stated, would be the reverse of the basic function of our present system. Urban societies presently seem to amplify deviance by formalizing the reaction to deviance and by cutting deviant actors out of the social system. Centralized in small groups, as in prisons, deviants tend to be perceived as, and to behave as, increasingly deviant people. In the long run, this kind of reaction to deviance tends to make the social system unstable because it creates subsystems with conflicting values, the needs of which cannot be met within the existing social system. The new correctional model would focus on *deviance* rather than *deviants* by treating both the community and the individual as clients with resolvable problems. We could accurately call this a model of a *correctional* system because the system would provide feedback to the community, so that community structure could be continually reorganized to meet the needs of a greater proportion of its people.

THE RADICALIZED ORGANIZATION

The proposal of this new model for dealing with community problems brings us full circle to a discussion of the function of corrections in a social system. This is an area, as we said in Chapter 1, where we do not have much confidence in the kinds of analysis and kinds of theory building that have been conducted so far. What observer can stand far enough away from the encompassing social complex in which he lives to be able to say that corrections carries on a political or an educative function? Although this kind of thinking has been very important to the teaching of introductory sociology, it has not helped social scientists and administrators to deal with the actual problems of operating organizations. A nineteenth-century British poet suggested that in the "sinless" society, religion and politics would be the same: brotherhood. We might add that in such a reconstructed society, politics and education are basically the same, since both would deal with the problems of social integration under conditions of uncertainty.

But without becoming so utopian and otherworldly as that, we think we can compare some of the current outputs or functions of corrections with outputs or functions to be performed by the new model. The basic difference would be that rather than take up problem solution in a conservative or liberal light, the new organization would be identified (from our present time perspective) as radical; i.e., the new correctional model would perceive problems as they are related to system structure. Rather than dealing with individual deviants, it would deal with the interaction between community and individual behavior, within the context of the community. Rather than attempting to make certain individuals adapt to the present situation, where their opportunities are systematically reduced, it would attempt to increase the opportunities for goal achievement among all the groups of a community.

There is much that corrections can do to help individuals more effectively within our present social structure. But helping individuals reenter the marketplace does nothing to change the basic mode of exchange in the market. Thus, if it is a goal of corrections to reduce crime rather than merely to help individual criminals, corrections must be reorganized so that it can deal with deviance-generating patterns of behavior, rather than focusing on the deviant behavior of individuals who have already been caught and isolated. In short, corrections, to be a crime-reducing institution of society, must be in a position to change society.

NOTES

1. Herbert Packer, "Two Models of the Criminal Process," *University of Pennsylvania Law Review* 113 (1964): 1.
2. Herbert Packer, *The Limits of the Criminal Sanction* (Stanford: Stanford University Press, 1968).
3. Justice Frankfurter's plurality opinion in Culombe v. Connecticut 367 U.S. 568 (1961); Yale Kamisar, "Equal Justice in the Gate Houses and Mansions of American Criminal Procedure," in Kamisar, Inbau and Arnold, *Criminal Justice in Our Time* (Charlottesville: University of Virginia Press, 1965), pp. 443–510.
4. John Griffiths, "Ideology in Criminal Procedure or a Third Model of the Criminal Process," *Yale Law Journal 79*, no. 3 (January 1970): 359–417.
5. Ibid., pp. 367–371.
6. Packer, note 2, supra, pp. 160–163.
7. Ibid., pp. 164–166.
8. Jonathan Casper, *American Criminal Justice* (Englewood Cliffs, N.J.: Prentice-Hall, 1970).
9. Griffiths, note 4, supra, pp. 172–173.
10. Karl Menninger, *The Crime of Punishment* (New York: Viking Press, 1969); Matthew Dumont, *The Absurd Healer* (New York, Jason Aronson, 1968); and Ramsey Clark, *Crime in America* (New York: Pocket Books, 1971).
11. See David J. Rothman, *The Discovery of the Asylum* (Boston: Little, Brown,

1969); Elliot Studt, "Reintegration from the Parolee's Perspective," in *Reintegrating the Offender into the Community—Justice Monograph* (Washington, D.C.: U.S. Department of Justice, June 1973), pp. 42–52.

12. For an analysis of athletics given as an analogy of information control and variability see Stafford Beer, *Decision and Control* (New York: Wiley, 1966).

13. See Leslie Wilkins, *Social Deviance* (Englewood Cliffs, N.J.: Prentice-Hall, 1965), Chapter 4.

14. Donald Cressey, "Achievement of an Unstated Organizational Goal: An Observation on Prisons," *Pacific Sociological Review* 1 (Fall 1958): 43–49; "The Nature and Effectiveness of Correctional Techniques," *Law and Contemporary Problems* 23 (Autumn 1958): 754–771; "Contradictory Directives in Complex Organizations: The Case of the Prison," *Administrative Science Quarterly* 4 (June 1959): 1–19.

15. Harold Bradley, "Designing for Change: Innovation in Corrections," *Annals of the American Academy of Political and Social Science* 381 (January 1969): 89–98.

16. David Street, Robert Vinter, and Charles Perrow, *Organization for Treatment* (New York: Free Press, 1966), pp. 4–6.

17. Bradley, note 15, supra.

18. Ibid.

19. See David Duffee, "The Use of Organizational Variables in the Periodic Assessment of Correctional System Effectiveness" (Paper presented at the Project SEARCH Symposium, San Francisco, 1 May 1974).

20. George Dession, "Psychiatry and the Conditioning of Criminal Justice," *Yale Law Journal* 47 (1933): 319.

21. George Jackson, *Soledad Brother* (New York: Bantam Books, 1970).

22. F.E. Emery and E.L. Trist, "The Causal Texture of Organizational Environments," in F.E. Emery, ed., *Systems Thinking* (Baltimore, Penguin Books, 1970), pp. 241–258.

23. See Richard Korn, "Of Crime, Criminal Justice and Corrections," *University of San Francisco Law Review* 6 (October 1971): 27–75.

24. In general, a good review of ineffective and effective change attempts is available in Daniel Katz and Robert Kahn, *The Social Psychology of Organizations* (New York: Wiley, 1966), Chapter 13.

25. See David Duffee, "The Correctional Officer Subculture and Organizational Change," *Journal of Research in Crime and Delinquency* 11, no. 2 (July 1974): 155–172.

26. Gresham M. Sykes, *The Society of Captives* (Princeton, N.J.: Princeton University Press, 1971).

27. See David Duffee, *Correctional Policy and Prison Management* (Beverly Hills, Calif.: Sage-Halstead, 1975).

28. David Duffee and Richard Steinert, "Correctional Officers as Organizational Problem Solvers" (Paper, Pennsylvania State University, 1974).

29. Duffee, note 27, supra.

Bibliography

All the materials cited in the text are listed below under eleven different headings. We have attempted to categorize the works in a helpful manner, although there has been no attempt to make the categories mutually exclusive. In some instances, an item cited under one heading is clearly relevant in one or two of the other areas as well. The headings are:

1. Cases Cited
2. Corrections (General)
3. Courts
4. Criminal Justice
5. Criminology

6. Juvenile Correction and Delinquency
7. Parole and Probation
8. Police
9. Prisons
10. Reintegration (including community studies)
11. Other

Cases Cited

Culombe v. Connecticut, 367 U.S. 568 (1971)
Furman v. Georgia, 408 U.S. 238 (1972)
Gideon v. Wainwright, 372 U.S. 335 (1963)
Holt v. Sarver, 309 F. Supp. 362 (E.D. Ark. 1970)
In re Gault, 387 U.S. 1 (1967)
Jackson v. Hendrick, 40 Law Week 2710 (Ct. Comm. Pls. Pa. 1972)
Mempa v. Rhay, 389 U.S. 128 (1967)
Miranda v. Arizona, 384 U.S. 436 (1966)
Morrissey v. Brewer, 408 U.S. 471 (1972)
Santobello v. N.Y., 404 U.S. 257 (1971)
Terry v. Ohio, 392 U.S. 1 (1968)
U.S. v. Wade, 388 U.S. 218 (1967)
White v. Maryland, 373 U.S. 59 (1963)

Corrections (General)

Adams, Stuart. "Evaluative Research in Corrections: Status and Prospects." *Federal Probation* 38, 1 (March 1974): 14–21.
American Correctional Association. *Manual of Correctional Standards.* Washington, D.C.: ACA, 1969.
American Law Institute. *Model Penal Code.* Philadelphia: ALI, 1962.
American Psychiatric Association and National Association for Mental Health. *The Treatment of Drug Abuse: Programs, Problems, Prospects.* Washington, D.C.: Joint Information Service, 1972.
Axilbund, Melvin T. "New Pep for Corrections." *American Journal of Corrections* 33, 5 (September–October 1971): 30–31.
Bailey, W.C. "Correctional Treatment: An Analysis of One Hundred Correctional Outcome Studies." *Journal of Criminal Law, Criminology and Police Science* 57, 2 (1966): 153–160.
Barnes, Harry Elmer. *The Story of Punishment.* Montclair, N.J.: Patterson Smith, 1972.

Bedau, Hugo A. *The Death Penalty in America: An Anthology.* Garden City: Doubleday, 1964.
Bradley, Harold B. "Designing for Change: Problems of Planned Innovation in Corrections." *The Annals* 381 (January 1969): 89–99.
Burdman, Milton. "Ethnic Self-Help Groups in Prison and on Parole." *Crime and Delinquency* 20, 2 (April 1974): 107–118.
Carney, Louis P. *Introduction to Correctional Science.* New York: McGraw-Hill, 1974.
Cohen, Fred. *The Legal Challenge to Corrections.* Washington, D.C.: GPO, 1967.
Cohen, Morris R. "Moral Aspects of the Law." In *Crime and Justice.* Vol. 2. *The Criminal in the Arms of the Law,* edited by Radzinowitz and Wolfgang. New York: Basic Books, 1971.
Conrad, John. *Crime and its Treatment.* Berkeley: University of California Press, 1965.
Cressey, Donald. "Achievement of an Unstated Organizational Goal: An Observation on Prisons." *Pacific Sociological Review* 1 (Fall 1958): 43–49.
_____. "Contradictory Directives in Complex Organizations: The Case of the Prison." *Administrative Science Quarterly* 4 (June 1959): 1–19.
_____. "The Nature and Effectiveness of Correctional Techniques." *Law and Contemporary Problems* 23 (Autumn 1958): 754–771.
Dickover, Robert M.; Maynard, Verner E.; and Painter, James A. "A Study of Vocational Training in the California Department of Corrections." *Research Report number 40.* Sacramento: Research Division, Department of Corrections, January 1971.
Duffee, David. *Correctional Policy and Prison Management.* Beverly Hills: Sage, 1975.
_____. "The Use of Organizational Variables in the Periodic Assessment of Correctional System Effectiveness." Paper presented at the Project SEARCH Symposium, San Francisco, 1 May 1974.
Duffee, David, and O'Leary, Vincent. "Models of Correction: An Entry in the Packer–Griffiths Debate." *Criminal Law Bulletin* 7, 4 (May 1971): 329–352.

Dupont, Robert L. "How Corrections Can Bear the High Cost of Heroin Addiction." *Federal Probation* 35, 2 (June 1971): 43–50.

Fogel, David, et al. "Restitution in Criminal Justice: A Minnesota Experiment." *Criminal Law Bulletin* 8, 8 (October 1972): 682–683.

Foote, Caleb. "The Sentencing Function." In *A Program for Prison Reform, The Final Report*. Annual Chief Justice Earl Warren Conference on Advocacy in the United States, 9–10 June 1972.

Geerken, Michael, and Grove, Walter R. "Systems of Deterrence: Some Theoretical Considerations." Paper prepared for the Study of Social Problems Conference, Montreal, August 1974.

Glaser, Daniel. *The Effectiveness of a Prison and Parole System*. Indianapolis: Bobbs-Merrill, 1969.

Glasser, William. *Reality Therapy: A New Approach to Psychiatry*. New York: Harper & Row, 1965.

Gottfredson, Don. *Measuring Attitudes Toward Juvenile Detention*. New York: NCCD, 1968.

Heyns, Garrett. "Patterns of Correction." *Crime and Delinquency* 13, 3 (July 1967): 421–431.

Jones, Howard. "Punishment and Social Values." In *Criminology in Transition: Essays in Honour of Hermann Mannheim*, edited by Grygier et al. London: Tavistock, 1965.

Keating, Michael, Jr. "Preventive Mediation in Corrections." *Conflict* 2,1. Institute for Mediation and Conflict Resolution, November 1974.

Kelman, Herbert. "Compliance, Identification and Internalization: Three Processes of Attitude Change." *Journal of Conflict Resolution* (April 1958): 51–60.

Kerper, Hazel, and Kerper, Janeen. *Legal Rights of the Convicted*. St. Paul: West, 1974.

Kittrie, Nicholas. *The Right to Be Different*. Baltimore: Penguin, 1973.

Koestler, Arthur. *Reflections on Hanging*. New York: Macmillan, 1957.

Korn, Richard. "Of Crime, Criminal Justice and Corrections." *University of San Francisco Law Review* 6 (October 1971): 27–75.

Menninger, Karl. *The Crime of Punishment*. New York: Viking, 1969.

Mueller, Gerhard, O.W. "Imprisonment and Its Alternatives." In *A Program for Prison Reform, The Final Report*. Annual Chief Justice Earl Warren Conference on Advocacy in the United States, 9–10 June 1972.

National Advisory Commission on Criminal Justice Standards and Goals. *Task Force on Corrections*. Washington, D.C.: GPO, 1974.

National Council on Crime and Delinquency. *Corrections in the United States*. New York: NCCD, 1966.

Nicolau, George. *Grievance Arbitration in a Prison: The Holton Experiment*. New York: Institution for Mediation and Conflict Resolution, 1974.

O'Leary, Vincent. *The Correctional Policy Inventory*. Hackensack, N.J.: NCCD, 1970.

O'Leary, Vincent, and Duffee, David. "Correctional Policy: A Classification of Goals Designed for Change." *Crime and Delinquency* 17, 4 (October 1971): 373–386.

Rector, Milton G. "Heroin Maintenance: A Rational Approach." *Crime and Delinquency* 18, 3 (July 1972): 241–242.

Scheurnell, Robert P. "Valuation and Decision Making in Correctional Social Work." *Issues in Criminology* 4, 2 (Fall 1969): 101–108.

Schrag, Clarence. "Contemporary Corrections—An Analytical Model." Consultant paper prepared for President's Commission on Law Enforcement and the Administration of Justice, 1966.

Schwitzgabel, Ralph. "Limitations on the Coercive Treatment of Offenders." *Criminal Law Bulletin* 8, 4 (1972): 267–320.

Shelly, Joseph A., and Bassin, Alexander. "Daytop Lodge: Halfway House for Drug Addicts." *Federal Probation* 28, 4 (December 1964): 46–54.

Singer, Linda R., and Keating, J. Michael. "Prisoner Grievance Mechanisms." *Crime and Delinquency* 19, 3 (July 1973): 367–377.

Stubblefield, Keith A., and Dye, Larry L. Introduction to *Offenders as a Correctional Manpower Resource*, Joint Commission on Correctional Manpower and Training. Washington, D.C.: GPO, 1968.

Szasz, Thomas S. *Ideology and Insanity.* Garden City: Doubleday, 1970.
_____. *The Myth of Mental Illness.* Indianapolis: Bobbs-Merrill, 1960.
Venezia, Peter S. "Unofficial Probation: An Evaluation of Its Effectiveness." *Journal of Research in Crime and Delinquency* 9, 2 (July 1972): 149–170.
Wilkins, Leslie. *The Evaluation of Penal Measures.* New York: Random House, 1971.
Yablonsky, Lewis. *The Tunnel Back: Synanon.* New York: Macmillan, 1965.

Courts

The American Bar Association. *Sentencing Alternatives and Procedures.* Approved draft, 1968.
Ares, Charles E.; Rankin, Anne; and Sturz, Herbert. "The Manhattan Bail Project: An Interim Report on the Use of Pre-Trial Parole." *New York University Law Review* 38 (January 1963): 71–79, 81–92.
Bing, Stephen, and Rosenfeld, S. Stephen. *The Quality of Justice in the Lower Criminal Courts of Metropolitan Boston.* Boston: Governor's Committee on Law Enforcement and the Administration of Justice, 1970.
Blumberg, Abraham. *Criminal Justice.* Chicago: Quadrangle, 1970.
Board of Directors, NCCD. "The Nondangerous Offender Should Not be Imprisoned: A Policy Statement." *Crime and Delinquency* 19, 4 (October 1973): 456.
Chute, Charles Lionel, and Bell, Marjorie. *Crime, Courts and Probation.* New York: Macmillan, 1956.
Commentaries on the Laws of England, 1965-1969. Albany: Banks & Co., 1900.
Council of Judges, National Council on Crime and Delinquency. "Model Sentencing Act: Second Edition." *Crime and Delinquency* 18, 4 (October 1972): 356–357
Duffee, David, and Siegel, Larry. "The Organization Man: Legal Counsel in Juvenile Court." *Criminal Law Bulletin* 7, 6 (July–August 1971): 544–553.
Feit, Michael. "Before Sentence Is Pronounced." *Criminal Law Bulletin* 9, 2 (March 1973): 140–157.

Goldstein, Abraham. "The State and the Accused: Balance of Advantage in Criminal Procedure." *Yale Law Journal* 69 (1960): 1149–1194.
"I Have Nothing to do with Justice." *Life* 70 (March 12, 1971): 56–58.
Kaplan, John. "The Prosecutorial Discretion—A Comment." *Northwestern Law Review* 60 (1965): 174–193.
Larkins, Norm. "Presentence Investigation Report Disclosure in Alberta." *Federal Probation* (December 1972): 59–62.
Merrill, Dean C. "Using the PROMIS Tracking System for Criminal Justice Evaluation." *Project SEARCH Symposium Proceedings* (Sacramento: California Crime Technology Research Foundation, 1972): 231–234.
Newman, Donald J. *Conviction: The Determination of Guilt or Innocence Without Trial.* Boston: Little, Brown, 1967.
_____. "Role and Process in the Criminal Court." In *Handbook of Criminology*, edited by Glaser. New York: Rand McNally, 1974.
President's Commission on Law Enforcement and the Administration of Justice. *Task Force Report: The Courts.* Washington, D.C.: GPO, 1967.
San Francisco Committee on Crime. *Report on the Courts.* San Francisco, 1970.
Wice, Paul B. "Bail Reform in American Cities." *Criminal Law Bulletin* 9, 9 (November 1973): 770–797.
Woodman, Horatio, ed. *Reports of Criminal Cases Tried in the Municipal Court of the City of Boston Before Peter Oxenbridge Tacher, Judge of the Court From 1823–1843.* Boston: 1845.
Zastrow, William G. "Disclosure of the Presentence Investigation." *Federal Probation* (December 1971): 20–22.

Criminal Justice

Arnold, Thurmond. "Law Enforcement—An Attempt at Social Dissection." *Yale Law Journal* 42 (1932): 1–30.
Blumstein, Alfred. "Systems Analysis and the Criminal Justice System." *Annals* 374 (November 1967): 92–100.

Casper, Jonathan. *American Criminal Justice.* Englewood Cliffs: Prentice-Hall, 1970.

Clark, Ramsey. *Crime in America.* New York: Pocket Books, 1971.

Davis, Kenneth Culp. *Discretionary Justice.* Baton Rouge: Louisiana State University Press, 1969.

Dession, George. "Psychiatry and the Conditioning of Criminal Justice." *Yale Law Journal* 47 (1938): 319–340.

Governor's Special Committee on Criminal Offenders. *Preliminary Report.* State of New York, 1968.

Griffiths, John. "Ideology in Criminal Procedure or a 'Third' Model of the Criminal Process." *Yale Law Journal* 79, 3 (January 1970): 359–417.

Kamisar, Yale. "Equal Justice in the Gate Houses and Mansions of American Criminal Procedure." In *Criminal Justice in Our Time,* edited by Kamisar, Inbau, and Arnold. Charlottesville: University of Virginia Press, 1965.

Kaplan, John. *Criminal Justice.* Minneola, New York: Foundation Press, 1973.

Kerper, Hazel B. *Introduction to the Criminal Justice System.* St. Paul: West, 1972.

Law Enforcement Assistance Administration. *Third Annual Report.* Washington, D.C.: GPO, 1971.

Packer, Herbert. *The Limits of the Criminal Sanction.* Stanford: Stanford University Press, 1968.

———. "Two Models of the Criminal Process." *University of Pennsylvania Law Review* 113 (1964): 1–23.

President's Commission on Law Enforcement and the Administration of Justice. *Challenge of Crime in a Free Society.* Washington, D.C.: GPO, 1967.

———. *Task Force Report: Science and Technology.* Washington, D.C.: GPO, 1967.

Project SEARCH, Technical Report no. 5. Sacramento: California Crime Technological Research Foundation, 1973.

Remington, Frank; Newman, Donald J.; Kimball, Edward L.; Melli, Margold; and Goldstein, Herman. *Criminal Justice Administration.* Indianapolis: Bobbs-Merrill, 1969.

Tappan, Paul W. *Crime, Justice and Correction.* New York: McGraw-Hill, 1960.

Wilkins, Leslie. "Crime and Justice at the Turn of the Century." Paper presented at the 77th Annual Meeting of the American Academy of Political and Social Service, Philadelphia, 13 April 1973.

Criminology

Barnes, Harry Elmer, and Teeters, Negley K. *New Horizons in Criminology.* Englewood Cliffs: Prentice-Hall, 1955.

Beccaria, Cesare. *Of Crimes and Punishment.* London, Oxford University Press, 1964.

Cressey, Donald. *Theft of the Nation.* New York: Harper & Row, 1969.

Gordon, David. "Capitalism, Class, and Crime in America." *Crime and Delinquency* 19, 2 (April 1973): 163–186.

Haskell, Martin B., and Yablonsky, Lewis. *Crime and Delinquency.* Chicago: Rand McNally, 1970.

Johnson, Elmer H. *Crime, Correction, and Society.* Homewood, Ill.: The Dorsey Press, 1968.

Korn, Richard R., and McCorkle, Lloyd W. *Criminology and Penology.* New York: Holt, Rinehart, and Winston, 1959.

Schrag, Clarence. "A Preliminary Criminal Typology." *Pacific Sociological Review* 4 (Spring 1961): 11–16.

Sutherland, Edwin H., and Cressey, Donald R. *Criminology.* New York: Lippincott, 1970.

Taft, Donald R., and England, Ralph W., Jr. *Criminology.* 4th ed. New York: Macmillan, 1964.

Taylor, Ian; Walton, Paul; and Young, Jack. *The New Criminology: For a Social Theory of Deviance.* London: Rutledge and Keegan Paul, 1973.

Wilkins, Leslie. *Social Deviance.* Englewood Cliffs, N.J.: Prentice-Hall, 1965.

Wolfgang, Marvin; Savitz, Leonard; and Johnston, Norman. *The Sociology of Crime and Delinquency.* New York: Wiley, 1962.

Juvenile Correction and Delinquency

Cloward, Richard, and Ohlin, Lloyd. *Delinquency and Opportunity.* Glencoe, Ill.: Free Press, 1960.

The Detroit Foster Homes Project for the Merrill-Palmer Institute. *Current Pro-*

ject. Project No. P487 in Information Center Files.

Elias, Albert, and Pilnick, Saul. "The Essexfield Group Rehabilitation Project for Youthful Offenders." *Correction in the Community: Alternatives to Incarceration.* Monograph no. 4. Sacramento: Corrections Board, State of California, 1964.

Empey, Lamar T., and Ralsow, Jerome. "The Provo Experiment in Delinquency Rehabilitation." *American Sociological Review* 26 (October 1961): 683–694.

Empey, Lamar T.; Erickson, Maynard; and Scott, Max. "The Provo Experiment: Evaluation of a Community Program." *Correction in the Community: Alternatives to Incarceration.* Monograph no. 4. Sacramento, Corrections Board, State of California, 1964.

Gemignani, Robert J. "Youth Services Systems." *Federal Probation* 30, 4 (December 1972): 48–53.

Harlow, E.R. Welser, and Wilkins, Leslie T. "Community-Based Correctional Programs." *Crime and Delinquency Topics: A Monograph Series.* National Institute of Mental Health Center for Studies of Crime and Delinquency. Washington, D.C.: GPO, 1971.

Herschi, Travis, and Selvin, Hanan. *Delinquency Research.* New York: Free Press, 1967.

Howlett, Frederick. "Is the Youth Service Bureau All It's Cracked Up to Be?" *Crime and Delinquency* 19, 4 (October 1973): 485–492.

Katkin, Daniel; Hyman, Drew; and Kramer, John. *Juvenile Justice: Love Them or Leave Them.* Paper prepared for the Society for the Study of Social Problems, New York City, August 1973.

McCorkle, Lloyd W.; Elias, Albert; and Bixby, F. Lovell. *The Highfields Story.* New York: Henry Holt, 1958.

Pickett, Robert S. *House of Refuge: Origins of Juvenile Reform in New York State 1815-1857.* Syracuse: Syracuse University Press, 1969.

Platt, Anthony. "The Rise of the Child-Saving Movement: A Study in Social Policy and Correctional Reform." *The Annals* 381 (January 1969): 25–28.

Southfields Residential Group Center, A

Four Year Report. Anchorage, Kentucky: Southfields, March 1966.

Stephenson, Richard M., and Scarpitti, Frank R. *The Rehabilitation of Delinquent Boys.* A Final Report to the Ford Foundation. New Brunswick, N.J.: Rutgers University, 1967.

Sullivan, Clyde; Grant, Marguerite Q.; and Grant, J. Douglas. "The Development of Interpersonal Maturity Applications to Delinquency." *Psychiatry* 20, 4 (November 1974): 373–385.

Underwood, William. *A National Study of Youth Service Bureaus.* Washington, D.C.: U.S. Youth Development and Delinquency Prevention Administration, 1975.

Weeks, Ashley H. *Youthful Offenders at Highfields.* Ann Arbor: University of Michigan Press, 1958.

Werthman, Carl. "The Function of Social Definitions in the Development of Delinquent Careers." In President's Commission on Law Enforcement and the Administration of Justice. *Task Force Report: Juvenile Delinquency and Youth Crime.* Washington, D.C.: GPO, 1967.

Parole and Probation

Adams, Stuart. "Some Findings From Correctional Caseload Research." *Federal Probation* 31, 4 (December 1967): 48–57.

Berecochea, John E.; Jamen, Dorothy R.; and Jones, Walton A. *Time Served in Prison and Parole Outcome: An Experimental Study.* Research Report no. 49. Sacramento: California Department of Corrections, 1973.

Bruce, Burgess, and Hano. *The Working of the Indeterminate Sentence Law and the Parole System in Illinois.* Springfield, Ill.: Illinois Board of Parole, 1928.

California State Department of Corrections. *Parole Work Unit Program: An Evaluative Report.* Sacramento: California Department of Corrections, 1966.

Cromwell, Terry A. "Supervision of Parole and Probation Cases." In Killinger and Cromwell. *Corrections in the Community.* St. Paul: West, 1974.

Division of Adult Parole, Adult Authority. *Special Intensive Parole Unit,*

Phase I: Fifteen-Man Caseload Study. Sacramento: State of California, 1956.

Glueck, Sheldon, and Glueck, Eleanor. *Five Hundred Criminal Careers.* New York: Alfred A. Knopf, 1937.

————. *Criminal Careers in Retrospect.* New York: The Commonwealth Fund, 1943.

————. *One Thousand Juvenile Delinquents.* Cambridge: Harvard University Press, 1934.

————.*Five Hundred Delinquent Women.* New York: The Commonwealth Fund, 1940.

Greensburg, David F. "Parole Recidivism and the Incapacitative Effects of Imprisonment." Paper prepared in the Society for the Study of Social Problems, Conference, Montreal, August 1974.

Havel, Joan. *Special Intensive Parole Unit, Phase IV: The Parole Outcome Study.* Research Report no. 13. Sacramento: California Department of Corrections, September 1965.

Havel, Joan, and Sulka, Elaine. *Special Intensive Parole Unit, Phase III.* Research Report no. 3. Sacramento: California Department of Corrections, March 1962.

Keve, Paul W. *Imaginative Programming in Probation and Parole.* Minneapolis: University of Minnesota Press, 1967.

Mannheim, Hermann, and Wilkins, Leslie T. *Prediction Methods in Relation to Borstal Training.* London: HMSO, 1955.

National Probation and Parole Institutes. *Uniform Parole Reports.* New York: NCCD, 1972.

Newman, Charles L. *Sourcebook on Probation, Parole, and Pardons.* Springfield, Ill.: Charles C Thomas, 1968.

New York State Division of Parole. *Manual for Parole Officers* (1953). In *Corrections in the Community,* edited by Killinger and Cromwell. St. Paul: West, 1974.

Ohlin, Lloyd. *Selection for Parole: A Manual of Parole Prediction.* New York: Russell Sage, 1951.

Pennsylvania Board of Parole. *15th Annual Report.* Harrisburg: Board of Parole, 1958.

Sparkes, R.F. "Research on the Use and Effectiveness of Probation Parole and Measures of After-Care." In *The Practical Organization of Probation and After-Care Services.* Strasbourg: The Council of Europe, 1968.

Police

Bittner, Egon. *The Functions of the Police in a Modern Society.* Public Health Service Publication No. 2059. Chevy Chase, Md., National Institute of Mental Health, 1970.

Black, Algernon. *The People and the Police.* New York, McGraw-Hill, 1968.

Goldstein, Herman. "Administrative Problems in Controlling the Exercise of Police Authority." *Journal of Criminal Law, Criminology, and Police Science,* 58 (1967): 160–170.

Katz, Michael. "Patterns of Arrest and the Dangers of Public Visibility." *Criminal Law Bulletin* 9, 4 (1973): 311–324.

Knapp Commission. *Report.* New York: George Brazillier, 1973.

Munro, Jim. *Administrative Behavior and Police Organization.* Cincinnati: Anderson, 1974.

National Advisory Commission on Criminal Justice Standards and Goals. *Task Force on Police.* Washington, D.C.: GPO, 1974.

O'Neill, Michael. *The Role of the Police—Normative Role Expectation in a Metropolitan Police Department.* Unpublished doctoral dissertation, State University of New York at Albany, 1974.

President's Commission on Law Enforcement and the Administration of Justice. *Task Force Report: The Police.* Washington, D.C.: GPO, 1967.

Skolnick, Jerome. *Justice Without Trial.* New York: Wiley, 1967.

Tiffany, McIntyre, and Rotenberg. *Detection of Crime.* Boston: Little, Brown, 1967.

Wilson, J.Q. *Varieties of Police Behavior.* Cambridge: Harvard University Press, 1968.

Prisons

Baker, Donald P. "The Prisoner of Patuxent." *The Washington Post,* 24 March 1974, pp. C-l and C-5.

Baker, J.E. "Inmate Self-Government."

Journal of Criminal Law, Criminology, and Police Science 55, 1 (1964): 39–67.

Belbenoit, René. *Dry Guillotine*. New York: Bantam, 1971.

Carter, Robert M.; Glaser, Daniel; and Wilkins, Leslie T. *Correctional Institutions*. New York: Lippincott, 1972.

Chaneles, Sol. "Open Prisons: Urban Convicts Can Turn Ghost Towns into Rural Communities." *Psychology Today* 7, 4 (April 1974): 30, 90–93.

Clemmer, Donald. *The Prison Community*. New York: Holt, Rinehart and Winston, 1958.

Cloward, Richard, et al. *Theoretical Studies in Social Organization of the Prison*. New York: Social Science Research Council, 1960.

Cressey, Donald. "Contradictory Directives in Complex Organizations: The Case of the Prison." *Administrative Science Quarterly* 4 (June 1959): 1–19.

Cressey, Donald, ed. *The Prison: Studies in Institutional Organization and Change*. New York: Holt, Rinehart and Winston, 1960.

Duffee, David. "The Correctional Officer Subculture and Organizational Change." *Journal of Research in Crime and Delinquency* 11, 2 (July 1974): 155–172.

Duffee, David; Steinert, Richard; and Dvorin, Robert. "Correctional Officers as Organizational Problem Solvers." Unpublished paper, Pennsylvania State University, 1974.

Goffman, Erving. *Asylums*. Garden City: Doubleday, 1969.

Grant, Douglas, and Grant, Marguerite. "A Group Dynamics Approach to Non-Conformity in the Navy." *Annals* 322 (March 1959): 126–155.

Hopper, Columbus. *Sex in Prison: The Mississippi Experiment With Conjugal Visiting*. Baton Rouge: Louisiana State University Press, 1969.

Jackson, George. *Soledad Brother*. New York: Bantam, 1970.

Knight, Etheridge. *Black Voices From Prison*. New York: Pathfinder Press, 1970.

Manocchio, Anthony J., and Dunn, Jimmy. *The Time Game*. New York: Dell, 1970.

McCorkle, Lloyd W., and Korn, Richard. "Resocialization Within Walls." The

Annals 293 (May 1954): 88–98.

McGee, Richard A. "Our Sick Jails." *Federal Probation* 35, 1 (March 1971): 3–8.

McKelvey, Blake. *American Prisons: A Study of American Social History Prior to 1915*. Montclair, N.J.: Patterson Smith, 1972.

McKendrick, Charles. "Custody and Discipline." In *Contemporary Corrections*, edited by Paul Tappan. New York: McGraw-Hill, 1951.

President's Commission on Law Enforcement and the Administration of Justice. *Task Force Report: Corrections*. Washington, D.C.: GPO, 1967.

Rothman, David. *The Discovery of the Asylum: Social Order and Disorder in the New Republic*. Boston: Little, Brown, 1971.

Street, David; Vinter, Robert; and Perrow, Charles. *Organization for Treatment*. New York: Free Press, 1966.

Sykes, Gresham. "The Corruption of Authority and Rehabilitation." *Social Forces* 34 (March 1956): 257–262.

———. *The Society of Captives*. Princeton: Princeton University Press, 1971.

U.S. Bureau of Prisons. *Annual Report*. Washington, D.C.: GPO, 1969.

Wheeler, Stanton. "Socialization in Correctional Communities." In *Prison Within Society*, edited by Hazelbrigg. Garden City: Doubleday, 1969.

Reintegration

Baker, J.E. "Preparing Prisoners for Their Return to the Community." In *Correctional Institutions*, edited by Carter, Glaser, and Wilkins. New York: Lippincott, 1972.

Beam, Kenneth S. "The Coordinating Council Movement." *Yearbook*. National Probation Association, 1935.

———. "Community Coordination for Prevention of Delinquency." *Yearbook*. New York: National Probation Association, 1936.

Committee for Economic Development. *Education of the Urban Disadvantaged*. New York: CEP, 1971.

Dumont, Matthew. *The Absurd Healer*. New York: Jason Aronson, 1968.

Fitch, Robert Forest. *The Work Furlough Program in California*. Unpublished master's thesis, Berkeley, University of California, 1967.

Irwin, John. *The Felon*. Englewood Cliffs, N.J.: Prentice-Hall, 1970.

Keller, Oliver J., and Alper, Benedict S. *Halfway Houses: Community Centered Correction and Treatment*. Lexington, Mass.: Heath and Company, 1970.

Killinger, George C., and Cromwell, Paul F., Jr. *Corrections in the Community: Alternatives to Imprisonment*. St. Paul: West, 1974.

McCartt, John H., and Mangogna, Thomas. *Guidelines and Standards for Halfway Houses and Community Treatment Centers*. Washington, D.C.: U.S. Department of Justice, May 1973.

Miller, Herbert S. "The Citizen's Role in Changing The Criminal Justice System." *Crime and Delinquency* 19, 3 (July 1973): 344–345.

National Advisory Commission on Civil Disorders. *Final Report*. New York: Bantam Editions, 1968.

Scudder, Kenyon J. "The Coordinating Council at Work." *Yearbook*, pp. 67–77. New York: National Probation Association, 1936.

Studt, Elliott. "Reintegration From the Parolee's Perspective." In *Reintegrating the Offender into the Community*. Criminal Justice Monograph, pp. 42–52. Washington, D.C.: U.S. Department of Justice, 1973.

U.S. Attorney General's Office. "Progress Report on Work Release Program—Prison Rehabilitation Act of 1965," 12 September 1966.

U.S. Bureau of Prisons. "Community Centered Correctional Programs." In *Trends in the Administration of Justice and Correctional Programs in the United States*. Washington, D.C.: GPO, 1965.

U.S. Dept. of Justice. *Questions and Answers about Work Release, Questions and Answers about Unescorted Furloughs, and Work Furlough Release*. Washington, D.C.: GPO, 27 January 1967.

Warren, Marguerite. "The Community Treatment Project: History and Prospects." *Law Enforcement Science and Technology* 1 (1967): 191–200.

Other

Beer, Stafford. *Decision and Control*. New York: Wiley, 1966.

Brown, Claude. *Manchild in the Promised Land*. New York: Signet, 1965.

Durkheim, Emile. *The Rules of the Sociological Method*. Glencoe, Ill.: Free Press, 1950.

Emery, F.E., and Trist, E.L. "The Causal Texture of Organizational Environments." In *Systems Thinking*, edited by Emery. Baltimore: Penguin, 1970.

Etzioni, Amitai. *The Active Society*. New York: Free Press, 1970.

———. *Complex Organizations*. New York: Free Press, 1961.

Gellhorn, Walter. "The Ombudsman Concept in the United States." In *Readings in Sociology*, edited by Schuler, Hoult, Gibson, and Brookover. New York: Thomas T. Crowell, 1971.

Katz, Daniel, and Kahn, Robert. *The Social Psychology of Organizations*. New York: Wiley, 1966.

Lord, Walter. *The Good Years*. New York: Harper and Row, 1962.

Newman, Oscar. *Defensible Space*. New York: Collier, 1973.

Merton, Robert. *Social Theory and Social Structure*. Glencoe, Ill.: Free Press, 1949.

Parsons, Talcott. *The Social System*. New York: The Free Press, 1964.

Smith, Gilbert. *Social Work and the Sociology of Organizations*. Boston: Rutledge & Kegan Paul, 1967.

Warner, W. Keith, and Havens, A. Eugene. "Goal Displacement and the Intangibility of Organizational Goals." *Administrative Science Quarterly* 12, 4 (March 1968): 539–555.

Index of Subjects

Index of Names